T0331115

The United States faces enormous challenges in the energy area. Climate change, biofuels policy, energy security, and environmental degradation are all intimately bound up with energy production and consumption. Historically, the federal government has relied on tax subsidies to effect energy policy. With mounting federal deficits, policy makers and advocates are increasingly calling for a rethinking of our energy tax policy.

How can the federal tax code strengthen environmental policy and reduce security concerns in the area of energy? This book brings together leading tax scholars to answer this question. The authors tackle such difficult problems as climate change, efficient taxation of oil and gas, and optimal oil tax policy in a world in which OPEC oil producers dominate the world oil supply.

This volume presents a number of innovative policy suggestions backed by sophisticated and cutting-edge research carried out by leading scholars in the area of energy taxation. Scholars and policy makers alike will appreciate the incisive analysis and discussion of critical issues that are part of the energy challenge in the twenty-first century.

Gilbert E. Metcalf is Professor of Economics at Tufts University, Massachusetts, and a Research Associate at the National Bureau of Economic Research. He is also a Research Associate in the Joint Program on the Science and Policy of Global Change at MIT and is currently a Visiting Professor in the Department of Economics at MIT, where he teaches a class on the economics of energy markets.

Professor Metcalf recently served as a member of the U.S. National Academy of Sciences's Committee on Health, Environmental, and Other External Costs and Benefits of Energy Production and Consumption, and the peer-review team of the U.S. Environmental Protection Agency's climate modeling efforts. He has also been a consultant on energy matters to numerous government agencies and is a Lead Author for the Intergovernmental Panel on Climate Change's Fifth Assessment Report that is scheduled for release in 2014. Professor Metcalf also serves on the Advisory Board for the SECURE (Security of Energy Considering Its Uncertainty, Risk, and Economic Implications) Project funded by the European Commission. An associate editor of the *Journal of Economic Perspectives* and a member of the editorial board of the *Berkeley Electronic Journal of Economic Analysis and Policy*, Professor Metcalf is the author of more than seventy papers in academic and professional journals, including the *Journal of Political Economy*, the *Economic Journal*, *Journal of Public Economics*, and the *Review of Economics and Statistics*. He coedited *Behavioral and Distributional Effects of Environmental Policy* (2001, with Carlo Carraro) and *The Distribution of Tax Burdens* (2003, with Don Fullerton). Professor Metcalf's primary research area is applied economics with particular interests in taxation, energy, and environmental economics.

U.S. Energy Tax Policy

Edited by

GILBERT E. METCALF
Tufts University, Massachusetts

CAMBRIDGE
UNIVERSITY PRESS

32 Avenue of the Americas, New York NY 10013-2473, USA

Cambridge University Press is part of the University of Cambridge.

It furthers the University's mission by disseminating knowledge in the pursuit of education, learning and research at the highest international levels of excellence.

www.cambridge.org
Information on this title: www.cambridge.org/9781107436022

© Cambridge University Press 2011

First published 2011
First paperback edition 2014

A catalogue record for this publication is available from the British Library

Library of Congress Cataloguing in Publication data

U.S. energy tax policy / edited by Gilbert E. Metcalf.
p.   cm.
Includes index.
ISBN 978-0-521-19668-0 (hardback)
1. Energy tax – United States.   2. Energy policy – United States.   I. Metcalf, Gilbert E.   II. Title.
HD9502.U52U1734   2010
336.2′78333790973–dc22   2010041741

ISBN 978-0-521-19668-0 Hardback
ISBN 978-1-107-43602-2 Paperback

Contents

Conference Participants

The papers in this volume were written for a conference sponsored by the American Tax Policy Institute and held in Washington, D.C., on October 15 and 16, 2009. Conference authors and discussants are as follows:

Roseanne Altshuler, Co-Director, Tax Policy Center, The Urban Institute, Washington, D.C.

Joshua Blonz, Research Assistant, Resources for the Future, Washington, D.C.

Dallas Burtraw, Senior Fellow, Resources for the Future, Washington, D.C.

Curtis Carlson, Financial Economist, Office of Tax Analysis, U.S. Department of the Treasury, Washington, D.C.

Ujjayant Chakravorty, Professor and Canada Research Chair, School of Business and Department of Economics, University of Alberta, Edmonton, Alberta, Canada

Harry de Gorter, Professor, Department of Applied Economics and Management, Cornell University, Ithaca, New York

Terry M. Dinan, Senior Advisor, Congressional Budget Office, Washington, D.C.

Susan Esserman, Partner, Steptoe and Johnson, LLP, Washington, D.C.

Don Fullerton, Gutgsell Professor of Finance, University of Illinois, Urbana-Champaign, Champaign, Illinois

Shelby Gerking, Galloway Professor of Economics, University of Central Florida, Orlando, Florida

Lawrence Goulder, Shuzo Nishihara Professor of Environmental and Resource Economics, Stanford University, Stanford, California

Dan Greenbaum, President, Health Effects Institute, Boston, Massachusetts

Kevin Hassett, Senior Fellow and Director of Economic Policy Studies, American Enterprise Institute, Washington, D.C.

David R. Just, Associate Professor, Department of Applied Economics and Management, Cornell University, Ithaca, New York

Louis Kaplow, Finn M. W. Caspersen and Household International Professor of Law and Economics, Harvard Law School, Cambridge, Massachusetts

Andrew Leach, Assistant Professor, School of Business, University of Alberta, Edmonton, Alberta, Canada

Charles E. McLure, Jr., Senior Fellow (emeritus), Hoover Institution, Stanford University, Stanford, California

Gilbert E. Metcalf, Professor, Department of Economics, Tufts University, Medford, Massachusetts

Richard D. Morgenstern, Senior Fellow, Resources for the Future, Washington, D.C.

Adele Morris, Fellow and Policy Director for Climate and Energy Economics, Brookings Institution, Washington, D.C.

Sergey Paltsev, Principal Research Scientist, MIT Joint Program on the Science and Policy of Global Change, Cambridge, Massachusetts

Ian W. H. Parry, Allen Kneese Senior Fellow, Resources for the Future, Washington, D.C.

Sebastian Rausch, Research Scientist, MIT Joint Program on the Science and Policy of Global Change, Cambridge, Massachusetts

John M. Reilly, Co-Director, MIT Joint Program on the Science and Policy of Global Change, Cambridge, Massachusetts

Stephen Salant, Professor of Economics, University of Michigan, Ann Arbor, Michigan

Jon Strand, Development Research Group, Environmental Energy Team, The World Bank, Washington, D.C., and Department of Economics, University of Oslo, Oslo, Norway

Eric Toder, Institute Fellow, The Urban Institute, Washington, D.C.

Margaret Walls, Senior Fellow, Resources for the Future, Washington, D.C.

David Weisbach, Walter J. Blum Professor, University of Chicago Law School, Chicago, Illinois

Roberton C. Williams III, Associate Professor of Agricultural and Resource Economics, University of Maryland, College Park, Maryland

Brent Yacobucci, Specialist in Energy and Environmental Policy, Congressional Research Service, Washington, D.C.

ONE

Introduction

Gilbert E. Metcalf

Anyone interested in understanding U.S. energy policy must begin from the premise that policy seeks to achieve multiple and often conflicting goals. Policy makers, for example, wish to encourage the reduction of greenhouse gas emissions (predominantly carbon dioxide from energy consumption) but at the same time reduce our reliance on oil consumption. Although at first glance these goals appear to be complementary, a leading contender for a replacement for the internal combustion engine in vehicles is a plug-in hybrid, which in turn could lead to an increase in demand for coal-fired electricity. Coal emits the most carbon dioxide per BTU of any energy source and so is a prime target for environmentalists who wish to reduce emissions.

Concerns with climate change, energy security, and pollution associated with the production and consumption of energy top the list of concerns about our use of energy; in addition, there are complex distributional considerations. The damages, for example, from coal combustion for electricity production vary widely across plants, with one recent study suggesting that the damages per kilowatt hour (kWh) from criteria pollutants range from less than 0.19 cents to more than 12 cents (National Research Council 2009). Meanwhile, policies to discourage the consumption of coal could have sharp distributional consequences. Just to focus on one fact, three states – Montana, Wyoming, and Illinois – account for over one-half of all recoverable reserves of coal in the United States. Whether the impacts of policies to reduce coal consumption would disproportionately fall on residents of these states is another question – a question that, among others, is addressed in this book.

This book contains a number of chapters that undertake economic analyses of some aspect of current or proposed energy policy. Much of the attention will be on fiscal policies – for example, market-based instruments

1

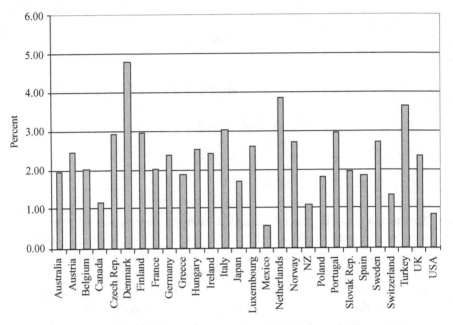

Figure 1.1. Environmental Taxes as a Percentage of GDP in 2006.

to reduce greenhouse gas emissions. To place the analyses in some context, it may be useful to review a few facts about energy-related fiscal policy.

Figure 1.1 reports environmental tax revenues as a percentage of GDP for a number of developed countries in 2006. The share of environmental tax revenues in GDP across OECD countries (weighted by GDP) was 1.71 percent in 2006. The share for the United States was 0.86 percent – the lowest rate among all OECD countries. In contrast, the share for the United Kingdom was 2.37 percent, 2.40 percent for Germany, and 4.79 percent for Denmark.

Figure 1.2 helps explain the unusually low share of environmental taxes in GDP for the United States. This figure reports the excise tax rate on gasoline as of January 1, 2009. The U.S. excise tax rate (federal and state) ranges from 10 to 34 percent of the tax rate of other countries (excepting Canada). It is half the Canadian rate. Clearly, the United States is an outlier on gasoline taxes.

Congress has been more active in providing subsidies for energy production to encourage desired activities. The Office of Management and Budget (2009) listed twenty-four federal tax expenditures related to energy, not including the excise tax credits for alcohol fuel (ethanol)

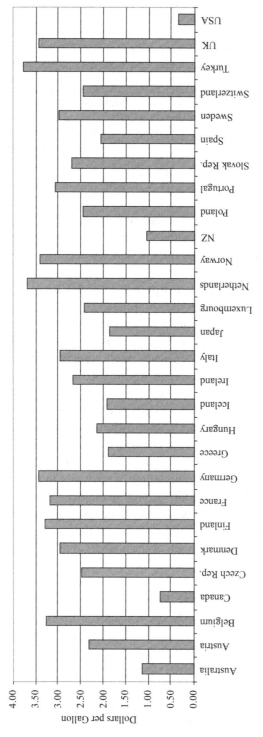

Figure 1.2. Tax Rate on Unleaded Gasoline in 2009.

Table 1.1. *Energy-related tax expenditures*

Category	2009–2013
Expensing of Exploration and Development Costs	1,550
Excess of Percentage Over Depletion Costs	4,430
New Technology Production and Investment Tax Credits	5,010
Alcohol Fuels Tax Credit	10,630

Tax expenditures are in millions of dollars.
Source: Office of Management and Budget (2009).

production.[1] Table 1.1 lists the four most important reductions in federal tax revenue related to energy. The first two items are tax preferences largely received by oil and gas drillers, and the next two are for renewable fuels.[2]

The reliance on accelerated depreciation and other deductions along with income and excise tax credits complicates the analysis of federal energy policy. Many of the contributions in this book dig deeply into the tax code to understand how energy supply or consumption is affected as well as to assess the distributional and efficiency implications of policy.

The chapters in this book fall broadly into two categories: assessments of possible policies to reduce our reliance on fossil fuels as part of a climate change policy and assessments of current energy tax policies. In addition to the chapters themselves, the volume includes a number of contributions by discussants at the conference at which these chapters were presented. We have included commentaries in this volume in those instances in which the discussants wished to say something of substance in print that enriches understanding of the topic addressed in the chapter.

Chapters 2 and 3 consider the distributional impacts of policies to impose a price on greenhouse gas emissions. Although the focus in these chapters is on cap-and-trade policies, much of the analysis applies to carbon charges. These chapters start from a very basic premise: a federal cap-and-trade system (like a carbon charge) has the potential to raise billions of dollars in revenue for the government. Free allocation of permits is equivalent to auctioning them and returning the revenues to firms and consumers in some lump-sum fashion. Although the burden of carbon pricing through

---

[1] The ethanol tax credit is not treated as a tax expenditure in the President's budget submission, because it is a reduction in excise tax revenue rather than income tax revenue.

[2] Energy Information Administration (2008) describes the various federal subsidies for energy production or consumption as well as subsidies to reduce energy use in detail. Metcalf (2007, 2009) provides an assessment of federal energy tax policy.

the cap-and-trade system is determined by the carbon intensity of goods and services consumed by households along with the capital intensity of carbon-intensive industries, the full burden of carbon pricing must account for the use of proceeds (or distribution of free permits) from the cap-and-trade-system.

Chapter 2, by Burtraw, Walls, and Blonz, considers the distributional implications of carbon pricing arising through policies to allocate permits to consumers through electricity and natural gas local distribution companies (LDCs), as has been proposed in the American Clean Energy and Security Act of 2009 (H.R. 2454), popularly known as the Waxman-Markey bill. Allocation of allowances to LDCs is an effort in large part to equalize costs to electricity users across different regions of the country. Burtraw, Walls, and Blonz show that alternative allocation mechanisms can achieve lower household costs on average and effect a more balanced set of impacts across regions than would occur under the system set out in H.R. 2454. A key message in their analysis is that administrative details matter. How LDCs distribute the value of the permits they receive to rate payers has significant efficiency costs. This message is echoed and amplified in the next chapter in the book.

In Chapter 3, Rausch and colleagues also undertake a distributional analysis of carbon pricing policy using a new computable general equilibrium model of the U.S. economy that offers rich detail about household income and location. The USREP model provides results for the near-term general equilibrium impact of carbon pricing for a number of different scenarios. Whereas Chapter 2 focuses specifically on allowance allocation in the electricity sector, with detailed attention to key provisions of the Waxman-Markey bill, Chapter 3 considers more stylized proposals in a general equilibrium context in which both factor prices and consumer prices can adjust.[3]

Allowing for backward shifting, Rausch and colleagues find that carbon pricing by itself (ignoring the return of revenue) is modestly progressive owing to the policy's impact on capital income. This stands in contrast to most studies that assume full forward shifting of a carbon price into higher consumer prices; these studies find that carbon pricing is quite regressive. The authors find, as do Burtraw, Walls, and Blonz, that policy design matters. Despite proscriptions in H.R. 2454 against using the value

---

[3] Using some public finance terminology, forward shifting occurs when consumer prices rise in response to carbon pricing, whereas backward shifting occurs when factor prices fall. Chapter 2, by Burtraw, Walls, and Blonz, assumes forward shifting of the carbon price, whereas Chapter 3, by Rausch et al., allows for both forward and backward shifting, with the model determining the amount of each.

of LDC allowances to lower the marginal price of electricity, Rausch and colleagues find that if consumers misperceive the free allowance value as lowering the price, then the costs of climate policy rise sharply. Minor differences in the design of the electricity bill could lead electricity customers to confuse a reduction in the average price of electricity with an increase in the marginal price.

The next three chapters address important design features of carbon pricing. Economists in large measure have long favored a carbon tax, whereas politicians and environmental advocates have favored cap-and-trade systems. In Chapter 4, Weisbach analyzes the choice between taxes and cap-and-trade systems and argues that in a domestic context the two systems can be made to be functionally identical. The oft-stated differences – taxes fix prices but let emissions vary, whereas cap and trade fixes emissions but let prices vary – ignore flexible design principles under either a tax or permit system that can blur or eliminate the distinctions. In the international context, however, Weisbach argues that important differences remain and that taking coordination, monitoring, and verification problems into consideration leads to a distinct preference for taxes over cap and trade.

Much of the debate over carbon taxes versus cap-and-trade systems has hinged on the seminal paper by Weitzman (1974). A key point in Weisbach's chapter is that the Weitzman analysis for the climate problem is incomplete and that inappropriate conclusions can be drawn from applying Weitzman's model to the climate change instrument choice problem. Chapter 5, by Kaplow, elaborates on Weisbach's argument. Kaplow – as well as Weisbach – argues that the Weitzman model has two key limitations: its reliance on linear instruments, and the assumption that policy cannot be revisited in the future. Once one relaxes those assumptions, either approach can be used and, most importantly, the carbon price can be designed to match the marginal damage of emissions at any point on a nonlinear marginal damage curve. In other words, we needlessly limit ourselves in requiring the use of linear instruments.[4] The Kaplow chapter was originally commissioned as a set of comments on the Weisbach contribution to this book at the Washington, D.C., conference at which these papers were presented. Kaplow expanded on his conference comments to such an extent that what were originally intended to be comments on the Weisbach chapter in the book became a fully freestanding and substantive chapter.

---

[4] Some might argue that linear systems are simpler, but the nonlinear nature of the personal income tax (marginal tax rates increasing with income) is among the least complex aspects of the tax code.

A major concern for policy makers considering the design of U.S. climate policy is the possibility of "leakage." Leakage occurs when the policy-induced higher costs of carbon-intensive manufacturing lead firms to shift production from a country that imposes a carbon price to one that doesn't. If the manufactured goods now produced in a country with no carbon price in place are exported to the United States and no tariff is placed on their embedded carbon, then a domestic carbon tax will have no impact on emissions but will simply lead to a loss of domestic jobs.[5] An obvious solution to this problem is to levy a tariff on embedded carbon in imported goods from countries that do not impose a carbon price. This solution, however, runs up against two obstacles: first, it is not obvious what the tariff rate should be on the imported products; second, any such tariff needs to be made compatible with international trade agreements. Chapter 6, by McLure, addresses these complex issues.

Drawing on a vast literature on border adjustments for value-added taxes, McLure describes the various ways in which border adjustments could be made and carefully walks the reader through how they would operate. His careful analysis makes clear the difficult task facing lawmakers to construct a border-adjustment system that takes into account the varying carbon-pricing regimes in other countries and avoids creating any number of distortions and unintended consequences. McLure dissects various arguments for and against different border-adjustment approaches and clearly distinguishes irrelevant from crucially important issues.

Chapter 7, by Strand, revisits the cap and trade versus tax debate from an entirely new perspective. Whereas Weisbach and Kaplow show that most of the differences between these two instruments are overstated, Strand raises an important difference in a world in which some countries export energy goods (e.g., oil) to other countries and have market power. Carbon taxes and cap-and-trade policies are no longer equivalent in the Weisbach and Kaplow sense. A carbon-tax system in oil-importing countries enhances the strategic position of the oil-importing countries relative to a cap-and-trade system. In short, the tax is more efficient than a cap-and-trade system at extracting monopoly rents from oil-exporting countries. Which system a country prefers then depends on whether it is an oil-exporting or an oil-importing country.

The next three chapters in the book turn to broader environmental issues in energy markets. In large measure, they are assessments of existing

---

[5] If foreign production technologies are less efficient than domestic technologies, global emissions could, in fact, rise.

energy policy rather than assessments of possible policy. Chapter 8, by Parry, constructs estimates of the optimal tax on gasoline and diesel in the United States. The analysis draws on earlier work by the author but takes into account up-to-date estimates of the damages from transportation fuel use, including the damages from climate change. In addition, technology has made new instruments possible so that more precisely targeted instruments can be employed (e.g., electronic metering and pay-as-you-drive insurance). As discussed by Fullerton, Hong, and Metcalf (2001), the efficiency gains from more precisely targeted environmental instruments can be large. Parry considers how the optimal tax on gasoline and diesel is affected by the ability to charge directly for externalities related to mileage (as opposed to fuel).

There has been considerable debate over the past decade about the tax treatment of oil and gas producers in the United States. Although most of the discussion has occurred at the federal level, an important driver of oil-production activity is state severance tax policy. Chapter 9, by Chakravorty, Gerking, and Leach, provides a very helpful overview of state oil tax systems and the interplay between state and federal energy taxes. They then embed taxes in a Hotelling model of production to examine how producers adjust the time profile of production in response to taxes. Calibrating their model to U.S. data they find that production is relatively insensitive to changes in state severance tax rates or federal percentage depletion rules. Increasing severance tax rates or further restricting the use of percentage depletion thus is likely to raise new revenues, although whether the federal government or states receive the revenue depends on which tax instrument is changed. Moreover, although the expensing of intangible drilling costs does appear to increase drilling activity, the authors are pessimistic that it will lead to appreciably more oil, given the already extensive drilling activity that has occurred in the continental United States.

Chapter 10, by de Gorter and Just, investigates the complex interactions of the different U.S. biofuels policies. The two key policies are an excise tax credit for ethanol blending in gasoline and mandates for biofuel use in transport fuels. These interact with each other and with existing gasoline excise taxes. The chapter considers how mandates and credits interact with optimal and suboptimal gasoline excise tax rates (accounting for the externalities discussed in Parry's contribution to this volume). The authors confirm previous results that mandates dominate excise tax credits in the presence of optimal fuel taxes. Importantly, they show that the efficiency advantage of mandates over excise tax credits increases sharply if fuel taxes are levied at a suboptimal level. Given the political difficulties with raising the gasoline tax in the United States, these results are highly relevant.

Taken as a whole, the contributions in this book enhance our understanding of the current fiscal treatment of energy and clarify the policy options available to address significant environmental and security issues in our use of energy resources in the twenty-first century. We hope the research reported in this book will aid policy makers in crafting sensible energy policy and stimulate future research.

These chapters grew out of a conference sponsored by the American Tax Policy Institute (ATPI) that was held in Washington, D.C., in October 2009. I am deeply grateful to ATPI for its financial support and to Mike Schler, Victoria Perry, and Dennis Zimmerman from ATPI for their encouragement of this project. Mila Albertson provided able logistical support at the conference itself. I also want to thank the many members of the Washington, D.C., academic and policy community that came to the two-day conference and contributed thoughtful questions and commentary on the papers.

References

Energy Information Administration. 2008. *Federal Financial Interventions and Subsidies in Energy Markets 2007*. Washington, D.C.: Energy Information Administration.

Fullerton, Don, Inkee Hong, and Gilbert E. Metcalf. 2001. A tax on output of the polluting industry is not a tax on pollution: The importance of hitting the target. In *Behavioral and Distributional Effects of Environmental Policy*, Carlo Carraro and Gilbert. E. Metcalf (eds.), pp. 13–38. Chicago: University of Chicago Press.

Metcalf, Gilbert E. 2007. Federal tax policy toward energy. *Tax Policy and the Economy* 21: 145–184.

Metcalf, Gilbert E. 2009. Tax policies for low-carbon technologies. *National Tax Journal* 62 (3): 519–533.

National Research Council. 2009. *Hidden Costs of Energy: Unpriced Consequences of Energy Production and Use*. Washington, D.C.: National Academies Press.

Office of Management and Budget. 2009. *Budget of the United States Government, Fiscal Year 2010*. Washington, D.C.: Government Printing Office.

Weitzman, Martin. 1974. Prices vs. quantities. *Review of Economic Studies* 41 (4): 477–491.

TWO

Distributional Impacts of Carbon Pricing
Policies in the Electricity Sector

Dallas Burtraw, Margaret Walls, and Joshua Blonz

2.1 Introduction

It is well recognized that a carbon tax or cap-and-trade program will have its greatest impact on the electricity sector, which currently accounts for 40 percent of carbon dioxide (CO_2) emissions in the United States. The sector is also a focus of concerns about the costs that climate policy will impose on households. An average household spends approximately $1,315 per year on electricity, which is 31.2 percent of total direct energy expenditures (for electricity, gasoline, natural gas, and heating oil) and 2.25 percent of average household income. In some regions of the country, these numbers are even higher, and for lower-income households the expenditures make up a considerably larger fraction of the annual income (estimates updated from Burtraw, Sweeney, and Walls [2009]).

These factors have led researchers, advocates, and policy makers to suggest a variety of approaches to reducing the impact of climate policy on consumers and alleviating regional disparities. These approaches include assorted ways of redistributing the revenue from auctioned allowances under a cap-and-trade system (or revenue from a carbon tax) and alternative means of allocating allowances under cap and trade. Most recently, H.R. 2454, the Waxman-Markey bill, has proposed that some portion of allowances under a cap-and-trade system be allocated to electricity and natural gas local distribution companies (LDCs) based on current patterns

This research was supported by grants from the National Commission for Energy Policy, the Doris Duke Charitable Foundation, Mistra's Climate Policy Research Program, and the American Tax Policy Institute. We are indebted to Erin Mastrangelo, Karen Palmer, Anthony Paul, and Richard Sweeney for assistance and guidance with our work. We also appreciate the helpful comments of Terry Dinan, Don Fullerton, and participants in the American Tax Policy Institute Conference on U.S. Energy Taxes.

of consumption and emissions. Local distribution companies are retail providers that distribute energy to homes and businesses and are responsible for billing consumers for all the costs of delivered energy. For electricity, these costs include the costs associated with generation, transmission, and distribution, and for natural gas, they include well-head costs, transportation, and distribution. Because they are regulated entities, the thinking is that LDCs will act as trustees on behalf of consumers and will use the allowance value to lessen the burden of climate policy. Under H.R. 2454, electricity LDCs would receive about 30 percent and natural gas LDCs 9 percent of the value of emissions allowances over the next decade. The allocation would phase out between 2026 and 2030.

If LDCs indeed act as trustees on behalf of consumers, then we can expect the electricity and natural gas bills that customers see under this approach to be lower than they would be in a full auction of allowances. The question, then, is how exactly the bills are affected. If the variable price of electricity is lower, then electricity consumption will be higher than in a full auction, and other energy sectors, such as transportation and industry, will have to pick up the slack.[1] The price of CO_2 in this case will be higher than in the full-auction scenario. This leads to higher prices for all goods and services, making it unclear whether households in any given region or income group are actually better off or worse off as a result of the decision to subsidize electricity consumption through allocation to LDCs.

It is possible, though, that electricity LDCs will pass on the value to customers through a fixed-charge component rather than the variable electricity price. This would preserve the marginal price signal, providing a stronger incentive to reduce electricity consumption while, in principle, providing lump-sum relief through lower electricity bills. Electricity bills have a fixed-cost component that covers the cost of providing service to a customer and a variable-cost component that covers the cost of acquiring electricity from the wholesale market, but the extent to which monthly bills actually separate fixed from variable charges varies around the country. In most jurisdictions, in fact, very little of the fixed cost is actually placed in a fixed charge; in cases in which fixed and variable charges are separated, the fixed charges are typically recovered on a volumetric basis. Bill reform would be necessary to provide billing that recovered fixed costs in a separate accounting from variable costs, but this is the domain of state public utility

---

[1] Alternatively, there may be a greater reliance on offsets, which are emissions reductions that are achieved outside the sectors covered by the cap-and-trade program. We do not address issues related to offsets in this chapter.

commissions. Moreover, even if fixed and variable charges were separated, it is a behavioral issue whether households and businesses would distinguish changes in the overall bill from changes in the marginal price.

These issues highlight the uncertainties that exist with the LDC approach to allocation. In this chapter, we analyze the effect of LDC allocation on households across a variety of scenarios and behavioral assumptions. We assess the distributional impacts across eleven regions of the country and ten income groups. We first look only at the 30 percent of the allowance value that is to be allocated to electricity LDCs under H.R. 2454, and we compare three alternative scenarios. In one case, we assume conventional electricity pricing and behavior for all customer classes. All consumers – residential, commercial, and industrial – receive the allocation of allowance value to LDCs as a reduction in the variable price of electricity over the full-auction scenario. In a second case, we assume that LDCs are able to separate entirely the fixed and variable charges for industrial and commercial customers and that these consumers respond rationally; residential customers, meanwhile, are assumed to perceive the reduction in the fixed charge (and commensurately in their overall bill) as a reduction in the variable price of electricity. We compare theses two cases to a third in which there is no free allocation to LDCs at all; rather, the value is returned to households as a per capita, nontaxable dividend.

We investigate whether the LDC approach does a better job of protecting low- and middle-income households and/or reduces regional disparities. We also analyze if the benefits from lower electricity prices are offset by the higher allowance price and impacts in other sectors. The results shed light on a familiar trade-off between distributional and efficiency goals in policy design and allow us to describe the efficiency cost of this attempt to address distributional concerns.

Finally, we focus more narrowly on the specific design in the proposed legislation H.R. 2454. In addition to the allocation to electric LDCs, we incorporate the 9 percent allocated to natural gas LDCs, the 1.5 percent to home heating-oil providers, and the 15 percent that goes to low-income households. Together, these features of the bill account for an additional 26 percent of emissions allowances, to bring the total to 56 percent. We compare this approach to full auction and per capita dividend, and to a more incremental reform for H.R. 2454 that preserves allocation to LDCs for residential-class customers only.

Our analysis suggests that households on net are made worse off as a consequence of the LDC allocation policy compared to one in which the revenue is distributed directly back to households on a per capita basis.

Assuming that commercial and industrial customers respond rationally to the fixed/variable distinction reduces the burden somewhat, but even in that case, the LDC approach is more costly to households than an auction-and-dividend option. We also note some interesting regional differences in results between the LDC allocation scheme and auction and dividend. Finally, we find that an incremental reform, which allocates some allowances to LDCs based on residential consumption and the remainder as a per capita dividend, does a better job of achieving the distributional and regional goals of H.R. 2454 than does the approach in the bill, which allocates more to electricity and natural gas LDCs, home heating-oil providers, and low-income households. Moreover, our reform does so at a lower efficiency cost.

We hasten to point out that our analysis focuses on household consumption behavior and the impacts of carbon pricing that are felt through higher prices and expenditures, as well as the impacts of the allocation schemes. In fact, the latter is our focus here. However, we do not assess any general equilibrium effects, impacts on specific industries, and impacts felt through worker dislocations. We also do not consider the benefits of reducing CO_2 emissions and the distribution of those benefits across income groups and regions. Furthermore, we focus on annual income as a measure of ability to pay, rather than a measure of lifetime income.[2] In our earlier work, we used a measure of lifetime income (Burtraw, Sweeney, and Walls 2009).

In the next section, we briefly discuss other literature that has assessed the distributional impacts of climate policy. Following that discussion, we review the evolution in policy with respect to allocation of emissions allowances and provide the rationale behind the LDC approach given the current landscape of electricity regulation in the United States. Section 2.4 describes our data and methodology, including the Haiku electricity market model used to assess impacts of carbon pricing in the electricity sector. Section 2.5 presents results with respect to general approaches to allocation. In Section 2.6 we consider in more detail the Waxman-Markey proposal (H.R. 2454) as a case study in current policy. Section 2.7 provides concluding remarks.

2.2 Literature Review

It is now fairly well established that putting a price on CO_2 emissions disproportionately harms low-income households. Pricing CO_2 increases

---

[2] See Fullerton (2009) for a discussion of the various distributional aspects of taxes.

energy prices; whereas higher-income households tend to spend more on energy than do low-income households, they spend less as a fraction of income. Thus, low-income households tend to be harmed relatively more when energy prices rise. Even accounting for the indirect effect on nonenergy goods and services, this finding tends to hold (Hassett, Mathur, and Metcalf 2009). Agreement on this point has contributed to a focus in recent years on the allocation of allowance value in a cap-and-trade program or distribution of revenues raised with a carbon tax or auctioned allowances. Findings in the literature now emphasize the importance of allocation to the overall efficiency and equity of the program.

Dinan and Rogers (2002) find that distributional effects hinge crucially on whether allowances are grandfathered or auctioned and whether revenues from allowance auctions, or from indirect taxation of allowance rents, are used to cut payroll or corporate taxes or provide lump-sum transfers to households. For example, they estimate that households in the lowest-income quintile would see their average after-tax income reduced by 6 percent under grandfathered allowances, whereas households in the top quintile would see a gain of 1.2 percent. Grandfathering tends to benefit high-income households because the value accrues to shareholders, who are primarily in the upper-income groups. This result was also found in Parry (2004) in a calibrated analytical model. In contrast, Dinan and Rogers (2002) find that if allowances are auctioned with revenues returned in equal lump-sum rebates for all households, then the distribution of costs across income levels would be reversed. Households in the bottom quintile would see average after-tax income rise by 3.5 percent, whereas households in the top quintile would lose 1.6 percent. Using auction revenues to cut payroll or corporate taxes is found to be regressive, although less so than grandfathering.

Metcalf et al. (2008) assess the overall impacts of three recent CO_2 tax bills introduced in Congress, assuming that revenues are returned as per capita dividends. They focus on the question of whether the tax is passed forward to consumers or borne in part by producers. Specifically, they look at three scenarios: one in which the burden of the tax is fully passed forward to consumers in the form of higher energy and product prices, and two scenarios in which a share of the burden is borne by producers, that is, shareholders of firms.[3] The tax alone, assuming full forward shifting, is highly regressive, but returning revenues lump sum makes it progressive.

---

[3] The backward-shifting analysis is informed by runs from the MIT Emissions Prediction and Policy Analysis model. See Paltsev et al. (2007) for a description of the model.

Households in deciles 1 through 6 are actually better off with the policy; only the two highest-income deciles experience a net loss. Shifting the burden back to shareholders also reduces the regressivity of the tax, as shareholders are predominantly in the higher-income groups.

Metcalf (2009) assesses the impact of a CO_2 tax coupled with a reduction in payroll taxes. Specifically, he gives each worker in a household a tax credit equal to the first $560 of payroll taxes; this would be equivalent to exempting from the payroll tax the first $3,660 of wages per worker. Metcalf (2009) finds that this option leads to an outcome that is approximately distributionally neutral. He then analyzes an option that couples this rebate with an adjustment to Social Security payments that benefits the lowest-income households. This makes the CO_2 policy more progressive. Finally, he compares these options to a lump-sum redistribution of the CO_2 tax revenues and finds that this last option is the most progressive of all.

Studies that also analyze the regional impacts of climate policy include Hassett, Mathur, and Metcalf (2009), Boyce and Riddle (2009), and Burtraw, Sweeney, and Walls (2009).[4] Hassett, Mathur, and Metcalf (2009) use data from the Bureau of Labor Statistics' Consumer Expenditure Survey (CES) for 1987, 1997, and 2003 and assess the impacts of a carbon tax if it were enacted in each of those years. They find that the direct component of the tax – the impact felt through direct energy consumption – is significantly more regressive than the indirect component – the impact felt through consumption of energy-using goods and services. They also find, as have several other studies, that the regressivity of the tax is muted when a measure of lifetime income is used rather than annual income. The authors find only small differences in the incidence of the tax across regions. However, they only look at impacts on average households in each region and not across income groups.

Boyce and Riddle (2009) assess the state-by-state net impact on households of a cap-and-dividend option in which the government auctions all CO_2 emissions allowances and returns the revenue as a per capita dividend. The authors estimate state-level impacts by adjusting national-level CES data on the basis of state-level income, an estimate of emissions intensity of electricity consumption in each state, and information on regional

---

[4] Pizer, Sanchirico, and Batz (2010) also look at regional impacts but do not consider differences across income groups. Moreover, they look only at direct energy use; the other studies described here, as well as our own, include both direct and indirect energy consumption.

consumption patterns from Burtraw, Sweeney, and Walls (2009). The authors conclude that differences across states are relatively small compared to differences across income brackets. They find that within each state, for a program with a $25 per metric ton CO_2 ($mtCO_2$) allowance price, at least 60 percent of households receive net benefits; that is, the per capita dividends more than offset the impact of carbon pricing on expenditures.

Burtraw, Sweeney, and Walls (2009) assess the incidence of a cap-and-trade proposal similar to the Lieberman-Warner proposal (S. 2191), which results in a $20.91/$mtCO_2$ allowance price, with five alternatives for distributing the allowance value: two cap-and-dividend scenarios, one in which dividends are taxed and one untaxed, and three options that would change preexisting taxes – reducing the payroll tax, reducing the personal income tax, and expanding the Earned Income Tax Credit (EITC). The authors find that the cap-and-dividend options and the EITC alternative reverse the regressivity of carbon pricing. Reducing payroll or income taxes, however, exacerbates the regressivity. Regional differences are small for average households for all of the options but are significantly larger for lower-income households.

The recent debate and passage of H.R. 2454 have resulted in analyses from the Energy Information Administration (EIA) (2009), the Congressional Budget Office (CBO) (2009), and the Environmental Protection Agency (EPA) (2009). These analyses differ from the aforementioned journal articles in that they narrowly analyze only the provisions detailed in the legislation. The EIA, CBO, and EPA all used different models and different underlying assumptions in those models. The studies yield average costs of $134 (EIA), $175 (CBO), and $105 (EPA) per household in 2020. These cost estimates are for the national average household in the United States, with only the CBO providing a breakdown of effects across the income distribution. The CBO finds that households in the lowest-income quintile would see a net benefit of $40, with households in the highest quintile experiencing a net cost of $245.

2.3 Allocation in Cap-and-Trade Programs

The economics literature finds significant efficiency advantages from distribution of emissions allowances through an auction rather than free allocation. Some benefits are qualitative: an auction is administratively simple, it helps to maintain transparency and the perception of fairness, and it leads to more efficient pricing of goods in the economy, which reduces the cost of the policy (Binmore and Klemperer 2002; Burtraw et al. 2007).

In contrast, especially in regulated electricity markets, free allocation can move consumer prices away from the marginal social cost of production and therefore distort resource allocation in the wider economy away from the efficient optimum (Burtraw et al. 2002).

Another forceful reason why economists favor the use of an auction (or an emissions tax) is that it generates funds that can be used to help reduce the cost of policy. One use of funds might be to invest in program-related goals such as energy efficiency (Ruth et al. 2008). The public finance literature has focused on dedicating the use of revenue from an auction to reduce preexisting taxes. Like any new regulation, climate policy imposes a cost on households and firms that acts like a virtual tax, reducing the real wages of workers. However, revenue from an auction, if dedicated to reducing other preexisting taxes, can reduce this cost. This so-called revenue recycling would have substantial efficiency advantages compared with free distribution (Bovenberg and Goulder 1996; Parry, Williams, and Goulder 1999).

In practice, however, most previous emissions trading programs have distributed emissions allowances for free. The most well-known example may be the so-called grandfathering of allowances in the sulfur dioxide (SO_2) trading program initiated under the 1990 Clean Air Act Amendments in the United States. This program freely allocates emissions allowances to incumbent emissions sources based on a formula that multiplies heat input during a base period (1985–1987) by a target emissions rate (measured in tons per million British thermal units heat input). The allocation does not adjust over time, which avoids creating incentives for investment behavior to deviate from what is otherwise efficient. However, that rule leads to the result that facilities that retire continue to receive their allocation decades into the future.

Other trading programs that freely allocate allowances, such as the nitrogen oxide (NO_x) budget program in the United States, typically have such adjustments. Individual states determine the allocation of NO_x allowances, and most have set-asides for new sources, whereas sources that retire lose their allocations. Adjustments in the allocation to new sources or to remove allowances from retired sources also have been common in the European Union Emissions Trading Scheme (Åhman et al. 2007). The downside of this scheme is that it can bias investment toward higher-emitting generating sources because of the value of the subsidy received (Åhman and Holmgren 2006). Furthermore, the removal of allocations from sources that retire provides a financial incentive to continue the operation of existing facilities that otherwise would retire.

The suggestion of free distribution through grandfathering to incumbent emitters without adjustment should be the most popular approach for industry because it awards an asset worth tens of billions of dollars. In the electricity sector, which is the focus of our study, such an approach would lead to substantial net profits (windfall profits) as a result of climate policy (Burtraw and Palmer 2008). This occurs because the increase in revenues associated with the increase in electricity price would greatly outweigh the increase in costs resulting from compliance with the program when emissions allowances are given away for free. Experience in the E.U. system also indicates that the net profits that resulted from free allocation to the electricity sector emerged as one of the most politically controversial aspects of the program.

Nonetheless, the suggestion of free distribution through grandfathering to incumbent emitters poses a dilemma that has divided opinions within the electricity industry in the United States. The industry is split into two camps along geographic lines that correspond to regulatory status. Before the 1992 Energy Policy Act, the industry was fully regulated for all services, including generation, transmission, and distribution, and typically these services were delivered by a single vertically integrated firm in each service territory. Under regulation, electricity prices are set to recover total costs, and although exceptions abound, the rule of thumb is that prices are set at the average cost of service; that is, total costs divided by total sales should equal the average electricity price.

Since the mid-1990s, roughly half the nation has moved away from cost-of-service regulation to the use of market-based prices for generation services. In these regions – the northeast states, Texas, and, to varying degrees, parts of the Ohio Valley – generation costs are determined by the marginal cost of providing power in the wholesale power market. The marginal cost can vary significantly over the time of day and season of the year as different generation units are brought into service that have different fuel costs and different emissions rates for CO_2.

The way prices are determined varies greatly under these two market structures; consequently, the effect of grandfathered allowances on electricity prices varies as well. In a competitive market, firms are expected to recognize the opportunity cost of using an allowance for compliance even if they received the allowance for free, and that opportunity cost should be reflected in the marginal cost of providing electricity. Hence, in market-based regions, the price of power should increase to reflect not only the resource costs of reducing emissions, but also the value of allowances that are used for compliance, even if those allowances were received for free.

A different outcome results in regulated regions, where allowances are added to total recoverable costs at their original cost of zero under grandfathering. Hence, in these regions the cost of service would increase by the cost of achieving emissions reductions through fuel switching, using more efficient facilities, and so forth, but the cost would not include emissions allowances. The value of allowances is several times greater than the resource costs associated with reducing emissions, so the exclusion of that value in electricity prices means that prices would increase by much less than if the firm had to acquire their allowances in an auction.

As a consequence of the differences in regulation and market structure in different states, the effect on retail electricity prices of climate policy using grandfathering varies across regions. In fact, the difference in the change in prices depends much more on the regulation that is in place than on the actual emissions intensity of electricity. Paul, Burtraw, and Palmer (2010) estimate the effect on prices from the introduction of an emissions cap in the electricity sector commensurate with the Lieberman-Warner proposal as modeled by the EIA (2008). They find an auction would cause electricity prices to increase by $7/MWh in 2020 on average (2004 dollars), with regulated regions experiencing an increase of $6.10 and market-based regions experiencing an increase of $8.50. Under grandfathering, however, the change in prices on average for the nation would be just $2.70. Prices would actually fall by $1 in regulated regions compared to the absence of climate policy, whereas they would rise by $9.90 in market-based regions.

The difference in the potential price increases of grandfathering has fueled a dissonance in the industry, with widely divided views about the merits of climate policy. Over the last couple of years an alternative proposal has emerged that provided a way out of this dilemma for the industry: free allocation to electricity consumers rather than to electricity generators. This proposal also appeals to consumer advocates, and it won the endorsement of the National Association of Regulatory Utility Commissioners (April 21, 2008). Free allocation to consumers could be achieved by allocating not to generation companies, which are the historic emitters, but to the LDCs that deliver retail power to households and businesses. These companies are regulated throughout the nation and charge electricity prices that are a combination of expenses incurred from purchasing generation and transmissions services and their own costs of distribution. Because these companies are regulated, they might be expected to act as trustees on behalf of customers and to pass on, in some form, the value of emissions allowances they receive for free. This proposal has emerged as a key piece of proposed legislation, including the Waxman-Markey proposal (H.R. 2454).

In effect, free allocation to LDCs looks like grandfathering for regulated regions of the country, because the value of CO_2 allowances is not reflected in prices in these regions under grandfathering. Moreover, this effect is carried over to market-based regions under free allocation to LDCs. Paul, Burtraw, and Palmer (2010) indicate that free allocation on the basis of population served by the LDCs would lead to no increase in electricity prices in regulated regions and to an increase of just \$1.80/MWh in competitive regions, with national average electricity prices increasing by just \$0.60/MWh by 2020. This difference in the change in prices is broadly consistent with the emissions intensity of generation in these regions and, hence, would seem to offer a consistent economic signal.

A problem, however, is that the economic signal that is offered is weakened and does not provide adequate information about the opportunity cost of CO_2 emissions to electricity consumers. The award of free allowances to LDCs constitutes a subsidy to electricity consumption, resulting in lower prices and greater levels of electricity use. Consequently, other covered sectors are required to make additional, less efficient, reductions. For the same emissions, this raises the price of emissions allowances by roughly 15 percent (Paul, Burtraw, and Palmer 2010).[5] Ultimately, LDC allocation provides both advantages and disadvantages that must be well understood and balanced if it is to be used.

The second issue associated with allocation to LDCs is how to determine the apportionment among LDCs of the allowance value to be distributed. Paul, Burtraw, and Palmer (2010) consider three possible metrics with apportionment on the basis of population, emissions, or electricity consumption, and they find that this choice can change the price impact in various regions by over \$10/MWh. For example, regions that have relatively high populations and relatively low emissions, such as California or the Northeast, would benefit from allocation on the basis of population, whereas regions with relatively high emissions would prefer allocation on the basis of emissions. These large regional effects are an important determinant of a national compromise.

---

[5] The EIA has targeted this provision in H.R. 2454 as lowering the direct energy costs households face while simultaneously increasing the cost of the program. "The analysis shows that the free allocation of allowances to electricity and natural gas distributors significantly ameliorates impacts on consumer electricity and natural gas prices prior to 2025, when it starts to be phased out. While this result may serve goals related to regional and overall fairness of the program, the overall efficiency of the cap-and-trade program is reduced to the extent that the price signal that would encourage cost-effective changes by consumers in their use of electricity and natural gas is delayed" (EIA 2009).

The third issue associated with allocation to LDCs is exactly how they can be expected to act on behalf of consumers. The estimates are built on the assumption that the award of allowance value would be used by the LDCs to reduce the electricity price, which leads to expanded consumption. However, the way that the value is used will be determined at the state level, where public utility commissions have the prerogative to determine electricity rates for cost recovery of the LDCs. Language inserted into the Waxman-Markey legislation, which we discuss later, would attempt to ensure that all customers are treated fairly, or to circumvent the expected increase in electricity consumption associated with lower prices by directing value to be applied to reducing the fixed costs rather than variable costs, in some cases. Whether this is plausible, and how it might be implemented, is an open question that, in practical terms, appears beyond the reach of Congress. Consequently, the outcome of allocation to LDCs is uncertain, and we explore the possibilities in our simulation analysis.

2.4 Data and Methodology

We base our analysis on CES data from 2004 through 2006. The population sampled in the CES includes 97,519 observations for 39,839 households; an observation equals one household in one quarter. We use these observations to construct national after-tax income deciles, but because we are interested in regional analyses, we examine the CES data with state-level indicators. This leaves us with a sample for examining regional effects that includes 82,033 observations for 33,234 households in forty-three states plus the District of Columbia. We aggregate the observations into eleven regions (the twenty-one regions in the Haiku model are mapped into these eleven regions). Although observations with missing state identifiers are not used in our regional-level calculations, they are included in our calculations at the national level.

We account for direct energy expenditures and indirect expenditures through the purchase of goods and services.[6] We focus the analysis on 2015, assuming that consumption patterns are the same as in our data period with two exceptions. One is personal transportation; we account for changes in the vehicle fleet expected to result by 2015 from the 2007 Energy Independence and Security Act. In addition, we allow for technological and economic changes in electricity markets that are expected by 2015. Our electricity consumption patterns are obtained from Resources for the

---

[6] Indirect consumption accounts for approximately 49 percent of an average household's carbon emissions.

Table 2.1. *Haiku modeling results for 2015 under a baseline and with the introduction of a price of $20.91/metric ton CO_2*

Region	States	Baseline CO_2 emissions per MWh of generation ($mtCO_2$/KWh)	Post-cap CO_2 emissions per MWh of generation ($mtCO_2$/KWh)	Price Change	Change in consumption
Southeast	AL, AR, DC, GA, LA, MS, NC, SC, TN, VA	0.583	0.464	13%	−5%
California	CA	0.170	0.166	7%	−2%
Texas	TX	0.549	0.549	15%	−5%
Florida	FL	0.538	0.448	15%	−4%
Ohio Valley	IL, IN, KY, MI, MO, OH, WV, WI	0.794	0.654	27%	−8%
Mid-Atlantic	DE, MD, NJ, PA	0.573	0.512	18%	−3%
Northeast	CT, ME, MA, NH, RI	0.372	0.317	12%	−4%
Northwest	ID, MT, OR, UT, WA	0.344	0.195	8%	−3%
New York	NY	0.308	0.288	16%	−1%
Plains	KS, MN, NE, OK, SD	0.835	0.749	20%	−9%
Mountains	AZ, CO, NV	0.627	0.471	18%	−7%
National		0.596	0.492	16%	−5%

Future's Haiku electricity model. The Haiku model solves for electricity market equilibria in twenty-one regions of the country, accounting for price-sensitive demand, electricity transmission between regions, system operation for three seasons of the year (spring and fall are combined) and four times of day, and changes in capacity investment and retirement over a 25-year horizon (Paul, Burtraw, and Palmer 2009). The Haiku model also captures differences in the regulatory environment across regions and allows us to model different behavioral assumptions corresponding to fixed and variable charges for residential, commercial, and industrial customers, as we explained in the introduction. Table 2.1 reports the electricity sector results for the eleven regions of the country that we model, with an indication of how states are aggregated into these regions.[7]

---

[7] The forty-eight contiguous states and the District of Columbia are included in the electricity modeling; as noted, five states (Iowa, New Mexico, North Dakota, Vermont, and

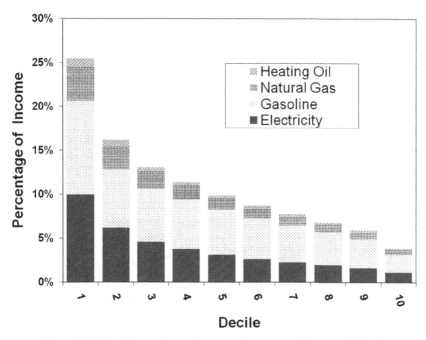

Figure 2.1. Direct Energy Expenditure as a Percentage of Income by Decile.

National baseline emissions of 0.596 tons of CO_2 emissions per megawatt-hour reflect model results for 2015 in the absence of any climate policy. After the introduction of an emissions cap leading to a price of $20.91/mtCO_2 (2006 dollars), the allowance price for 2015 predicted by EIA (2008) to result under the Lieberman-Warner proposal, emissions fall to 0.492 tons/MWh. Table 2.1 also reports the change in electricity price on a regional basis and the change in consumption that is expected to result from the introduction of the price on CO_2 emissions.

Household direct energy expenditures include electricity, gasoline, natural gas, and heating oil. Figure 2.1 shows expenditures in each of these categories as a fraction of annual income for average households in each income decile.

Spending on electricity does not vary substantially in absolute terms across deciles, but it does vary as a share of income, ranging from 10.0 percent for the lowest decile to 1.2 percent for the highest. On average, across all deciles, households spend 2.25 percent of income directly on electricity.

Wyoming) are dropped when calculating effects on households at the regional level. However, national estimates always include these five states.

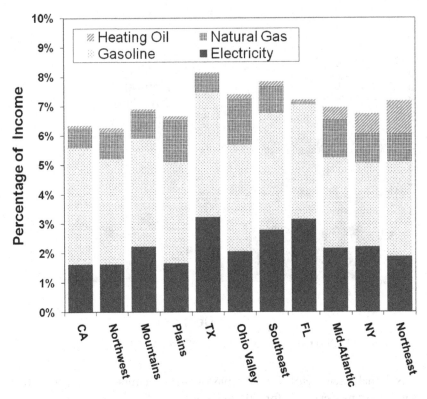

Figure 2.2. Average Direct Energy Expenditure as a Percentage of Income.

Regionally, we find some differences in spending as a fraction of income, but they are not large for average households. Results are shown in Figure 2.2.

The average total expenditure ranges from a low of 6.4 percent of annual income in California to a high of 8.1 percent in Texas. Categories of expenditure vary considerably across regions, however. For example, in New York and the Northeast, home heating contributes importantly to expenditures; electricity expenditures are substantially greater as a percentage of income in the South than for other regions, as are gasoline expenditures.[8]

Our model uses these consumption patterns by region and decile to estimate household-level emissions, which are scaled to per capita emissions

---

[8] In earlier work (Burtraw, Sweeney, and Walls 2009), we looked at the impacts by income decile within each region and showed that the regional differences are greater for low-income households. In this paper, our regional analysis focuses only on average households.

from the EIA analysis of the Lieberman-Warner proposal (S. 2191) and from Haiku for the electricity sector. Per capita precap emissions are estimated to be 16.4 tons of CO_2 per year, with approximately 49 percent of this due to indirect consumption. Government accounts for an additional 2.7 tons of CO_2 per year.

The model also estimates household-level consumer surplus loss that results from a cap-and-trade program. Initial consumer surplus loss (before any revenue is returned) is scaled to total the area under the marginal abatement cost curve at the given CO_2 price as estimated by EIA in its Lieberman-Warner analysis for all sectors except electricity. The electricity sector marginal abatement cost curves are taken from Haiku and vary across scenarios. The initial consumer surplus loss is combined with estimates of the value of the allowances under the various distribution schemes to obtain our estimates of net consumer surplus loss.

2.5 Allocating 30 Percent of Allowances to LDCs

The primary set of scenarios is set up to isolate the effects of two potential LDC allocation outcomes and to compare the results to an auction case in which the allowance value is returned as per capita dividends. We analyze three approaches to distributing 30 percent of the total allowance value. In case 1, we assume conventional electricity pricing with the subsidy placed in the variable portion of the bill. It is equivalent for practical purposes to assume what we describe as conventional economic behavior. By this we mean that for all customer classes we assume that even if regulators try to preserve the CO_2 price as a component of variable prices and assign the allowance value to reduce fixed costs, customers are unable to distinguish between a change in their bill and a change in their price. Under what we characterize as conventional behavior, all customers perceive the allocation of allowance value to LDCs as a reduction in the variable price of electricity from the full-auction case.

In case 2, we assume that LDCs are able to entirely separate the fixed and variable charges and pass on the allowance value by lowering the fixed charge; variable electricity prices are assumed to rise, reflecting the CO_2 price, as in the auction case. We assume further in case 2 that industrial and commercial customers exhibit rational behavior, that is, they distinguish a change in their bill from a change in the price and do not change their electricity consumption in response to changes in fixed charges. They are assumed to pass on the value of the allowances to shareholders. Residential customers, on the other hand, continue to exhibit conventional behavior and

Table 2.2. *Differences in climate policy costs per household with allocation to local distribution companies compared to auction-and-dividend, by income decile* [a]
(2006 Dollars)

National income decile	Average household income	Case 1: Value applied to variable price (Allowance price = $26.90/mt CO_2$)	Case 2: Value applied to fixed charge for industrial/commercial (Allowance price = $22.72/mtCO_2$)
1	7,030	104	112
2	15,372	112	133
3	23,038	130	152
4	31,036	144	162
5	39,553	163	177
6	49,596	167	161
7	61,558	184	165
8	77,074	188	157
9	100,267	200	109
10	178,677	175	−673
Avg.	58,321	157	66

Note: Deciles constructed at the national level.

[a] Differences in costs when 30 percent of total permits are allocated to LDCs rather than through an auction-and-dividend approach. The remaining revenue effectively disappears.

do not perceive the fixed/variable difference, and respond as if electricity prices are lower (as in case 1). We compare these outcomes with a third scenario in which there is no free allocation to LDCs, and the same share of allowance value that would be given to LDCs is returned to households as a per capita, nontaxable dividend. We label this third case auction and dividend.

2.5.1 Impacts on Costs and Incidence across Income Groups

Table 2.2 shows the difference in net consumer surplus loss for cases 1 and 2 as compared with the auction-and-dividend scenario.

The differences are shown for average households in each of ten income deciles as well as the national average across all households.[9] Keep in mind that these are the differences in net consumer surplus losses that result when 30 percent of the allowance value is distributed in alternative ways. Of the remaining 70 percent, we assume that 14 percent is withheld by

[9] National averages include five states that are not included in the regions.

government to account for its own changes in direct energy costs at the federal, state, and local levels; the remaining 56 percent is not accounted for in our model (e.g., it may include free allocation to emitters or be used to fund other government expenditures). The allowance price that results in each case is also shown in Table 2.2. The full consumer surplus loss before any of the allowance value is returned to consumers averages $829 per household when the allowance price is $20.91/mtCO$_2$.[10] This is the allowance price that obtains in the auction-and-dividend scenario that we examine as well. Although we focus on just 30 percent of the allowance value that might be distributed in various ways, for a point of comparison we note that if all of the allowance value is returned to households as a per capita dividend (except for the 14 percent retained by government), the net consumer surplus loss averages $130 per household.

Case 1, in which all customer classes perceive a reduction in the price of electricity compared with the auction-and-dividend scenario, leads to the highest allowance price – $26.90/mtCO$_2$, as compared with $20.91/mtCO$_2$ with the per capita dividend. The higher allowance price results because electricity prices are held down in this scenario. Electricity consumption and emissions are consequently higher, and to achieve the same aggregate emissions economy-wide, emissions reductions must be achieved in other sectors of the economy in which they are more costly. This leads, in turn, to higher costs for other goods and services and raises the net consumer surplus loss of the average household by $157 compared with the auction-and-dividend scenario. Thus, although electricity expenditures are held down, the benefits to households are more than offset by higher costs elsewhere in their consumption bundle.

In case 2, in which only residential customers perceive a lower electricity price in comparison with the full-auction approach, industrial and commercial customers respond to their higher variable electricity price by reducing consumption and thus emissions. This leads to a smaller allowance price than in case 1 ($22.72/mtCO$_2$), but it still raises the net consumer surplus loss for an average household over the auction-and-dividend case by $66.

As the third column of Table 2.2 makes clear, the difference in burdens between case 1 and the auction-and-dividend scenario grows as we move up the income distribution; however, as a fraction of household income, the numbers become smaller. Our earlier research showed that the auction-and-dividend approach is quite progressive in that households in the lower-income deciles see a net gain from climate policy once revenues are returned

[10] All results are reported in 2006 dollars.

in a lump sum, per capita payment (Burtraw, Sweeney, and Walls 2009).[11] Moving to the LDC allocation approach dampens that progressivity by raising costs overall and redistributing some of the costs from higher-income to lower-income households.

This distributional effect is especially evident when comparing across the two LDC allocation scenarios. In case 2, the scenario with separate fixed and variable pricing, commercial and industrial customers are assumed to take the subsidy on the fixed portion of their bill and pay it out as a dividend to their shareholders. The higher variable costs, however, are passed on to their customers in the form of more expensive goods and services. Although this impacts all households, the majority of shareholders are in the top income decile.[12] On the national level, the top income decile fares $673 better than under the auction-and-dividend allocation scheme. This increase is at the expense of households in the lowest five deciles, who do not own much equity but are still faced with higher prices for goods and services. The average household in each of the lowest five deciles is worse off under case 2 than case 1, even though the average household overall is better off.

2.5.2 Regional Impacts

A partial motivation for the LDC approach was to balance the impacts of climate policy across regions. As we explained in Section 2.4, differences in regulation across regions as well as differences in fuel mix are likely to create differences in costs for households. How the full effects play out once we account for consumption patterns across regions and the impact of the LDC approach on prices of all goods and services is unclear. Table 2.3 shows our findings by region.

As in Table 2.2, we show the difference in net consumer surplus loss for case 1 and case 2 over the auction-and-dividend approach for average households; Table 2.3 shows the results for each of eleven regions of the country.

There are substantial differences in the costs of the different approaches across regions. Average households in California and the Northwest are

---

[11] It is important to note that the strong progressivity of cap and dividend in Burtraw, Sweeney, and Walls (2009) results from 86 percent of the revenue being returned as a dividend.

[12] Several studies have emphasized this point; see the analysis of grandfathering of allowances in Dinan and Rogers (2002) and Parry (2004), for example. We use the Federal Reserve Board's 2004 *Survey of Consumer Finances* to determine allocations to shareholders (http://www.federalreserve.gov/PUBS/oss/oss2/2004/scf2004home.html).

Table 2.3. *Differences in climate policy costs per household with allocation to local distribution companies compared to auction-and-dividend, by region*[a] *(2006 Dollars)*

Region	Average household income	Case 1: Value applied to variable price (Allowance price = $26.90/mtCO_2$)	Case 2: Value applied to fixed charge for industrial/commercial (Allowance price = $22.72/mtCO_2$)
Southeast	56,528	148	75
California	69,317	265	135
Texas	58,586	170	56
Florida	54,325	124	52
Ohio Valley	60,237	97	1
Mid-Atlantic	66,037	134	0
Northeast	69,702	185	52
Northwest	61,572	226	141
New York	66,930	168	25
Plains	63,131	145	58
Mountains	58,202	135	67
National	58,321	157	66

Note: Deciles constructed at the national level. Negative welfare losses reflect a net increase in welfare after CO_2 revenues are redistributed.

[a] Differences in costs when 30 percent of total permits are allocated to LDCs rather than through an auction-and-dividend approach. The remaining revenue effectively disappears.

much worse off under the LDC approach, under either case 1 or 2 assumptions, than with a per capita dividend. In case 1, the average household in California loses an additional $265 in consumer surplus and the average household in the Northwest an additional $226. This compares to the average additional loss across all regions of $157. Similarly, in case 2, in which industrial and commercial customers experience a drop in fixed charges on their electricity bill and pass that on to shareholders, households in California and the Northwest are harmed relatively more. By contrast, average households in the Ohio Valley and Mid-Atlantic regions fare equally under the LDC approach under case 2 assumptions and the auction-and-dividend approach.

The explanation for these disparities hinges in large part on the way that allowances are apportioned to the states and their LDCs. The three main criteria by which allowances could be distributed are consumption, emissions, and population. Because each one would affect states differently, the allocation system can dramatically shape regional distributions. All cases in this chapter use a fifty-fifty split between consumption and emissions as stipulated in H.R. 2454. Regions such as the Ohio Valley and the Mid-Atlantic have among the highest emissions intensity of electricity generation (see Table 2.1), so placing 50 percent weight in the apportionment on emissions benefits these regions relative to others. Another factor that affects the distribution of effects is the portion of electricity consumption by each customer class. The Plains region has the nation's lowest share of consumption by residential customers compared to industrial and commercial classes; consequently, relatively fewer of the benefits to residential-class customers under the LDC allocation accrue in this region.

2.6 Limitations of Analysis on Only 30 Percent of Allowance Value

An important consideration is how the remaining revenue not directed to LDCs is allocated (e.g., the remaining 70 percent less the 14 percent to government). How one accounts for this portion of the allowance value affects the calculation of the burden on households. The reason is that its value changes under the different cases we evaluate. For example, allocating revenue to LDCs is likely to lower electricity prices, which leads to expanded electricity consumption. Greater electricity consumption leads to an increase in allowance prices. This consequently increases the total monetary value of the revenue not directed to LDCs. Thus, under an allocation to LDCs, the available potential rebate grows with the allowance price and can offset some of the increased burden felt by households. By focusing only on the 30 percent of allowance value, we ignore this impact.

The increased value of the revenue not directed to LDCs, however, does not totally offset the extra burden on households from the increase in the allowance price. The difference is the efficiency loss that results from other sectors having to make more expensive abatement decisions owing to the expansion of consumption of electricity and greater emissions in the electricity sector. In case 1, the average additional welfare loss to households over the auction-and-dividend scenario is $157; of this amount, $36 constitutes a direct loss in efficiency. The remaining $121 is collected by the government.

Figure 2.2 illustrates the difference in revenue between case 1, in which full LDC allocation is used, and the auction-and-dividend approach. The two scenarios have different slopes as a result of the less-efficient abatement opportunities in case 1. The efficiency loss of $36 per household is signified by the green area between the two curves. The increased allowance price in case 1 generates revenue equal to the increase in the allowance price multiplied by the total emissions. The orange rectangle, equal to 30 percent of this new revenue, is dedicated to the electricity LDC allocation. The remaining 70 percent, or $121 per household, represented by the blue rectangle, is additional revenue collected by the government.[13]

The additional funds resulting from the increase in the allowance price were not explicitly rebated in our analysis in order to isolate the impacts of the LDC allocation, and not to confound those impacts with the distribution of the additional revenue. However, our $157 per household estimate of the extra burden on households should be considered an upper bound on the true burden. Likewise, $36 per household is the lower bound, assuming all of the additional revenue goes back to households. Without any specific direct rebate provisions, the distributional and regional impacts of this money remain uncertain as well.

2.7 A Case Study in Current Policy: LDC Allocation in the Waxman-Markey Proposal and Potential Incremental Reform

Thus far we have analyzed the impacts of the 30 percent of allowances that would go to electricity LDCs under H.R. 2454 without accounting for the remainder of the allowance value. In this section, we place this special treatment for the electricity sector in a broader context. In the bill, over the first couple of decades of the program, 56 percent of emissions allowances would be directed back to consumers and businesses in a way that is intended to rectify disparate impacts among income groups and regions. This allocation is directed to electricity LDCs (30 percent), natural gas LDCs (9 percent), home heating-oil providers (2 percent), and direct compensation to low-income families (15 percent). Although we now account for 56 percent of the allowance value, we do not account for the remaining 44 percent.

We characterize all of these provisions under the assumption in case 1 – that is, that the allocation to LDCs is reflected in a reduction in the variable costs for all customer classes. In fact, the proposed legislation indicates that the allowance value may be directed to reduce the fixed part of the bill "to the maximum extent practicable," but it also indicates that notwithstanding this direction, for industrial-class customers the value may be applied to the variable part of the bill.[14] We assume broadly that residential-class customers

---

[13] We are indebted to Terry Dinan for her comments on this point.

[14] The language says with respect to directing the allowance value to the fixed portion of the bill that "if compliance with the requirements of this title results (or would otherwise result) in an increase in electricity costs for industrial retail ratepayers of any given electricity local distribution company . . . , such electricity local distribution company – . . . may do so based on the quantity of electricity delivered to individual industrial retail ratepayers."

would not be able to distinguish between changes in the price and the bill, and would behave in either case as though electricity is cheaper as a result of the LDC allocation. For commercial-class customers, the implementation of a reduction in the fixed part of the bill is problematic because it introduces moral hazard in the form of incentives to split accounts and open new accounts. Consequently, we represent the allocation to LDCs as a reduction in the variable portion of the bill as the most likely outcome under the proposed legislation.

In this analysis, we compare the results from the Waxman-Markey approach to an alternative incremental reform of the allocation of the 56 percent that limits allocation to LDCs on behalf of only residential consumers of electricity and natural gas. In the reform proposal, the allowance value that was scheduled to go to LDCs on behalf of commercial and industrial electricity and natural gas consumers, as well as the portion scheduled to go to home heating-oil providers and low-income households, would instead be given directly to households in the form of a taxable per capita dividend. This incremental reform thus preserves some aspects of the LDC approach but reduces the allocation to LDCs and removes the other special provisions in favor of cap and dividend. It also allocates 15 percent of the allowance value to residential electricity and natural gas customers, consistent with H.R. 2454, and the remaining 41 percent as a per capita dividend.

2.7.1 Impacts on Costs and Incidence across Income Groups

The difference in the net loss in consumer surplus between the Waxman-Markey allocation and the reform proposal is reported in Table 2.4.

On a national-average basis, the cost per household declines by $78 in the reform proposal owing to the efficiency gain associated with limiting the allocation to LDCs. The allowance price falls from a value of $27.39 when accounting for 56 percent of the allowance value under Waxman-Markey to a value of $23.01 under the reform proposal.

Across income groups, the reform proposal raises the costs for the bottom three income groups and most significantly for the top income group; however, it reduces the costs even more significantly for the middle six income groups. Although households in the first income decile are $80 worse off, on average, under the reform proposal than with H.R. 2454, they still receive an average net gain of $87 under the reform policy. The greatest benefit accrues to the seventh income decile, which has an average income of $61,558. This group would see a reduction in costs of $255 compared to H.R. 2454.

Table 2.4. *Differences in climate policy cost per household of reform proposal compared to H.R. 2454, by decile (2006 Dollars)*

National income decile	Average income	Alternative: Residential electricity and household natural gas LDC allocation (15%) with 41% income dividend[a] (Allowance price = $23.01/mtCO_2$)
1	7,030	80
2	15,372	16
3	23,038	23
4	31,036	−53
5	39,553	−172
6	49,596	−219
7	61,558	−255
8	77,074	−247
9	100,267	−221
10	178,677	191
Avg.	58,321	−78

Note: All negative welfare losses reflect a net increase in welfare compared to H.R 2454. Deciles constructed at the national level.

[a] Results only account for allocation of 56 percent of allowance value. The remaining revenue effectively disappears.

The advantages of the reform are well illustrated in Figure 2.3, which shows the impact on households organized by income deciles.

The status quo allocation of the 56 percent of allowances in H.R. 2454 is displayed in the left panel. The darker blue reports the loss to households from introducing a price on CO_2 before accounting for any of the allowance value. The lighter blue reveals the loss to households after accounting for the 56 percent that we model as a representation of the Waxman-Markey proposal. The lighter blue reveals an inverted "U" with respect to the distribution of costs across household income groups. The status quo allocation in Waxman-Markey would do a good job of protecting the bottom 20 percent of households and the top 10 percent. The dotted horizontal line represents the average loss that we estimate under the proposal.

The right panel in Figure 2.4 displays the incremental reform, which would smooth out the burden across household income groups.

Simultaneously, the reform proposal lowers the overall costs of the program, resulting in every income group performing "above average," that is, with costs below average, when compared to the average loss as a share of income (shown in the left-hand panel). Figure 2.4 also indicates that the reform proposal is somewhat less progressive with respect to the impact

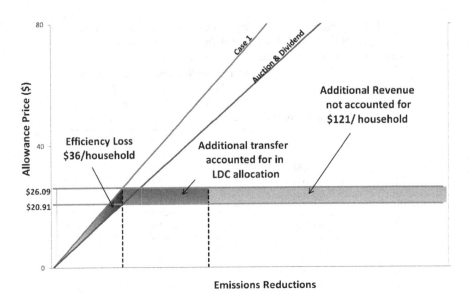

Figure 2.3. Change in Total Allowance Value with Free Allocation to Local Distribution Companies.

on the bottom three income deciles, but the bottom decile remains a net winner under the policy and the second decile nearly breaks even. On net, the proposal appears to do well in protecting low-income households and provides a potent correction to the inverted "U" that appears under the

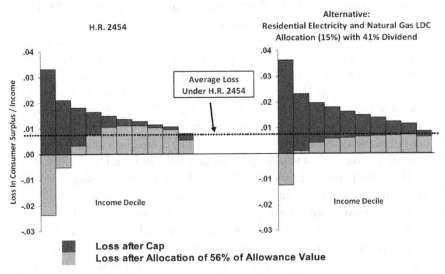

Figure 2.4. Comparison of the Distributional Burden under Alternative Proposals.

Table 2.5. *Differences in climate policy cost per household of reform proposal compared to H.R. 2454, by region (2006 Dollars)*

Region	Average income	Alternative: Residential electricity and natural gas LDC allocation (15%) with 41% dividend[a] (Allowance price = $23.01/mtCO_2$)
Southeast	56,528	−69
California	69,317	−86
Texas	58,586	−129
Florida	54,325	−68
Ohio Valley	60,237	−91
Mid-Atlantic	66,037	−77
Northeast	69,702	−47
Northwest	61,572	−81
New York	66,930	−83
Plains	63,131	−68
Mountains	58,202	−85
National	58,321	−78

Note: All negative welfare losses reflect a net increase in welfare compared to H.R 2454. Deciles constructed at the national level.

[a] Results only account for allocation of 56 percent of allowance value. The remaining revenue effectively disappears.

Waxman-Markey approach, thereby removing the appearance that climate policy imposes a disproportionate tax on the middle class.

2.7.2 Regional Impacts

Free allocation to LDCs may have a justification in reducing regional disparities. However, the reform proposal that would limit LDC allocation to residential customers only does at least as well in this regard. Table 2.5 indicates that the average household in all regions is better off as a result of the reform.

Moreover, those regions with the greatest emissions intensity of electricity generation are among those that benefit the most from the reform. In particular, although costs fall by $78 on average for the nation, they fall by $91 in the Ohio Valley. Among other relatively emissions-intensive regions, costs fall by $68 in the Plains, less than the national average, and by $85 in the Mountain region, greater than average. Household costs are reduced in all of the regions. On net the reform proposal appears to be sufficient to level the playing field across geographic regions as well as to protect low-income households, while reducing the overall costs of the program.

2.8 Conclusion

The introduction of a price on CO_2 will have important effects on the economy, and especially important effects on the electricity sector. This chapter examines alternative approaches to the distribution of allowance value to the sector, including free allocation to consumers through LDCs and direct per capita dividends. Consideration of allocation to LDCs has emerged as an important possibility in just the last three years as the United States has struggled to identify a political compromise that would enable a majority opinion to support climate policy. Allocation to LDCs may contribute to that outcome, but because it represents special treatment of one sector of the economy, it can be expected to raise the overall cost of climate policy. Furthermore, there is uncertainty about how an allocation to LDCs might actually be implemented.

We present the results from a pairing of models. One is built on CES data and provides an understanding of how the introduction of a price on CO_2 will affect households in different regions and income groups. We pair that with a detailed model of the electricity sector, and use this suite of models to analyze the effects of allocation to LDCs.

Compared to an auction with revenues returned on a per capita basis, we find that allocating 30 percent of the allowance value to LDCs raises the allowance price by as much as 29 percent; however, the actual outcome will depend heavily on what is done with the remaining 70 percent of the allowance value. We directly compare two formulations of the way that allocations to LDCs may benefit households. In one case, the allowance value is used by LDCs to directly reduce electricity prices, and we find this would raise the average consumer surplus loss per household by $157 over a case with an auction coupled with a per capita dividend. In the other case, the allowance value is directed toward reducing the fixed portion of electricity bills for industrial- and commercial-class customers, but is used to reduce the electricity price for residential-class customers. We find this would have less of an effect on the overall allowance price, raising it by just $66 over the auction-and-dividend case, suggesting the efficiency cost of this outcome would be less. However, because the reduction in the fixed part of electricity bills would work to the benefit of shareholders of the firms that constitute the LDC's industrial- and commercial-class customers, it has a regressive effect on the distribution of costs over the population, thereby undermining the objective of the allocation to LDCs.

In the last section, we characterize a large part of the allocation scheme in the Waxman-Markey proposal, describing 56 percent of the allocation formula, including provisions that are specifically aimed at correcting income group and regional disparities. This exercise provides a useful insight into the cost of achieving distributional goals from the standpoint of raising the overall cost of the program; even more importantly, it indicates that the same goals can be substantively achieved at much less cost. The proposed reform we model would redirect 44 percent of the allowance value away from its narrowly defined constituents and direct it toward per capita dividends, leaving 15 percent to remain as allocation to electricity and natural gas LDCs that is targeted to residential-class customers only.

This incremental reform results in savings of $78 per year for the average American household compared to the allocation scheme in H.R. 2454. Further, it would protect households in the bottom quintile of the income distribution in a manner similar to H.R. 2454. The middle class, which bears a large portion of the burden under H.R. 2454, would receive substantial relief with the alternate approach. The reform also improves upon H.R. 2454 in addressing regional disparities by further compensating residential electricity consumers in the Ohio Valley region while reducing households burdens overall. The average household in the Ohio Valley region experiences savings of $91 under the reform proposal compared to H.R. 2454, which is even greater than the benefit on average across the nation from this incremental reform.

Another feature of this reform is that it better achieves administrative simplicity and consistency than H.R. 2454. It is unclear how LDC allocation on behalf of industrial and commercial customers will flow to them, or whether the benefits will accrue to shareholders or be reflected in lower prices of goods and services for households. The outcome depends heavily on regulatory decisions by state public utility commissions. The reform we model removes this uncertainty by directly rebating the money as a dividend. The simple approach of direct dividends also avoids the appearance of favoritism by distributing to households an equal share of the value of a new property right that is created under a cap-and-trade program.

Our model has important limitations that could lead to misinterpretation of results, and we have tried to guard against that. The model does not directly replicate H.R. 2454. In the analysis of a reform to the proposed legislation, we use a characterization of LDC allocation that passes value through to all customer classes in the variable charge. Especially important, this analysis also does not account for the remaining 44 percent of the allowance value in any manner. If that value is returned as a per capita dividend or otherwise works to directly reduce the costs of the program for households, then it also lessens the impact of allocation to LDCs on overall cost. If the value is directed to other purposes, however, such as free allocation to industry or expenditure on unrelated programs, then it raises the cost of the allocation to LDCs. Further, we model a limited role for CO_2 offsets and hold that level constant across various scenarios when examining alternative approaches to allocation. Under H.R. 2454, expanded use of offsets early in the program shifts the costs associated with domestic abatement to later years. If the supply of offsets is elastic, then the use of offsets could expand in response to an increase in the allowance price, thereby offsetting part of that increase.

In conclusion, the way that emissions allowances are distributed will have significant efficiency and distributional effects. The way these effects are felt or perceived could have great consequence for the popularity and evolution of climate policy as well as the performance of the economy. This research illustrates that the allocation to LDCs poses a familiar trade-off between efficiency and distributional goals. Although distributional outcomes may be worth the price, we find in our analysis of a reform proposal that similar distributional outcomes may be achieved at much less cost by incrementally substituting toward per capita dividends.

References

Åhman, Markus, Dallas Burtraw, Joe Kruger, et al. 2007. A ten-year rule to guide the allocation of EU emission allowances. *Energy Policy* 35 (3): 1718–1730.

Åhman, Markus, and Kristina Holmgren. 2006. New entrant allocation in the Nordic energy sectors: Incentives and options in the EU ETS. *Climate Policy* 6: 423–440.

Binmore, Kenneth, and Paul Klemperer. 2002. The biggest auction ever: The sale of the British 3G telecom licenses. *The Economic Journal* 112: C74–C76.

Bovenberg, A. Lans, and Lawrence H. Goulder. 1996. Optimal environmental taxation in the presence of other taxes: General equilibrium analyses. *American Economic Review* 86 (4): 985–1000.

Boyce, James and Matthew Riddle. 2009. Cap and dividend: A state-by-state analysis. Political Economy Research Institute, University of Massachusetts, Amherst.

Burtraw, Dallas, Richard Sweeney, and Margaret Walls. 2009. The incidence of U.S. climate policy: Alternative uses of revenues from a cap-and-trade auction. *National Tax Journal* 62 (3): 497–518.

Burtraw, Dallas, and Karen Palmer. 2008. Compensation rules for climate policy in the electricity sector. *Journal of Policy Analysis and Management* 27 (4): 819–47.

Burtraw, Dallas, Jacob Goeree, Charles Holt, et al. 2007. *Auction Design for Selling CO2 Emission Allowances under the Regional Greenhouse Gas Initiative.* Report to the New York State Energy Research and Development Authority. Washington, D.C.: Resources for the Future.

Burtraw, Dallas, Karen Palmer, Anthony Paul, et al. 2002. The effect on asset values of the allocation of carbon dioxide emission allowances. *The Electricity Journal* 15 (5): 51–62.

Congressional Budget Office. 2009. *The Estimated Costs to Households from the Cap-and-Trade Provisions of H.R. 2454.* Washington, D.C.: Congressional Budget Office. http://energycommerce.house.gov/Press_111/20090620/cbowaxmanmarkey.pdf (accessed August 10, 2009).

Dinan, Terry, and Diane Rogers. 2002. Distributional effects of carbon allowance trading: How government decisions determine winners and losers. *National Tax Journal* 55 (2): 199–221.

Energy Information Administration. 2009. *Energy Market and Economic Impacts of H.R. 2454, the American Clean Energy and Security Act of 2009.* SR/OIAF/2009–05. Washington, D.C.: Energy Information Administration. http://www.eia.doe.gov/oiaf/servicerpt/hr2454/pdf/sroiaf(2009)05.pdf (accessed August 20, 2009).

Energy Information Administration. 2008. *Energy Market and Economic Impacts of S. 2191, the Lieberman-Warner Climate Security Act of 2007.* SR/OIAF/2008–01. Washington, D.C.: Energy Information Administration. http://www.eia.doe.gov/oiaf/servicerpt/s2191/pdf/sroiaf(2008)01.pdf (accessed March 10, 2009).

Environmental Protection Agency. 2009. *EPA Analysis of the American Clean Energy and Security Act of 2009 H.R. 2454 in the 111th Congress.* Washington, D.C.: Environmental Protection Agency. http://www.epa.gov/climatechange/economics/pdfs/HR2454_Analysis.pdf (accessed August 5, 2009).

Fullerton, Don. 2009. *The Distributional Effects of Environmental and Energy Policy,* Don Fullerton (ed.). Aldershot, UK: Ashgate Publishers.

Hassett, Kevin, Aparna Mathur, and Gilbert Metcalf. 2009. The incidence of a U.S. carbon tax: A lifetime and regional analysis. *Energy Journal* 30 (2): 155–177.

Metcalf, Gilbert. 2009. Designing a carbon tax to reduce U.S. greenhouse gas emissions. *Review of Environmental Economics and Policy* 3 (1): 63–83.

Metcalf, Gilbert, Jennifer Holak, Henry Jacoby, Sergey Paltsev, and John Reilly. 2008. *Analysis of U.S. greenhouse gas tax proposals.* Working Paper No. 13980, NBER, Cambridge, MA.

Paltsev, Sergey, John Reilly, Henry Jacoby, et al. 2007. *Assessment of U.S. Cap-and-Trade Proposals. Report No. 146,* MIT Joint Program on the Science and Policy of Global Change. Cambridge: Massachusetts Institute of Technology.

Parry, Ian W.H. 2004. Are emissions permits regressive? *Journal of Environmental Economics and Management* 47 (2): 364–387.

Parry, Ian W.H., Roberton C. Williams III, and Lawrence H. Goulder. 1999. When can carbon abatement policies increase welfare? The fundamental role of distorted factor markets. *Journal of Environmental Economics and Management* 37 (1): 51–84.

Paul, Anthony, Dallas Burtraw, and Karen Palmer. 2010. Compensation for electricity consumers under a U.S. CO2 emissions cap. In *Reforming Rules and Regulations: Laws, Institutions and Enforcement,* Vivek Ghosal (ed.). Cambridge: MIT Press.

Paul, Anthony, Dallas Burtraw, and Karen Palmer. 2009b. *Haiku Documentation: RFF's Electricity Market Model Version 2.0.* Washington, D.C.: Resources for the Future.

Pizer, William, James Sanchirico, and Michael Batz. 2010. Regional patterns of U.S. household carbon emissions. *Climate Change* 99 (1–2): 47–63.

Ruth, Mathius, Steve Gabriel, Karen Palmer, et al. 2008. Economic and energy impacts from participation in the regional greenhouse gas initiative: A case study of the state of Maryland. *Energy Policy* 36: 2279–2289.

Comments

Don Fullerton

It is a joy to read and comment on a chapter like this one, written by Dallas Burtraw, Margaret Walls, and Joshua Blonz. They use comprehensive data and modeling to account for many complications in their major effort to measure the effects on ten different income groups from the way in which a cap-and-trade climate policy like the Waxman-Markey bill that passed the U.S. House of Representatives is likely to raise the price of electricity and generate value from permits that may be distributed to households. The result is well written, clear, and convincing. In particular, they employ 82,000 household observations from the Consumer Expenditure Survey from 2004 to 2006, allocate those households into ten annual income deciles, and calculate the expenditure on electricity of each group. Then they use the "Haiku model," which includes specific differences in electricity pricing regulation in twenty-one different regions of the United States, "accounting for price-sensitive demand, electricity transmission between regions, system operation for three seasons of the year . . . and four times of day, and changes in capacity investment and retirement over a 25-year horizon."

Effects would be proportional if all groups spent their income in the same proportions, but the data show that the poorest group spends ten percent of their income on electricity, whereas the richest group spends only 1.2 percent of income on electricity; hence, the effects are regressive. The main question addressed, however, is about the effects of alternative uses of the permit value to help low-income families.

As a baseline, they calculate the effects on each group from a version of the policy that uses 30 percent of permit value to provide a lump sum per capita (called "cap and dividend"). Then they show the change in those effects from a version in which that permit value is returned to customers via price reductions ("conventional behavior") and from a version that reduces the fixed portion of electricity costs for industrial and commercial customers (in which households only think marginal prices are reduced).

I think that the result about regressivity would be a bit more clear if the authors showed all three cases, and not just the two latter variants relative to the first baseline. Also, their initial tables show dollar effects on each group that need to be divided by income to get relative burdens that would show whether any tax is proportional, progressive, or regressive. They do show those relative burdens in later figures, however, so I will leave my only quibbles to this one paragraph, and turn instead next to the main point I want to develop.

In my slide presentation at the conference where the paper was presented, I suggested that three words could be added to the beginning of the title, to clarify that the authors present "*Some of the* Distributional Impacts of Carbon Pricing Policies in the Electricity Sector." This is no major criticism of the paper, as *every* paper on any topic is always intended to cover only some effects and not others. It may help readers, however, to understand better which effects are covered here and which are not.[1]

In particular, the chapter studies effects on output prices (called the "uses side" in standard tax incidence analysis), and it looks at part of the distribution of the scarcity rents (the 30–50% of permit value that is returned to households). Those represent about one and a half of what I describe as *six* different categories of distributional effects in Fullerton (2009). And the other four might be big!

To categorize the six distributional effects, consider the market for electricity in Figure 2.5, where demand reflects private marginal benefits (PMB), and production has rising private marginal costs (PMC). For simplicity assume fixed pollution per unit of output, so that social marginal costs (SMC) include marginal environmental costs (MEC). In this diagram, the private market with no policy restriction would produce to the point where PMB = PMC, namely, output $Q°$. The optimal output is where SMB = SMC, at Q'. A permit policy could restrict output to Q', and we can now categorize distributional effects.

First, this policy raises the equilibrium output price to a new "gross" price, P^g, and it reduces consumer surplus by the trapezoid area A + D. The amount of this price increase and resulting burden is relatively large, as drawn, because the elasticity of demand for this output is low compared

---

[1] Another good review of environmental policy incidence is in Parry, Sigman, Walls, et al. (2006).

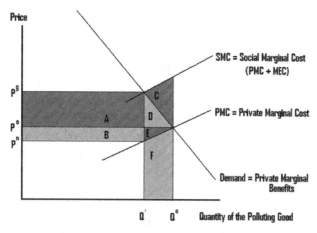

Figure 2.5. Categories of Gains and Losses.

to the elasticity of supply. This first effect is regressive, as captured in the model of Burtraw, Walls, and Blonz.

Second, the permit policy may also impose burdens on producers or on factors of production. Figure 2.5 shows a simple partial equilibrium model, in which the loss in producer surplus (area B + E) is relatively small because the supply curve (PMC) is relatively elastic. These losses could be larger if instead production involves industry-specific resources in relatively fixed supply, such as a specific type of energy, land with specific characteristics, or labor with industry-specific skills. If so, then the cutback in production burdens the owners of those limited resources. A general equilibrium model could be used to solve for the new economy-wide wage, rate of return, or land rents, and a more sophisticated dynamic general equilibrium model could be used to solve for short run effects, capital deepening, and the transition to a new balanced growth path with a new labor/capital ratio.[2]

Third, when the quantity of the polluting good is restricted in Figure 2.5, the restriction makes the good scarce and gives rise to scarcity rents (area A + B). To the extent that the permits are auctioned, the government captures some of those scarcity rents as revenue that can be used for any purpose, such as rebates to households. The chapter considers 30 to 50 percent

[2] Rausch et al. (see Chapter 3) build a general equilibrium model of carbon pricing that incorporates factor price effects on the sources side as well as output price effects on the uses side. Although the effects through output prices are decidedly regressive for reasons explained previously, the effects through reduced capital returns and wage rates are progressive and completely offset the uses side.

of permit value that is returned to households, but Waxman-Markey hands out a lot of permits to industry, so much of area A + B becomes profit.[3]

Fourth, a policy to abate pollution also provides environmental benefits. In Figure 2.5, the gains are represented by area C + D + E, the sum of "marginal environmental costs" over the range that pollution is reduced (from Q° to Q'). Indeed, the main reason for a carbon policy is to reduce greenhouse gas emissions that cause global warming. The benefits of the policy are reduced disruption to agriculture, sea-level rise, and extreme weather events like hurricanes, floods, or droughts. Different income groups may benefit to different degrees. For example, the rich might own more beachfront property that would be saved by an international agreement to reduce emissions.

Fifth, households may be differentially affected by adjustment and transition costs. In Figure 2.5, area E + F represents the value of inputs no longer employed in this industry. They are often assumed to be re-employed elsewhere, with no loss. Yet a change in policy can be very disruptive, especially for a local economy highly dependent on extracting a particular resource used in electricity generation. Coal mining is often a predominant occupation in a town that can be virtually annihilated by environmental protection. Those individuals may acquire a great deal of industry-specific human capital, the value of which is lost by the shrinking of that industry. This human capitalization effect can imply a much larger percentage loss for individuals than other asset price capitalization effects of environmental policy.

Finally, any of the first five effects might be capitalized into stock prices or land prices, in a way that magnifies gains or losses to particular individuals. The expected future handout of permits or "scarcity rents" (area A + B) is capitalized into corporate stock prices, and the benefits from environmental protection (area C + D + E) is capitalized into land prices. Certainly the saving of beachfront property has an effect on those house prices! The entire present value of the gains described in the preceding section can be captured by whoever owns a house site at the time of the change. Capitalization effects also apply to human capital, with even greater proportional gains and losses to individuals.

Interestingly, these capitalization effects move the gains and losses around, sometimes in unpredictable ways. A new environmental mandate

---

[3] Parry (2004) uses a stylized analytical model with explicit formulas that show impacts of underlying parameters. He also looks at other pollutants (SO_2 and NO_X) and other policies (performance standards, technology mandates, and taxes on dirty inputs). He finds that grandfathered permits benefit stockholders and thus can provide gains to high-income groups while imposing large costs on the poor.

on firms imposes costs on shareholders at the time of enactment, not on those who buy later and actually write the check for the pollution abatement equipment. Any gains or losses on waterfront property affect owners at the time, not those who buy later (at a premium or discount).

In general, as pointed out by Burtraw, Walls, and Blonz, higher electricity prices have regressive effects, and rebates to low-income households can offset those regressive effects and allow for environmental protection without adverse distributional consequences. More permits might need to be auctioned, to acquire the revenue necessary to offset these and other unintended distributional effects of climate policy. This point makes it all the more important to use emissions taxes or the auction of permits, rather than to hand out permits to firms in a way that benefits relatively wealthy stockholders.

References

Burtraw, Dallas, Margaret Walls, and Joshua Blonz. 2011. Distributional impacts of carbon pricing policies in the electricity sector. Chapter 2. In *U.S.Energy Tax Policy*, Gilbert E. Metcalf (ed.). Cambridge, UK: Cambridge University Press.

Fullerton, Don. 2009. Introduction. In *The Distributional Effects of Environmental and Energy Policy*, Don Fullerton (ed.), pp. xi–xxvii. Aldershot, UK: Ashgate Publishers.

Parry, Ian. 2004. Are emissions permits regressive? *Journal of Environmental Economics and Management* 47 (2): 364–387.

Parry, Ian, Hilary Sigman, Margaret Walls, et al. 2006. The incidence of pollution control policies. In *International Yearbook of Environmental and Resource Economics 2006/2007*, H. Folmer and T. Tietenberg (eds.). Cheltenham, UK: Edward Elgar Publishers.

Rausch, Sebastian, Gilbert E. Metcalf, John M. Reilly, et al. 2011. Distributional impacts of a U.S. greenhouse gas policy: A general equilibrium analysis of carbon pricing. Chapter 3. In *U.S. Energy Tax Policy*, Gilbert E. Metcalf (ed.). Cambridge, UK: Cambridge University Press.

Comments

Terry M. Dinan

A cap-and-trade program for greenhouse gas emissions would provide economy-wide incentives for households and businesses to reduce their consumption of energy and energy-intensive goods and services. Those incentives are crucial to the program's success in minimizing the cost of achieving the desired cap on emissions. The chapter by Burtraw, Walls, and Blonz offers valuable insights into the potential efficiency cost associated with allocating emission allowances in a manner that undermines incentives for households and businesses to reduce their emissions. As a case study in current policy, the authors consider the implications of allowance allocations to LDCs providing electricity, natural gas, and home heating oil in 2015 under the provisions of H.R. 2454, the American Clean Energy and Security Act of 2009, which was passed by the House of Representatives on June 22, 2009.

Burtraw, Walls, and Blonz assumed that those free allocations, which would account for 41 percent of all emission allowances provided under the act in 2015, would offset the price increases that the customers served by those LDCs would otherwise have faced under the cap-and-trade program. As a result, the authors found that allocations to LDCs would raise the price of allowances by \$4.38 compared with what the price would have been if policy makers had given the allowances away in a manner that did not reduce incentives for households and businesses to conserve energy.

These comments draw upon analyses conducted by the Congressional Budget Office (CBO). Many people contributed to those analyses, including Ed Harris, Robert Johansson, Kevin Perese, Frank Sammartino, Robert Shackleton, Natalie Tawil, and David Wiener. However, the views expressed in this comment are my own and should not be interpreted as those of CBO.

I offer three observations here that supplement the findings that Burtraw, Walls, and Blonz present:

- The efficiency cost of free allocations to LDCs under H.R. 2454 may be less than Burtraw, Walls, and Blonz estimated because provisions in the act that allow firms to bank allowances and to comply with the cap by using offset credits could dampen the effect that the LDCs' allocations would otherwise have had on allowance prices. (Offset credits are generated when domestic or international entities not otherwise covered by the cap reduce their emissions in approved ways.)
- To the extent that free allocations to LDCs increase the price of allowances, they also increase the transfer of income that occurs under a cap-and-trade program – that is, the amount of income that is transferred from households through the higher prices that they pay for the goods and services that they consume to households that ultimately receive the allowance value. Thus, an understanding of the distributional implications of any increase in allowance prices that might result from free allocations to LDCs requires accounting for the value of all of the allowances.
- Estimates of both the efficiency and distributional effects of allocations to LDCs depend crucially on assumptions about how LDCs would pass the allowances' value on to their customers. As a result, transferring the allowances' value to energy consumers indirectly through LDCs creates significant uncertainty about the effects of such a policy.

Provisions that Allow Banking and the Use of Offset Credits Could Dampen the Allowance Price Increase that Would Otherwise Result from Free Allocations

Under the cap-and-trade program that H.R. 2454 would establish, firms would be able to bank unused allowances in any given year to use in future periods – which would smooth their compliance costs over time. The bill would also allow firms to submit offset credits in lieu of up to two billion emission allowances each year.

Analyses that take allowance banking into account typically assume that such an approach will ultimately minimize the cost of meeting the cumulative cap on emissions and cause the price of allowances to rise over time at a rate that reflects the opportunity cost associated with banked allowances (which is typically assumed to be a real rate of return of between 5 percent and 7 percent). Because of banking, the availability of low-cost options for complying with the policy in future periods affects the price of allowances in early periods.

The combination of allowance banking and offset credits tends to reduce the price increases that would otherwise result from policies that dampened consumers' incentives to conserve energy. As that dampening began to push up the prices of allowances in the early years of the policy's implementation, firms would bank fewer of them, which would tend to lower allowance prices in that period, other things being equal. In addition, to the extent that dampening the incentive to conserve energy boosted allowance prices, it would also tend to increase the supply of domestic and international offset credits. (With a relatively flat supply curve, international offset credits in particular would probably be available in very large quantities, but only after the policy had been in place long enough for international agreements to be reached and the necessary provisions for monitoring and enforcement put in place.) That additional supply of offset credits, in turn, would reduce the price of allowances, other things being equal.

In estimating the price of allowances under H.R. 2454, the Congressional Budget Office (CBO) assumed that the allowances that were allocated to LDCs and passed on to residential customers in the form of fixed rebates on customers' bills would reduce households' energy consumption by half the amount that would result from an explicit decrease in the price of electricity. The CBO found, however, that the lessening of households' incentive to conserve energy had only a small effect on the price of allowances (e.g., less than $0.50 in 2020), once decreases in the amount of allowance banking and increases in the use of offset credits for compliance purposes were taken into account.

Allocations that Increase the Price of Allowances Would Increase the Total Amount of Income Transferred Under a Cap-and-Trade Program

Burtraw, Walls, and Blonz found that the free allocations to LDCs under H.R. 2454 would increase the price of allowances by $4.38 in 2015. Given that the bill would allocate 5,003 million allowances in that year, the amount of income transferred as a result of the free-allocation policy would increase by roughly $22 billion. In their distributional analysis, Burtraw, Walls, and Blonz accounted for 56 percent, or about $12 billion, of that additional income. The remaining 44 percent, or $10 billion, would be transferred from households based on the carbon content of the goods and services that they consumed to households that benefited from the 44 percent of allowances not allocated in the Burtraw, Walls, and Blonz analysis. Of the 44 percent of allowances not accounted for in their analysis, about 10 percent would be distributed via state and federal programs (e.g., to promote energy efficiency and assist workers); about 23 percent would be given to businesses either directly (e.g., as free allocations to trade-exposed, energy-intensive industries) or indirectly (e.g., as subsidies to electricity generators that capture and sequester carbon dioxide emissions); and 7 percent would be spent overseas (e.g., to help reduce deforestation, promote technology transfer, and assist developing countries to adapt to climate change). A full accounting of the effects of the free allocations to LDCs would entail examining not only the efficiency cost associated with the higher allowance price but also the full effects of the additional income transfer that would take place as a result of the price increase.

The Distributional Results of H.R. 2454 Are Sensitive to Assumptions about Who Ultimately Benefits from the Allowances Given to LDCs

Indirectly providing allowances – through such intermediaries as LDCs – to entities (such as consumers of electricity) that policy makers might wish to compensate for the effects of a policy would create significant uncertainty about the policy's ultimate distributional effects. That uncertainty can be illustrated by examining how a measure of the direct cost of H.R. 2454 would be distributed across households in different income brackets using alternative assumptions about the ultimate beneficiaries of the value of the allowances given to LDCs and passed on to commercial and industrial customers.

The direct cost measure used in demonstrating this point is an estimate of the loss in purchasing power that households would experience as a result of the cap-and-trade program defined in H.R.2454. That loss in purchasing power equals the costs of purchasing allowances, offset credits, and reducing emissions (costs that businesses would generally pass on to consumers in the form of higher prices) minus the compensation that would be received as a result of the policy, including the free allocation of allowances, the proceeds from the sale of allowances, and the profits earned from producing offsets. Once the compensation received by U.S. households is deducted from the costs of compliance, the remaining loss in purchasing power stems from the cost of reducing emissions and producing domestic offsets, from expenditures on international offsets, and from the value of allowances that would be directed overseas. The distribution of the loss in

Terry M. Dinan

Table 2.6. *Average net loss in purchasing power from the greenhouse gas cap–and–trade program in H.R. 2454 under alternative assumptions about the distribution of allowance value given to LDCs for commercial and industrial customers*

	(1) Net gain or loss in purchasing power if LDC allowances for commercial and industrial customers benefit shareholders[a] (In dollars and as a percentage of after-tax income)		(2) Net gain or loss in purchasing power if LDC allowances for commercial and industrial customers benefit consumers of final goods[b] (In dollars and as a percentage of after-tax income)		Net gain or loss in purchasing power under assumption (2) relative to net gain or loss under assumption (1)[b] (Ratio)
First Quintile	$125	(0.7%)	$190	(1.1%)	1.5
Second Quintile	−150	(−0.4)	−70	(−0.2)	−0.5
Third Quintile	−310	(−0.6)	−225	(−0.4)	−0.7
Fourth Quintile	−375	(−0.5)	−315	(−0.4)	−0.8
Fifth Quintile	−165	(−0.1)	−455	(−0.2)	−2.8
Unallocated	10[c]	(0)	10[c]	(0)	N.A.
All Households	−160	(−0.2)	−160	(−0.2)	N.A.

Note: The figures in the table reflect the policy in 2020 measured at 2010 income levels and as a percentage of after-tax income. (The 2010 income levels are based on the 2006 distribution of income and expenditures.) Households are ranked by adjusted household income. Each quintile contains an equal number of people. Households with negative income are excluded from the bottom quintile but are included in the total. Compliance costs are distributed to households on the basis of their carbon consumption.

[a] Congressional Budget Office. September 2009. *The Economic Effects of Legislation to Reduce Greenhouse-Gas Emissions*, Table 2. Washington, D.C.: Congressional Budget Office.

[b] Author's calculations.

[c] The government's share of compliance costs was not distributed across households. In addition, allowances for which the recipients were not specified were not distributed. On net, the value of the allowances that were not distributed across households exceeded the undistributed costs by $10.

purchasing power across households depends both on their consumption of goods and services (whose prices would increase as a result of the policy) and their share of the allowances' value and of the profits made from producing domestic offsets.[1]

In a recent analysis, the CBO estimated how the loss (or gain) in purchasing power, given the allocation of allowances defined by H.R. 2454 for 2020, would vary across households in different income brackets (see column 1 of Table 2.6). That analysis assumed that the allowances that were

[1] For details, see Congressional Budget Office (2009).

given to LDCs and whose value was then passed on to their commercial and industrial customers would ultimately benefit the shareholders of those businesses.

The distribution of the loss (or gain) in purchasing power across households from the same allocation of the same amount of allowances could look quite different under alternative assumptions. For example, column 2 of Table 2.6 indicates the outcome if the value of the allowances that were given to LDCs to use for the benefit of their commercial and industrial consumers was ultimately passed on to the final consumers of the goods produced by those entities. (Such an outcome could arise, for example, if LDCs issued rebates to commercial and industrial customers on the basis of the specific quantity of electricity that they purchased.) That outcome is modeled by distributing the allowance value among households in the form of lower prices for the non-direct energy-related goods and services that they consume.

Variations in the assumption about how the value of the allowances that businesses indirectly receive through LDCs ultimately benefits households would significantly affect the way losses in purchasing power would be distributed among households. For example, the loss in purchasing power (measured at 2010 levels of income) experienced by households in the second quintile of the income distribution would be roughly 50 percent less if the allowances given to LDCs, and passed on to businesses, ultimately reduced prices rather than increased profits. In contrast, the loss in purchasing power experienced by households in the highest quintile would be roughly 2.75 times as large in that case. The average household in the lowest income quintile would experience an increase in after-tax income under either assumption about the distribution of allowances to LDCs.

Uncertainty about the distributional effects of H.R. 2454 would be less in the latter years of the policy because a smaller fraction of the allowances' value would flow to households via private entities (such as LDCs). By 2050, most of the value of the allowances would flow to households directly, in the form of rebates from the federal government.

References

Burtraw, Dallas, Margarent Walls, and Joshua Blonz. 2010. Distributional impacts of carbon pricing policies in the electricity sector. Chapter 2. In *U.S. Energy Tax Policy*, Gilbert E. Metcalf (ed.). Cambridge, UK: Cambridge University Press.

Congressional Budget Office. September 2009. *The Economic Effects of Legislation to Reduce Greenhouse-Gas Emissions*. Washington, D.C.: Congressional Budget Office.

THREE

Distributional Impacts of a U.S. Greenhouse Gas Policy

A General Equilibrium Analysis of Carbon Pricing

Sebastian Rausch, Gilbert E. Metcalf, John M. Reilly,
and Sergey Paltsev

3.1 Introduction

The United States is moving closer to enacting comprehensive climate change policy. President Obama campaigned in 2008 in part on a platform of re-engaging in the international negotiations on climate policy and supported a U.S. cap-and-trade policy with 100 percent auctioning of permits. Congress moved rapidly in 2009, with the House of Representatives voting favorably on the American Clean Energy and Security Act of 2009 (H.R. 2454) in late June of that year. What will happen in the Senate is still unresolved as this is written.

H.R. 2454 establishes a cap-and-trade system to reduce greenhouse gas emissions 17 percent below 2005 levels by 2020 and 83 percent by 2050. Among other provisions, it contains new energy efficiency standards for various appliances and a renewable electricity standard that requires retail suppliers to meet 20 percent of their electricity demand through renewable sources and energy efficiency by 2020 (see Holt and Whitney [2009] for a detailed description of the bill).

This paper was written for the American Tax Policy Institute Conference on Energy Taxation held in Washington, D.C., on October 15 and 16, 2009. Without implication, we would like to thank Lawrence H. Goulder, Richard D. Morgenstern, Thomas F. Rutherford, and participants at the American Tax Policy Institute Conference on Energy Taxation, Washington, D.C., October 2009, and at the MIT Joint Program U.S. Modeling Meeting, October 2009, for helpful comments and discussion. We thank Dan Feenberg for providing data from the NBER TAXSIM simulator on marginal income tax rates. We thank Tony Smith-Grieco for excellent research assistance. We acknowledge support of MIT Joint Program on the Science and Policy of Global Change through a combination of government, industry, and foundation funding, the MIT Energy Initiative, and additional support for this work from a coalition of industrial sponsors.

Cap-and-trade legislation acts like a tax in raising the price of carbon-based fuels and other covered inputs that release greenhouse gases. The monies involved in a cap-and-trade program are significant. The Congressional Budget Office estimated in June 2009 that H.R. 2454 would increase federal revenues by nearly $850 billion between 2010 and 2019. Because the bulk of permits are freely allocated in the early years of the program, spending would also increase over that period by roughly $820 billion.[1] This chapter uses a new computable general equilibrium model of the U.S. economy, the MIT U.S. Regional Energy Policy (USREP) model, to assess the distributional impacts of carbon pricing, whether in the form of a cap-and-trade system or a carbon tax. Sectoral detail, production structure, and parameters of the USREP model are similar to those of the MIT Emissions Prediction and Policy Analysis (EPPA) model (Paltsev et al. 2005). Whereas the EPPA model is a global model, with the United States as one of its regions, the USREP model explicitly models only the United States. This sacrifice of global coverage allows explicit modeling of regions and states within the United States and multiple household income classes in each region. As with the EPPA model, the USREP model provides rich detail on energy production and consumption, making it particularly suitable for analyzing energy and climate change legislation.

Because it presents information on multiple regions and income classes, the USREP model is especially useful for evaluating the distributional effects of policy. Many of the provisions of H.R. 2454 are designed to blunt the impact of the legislation on lower- and middle-income households and to balance regional effects. Given the potential for the strong distributional effects of climate policy, whether something close to H.R. 2454 passes or not, attention to distributional impacts is likely to be an important feature of any eventual policy.[2] To date, much of the distributional analysis has been done as a side calculation based on the energy and CO_2 prices, simulated in models like EPPA, and on energy expenditure shares in different regions and among households of different income classes. Such analyses fail to take into account the distribution implications of changes in wages and returns on capital, or how CO_2 pricing will translate into different energy price impacts in different regions. The design of the USREP model allows direct consideration of these issues, endogenously calculating effects on

---

[1] See Congressional Budget Office (2009b). The CBO treats freely allocated permits as both revenue and spending. Ignoring impacts on other tax revenues, the free allocation of $100 of permits would be scored as $100 of revenue and $100 of spending. The CBO's scoring approach is described in Congressional Budget Office (2009a).

[2] See, for example, the testimony of Burtraw (2009) before the Senate Committee on Finance.

each household type. We consider a number of possible ways of using the revenue from carbon pricing to show how these strongly affect households at different income levels and in different regions.

Economists often focus on the efficiency of policy first; as diagramed in introductory economics texts, these efficiency considerations are reflected in "welfare triangles." Observers of the policy process in Washington often note that who gets what and who pays are far more important considerations in pushing policy forward or stopping it than efficiency considerations. In the diagrams of economic texts, who gets what and who pays are rectangles, of which the triangles are only a small fraction. A Washington economic policy quip is that rectangles trump triangles every time, a warning that to be relevant to policy the distributional effects are key. Moreover, who ends up bearing costs in a market system is also not automatically intuitive. Who writes the check for the tax bill has little to do with who actually bears the cost. Economists refer to this as the incidence of a tax, and it can be passed forward to consumers or backward to asset owners, and it can affect labor and capital returns. The USREP model offers the ability to examine such distributional effects.

3.2 Background

The impacts of carbon pricing are very similar to those of broad-based energy taxes – not surprising, because over 80 percent of greenhouse gas emissions are associated with the combustion of fossil fuels (U.S. Environmental Protection Agency 2009). The literature on distributional implications across income groups of energy taxes is extensive, and some general conclusions have been reached that help inform the distributional analysis of carbon pricing. First, analyses that rank households by their annual income find that excise taxes generally tend to be regressive (e.g., Pechman [1985], looking at excise taxes in general, and Metcalf [1999], looking specifically at a cluster of environmental taxes). The difficulty with this ranking procedure is that many households in the lowest income groups are not poor in any traditional sense that should raise welfare concerns. This group includes households that are facing transitory negative income shocks or who are making human capital investments that will lead to higher incomes later in life (e.g., graduate students). It also includes many retired households that may have little current income but are able to draw on extensive savings.

That current income may not be a good measure of household well-being has long been known and has led to a number of efforts to measure lifetime income. This leads to the second major finding in the literature.

Consumption taxes, including taxes on energy, look considerably less regressive when lifetime income measures are used than when annual income measures are used. Studies include Davies, St.-Hilaire, and Whalley (1984), Poterba (1989, 1991), Bull, Hassett, and Metcalf (1994), Lyon and Schwab (1995), and many others.[3]

The lifetime income approach is an important caveat to distributional findings from annual incidence analyses, but it relies on strong assumptions about household consumption decisions. In particular, it assumes that households base current consumption decisions knowing their full stream of earnings over their lifetime. Although it is reasonable to assume that households have some sense of future income, it may be implausible to assume that they have complete knowledge or that they necessarily base spending decisions on income that may be received far in the future.[4] It may be that the truth lies somewhere between annual and lifetime income analyses. This chapter takes a current income approach to sorting households.

Turning to climate policy, in particular, a number of papers have attempted to measure the distributional impacts of carbon pricing across household income groups. Dinan and Rogers (2002) build on Metcalf (1999) to consider how the distribution of allowances from a cap-and-trade program affects the distributional outcome. Both these papers emphasize that focusing on the revenue from carbon pricing (either a tax or auctioned permits) provides an incomplete distributional analysis. How the proceeds from carbon pricing are distributed have important impacts on the ultimate distributional outcome.

The point that use of carbon revenues matters for distribution is the basis for the distributional and revenue-neutral proposal in Metcalf (2007) for a carbon tax swap. It is also the focus of the analysis in Burtraw, Sweeney, and Walls (2009). This latter paper considers five different uses of revenue from a cap-and-trade auction, focusing on income distribution as well as regional distribution. A similar focus on income and regional distribution is done by Hassett, Mathur, and Metcalf (2009). This paper does not consider the use of revenue but does compare both annual and lifetime income measures as well as a regional analysis using annual income. Grainger and Kolstad (2009) do

---

[3] Most of these studies look at a snapshot of taxes in one year relative to some proxy for lifetime income – often current consumption based on the permanent income hypothesis of Friedman (1957). An exception is Fullerton and Rogers (1993), who model the lifetime pattern of tax payments as well as income.

[4] On the other hand, casual observation of graduate students in professional schools (business, law, and medicine) makes clear that many households are taking future income into account in their current consumption decisions.

an analysis similar to that of Hassett, Mathur, and Metcalf (2009) and note that the use of household equivalence scales can exacerbate the regressivity of carbon pricing. Finally, Burtraw, Sweeney, and Walls (2009) consider the distributional impacts in an expenditure-side analysis in which they focus on the allocation of permits to local distribution companies (LDCs), an issue to which we now turn.

All of the aforementioned papers assume that the burden of carbon pricing is shifted forward to consumers in the form of higher energy prices (and higher prices of energy-intensive consumption goods and services). That carbon pricing is passed forward to consumers follows from the analysis of a number of computable general equilibrium models. Bovenberg and Goulder (2001), for example, find that coal prices rise by over 90 percent of a $25 per ton carbon tax in the short and the long run (Table 2.4 in Bovenberg and Goulder [2001]).[5] This incidence result underlies their finding that only a small percentage of permits need be freely allocated to energy-intensive industries to compensate shareholders for any windfall losses from a cap-and-trade program. See also Bovenberg, Goulder, and Gurney (2005) for more on this issue.

Metcalf et al. (2008) consider the degree of forward shifting (higher consumer prices) and backward shifting (lower factor returns) over different time periods for a carbon tax policy begun in 2012 and slowly ramped up through 2050. The tax on carbon emissions from coal are largely passed forward to consumers in all years of the policy in roughly the same magnitude found by Bovenberg and Goulder (2001). Roughly 10 percent of the burden of carbon pricing on crude oil is shifted back to oil producers initially, with the share rising to roughly one-fourth by 2050 as consumers are able to find substitutes for oil in the longer run. Interestingly, the consumer burden of the carbon tax on natural gas exceeds the tax. This reflects a sharp rise in demand for natural gas. An initial response to carbon pricing is to substitute gas for coal in electricity generation. By 2050 the producer price is falling for reasonably stringent carbon policies.[6]

Fullerton and Heutel (2007) construct an analytic general equilibrium model to identify the various key parameters and relationships that

---

[5] They assume world pricing for oil and natural gas so that the gross of tax prices for these two fossil fuels rise by the full amount of the tax.

[6] Distributional results depend importantly on the stringency of policy. How stringent the policy is affects whether carbon-free technologies are adopted in the EPPA model and therefore what the relative demand for fossil fuels is. In the preceding text we are reporting carbon tax results for a policy that limits emissions to 287 billion metric tons over the control period.

determine the ultimate burden of a tax on a pollutant.[7] Although the model is not sufficiently detailed to provide a realistic assessment of climate change impacts on the U.S. economy, it illustrates critical parameters and relationships that drive burden results.

The general equilibrium models just discussed assume a representative agent in the United States, thereby limiting their usefulness to considering distributional questions. Metcalf et al. (2008) apply results from a representative agent model to data on U.S. households that allow them to draw conclusions about distributional impacts of policies, but the household heterogeneity is not built into the model.[8]

Several computable general equilibrium (CGE) models have been constructed to investigate regional implications of climate and energy in the United States. For example, the ADAGE model, documented in Ross (2008), has a U.S. regional module that is usually aggregated to five or six regions. The MRN-NEEM model described in Tuladhar et al. (2009) has nine U.S. regions. Both these models use a single representative household in each region.

The USREP model described in the next section marks an advance in the literature and climate change policy modeling by allowing for heterogeneity across income groups and regions in the United States. Among other things, the model allows us to test the reasonableness of previous model assumptions about complete forward shifting of carbon pricing to consumers. We turn to that model now.

3.3 The USREP Model

The USREP model merges economic data from IMPLAN (Minnesota IMPLAN Group 2008) with physical energy data from Energy Information Administration's State Energy Data System (SEDS). Most of the basic data are at the state level, so there is flexibility in the regional structure. We aggregate from the state level to regions, with the regional aggregations determined to capture difference in electricity costs and to help focus on how regions and states differ. A detailed technical description of the model and issues involved in merging these two datasets into a consistent

---

[7] The paper also provides a thorough summary of the literature on the incidence impacts of environmental taxes.

[8] A recent paper by Bento et al. (2009) marks an advance in the literature by allowing for household heterogeneity over income and location. That paper considers the impact of increased U.S. gasoline taxes, taking into account new and used car purchases along with scrappage and changes in driving behavior.

economic database are described in Appendices A through C in this chapter. In the following sections, we briefly describe the key components of the model.

3.3.1 Households

The USREP model is a multiregion, multisector, multihousehold CGE model of the U.S. economy for analyzing U.S. energy and greenhouse gas policies that has the capability to assess impacts on regions, sectors and industries, and different household income classes. As in any classical Arrow-Debreu general equilibrium model, our framework combines behavioral assumptions on rational economic agents with the analysis of equilibrium conditions, and represents price-dependent market interactions as well as the origination and spending of income for various economic agents based on microeconomic theory. Profit-maximizing firms produce goods and services using intermediate inputs from other sectors and primary factors of production from households. Utility-maximizing households receive income from government transfers and from supplying factors of production to firms that they spend on buying goods and services. The government collects tax revenue that is spent on consumption and household transfers. The USREP model implemented here is a static model calibrated to 2006 data. It distinguishes twelve regions that are aggregations of U.S. states as defined in Table 3.1 and visualized in Figure 3.1.[9] Consistent with the assumption of perfect competition on product and factor markets, production processes exhibit constant returns to scale and are modeled by nested constant-elasticity-of-substitution (CES) functions. A schematic overview of the nesting structure for each production sector is provided in Appendix A. Non-energy activities are aggregated into five sectors, as shown in Table 3.1.[10] The energy sector, which emits several of the non-CO_2 gases as well as CO_2, is modeled in more detail. The static USREP model is a first development phase toward a dynamic model that is similar to the EPPA model. In this analysis, we apply a relatively low CO_2 price, $15 per ton CO_2 equivalent, with the intent of showing results relevant to the first few years

---

[9] Alaska is a region in the model; we simulate policy in it, but we do not report results because we do not have the same degree of confidence in results for this region as we do for other regions. Alaska results are highly sensitive to minor changes in modeling scenarios because of the small population in the state. Merging Alaska with other regions, on the other hand, is problematic given the unique energy characteristics of the state.

[10] A detailed discussion of the adopted nesting structure and its empirical relevance to reflect substitution possibilities among various inputs, in particular with regard to fuels and electricity, can be found in Paltsev et al. (2005).

Table 3.1. *USREP model details*

Region[a]	Sectors	Factors
Alaska (AK)	**Non-Energy**	Capital
California (CA)	Agriculture (AGRIC)	Labor
Florida (FL)	Services (SERV)	Crude Oil Resources
New York (NY)	Energy-Intensive (EINT)	Natural Gas Resources
New England (NENGL)	Other Industries (OTHR)	Coal Resources
South East (SEAST)	Transportation (TRAN)	Nuclear Resources
North East (NEAST)	**Energy**	Hydro Resources
South Central (SCENT)	Coal (COAL)	
North Central (NCENT)	Crude Oil (OIL)	
Mountain (MOUNT)	Refined Oil (ROIL)	
Pacific (PACIF)	Natural Gas (GAS)	
	Electric: Fossil (ELEC)	
	Electric: Nuclear (NUC)	
	Electric: Hydro (HYD)	

[a] Model regions are aggregations of the following U.S. states: NENGL = Maine, New Hampshire, Vermont, Massachusetts, Connecticut, Rhode Island; SEAST = Virginia, Kentucky, North Carolina, Tennessee, South Carolina, Georgia, Alabama, Mississippi; NEAST = West Virginia, Delaware, Maryland, Wisconsin, Illinois, Michigan, Indiana, Ohio, Pennsylvania, New Jersey, District of Columbia; SCENT = Oklahoma, Arkansas, Louisiana; NCENT = Missouri, North Dakota, South Dakota, Nebraska, Kansas, Minnesota, Iowa; MOUNT = Montana, Idaho, Wyoming, Nevada, Utah, Colorado, Arizona, New Mexico; PACIF = Oregon, Washington, Hawaii.

of a climate policy. The static version of the model incorporates electricity generation from fossil fuel, nuclear and hydropower, and existing fuels, but not the array of advanced technologies in EPPA. Electricity outputs generated from different technologies are assumed to be perfect substitutes. We constrain the expansion of nuclear and hydropower to no more than a 20 percent relative to the benchmark level or, given this structure, production from these sources can expand without bound. Other advanced technologies would only be relevant at higher CO_2 prices and further into the future, so we believe that the static model, as formulated, is appropriate to study the effects of a relatively modest greenhouse gas emissions (GHG) pricing policy implemented in the near term.

Economic modeling often distinguishes between short- and long-run effects. In the short run agents have a limited ability to adjust to changed prices, whereas in the long run they adjust completely within the constraints of available technology. Because capital is fully mobile in the static USREP model, the analysis conducted here is closest to a long-run result. Although potential backstop technologies are not specified, they are unlikely to be

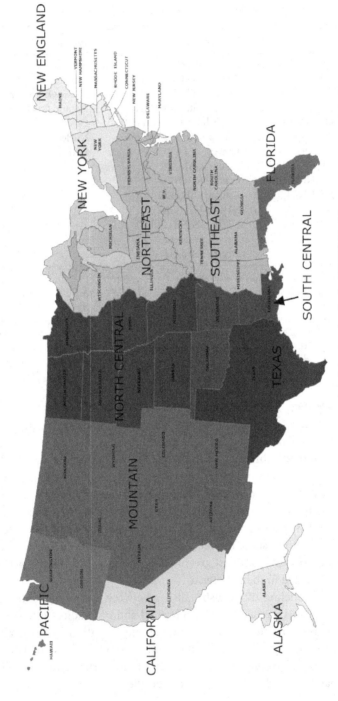

Figure 3.1. Regional Aggregation in the USREP Model.

Table 3.2. *Income classes used in the USREP model and cumulative population*

Income class	Description	Cumulative population for whole United States (in %)[a]
hhl	Less than $10,000	7.3
hh10	$10,000 to $15,000	11.7
hh15	$15,000 to $25,000	21.2
hh25	$25,000 to $30,000	31.0
hh30	$30,000 to $50,000	45.3
hh50	$50,000 to $75,000	65.2
hh75	$75,000 to $100,000	78.7
hh100	$100,000 to $150,000	91.5
hh150	$150,000 plus	100.0

[a] Based on Consumer Expenditure Survey Data for 2006.

relevant at a CO_2 price of $15. Hence, results of the USREP show the impact we would expect of implementing a CO_2 price of $15 (and maintaining it) and allowing 20 or 30 years for the economy to adjust to this level.[11]

We assume that labor is fully mobile across industries in a given region but is immobile across U.S. regions. Labor supply is determined by the household choice between leisure and labor (e.g., Babiker, Metcalf, and Reilly 2003). Capital is mobile across regions and industries. We assume an integrated U.S. market for fossil fuel resources and assume for the core model that the regional ownership of resources is distributed in proportion to capital income.[12] Savings enters directly into the utility function, which generates the demand for savings and makes the consumption-investment decision endogenous. We follow an approach by Bovenberg, Goulder, and Gurney (2005) distinguishing between capital that is used in production of market goods and services and capital used in households (e.g., the housing stock). We assume that income from the former is subject to taxation and that the imputed income from housing capital is not. A more detailed discussion of the nesting structure of total consumption can be found in Paltsev et al. (2005).

We distinguish nine representative household types for each region based on different income classes as defined in Table 3.2. We use a linearly homogeneous CES structure to describe preferences of households, implying that

[11] Immobility of labor among regions is consistent with an intermediate run. Note also that a comparative statics analysis can be set to capture long-run effects. It does not capture growth effects, which are important in the tax-recycling cases we investigate.

[12] Given the lack of data describing the regional ownership of fossil fuel resources in the U.S., we use capital income as a proxy.

the income elasticity is unity and does not vary with income.[13] Household heterogeneity refers to a different structure in terms of income sources as well as expenditures. The nesting structure is illustrated in Appendix A.

3.3.2 Government

Conventional tax rates are differentiated by region and sector and include both federal and state taxes. Revenue from these taxes is assumed to be spent in each region, proportional to its current levels. This takes account of varying state tax levels and the current distribution of the spending of federal tax revenue among the states. Different assumptions are possible, but the intent here is to focus on the implications of CO_2 pricing and revenue distribution, and not muddy that by assuming changes in distribution of other federal or state tax revenues. The USREP model includes ad-valorem output taxes, corporate capital income taxes, and payroll taxes (employers' and employees' contribution). These tax rates are calculated on the basis of IMPLAN, which provides data on inter-institutional tax payments. In the case of capital income taxes, this allows us to calculate average tax rates only. We incorporate marginal personal income tax rates based on data from the NBER TAXSIM tax simulator. We use the NBER data together with IMPLAN data on total personal income tax payments to estimate slope coefficients of a linear income tax schedule for each income class and region, capturing a nonlinear income tax across the entire income range.

3.3.3 Trade

Sectoral output produced in each region is converted through a constant-elasticity-of-transformation function into goods destined for the regional, national, and international markets. All goods are tradable. Depending on the type of commodity, we distinguish three different representations of intranational regional trade. First, bilateral flows for all non-energy goods are represented as "Armington" goods (Armington 1969), where like goods from other regions are imperfectly substitutable for domestically produced goods. Second, domestically traded energy goods, except for electricity, are assumed to be homogeneous products (i.e., there is a national pool that

---

[13]   We have experimented with a linear expenditure demand system in which consumption is measured relative to subsistence levels and have calibrated preferences to empirically plausible values for income elasticities ranging from 0 to 1. We found that this very slightly increases welfare costs for low-income classes. Overall, quantitative effects for the type of policy analyses that we consider here are negligible.

demands domestic exports and supplies domestic imports). This assumption reflects the high degree of integration of intra-U.S. markets for natural gas, crude and refined oil, and coal. Third, we differentiate six regional electricity pools that are designed to provide an approximation of the existing structure of independent system operators (ISO) and the three major NERC interconnections in the United States. More specifically, we distinguish the Western, Texas ERCOT, and Eastern NERC interconnections and identify AK, NENGL, and NY as separate regional pools.[14,15] We assume that within each regional pool traded electricity is a homogenous good and that there is no electricity trade between regional pools.

Analogously to the export side, we adopt the Armington (1969) assumption of product heterogeneity for imports. A CES function characterizes the trade-off between imported (from national and international sources) and locally produced varieties of the same goods. Foreign closure of the model is determined through a national balance-of-payments (BOP) constraint. Hence, the total value of U.S. exports equals the total value of U.S. imports, accounting for an initial BOP deficit given by the base-year statistics. The BOP constraint thereby determines the real exchange rate that indicates the (endogenous) value of the domestic currency vis-à-vis the foreign currency.

The U.S. economy as a whole is modeled as a large open economy, by specifying elasticities for world export demand and world import supply functions. Thus, although we do not explicitly model other regions, the simulations include terms of trade and competitiveness effects of policies that approximate results we would get with a full global model.

3.4 Scenarios and Analysis

We model a greenhouse gas policy that establishes a price on all greenhouse gases of $15 per metric ton of CO_2 equivalents.[16] We describe the scenarios

---

[14] We identify NY and NENGL as separate pools because electricity flows with contiguous ISOs represent only a small fraction of total electricity generation in those regions. For example, based on our own calculation from data provided by ISOs, net electricity trade between ISO New England and ISO New York accounts for less than 1 percent of total electricity produced in ISO New England. Interface flows between the New York and neighboring ISOs amount to about 6 percent of total electricity generation in ISO New York.

[15] The regional electricity pools are thus defined as follows: NENGL, NY, TX, AK. Each represents a separate pool. The Western NERC interconnection comprises CA, MOUNT, and PACIF. The Eastern NERC interconnection comprises NEAST, SEAST, and FL.

[16] The greenhouse gases are converted to CO_2 equivalents (CO_2e) using 100-year global warming potentials from the IPCC Second Assessment Report, those specified in most policy measures.

in terms of a cap-and-trade system but stress that the analysis applies equally to a carbon tax applied to the same base. A cap-and-trade system in which all permits are auctioned by the government is economically equivalent to a carbon tax. In both cases, carbon pricing raises the price of fossil fuels and carbon-intensive products while raising revenue for the federal government. A cap-and-trade system in which the permits are freely allocated according to some rule (or set of rules) can be decomposed into a two-part policy. In the first part, permits are fully auctioned, and in the second part, the auction revenue is distributed in a manner that mirrors the free distribution of permits. For that reason we do not focus on whether permits are auctioned; rather, we focus in the different scenarios on how the revenue is returned to the economy[17] – that is, returning revenue to agents in the economy is equivalent, for modeling purposes, to distributing allowances to them that they would then sell and receive payment for equal to the CO_2 price.[18] In order to facilitate comparisons across the various scenarios, we fix government revenue relative to GDP at the same level as in the reference (no policy) scenario, which we define as revenue neutrality.[19] This means that not all carbon pricing revenue is available for recycling purposes, because some is required to replace losses in other tax revenues as economic activity is affected by the policy. We impose this requirement as a constraint in the model to calculate endogenously in each simulation the amount needed to be held back, rather than assume a fixed percentage of revenue to cover losses in other tax revenues, as is done by the Congressional Budget Office (Congressional Budget Office 2009a). We consider seven different scenarios that differ in terms of how the revenues are returned to households. In all cases policy effects are assessed with respect to a reference scenario in which no policy changes apply.

Table 3.3 provides a full list of scenarios. In the LUMPSUM scenario the revenue from a carbon tax or cap-and-trade program is distributed by means of a uniform lump-sum transfer. Owing to tax base erosion, and given the revenue-neutrality constraint, only some part of total allowance revenue can be recycled. We endogenously determine the level of lump-sum

---

[17] Our two-part decomposition suggests a broader point, emphasized by Weisbach (2009), that the differences between taxes and cap-and-trade systems are, on many dimensions, more apparent than real.

[18] There may be political economy considerations in whether the allowances are distributed or the allowances are auction and the revenue distributed, but those do not affect the model results.

[19] Some analysts define revenue neutrality as the absolute level of revenue, but we observe that over time tax revenue has remained at about the same share of GDP.

Table 3.3. *Overview of scenarios*

Scenario	Description
LUMPSUM	Revenue is recycled through uniform lump-sum transfers per household.
PAYRTAX	Revenue is recycled through a uniform cut in payroll taxes.
MPITR	Revenue is recycled through a uniform cut in marginal personal income tax rates.
CAPTAX	Revenue is recycled through a uniform cut in average capital income tax.
CAPITAL	Revenue is allocated in proportion to capital income.
ELE_LS	Revenue is allocated in proportion to capital income except for revenue going to the electricity sector. Here revenue is allocated in proportion to electricity consumption.
ELE_SUB	Revenue is allocated in proportion to capital income except for allowances going to the electricity sector. Here revenue is assumed to subsidize the domestic consumer electricity price.

payment that satisfies revenue neutrality and give all households an equal transfer amount.[20]

The next three scenarios recycle climate revenue by lowering existing taxes. The PAYRTAX scenario uniformly reduces the payroll tax rate across all workers. The MPITR scenario reduces marginal tax rates for the personal income tax by the same amount (in percentage point terms). Finally, the CAPTAX scenario lowers capital income tax rates by the same amount (in percentage point terms). Although these three scenarios are perhaps most easily thought of in terms of a green tax reform, they are all possible with a cap-and-trade system with fully auctioned permits.

The final three scenarios return the revenue in ways intended to represent free allocation of allowances. The value of allowances allocated freely to industrial emitters or upstream producers of fossil fuels would generate a windfall gain for these firms, and those gains would accrue to equity owners of the firm. This would be equivalent to distributing the revenue from auctioned permits or taxes to the equity holders in these firms. The CAPITAL scenario assumes that the distribution of holdings is similar to the distribution of holdings of all capital income. We do not have data on how holdings of capital in carbon-intensive firms may differ

---

[20] The USREP model, as described, has a representative household for each income class in each region. To determine the distribution, we use data from the U.S. Census Bureau on the number of regional households in each income class, to weight the distribution to each income class by the actual number of households.

among regions or income levels, but this approach captures the fact that in general higher-income households own more equity than low-income households.

The American Clean Energy and Security Act of 2009 allocates a portion of permits to local gas and electricity distribution companies to be used to offset the higher costs of gas and electricity by retail customers. The legislation prohibits the use of the permit value for lowering gas or electricity rates, but leaves unclear how those funds will be distributed. It is also not clear how utilities subject to rate-of-return regulation will be treated in rate-setting proceedings at the state level. We assume that regulated rate-of-return industries would not be allowed to retain the windfall gain associated with the value of allowances distributed to them, but that the gain would go to ratepayers.

Although the legislation attempts to preserve the efficiency of passing through higher prices to consumers, an important question is whether or not that will be done in a way that consumers perceive as effectively lowering prices. If electricity bills include higher prices, and the funds are rebated separately (e.g., at the end of the year), consumers may indeed perceive higher electricity prices in their monthly bills. This possibility is modeled by treating the distribution as lump-sum rebates based on electricity expenditure in the ELE_LS scenario. However, if utilities rebate allowance value back to consumers in their monthly bill, even if they separately detail the electricity costs at high prices and the rebate, consumers may just see the low final bill and assume that reflects lower electricity rates. In the ELE_SUB scenario we assume that the value of electricity sector allowances is passed on to consumers by subsidizing the domestic consumer price for electricity at an endogenously determined rate to capture this possible response. In both scenarios, we assume that all non-electricity allowances are distributed on the basis of capital income. The ELE_SUB scenario is an effort to capture a possible behavioral response by consumers in which they misperceive the true price of electricity, or that the intent of the legislation, to have rates reflect the full CO_2 costs, is somehow frustrated by Public Utility Commission's rate setting.[21] We begin by reporting results from the model for the United States as a single region in which we focus on heterogeneity in income across households. We then consider regional variation and, finally, report results in which we allow for heterogeneity across households

---

[21] Burtraw, Sweeney, and Walls (2009) also consider different consumer responses to different LDC allocation schemes. Because they only focus on the electricity sector, they cannot assess the overall efficiency consequences of different allocation schemes.

Table 3.4. *Policy impacts on climate*

CO_2 Emissions	5,902.0
Non-CO_2 Emissions	1,055.7
Reduction in CO_2 Emissions from Reference Case	19.3%
Reduction in non-CO_2 Emissions from Reference Case	27.1%

Note: Emissions are reported for the Reference Case in million metric tons.

and regions. Before turning to those results, however, we report some summary impact measures for the climate policy analyses.

Table 3.4 reports greenhouse gas emissions in the reference (no policy) scenario as well as the reduction in emissions following the imposition of a $15 per metric ton carbon price. The bulk of the reduction in emissions comes from CO_2, although the percentage reduction in non-CO_2 emissions is higher. Aggregate emissions fall by 20.5 percent for the $15 carbon price. An important driver of the final burden of climate policy is its impact on fossil fuel prices. Table 3.5 reports prices for the various regions in our model as well as the carbon price as a percentage of that base price. Price data are taken from the Energy Information Administration database on state energy consumption and expenditures and include federal and state

Table 3.5. *Relationship between $15/mt CO_2e price and 2006 average fuel prices*

	Coal		Natural gas		Refined oil	
	Base price ($/short ton)	Added cost (%)	Base price ($/tcf)	Added cost (%)	Base price ($/gal)	Added cost (%0)
AK	43.42	66	4.77	17	2.10	6
CA	44.07	65	9.19	9	2.31	5
FL	52.81	54	9.43	9	2.08	6
MOUNT	28.70	100	9.54	9	2.36	5
NCENT	25.34	114	10.10	8	2.28	5
NEAST	36.00	80	12.20	7	2.33	5
NENGL	62.99	46	10.96	7	2.36	5
NY	50.14	57	11.54	7	2.19	6
PACIF	32.81	88	16.09	5	2.22	6
SCENT	29.97	96	8.46	10	2.19	6
SEAST	46.74	62	11.14	7	2.19	6
TX	30.73	94	7.21	11	2.04	6
US	40.31	71	10.05	8	2.22	6

Note: No adjustment for the effects of the policy on producer price. All prices are in 2006 dollars.
Source: Fuel prices are based on Department of Energy EIA price data and refer to average prices over all end-use categories and states in a given region.

Table 3.6. *Impacts on fuel prices inclusive and exclusive of GHG charge (in %)*

	Coal		Natural gas		Refined oil		Electricity
	Inclusive	Exclusive	Inclusive	Exclusive	Inclusive	Exclusive	Inclusive
AK	50.6	−15.0	14.8	−4.6	3.0	−2.4	3.5
CA	71.8	−6.4	10.2	−3.1	4.7	−0.2	8.5
FL	72.8	−5.4	11.5	−3.1	5.1	0.0	9.9
MOUNT	89.5	−10.6	9.9	−2.3	4.8	−0.2	14.8
NCENT	76.2	−6.8	11.1	−1.7	5.3	0.2	19.8
NEAST	69.4	−7.9	9.5	−3.3	5.1	0.0	14.2
NENGL	73.8	−4.5	9.5	−1.4	4.9	0.0	12.0
NY	71.8	−6.4	10.6	−0.7	5.0	0.0	7.5
PACIF	33.1	−4.2	13.5	−1.1	4.9	0.4	1.7
SCENT	81.5	−6.6	8.2	−2.8	5.0	0.0	12.3
SEAST	68.8	−7.4	9.3	−2.8	5.2	0.1	15.2
TX	76.5	−7.2	8.6	−4.2	5.0	−0.3	8.2
US	72.9	−6.9	9.8	−2.9	5.1	0.0	12.8

taxes on fuels. On average a $15 per metric ton carbon price would raise the price of coal by nearly three-quarters if the price is fully passed forward to consumers, whereas the prices of natural gas and refined oil would increase by less than 10 percent.

How much of the carbon price is passed forward to consumers in the form of higher prices for goods and services, as opposed to being passed back to factors of production (capital, labor) as well as resource owners, depends on a large number of economic parameters, including various supply and demand elasticities. Table 3.6 reports results from the USREP model on the extent of forward and backward shifting of carbon prices for a $15 per metric ton of CO_2 equivalent charge.

For the United States as a whole the carbon price on coal is predominantly passed forward to purchasers of coal (primarily electric utilities). This reflects the low level of rents in coal reserves given coal's abundance. Carbon pricing on natural gas is also largely passed forward but to a somewhat lesser extent than for coal. Whereas the consumer price for coal rises by over 90 percent of the carbon price, the consumer price for natural gas only rises by 75 percent. For this analysis, we assume that world oil prices are unaffected by U.S. carbon policy, so the entire impact is borne by consumers of refined oil products.[22] To the extent that carbon pricing

---

[22] U.S. oil consumption is sufficiently large that the assumption of zero impact is unrealistic. In other analyses in which we have explicitly modeled world oil production and consumption, we find that approximately 80 percent of the tax is passed forward in the form

is passed back to factors of production and resource owner, the burden of climate policy may differ significantly from the results of modeling in which carbon prices are fully passed forward. The USREP model allows us to disentangle both forward and backward shifting as well as which factors of production (labor or capital) and resource owners are disproportionately affected. In the model with regional disaggregation, we can also account for differences in impacts given the differences (albeit minor) among regions in the degree of forward and backward shifting, as shown in Table 3.6. In the model with an aggregate consumer and one region, we find that the wage falls by 0.6 percentage points and that the rental rate to capital falls by 0.8 percentage points. Although these are relatively small percentage changes relative to the changes in energy prices, wage and capital income makes up virtually all of a household's income, whereas changes in energy prices affect only a fraction of consumer expenditure. Hence, the changes in wages and returns to capital can be as important as changes in energy prices in determining distributional effects. With regional heterogeneity we find that wage rates fall by different amounts, as we discuss in Section 3.4.3. The last column of Table 3.6 shows how higher energy costs affect the price of electricity. Nationally, electricity prices rise by nearly 13 percent. The price increase varies across regions, which is not surprising given the different mixes of fuel sources for electricity across regions, as we discuss later.

The requirement that government spending as a share of GDP be unchanged means that not all of the revenue from carbon pricing can be recycled to households in the form of lower taxes or lump-sum subsidies. At the national level, a carbon price of $15 per metric ton of CO_2e would raise $83 billion in 2006 dollars. However, the change in economic activity due to the higher price of carbon-intensive goods and services leads to a decline in non-greenhouse gas revenue of $42.1 billion relative to the reference scenario. In the final equilibrium, just over half the revenue from carbon pricing is available for redistribution to households in some form or other.[23]

---

of higher crude oil prices, but that analysis also included measures in other developed countries, so the impact of just U.S. policy on oil price would be less than that.

[23] This contrasts to the CBO's assumption that 25 percent of the revenue from a cap-and-trade system or carbon tax would need to be set aside to offset declines in other tax collections. In simulations not reported here, we find the loss in tax revenue to be sensitive to the international trade closure assumptions – how much impact U.S. changes has on world prices. The larger the impact on world prices, the less the erosion of U.S. activity with less impact on tax revenue.

3.4.1 Sources vs. Uses Impacts of Carbon Pricing

It is a well-established fact that carbon pricing by itself is regressive if the analysis of the costs is based on income class–specific energy expenditure patterns (e.g., Metcalf 2007; Burtraw, Sweeney, and Walls 2009; and Hassett, Mathur, and Metcalf 2009). As already noted, we find that carbon pricing affects income through reduced factor prices for capital, labor, and fossil fuel resources; as a result, the relative sources of income of households at different levels of income will affect income distribution. At the lowest income levels, a larger fraction of income is from government transfers, and these transfers are not directly affected by carbon pricing. As discussed previously, the impact on capital returns is larger than the impact on wages, with higher-income households deriving more of their income from capital returns. These basic facts mean that sources side effects of carbon pricing are likely to be progressive, which will at least partly offset the regressive uses side effects. Sources side effects refer to burden impacts arising from changes in relative factor prices, whereas uses side effects refer to burden impacts arising from change in relative product prices. This terminology goes back to Musgrave (1959). The virtue of a general equilibrium framework is its ability to capture both expenditure and income effects in a comprehensive manner.

The core results we report all include distribution of the revenue in some manner. To eliminate the muddying effect of revenue distribution, we conduct simulations in which we do not recycle the revenue. Figure 3.2 provides welfare impacts across income groups for three scenarios designed to disentangle the contribution of sources and uses side effects on welfare. The line labeled "core model with true preferences and income shares" corresponds to our core model based on empirically observed expenditure and income data, and shows that the carbon tax is neutral to mildly progressive, especially at higher income levels. The line labeled "model with identical income shares" constructs a hypothetical case in which income shares across different income groups are equalized. As this scenario eliminates household heterogeneity on the income side, the distribution of costs is now shaped only by differences in energy expenditures across income groups. For this case, carbon pricing is distinctly regressive, consistent with previous research that has focused on the distributional implications only of energy expenditure patterns by households. Finally, the line labeled "model with identical preferences" eliminates heterogeneity in spending patterns across income groups. Hence, the distribution is determined by differences in the

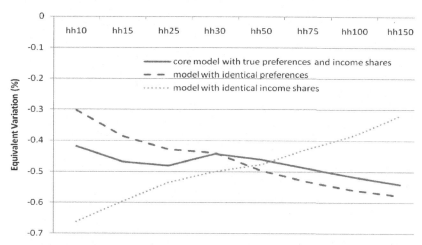

Figure 3.2. Relative Sources vs. Uses Side Impacts across Income Distribution (No Revenue Recycling).

source of income among income classes alone. In this case, the carbon tax is highly progressive.

Note that the two counterfactual cases do not eliminate the sources and uses drivers of incidence, but by eliminating household heterogeneity they suppress *differential* impacts across the income distribution. Harberger (1962) uses a similar analysis to identify the incidence of a corporate income tax. Also note that as we measure the *real* burden (i.e., the change in equivalent variation), our incidence calculation is independent of the choice of numéraire.

Our analysis finds that, in aggregate, the distributional effects on carbon pricing are near neutral to slightly progressive, which differs significantly from much of the literature. This comes about through the regressive effects that occur as a result of the pattern of energy expenditure by income class that are offset by the progressive impacts on returns to labor, capital, and resources. Also note that the estimates of welfare impact are quite large in these simulations (and larger than in the core results reported elsewhere). The larger impacts are attributable to the fact that revenue is not recycled to consumers but rather simply increases the government, which in our construction has no welfare benefit to the households. It is as if the revenue were thrown away. We made this assumption not to imply anything about the efficacy of government programs but only to disentangle the direct effects of carbon pricing from any plan to distribute allowances or revenue

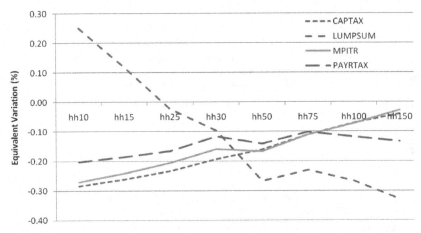

Figure 3.3. Welfare Impacts across Income Distribution of Various Tax Rebates.

from them. In the following sections, we return to the core results that more realistically involve different allowance revenue distributional approaches.

3.4.2 Distributional Effects of Carbon Pricing across Income Groups

Our first set of results focuses on the burden of carbon pricing across household groups focusing on differences in household income. These results are most comparable to those of Burtraw, Sweeney, and Walls (2009) and of Hassett, Mathur, and Metcalf (2009). We focus first on the LUMPSUM and tax rate reduction cases.

Figure 3.3 shows the LUMPSUM to be mildly progressive, whereas the tax rate cases are mildly regressive. That the LUMPSUM is mildly progressive is not surprising and is consistent with the findings for the cap-and-dividend program analyzed in Burtraw, Sweeney, and Walls (2009). Rebating the revenue through a reduction in the payroll tax (PAYRTAX) allows a reduction in the payroll tax rate of 1.1 percentage points. Metcalf (2009) examined a capped payroll tax reduction and found that to be distributionally neutral over most of the income distribution, as the cap at higher income levels shifts more of the benefit to lower-income households. Not surprisingly, the PAYRTAX reduction leads to the smallest costs for the low-income households and produces the least regressive outcome of the tax-recycling instruments analyzed here. At incomes in the highest brackets, the payroll tax limit is being exceeded, so cuts in that rate have proportionally less benefit for these income classes than do cuts in marginal personal income tax

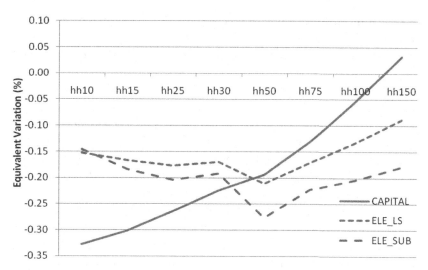

Figure 3.4. Welfare Impacts across Income Distribution of Free Allocation Schemes.

rates. The CAPTAX is somewhat more regressive at the lowest income levels but above hh50 mirrors closely the distributional effects of the MPITR.

Figure 3.4 illustrates that the distribution of revenues significantly affects the overall progressivity or regressivity of CO_2 pricing. Carbon pricing is decidedly progressive if a LUMPSUM distribution of the revenue is provided. The impact on the lowest three income groups ranges from +0.25 to −0.05 percent of income. In contrast, the impact on the highest four income groups is in the range of −0.20 to −0.30 percent of income.

We next consider the distributional impact of returning the revenue based on ownership of capital. No policy explicitly proposes to do this, but the free allocation of permits to covered industry groups on the basis of their emissions is equivalent to a lump-sum distribution of carbon tax revenues to equity holders in these industries. Note that this is the approach that has been used for the two major cap-and-trade systems to date – the U.S. SO_2 trading program under the Clean Air Act Amendments of 1990 and the European Union's Emission Trading Scheme for CO_2.

The line marked CAPITAL in Figure 3.4 distributes the revenue (or freely allocates permits) on the basis of capital income. Ideally, we would distribute the permits on the basis of holdings in carbon-intensive industries. As we do not have data on this distribution, we assume that the distribution of equity holdings in carbon-intensive industries is similar across income groups to the distribution of equity holdings in general and that both can be proxied by capital income for which we do have data.[24] The distribution based on this rebate policy is sharply regressive, with welfare falling by a third of 1 percent for the lowest income groups while rising slightly for the highest income groups.

Although we do not model H.R. 2454 here, an interesting feature of the bill is a complex permit allocation scheme that includes allocation of permits to local distribution companies for natural gas and electricity to be used to compensate utility consumers for the higher gas and electricity prices they will face from carbon pricing. Our cases, although they focus just on electricity, illustrate how such a system may work if consumers perceive the true electricity price (ELE_LS) or see the allowance value rebate as effectively reducing rates (ELE_SUB); note, however, that these cases, especially other aspects of them, were not designed to represent H.R. 2454. In the ELE_LS scenario, we model the distribution as a lump-sum allocation to households proportional to their electricity consumption, whereas in ELE_SUB we cut residential rates by the amount needed to reduce the total household electricity bills by the value of allowances distributed to LDCs. We determine the number of allowances allocated to LDCs to be just that needed to cover emissions from the electricity sector, so that they need to neither buy nor sell allowances. As Figure 3.3 indicates, this dampens the regressivity of the free allocation scenario considerably compared with the CAPITAL scenario.

In ELE_SUB, the distributional effects are dampened further so that the policy is nearer to neutral, slightly penalizing households in the upper middle income range. However, all households except the lowest income level are actually worse off than in ELE_LS. Subsidizing the electricity prices substantially – in a few regions electricity prices are actually lower than in the no-policy case – means that total residential electricity consumption is higher than in ELE_LS. Consumers have less incentive to reduce electricity use. They face low electricity bills, but someone in the economy must bear the cost of producing extra electricity. The fact that more electricity is produced raises the total cost of electricity by about $22 per household. Instead of households bearing the cost directly, it affects returns on capital, so the cost is disproportionately borne by higher income households. Thus, ELE_SUB achieves a nearly neutral or even slightly progressive result (comparing low to upper middle income households), but by making nearly all incomes groups worse off and none substantially better off. Because we

---

[24] This approach has been taken by Parry (2004) and Dinan and Rogers (2002), among others.

Table 3.7. *Equivalent variation by income class (in 2006 dollars/year)*

Income groups	LUMPSUM	PAYRTAX	MPITR	CAPTAX	CAPITAL	ELE_LS	ELE_SUB
hh10	140	−114	−152	−159	−183	−85	−81
hh15	73	−115	−149	−161	−186	−103	−113
hh25	−18	−128	−159	−181	−204	−137	−157
hh30	−99	−119	−163	−197	−229	−174	−196
hh50	−305	−163	−191	−185	−222	−241	−316
hh75	−304	−133	−145	−145	−172	−224	−292
hh100	−357	−159	−97	−95	−71	−178	−273
hh150	−506	−207	−42	−61	50	−136	−276

enforce tax revenue neutrality across all scenarios, the somewhat larger economic cost of the ELE_SUB policy lowers tax revenue, and more of CO_2 revenue must be retained to offset the loss in tax revenue. Thus, somewhat less of the revenue is available to be redistributed.

Table 3.7 shows the welfare impact of carbon pricing from the various scenarios reported in 2006 dollars per household per year. These are the same basic results in Figures 3.2 and 3.3, just reported in absolute dollar levels rather than as a share of income.

The results from this section are consistent with earlier research that assumes that the entire burden of carbon pricing is shifted forward to consumers in the form of higher prices. As shown previously, carbon pricing by itself is mildly progressive, and the use of the revenue significantly affects the ultimate distribution. Rebates that lower marginal tax rates in general lead to a regressive result of CO_2 pricing. A lump-sum distribution of the revenue that is uniform across households is progressive, although other lump-sum distributions can be devised (e.g., allocations to industry based on emissions) that are decidedly regressive.

Although distributional impacts of carbon pricing for different income levels are of concern to policy makers, regional impacts are also of concern. We turn next to an analysis of regional impact.

3.4.3 Distribution of Carbon Pricing across Regions

Different regions of the country vary in important ways that may affect the regional distribution of greenhouse gas policy impacts. Figure 3.5 presents information on carbon intensity (greenhouse gas emissions per dollar of GDP) and energy intensity (energy consumption per dollar of GDP) by region.

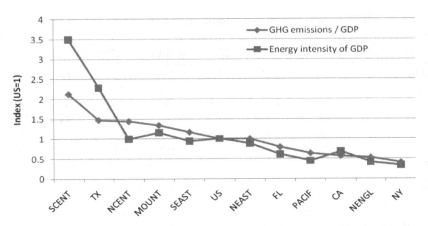

Figure 3.5. GHG and Energy Intensity by Region.

Energy intensity varies dramatically, with the South Central region of the country consuming over three times as much energy per dollar of GDP as the U.S. average; New England and New York consume roughly half the national average of energy per dollar of GDP. Variation in the intensity of greenhouse gas emissions is lower but tracks energy intensity reasonably closely.

Figure 3.6 presents data on electricity generation by fuel source for the various regions in the reference case scenario (no policy). Nationally, over half the electricity generated comes from coal, followed by natural gas and nuclear power (19 percent each), hydropower (6 percent), and refined oil (2 percent).[25] The regions that rely heavily on coal and have little nuclear or hydropower have higher than average greenhouse gas intensities.

Figure 3.7 shows greenhouse gas emissions by region, and Figure 3.8 shows the percentage reduction in emissions by region for the carbon pricing policy with lump-sum redistribution of revenues. Table 3.8 shows total emissions in the reference scenario and the reduction following the implementation of the policy. Not surprisingly, regions that are carbon intensive yield a larger percentage reduction in emissions than regions that are relatively less carbon intensive.

An important issue that affects regional economic impacts of the policy is the ownership of capital and resources, especially those most affected by climate policy. At issue is whether resources such as coal, oil, and gas

---

[25] These are production estimates from the reference case of the USREP model. The model does not include non-hydro renewable electricity. In 2006, non-hydro renewable power accounted for just under 2.5 percent of electricity generation.

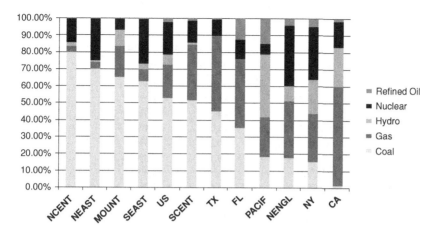

Figure 3.6. Regional Electricity Generation by Fuel Source.

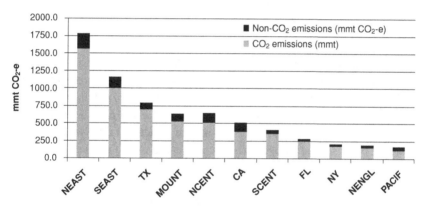

Figure 3.7. Greenhouse Gas Emissions in Reference Scenario.

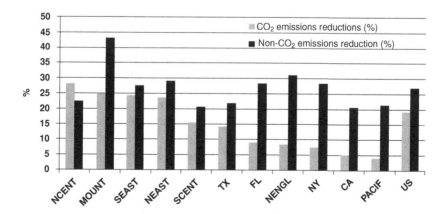

Figure 3.8. Reduction in Greenhouse Gas Emissions by Region.

Table 3.8. *Total emissions and
reductions by region*

	Total emissions	Reduction
US	6957.7	27.3%
NEAST	1788.4	24.3%
SEAST	1168.5	24.8%
TX	794.7	15.1%
MOUNT	639.5	28.3%
NCENT	649.1	27.0%
CA	514.8	8.9%
SCENT	415.0	16.2%
FL	286.6	11.8%
NY	214.9	10.8%
NENGL	199.1	12.6%
PACIF	176.1	8.9%

Note: Emissions are in millions of metric tons
of CO_2e for 2006.

within a region are mainly owned by households in the region or whether
those assets are owned equally by households across the country. The
IMPLAN and Consumer Expenditure Survey data do not have detailed
wealth data, and no other data exist that would allow us to attribute the
ownership of regional equity by region. For general equity, we assume a
national pool, so that households in each region own a proportion of the
national pool – they do not, for example, disproportionately own equity
of firms in their home region. For fossil energy resources, we have made
this same assumption, and constructed an alternative polar case in which all
regional resources are owned within the region.[26] There is most likely a positive correlation between resource and company ownership (if for no other
reason than some companies are organized as partnerships or sole propri-
etorships with owners living locally). Our base assumption, that resource
and company ownership simply mirrors national wealth-holding patterns,
ignores this correlation, but many of these resources are owned by large
publicly traded corporations whose shares are owned by investors across
the country. The right answer is somewhere between these cases, and we
suspect that it leans more towards the national ownership case. Thus, even
though the assumption that resource ownership is entirely local is extreme,
we construct such a scenario to show the sensitivity of results to regional
ownership patterns.

[26] We assume agricultural land resources in a region are owned regionally.

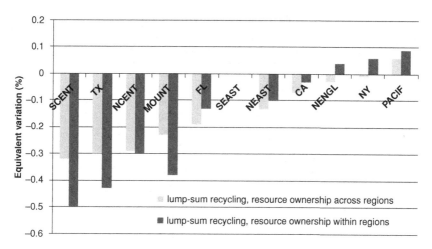

Figure 3.9. Welfare Impacts by Regions: Alternative Recycling Options.

Figure 3.9 shows the welfare impacts of the carbon pricing policy assuming lump-sum recycling of the revenue under these two scenarios of energy resource (coal, oil, gas) ownership, with the national ownership case labeled "resource ownership across regions" and the other labeled "resource ownership within regions." We focus on the LUMPSUM scenario for examining contrasting regional resource allocation assumption scenarios. The range is from a loss of 0.3 percent to a gain of just over 0.05 percent in the "resource ownership across regions" case. This widens to a loss of 0.5 percent to a gain of almost 0.1 percent in the "resource ownership within regions" case, in which those regions with significant fossil resources show greater losses and those without, lower losses or greater gains.

Table 3.9 shows the costs of electricity in the various regions for 2006 in the reference scenario; when generation source is compared with regional effects, it shows that regions with large shares of electricity generated from hydropower and/or nuclear power lose little or actually gain, and those that rely more on coal-generated electricity bear costs. Those states with the lowest welfare costs tend to be states with higher-than-average electricity prices pre-policy. This suggests that prior action that reduced carbon intensity in those regions (or favorable nonfossil resource conditions) contributes to the lower costs borne by residents of those regions.[27]

Figure 3.10 shows regional results for the different tax recycling cases compared against the LUMPSUM scenario shown in the previous figure.

---

[27] We are not suggesting that those prior actions were taken for GHG mitigation efforts, but the result of those actions has led to lower emissions and lower costs of any greenhouse gas pricing policy.

Table 3.9. *Regional electricity prices*

Region	Price ($/MMBTU)
NY	44.75
NENGL	39.69
CA	37.66
PACIF	32.70
FL	30.62
TX	30.52
NEAST	25.17
SCENT	22.20
SEAST	20.89
MOUNT	20.57
NCENT	19.35
US	30.15

Source: EIA SEDS. Prices are averages across
end-use categories for 2006.

These are the cases previously discussed for the United States as whole, in which revenue is recycled through reductions in capital income taxes, payroll taxes, or income taxes. Although the differences in impacts for the various recycling approaches are quite similar at the national level (the U.S. bars), the different recycling approaches have more heterogeneity across regions. These cases tend to amplify the regional spread we saw in the LUMPSUM case, especially the PAYRTAX case. In that case, the South Central region experiences a 0.55 percent reduction in welfare, up from

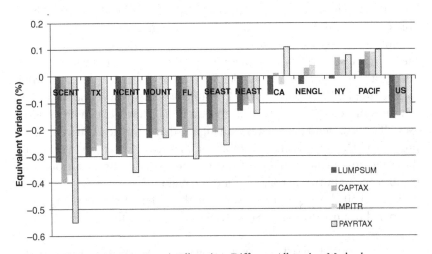

Figure 3.10. Free Permit Allocation: Different Allocation Methods.

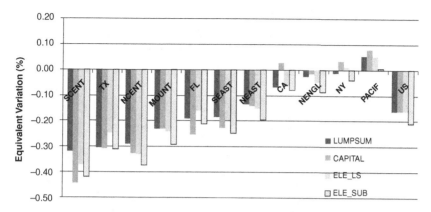

Figure 3.11. Welfare Impacts by Region.

about 0.3 percent in the LUMPSUM case, whereas California experiences a 0.11 percent gain, up from about a 0.05 percent loss. The spread rises from just over 0.3 percent to 0.66 percent. The effects of the CAPTAX and MPITR scenarios move in a similar direction but are less pronounced. Regions with higher incomes and, in the case of the PAYRTAX, a relatively larger share of the population employed, tend to benefit more from the tax-recycling cases, in which revenue is shifted to them from other states, whereas the LUMPSUM distribution is affected directly by population. The regional economic impacts we show in Figure 3.11 in the free allocation scenarios are even more varied; however, some of the large differences come about because the ELE_SUB simply has much larger costs in all regions. In that case, the spread across regions is 0.94 percent. Free allocation to covered industries (CAPITAL) leads to a spread equal to 0.66 percent. The ELE_LS is closest to the LUMPSUM case, with a maximal spread of 0.45 percent. The CAPITAL case favors the wealthier regions with larger ownership of capital. The ELE_LS and ELE_SUB differences from the CAPITAL case are driven by differences in household electricity consumption among regions, as that determines allowance allocation beyond that allocated to capital. Higher-income regions will tend, other things being equal, to use more residential electricity, but differences in climate as it affects air conditioning and heating will also have an effect.

    To further understand the effects of ELE_SUB and ELE_LS it is useful to examine the electricity price changes shown in Table 3.10. In ELE_SUB we directly allocate allowance revenue to households through reduction in electricity rates. As can be seen, in California, the Pacific region, Texas, and

Table 3.10. *Residential electricity price
(% change from reference case)*

	ELE_LS	ELE_SUB
CA	8.5	−0.1
FL	9.9	1.3
MOUNT	14.8	6.1
NCENT	19.8	10.9
NEAST	14.2	5.5
NENGL	12.0	3.4
NY	7.5	−1.0
PACIF	1.6	−6.7
SCENT	12.3	3.6
SEAST	15.2	6.5
TX	8.2	−0.4
US	12.8	4.1

New York electricity rates in this case actually fall compared with the no-policy baseline. Florida's electricity rates rise by only 1.3 percent, which is significantly below the U.S. average. These are regions in which the allocation of allowance revenue offsets more of the electricity cost rise than the U.S. average, so they all gain in the ELE_LS relative to the LUMPSUM case.

Figures 3.10 and 3.11, by showing the U.S. average cost, also show the efficiency effects of the different revenue allocation schemes. As should be expected, LUMPSUM, CAPITAL, and ELE_LS have an identical effect, and it is about 15 percent of total income. The tax-recycling cases reduce the cost by about 12 to 13 percent, with only slight differences among them. Some analyses have shown bigger gains from revenue recycling, especially when cuts are directed at capital taxation. In all cases, our assumption of revenue neutrality reduces the available revenue for recycling by about one-half. Analyses of revenue recycling that did not enforce revenue neutrality assumption would thus be expected to generate twice the gain. The revenue loss is also more substantial than has sometimes been estimated. In part this stems from specification of marginal tax rates on personal income. Lower GDP has a more than proportional effect on tax revenue.

We also find the revenue loss to be sensitive to how we close international trade in the model. Lower foreign trade supply elasticities lower the revenue loss to 30 to 40 percent of the auction revenue. With regard to capital taxation, its greater benefit in reducing the cost of the policy is typically due to its effect over time on the growth rate of the economy. In the static model we apply here, such growth effects are not captured. Although our

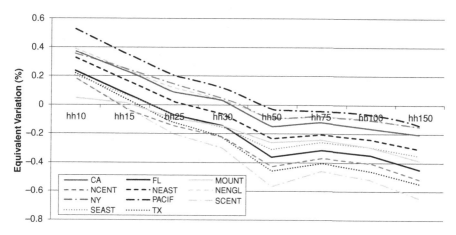

Figure 3.12. Income by Region Welfare Impacts.

analysis is relevant to the distributional effects of these policies with long-run adjustment of the capital stock to carbon pricing, to consider the full effects, especially of capital tax recycling over the longer term, a dynamic model that includes effects on growth would be required. ELE_SUB raises the welfare cost from 0.15 percent to 0.21 percent, a 40 percent increase in the policy cost, because it introduces inefficiency in the cap-and-trade system.[28] That is a substantial and perhaps surprisingly large increase in the cost. However, what this scenario essentially does is greatly reduce the incentive to conserve electricity in the residential sector, which accounts for approximately one-third of U.S. electricity consumption. That has further general equilibrium effects – not only is more electricity used but it is more costly electricity, because generators use more expensive lower CO_2 generation to avoid the CO_2 price. The larger economic loss leads to lower tax revenue, and then less of the CO_2 tax revenue is available to be redistributed to households.

Lastly, we consider how income heterogeneity interacts with regional heterogeneity. Figure 3.12 shows differences in welfare impacts among income groups by region where revenues are returned on an equal lump-sum basis to households. The broad pattern of the LUMPSUM results we saw at the national level, moderately progressive effects leading to positive income effects for the poorest households and costs for higher-income households, is the same in all regions. Thus, the most important reason for differences among regions for households in a particular household income level are

[28] All cases implemented a \$15/mtCO$_2$ price. An additional effect of reducing electricity prices is that economy-wide emissions are somewhat higher, and so the cost of achieving the same emissions level would be somewhat greater than we show here.

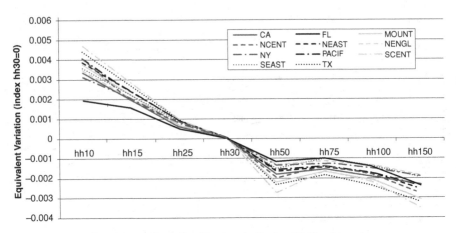

Figure 3.13. Normalized Income by Region Welfare Impacts.

differences for the region that affect all households in the region. This result is fairly intuitive; if climatic conditions lead to more or less energy consumption or the regions rely more or less on carbon-intensive electricity, all households are affected similarly.

To better see particular differences in the distribution effects among regions, we normalize each region's burden of impact for each income group by the impact on the hh30 group and show this result in Figure 3.13. In that way, we can focus specifically on the differences in within-region

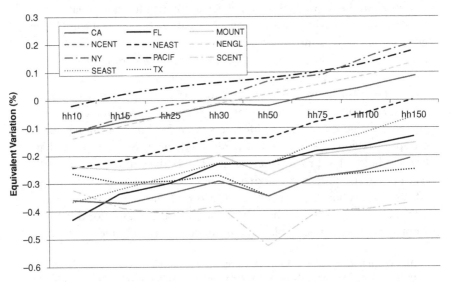

Figure 3.14. Income by Region Welfare Impacts: Reduction in Personal Income Tax.

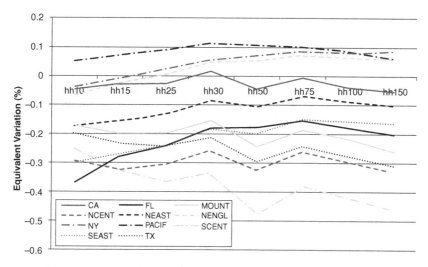

Figure 3.15. Income by Region Welfare Impacts: Reduction in Payroll Tax.

progressivity. The impact on households in Texas and the South Central states, for example, appears to be more progressive, whereas the impact in Florida is the least progressive. Other states and regions fall in between these cases.

Figures 3.14 through 3.19 show the distributions across households within regions for the other scenarios that we modeled. Again, for the

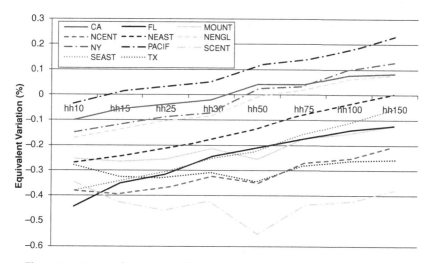

Figure 3.16. Income by Region Welfare Impacts: Reduction in Capital Income Tax.

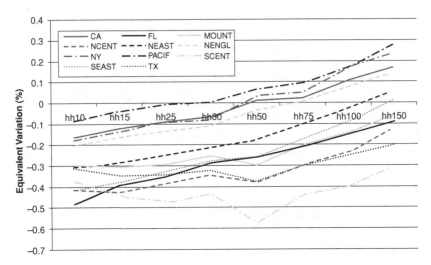

Figure 3.17. Income by Region Welfare Impacts: Freely Allocated Permits to Capital Owners.

most part, the different recycling schemes do not produce strongly different effects in different regions with regard to progressivity or regressivity. The personal income tax, capital tax, and lump-sum recycling to capital owners are generally regressive in most regions. An exception is the

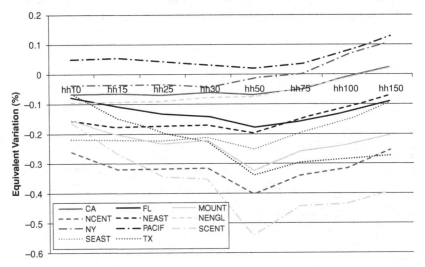

Figure 3.18. Income by Region Welfare Impacts: Freely Allocated Permits and Permits Directed to Electricity Consumers (Lump-sum).

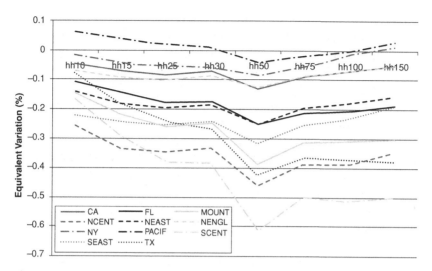

Figure 3.19. Income by Region Welfare Impacts: Freely Allocated Permits and Permits Directed to Electricity Consumers (Perceived as Price Reduction).

South Central region, where most of these schemes are fairly neutral across income classes. The allocations of allowances to households based on electricity use are fairly neutral in most regions. Again, the South Central region, where this allocation leads to a progressive result, is something of an exception.

On balance the losses across regions by income group do not appear to differ dramatically for most revenue-recycling approaches. The differences are most marked when benefits are mandated to be directed to electricity consumers, especially when those benefits are misperceived as a reduction in the price of electricity.

3.5 Conclusion

The USREP model was constructed with multiple regions and multiple households in each region to allow us to determine the distributional effects of a GHG mitigation policy endogenously. Past work has often used data on energy expenditure by region or household income class to estimate the cost incidence of policies based on increases in energy costs. Because higher energy costs affect the cost of all goods and the policy has effects on returns to capital and resources and on wages, basing distributional effects purely on energy expenditure of different households can be misleading.

Indeed when we focus just on the distributional impact of carbon pricing (ignoring the use of the revenue) we find that the progressive sources-side impacts more than outweigh the regressive uses-side impacts. In other words, carbon pricing is modestly progressive. This stands in sharp contrast to earlier studies that have only focused on the uses-side incidence.

In a model with a single representative household, a neutral assumption is to return auction revenue in a lump-sum manner to that household. With multiple households there is no obviously neutral way to distribute allowances or revenue from auctioning them. Giving allowances away for free benefits those who receive them or who own equity in firms that get the allowances. Direct distribution of the money to households or use of the revenue to reduce other taxes has different implications for costs borne by households of different income levels in different regions. We find that an equal lump-sum household payment leads to small net benefits for low-income households – the lump-sum payment more than offsets costs of the policy at these income levels. Higher-income households thus bear those costs. This allocation scheme was by far the most progressive one we analyzed.

Although there have been a few proposals calling for an equal lump-sum distribution of tax or allowance revenue from a GHG policy, most proposals have focused on more complex schemes to use this revenue. One set of proposals that is popular among economists focuses on using the revenue to reduce other tax rates on the basis that this will reduce the distortionary effects of taxes and thereby lower the overall cost of the policy. We examined using the revenue to reduce the payroll tax, the marginal personal income tax, and capital tax rates. We find modest efficiency gains from such revenue-recycling plans, but all are regressive, leading to higher percentage costs for the lowest-income households. Not surprisingly the payroll tax reduction is least regressive. The relatively modest efficiency gains from these appear to result from our revenue neutrality requirement. That, combined with formulation of marginal personal income taxes, allows only about one-half of the revenue to be recycled, because the rest must be retained to cover reduction in tax revenue.

Other proposals would give allowances away rather than cut taxes. Often, as in the European Trading Scheme or in the U.S. sulfur trading program, these are allocated to firms that would be required to turn in allowances on the basis that they "need" them. However, the incidence of mitigation costs are generally passed on to consumers or resource owners, so distributing allowances in this way leads to windfall gains for firms and mostly benefits equity owners. In H.R. 2454, which was recently passed by the House but is awaiting action in the Senate, a significant share of allowances is distributed to LDCs whose rates are set through public utility commissions. The presumption is that because rates are set to achieve a fair rate of return on capital, a lump-sum allocation of allowances of significant value would not lead to a windfall gain for the firms, but rather that value would be returned to the ratepayer. A concern with this approach, anticipated in H.R. 2454, is that it would result in lower electricity rates, which would undermine the efficiency of the cap-and-trade system by reducing the incentive for consumers to adopt electricity-saving measures. We did not attempt to simulate H.R. 2454 specifically, but we did structure a set of simulations that included a distribution of allowances "needed" by the LDCs to them. We returned this revenue to ratepayers either as a lump sum proportional to electricity consumption or as a reduction in electricity rates paid by households.

Among the free distribution schemes we analyzed, distribution to capital owners, which would be the result if firms were given allowances, was the most regressive; it actually lead to benefits for the highest-income households at the expense of low-income households. Because lower-income households spend a larger share of income on electricity (but derive a low share of income from capital returns), allocation of some of the allowances to LDCs would be expected to blunt the distributional effects. We find this case produced among the most neutral (by income) distributional results of the scenarios we considered. The simulation that reduced electricity rates did indeed undermine the efficiency of the policy, increasing costs for most households substantially compared to any other recycling policy. Thus, the language in H.R. 2454 instructing revenue to be returned to ratepayers in a manner that passes through higher electricity rates is important for retaining the efficiency of the policy. In that regard, it is crucial that ratepayers correctly perceive the higher rates. If a monthly bill is sent that includes an electricity charge at higher rates and reduces this by some amount of allowance value rebate, the consumer may very well just look at the bottom line of the bill, see not much increase, and not fully perceive that rates have gone up. We also note that with LDC distribution cases, public utility commissions could alter the distributional consequences through different formulae for distribution. Rather than distributing based on electricity consumption, they might do an equal lump sum to all households, favor lower-consumption households as a proxy for directing the value to lower-income households, or consider other mechanisms to distribute or use these funds. Our distributional results for this case are only illustrative of one possible way in which such revenue may be distributed. In reality, different public utility commissions in different regions of the country may pursue different strategies for using this allowance revenue with very different distributional implications.

Regionally, we find that California, the Pacific Coast, New England, and New York generally experience the lowest cost, and even benefit from the carbon pricing policy we examined, whereas the South Central, Texas, and Mountain states face the highest cost. Differences in costs among regions are driven by differences in CO_2 intensity of electricity production, the presence of energy-producing and energy-intensive industry, and income levels. Those regions that benefit do so not because abatement itself is beneficial. Abatement costs may be lower in these regions, but the reason for benefits is that the distributional scheme favors them. The regional results are relatively insensitive to the different revenue recycling approaches we explored; however, the lump-sum approach leads to the least difference in cost among regions. All the other approaches tend to benefit higher-income regions relatively more and increase the dispersion among regions. An important bottom line result is that the amount of revenue raised, even accounting for reduction in revenue from other taxes due to reduced economic activity, is large relative to costs borne by households. As a result, the cost impact on any household is determined as much or more by how the allowances are distributed or how auction revenue is used than the direct cost of the policy itself.

This initial exploration of distribution impacts was conducted using a static general equilibrium model of the U.S. economy. In further work we hope to embed this model in a recursive dynamic structure to better capture investment dynamics and capital market distortions, and simulate more realistic scenarios as other future conditions change. A recursive dynamic structure will also allow us to consider scenarios that more closely approach measures laid out in H.R. 2454 or other greenhouse gas legislation proposals.

APPENDIX A: MODEL STRUCTURE

This section provides an algebraic description of the static USREP model and lays out the equilibrium conditions. Following Rutherford (1995b) and Mathiesen (1985), we formulate the equilibrium as a complementarity problem and use the GAMS/MPSGE software (Rutherford 1999) and the

PATH solver (Dirkse and Ferris 1993) to solve for nonnegative prices and quantities. Our complementarity-based solution approach distinguishes price and demand equations, market clearance conditions, budget constraints, and auxiliary equations. We use constant returns to scale elasticity of substitution (CES) and constant elasticity of transformation (CET) functions to describe production and transformation activities.

A.1 Behavior of Firms

In each region (indexed by the subscript r) and for each sector (indexed interchangeably by i or j), a representative firm chooses a level of output y, quantities of capital and labor, resource factors (indexed by z), and intermediate inputs from other sectors j to maximize profits subject to the constraint of its production technology. By duality and the property of linear homogeneity, optimizing behavior of the representative firm requires that

$$p_{r,i} = c_{r,i}(pa_{r,j}, pl_r, pk, pr_z) \tag{A.1}$$

where $p_{r,i}$, $pa_{r,i}$, pl_r, pk and pr_z denote prices for domestic output, intermediate inputs, labor, capital, and resource factors, respectively. $c_{r,i}$ provides a generic representation of the unit cost function for sector i. Figures 3.20 through 3.24 provide a schematic overview of the adopted nesting CES structure for production sectors. Zero-profits conditions in (A.1) exhibit complementary slackness with respect to the activity level $y_{r,i}$. For each sector, ad-valorem sector- and region-specific output tax rates, denoted by $to_{r,i}$, enter at the top nest. Region-specific capital income tax rates, denoted by tk_r, and payroll tax rates, denoted by tl_r, enter in the value-added nest.

To illustrate how taxes enter the CES cost functions, consider the pricing equation for the agricultural sector (Figure 3.21). We write the equations in *calibrated share form* (Rutherford 1995a), where ϕ's denote respective benchmark value share parameters and an upper bar refers to the benchmark value of variables. Unit cost function is given by

$$\frac{(1 - to_{r,i})p_{r,i}}{(1 - \overline{to}_{r,i})\overline{p}_{r,i}} = \left[\phi_{r,i,RES}\left(\frac{p_{r,RESI}}{\overline{P}_{r,RESI}}\right)^{1-\sigma_{EVRA}} + \phi_{r,i,VA}\left(\frac{p_{r,VA}}{\overline{p}_{r,VA}}\right)^{1-\sigma_{EVRA}}\right]^{\frac{1}{1-\sigma_{EVRA}}} \tag{A.2}$$

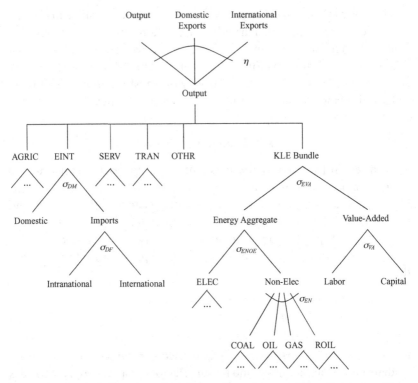

Figure 3.20. Services, Transportation, Energy-Intensive, and Other Industries. *Note:* Vertical lines in the input nest signify a Leontief or fixed coefficient production structure in which the elasticity of substitution is zero. Terminal nests with . . . indicate the same aggregation structure for domestic and imported goods as shown in detail for the EINT sector. Goods that are traded intranationally are modeled as homogeneous goods. The following figures provide greater detail over the production structure for subsectors of the economy.

where $p_{r,RESI}$ denotes the price for the resource-intensive input bundle. The price for the value-added composite, $p_{r,VA}$, is given by

$$\frac{p_{v,VA}}{\overline{p}_{r,VA}} = \left[\phi_{r,i,L} \left(\frac{(1+tl_r)pl_r}{(1+\overline{tl}_r)\overline{pl}_r} \right)^{1-\sigma_{VA}} + \phi_{r,i,K} \left(\frac{(1+tk_r)pk}{(1+\overline{tk}_r)\overline{pk}} \right)^{1-\sigma_{VA}} \right]^{\frac{1}{1-\sigma_{VA}}} \tag{A.3}$$

Elasticities are denoted by σ. Tables 3.11 and 3.12 provide a list of elasticity parameters used in the model.

By Shephard's Lemma, the demand for good j by sector i is

$$x_{r,j,i} = y_{r,i} \frac{\partial c_{r,i}}{\partial pa_{r,j}} \tag{A.4}$$

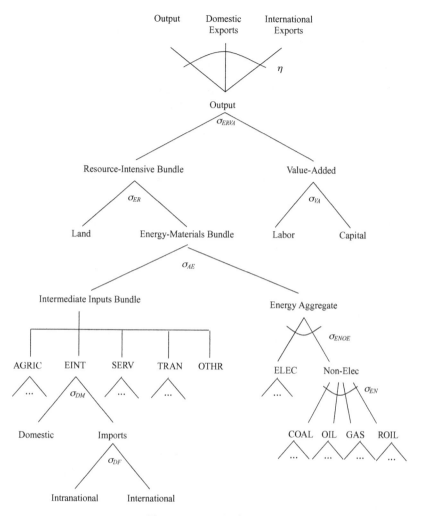

Figure 3.21. Agriculture.

and the demand for labor, capital, and resource factors is

$$ld_{r,i} = y_{r,i}\frac{\partial c_{r,i}}{\partial pl_r} \tag{A.5}$$

$$kd_{r,i} = y_{r,i}\frac{\partial c_{r,i}}{\partial pk} \tag{A.6}$$

$$rd_{r,i,z} = y_{r,i}\frac{\partial c_{r,i}}{\partial pr_{r,z}}. \tag{A.7}$$

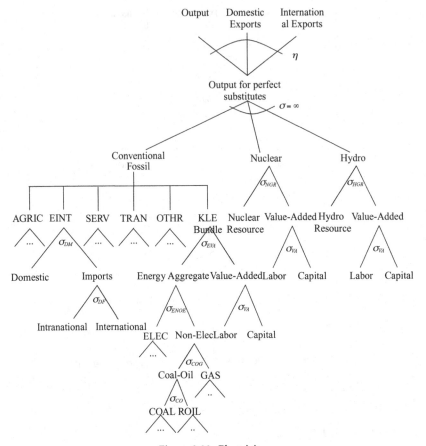

Figure 3.22. Electricity.

A.2 Domestic and Foreign Trade

We adopt the Armington (1969) assumption of product heterogeneity for imports and exports. Sectoral output produced in each region is converted through a CET function into goods destined for different markets. The associated unit cost function is given by

$$
\frac{p_{r,i}}{\overline{p}_{r,i}} = \left[\alpha_{r,i,d} \left(\frac{pd_{r,i}}{\overline{pdfx}_{r,,i}} \right)^{1+\eta} \right.
$$

$$
\left. + \alpha_{r,i,f} \left(\frac{pdfx_{r,i}}{\overline{pdfx}_{r,,i}} \right)^{1+\eta} + \alpha_{r,i,u} \left(\frac{pdx_{r,i}}{\overline{pdx}_{r,,j}} \right)^{1+\eta} \right]^{\frac{1}{1+\eta}} \quad (A.8)
$$

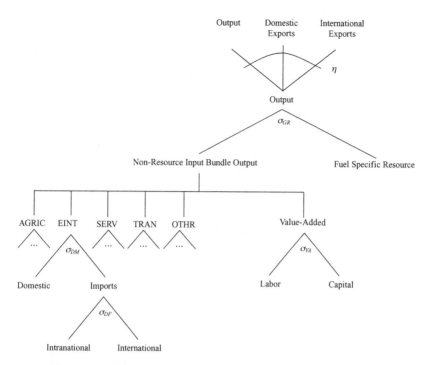

Figure 3.23. Primary Energy Sectors (Coal, Crude Oil, Natural Gas).

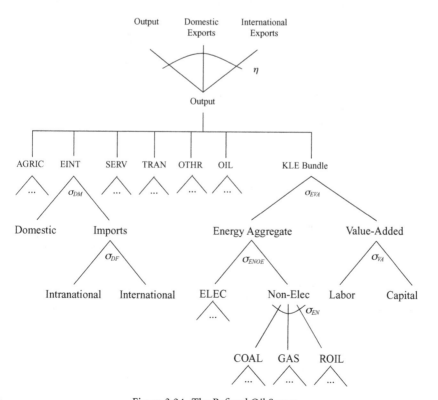

Figure 3.24. The Refined Oil Sector.

Table 3.11. *Reference values of production sector substitution elasticities*

Symbol	Description	Value	Comments
Energy Substitution Elasticities			
σ_{EVA}	Energy-Value Added	0.4–0.5	Applies in most sectors, 0.5 in EINT, OTHR
σ_{ENOE}	Electricity-Fuels Aggregate	0.5	All sectors
σ_{EN}	Among Fuels	1.0	All sectors except ELEC
σ_{EVRA}	Energy/Materials/Land-Value Added	0.7	Applies only to AGRI
σ_{ER}	Energy/Materials-Land	0.6	Applies only to AGRI
σ_{AE}	Energy-Materials	0.3	Applies only to AGRI
σ_{CO}	Coal-Oil	0.3	Applies only to ELEC
σ_{COG}	Coal/Oil-Gas	1.0	Applies only to ELEC
Other Production Elasticities			
σ_{VA}	Labor-Capital	1.0	All sectors
σ_{GR}	Resource-All Other Inputs	0.6	Applies to OIL, COAL, GAS sectors, calibrated to match medium run supply elasticity
σ_{NGR}	Nuclear Resource-Value Added	0.04–0.09	Varies by region, calibrated to match medium run supply elasticity
σ_{HGR}	Hydro Resource-Value Added	0.2–0.6	Varies by region, calibrated to match medium run supply elasticity
Armington Trade Elasticities			
σ_{DM}	Domestic-Aggregated Imports	2.0–3.0	Varies by good
		0.3	Electricity
σ_{MM}	National Imports-International Imports	5.0	Non-Energy goods
		4.0	Gas, Coal
		6.0	ROIL
		0.5	Electricity
η	Output produced for domestic, national, and foreign markets	2.0	Elasticity of transformation, uniform for all goods
γ, ν	Share parameters in world trade functions	0.01	Used to calibrate price elasticity of world export demand and word import supply.
σ_{GOV}	CES aggregator for government production	1.0	

Table 3.12. *Reference values for final demand elasticities*

Final Demand Elasticities for Energy			
σ_{EC}	Energy-Other Consumption	0.25	
σ_{EF}	Among Fuels and Electricity	0.4	
Other Final Demand Elasticities			
σ_{CS}	Consumption-Savings	0.0	
σ_{CL}	Consumption/Savings-Leisure	1	Calibrated to match labor supply elasticity of 0.25
σ_{SK}	Residential Investment-Other Investment	1	Calibrated to match capital supply elasticity of 0.3
σ_{C}	Among Non-Energy Goods	0.25–0.65	
σ_{CT}	Transportation-Other Consumption	1.0	

where $pd_{r,i}$, $pdfx_{r,i}$, and $pdx_{r,i}$ denote the price for domestic output, foreign exports, and intranational exports, respectively, and α's are value shares parameters. As described in the main part of the chapter, we use different market structures to model intra-U.S. trade for the following three subsets of goods: non-energy goods (indexed by *ne*) are traded on a bilateral basis, electricity (indexed by *ele*) is treated as a homogenous good within the six regional pools (indexed *pool*), and nonelectricity energy goods (indexed by *e*) are traded on an integrated U.S. market. In accordance with this market structure, we distinguish three prices for intranational exports:

$$
pdx_{r,i} = \begin{cases} pn_{r,i} & \textit{if } i \in ne \\ pnn_i & \textit{if } i \in e \\ pe_{pool} & \textit{if } i \in ele, \ r \in pool. \end{cases}
$$

Nested CES functions characterize the trade-off between imported (from national and international sources) and locally produced varieties of the same goods. The zero-profit condition that determines the level of Armington production, denoted by $a_{r,i}$, is given by

$$
\frac{p\,a_{r,i}}{\overline{p\,a}_{r,i}} = \left[\beta_{r,i,d} \left(\frac{pd_{r,i}}{\overline{pd}_{r,i}} \right)^{1-\sigma_{DM}} \right.
$$

$$
\left. + \left(\beta_{r,i,u} \left(\frac{pdx_{r,i}}{\overline{pdx}_{r,i}} \right)^{1-\sigma_{DF}} + \beta_{r,i,f} \left(\frac{pdfm_{r,i}}{\overline{pdfm}_{r,i}} \right)^{1-\sigma_{DF}} \right)^{\frac{1-\sigma_{DM}}{1-\sigma_{DF}}} \right]^{\frac{1}{1-\sigma_{DM}}}
$$

$$
(A.9)
$$

where $pdfm_{r,i}$ and β's denote the price for international imports and respective value share parameters, respectively.

The U.S. economy as a whole is modeled as a large open economy – that is, we assume that world export demand and world import supply functions for each traded good are elastic, implying that the United States can affect world market prices. Solving the model in the GAMS/MPSGE language (Rutherford 1999) constrains us to employ constant returns to scale functions. To model concave world trade functions, for each region and sector we introduce a fixed factor that enters as an input into a Cobb-Douglas export and import transformation function. A foreign consumer is endowed with the rents from fixed factors and demands foreign exchange. Let $pfix_{r,i}$ and $pfim_{r,i}$ denote the price for the fixed factor associated with export and imports, respectively, and let pfx denote the price for foreign exchange. The pricing equation for international exports of good i by region r is then given by

$$pfx = pdfx_{r,i}^{\gamma_{r,i}} pfix_{r,i}^{1-\gamma_{r,i}}. \tag{A.10}$$

Note that we can calibrate to any price elasticity of foreign demand for exports using the share parameter γ.[29] If $\gamma = 1$, the U.S. cannot affect world prices – that is, it is a small open economy. Analogously, the pricing equation for imports from international sources is

$$pdfm_{r,i} = pfx^{\nu_{r,i}} pfim_{r,i}^{1-\nu_{r,i}} \tag{A.11}$$

where $pdfm_{r,i}$ and ν denote the price for international imports and a share parameter, respectively.

A.3 Household Behavior

In each region, a representative agent in income class h chooses consumption, residential and nonresidential investment, and leisure to maximize

---

[29] To see this, consider the primal function associated with (A.10): $FX = X^\gamma R^{1-\gamma}$, where X and R denote the quantity of goods destined for the international markets and the fixed factor, respectively. The elasticity of foreign exchange revenue with respect to the quantity exported is then given by $\gamma = \frac{X}{FX} \frac{dFX}{dX}$. Foreign exchange revenue can be written as $FX = p(X)X$, where $p(X)$ denotes the inverse world demand function for U.S. exports. From this it follows that $\frac{dFX}{dX} = p + X \frac{dp}{dX}$, and $\frac{dFX}{dX} \frac{X}{FX} = 1 + \frac{X}{p} \frac{dp}{dX} = 1 + \frac{1}{\kappa}$, where κ denotes the inverse price elasticity of world demand for U.S. exports. Thus, we have $\gamma = 1 + \frac{1}{\kappa}$. In the small open economy case, world import demand is perfectly elastic, implying $\kappa \to \infty$ and hence $\gamma = 1$.

utility subject to a budget constraint given by the level of income $M_{r,h}$. Income is defined as

$$M_{r,h} = (pk\overline{K}_{r,h} + pl_r\overline{L}_{r,h})(1 - tinc_{r,h}) + pk\overline{RK}_{r,h}$$
$$+ \sum_z pr_z\overline{F}_{r,h,z} + \overline{TR}_{r,h} \quad (A.12)$$

where $\overline{K}_{r,h}$, $\overline{L}_{r,h}$, $\overline{F}_{r,h,z}$, and $\overline{RK}_{r,h}$ denote the initial endowment of non-residential capital, labor (including leisure time), fossil fuel resources, and residential capital, respectively. $tinc_{r,h}$ and $\overline{TR}_{r,h}$ denote the region- and household-specific marginal personal income tax rate and transfer income, respectively.

Preferences are represented by a CES function, and Figure 3.25 provides a schematic overview of the adopted nesting structure for household utility. By duality and the property of linear homogeneity, optimizing behavior of households requires that

$$pw_{r,h} = E_{r,h}(pa_{r,i}, pl_r, pk, pinv_r) \quad (A.13)$$

where $pw_{r,h}$ denotes a utility price index. $pinv_r$ denotes the price for the investment good in region r that is produced with fixed production coefficients according to

$$\frac{pinv_r}{\overline{pinv}_r} = \sum_i \phi_{r,i,INV}\frac{pa_{r,i}}{\overline{pa}_{r,i}}. \quad (A.14)$$

By Shephard's Lemma, the compensated final demand for good i by household h in region r is given by

$$d_{r,h,i} = \overline{M}_{r,h}\frac{\partial E_{r,h}}{\partial pa_{r,i}} \quad (A.15)$$

and leisure and residential and nonresidential investment demand are given by

$$leis_{r,h} = \overline{M}_{r,h}\frac{\partial E_{r,h}}{\partial pl_r} \quad (A.16)$$

$$rsd_{r,h} = \overline{M}_{r,h}\frac{\partial E_{r,h}}{\partial pk} \quad (A.17)$$

$$nrd_{r,h} = \overline{M}_{r,h}\frac{\partial E_{r,h}}{\partial pinv_r}. \quad (A.18)$$

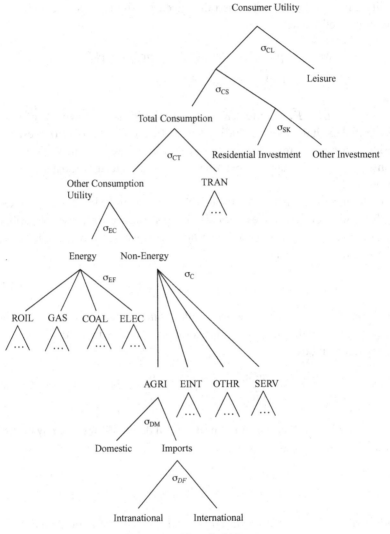

Figure 3.25. Household Sector.

A.4 Government

The federal government agent demands regional government goods in fixed proportions

$$\frac{pg}{\overline{pg}} = \sum_r \psi_r \frac{pgov_r}{\overline{pgov}_r} \qquad (A.19)$$

where ψ_r denotes benchmark value shares, and the regional government good is a CES aggregate of Armington goods whose price is given by

$$\frac{pgov_r}{\overline{pgov}_r} = \left[\sum_i \xi_{r,i} \left(\frac{pa_{r,i}}{\overline{pa}_{r,i}} \right)^{1-\sigma_{GOV}} \right]^{\frac{1}{1-\sigma_{GOV}}}, \tag{A.20}$$

and where $\xi_{r,i}$ denote value shares parameters. The government budget constraint is given by

$$GOV = \sum_{r,i} (to_{r,i} p_{r,i} y_{r,i} + tl_r pl_r k_{r,k,i} + tk_r k_{r,k,i} pk)$$

$$+ \sum_{r,h} tinc_{r,h} (pl_r (\overline{L}_{r,h} - leis_{r,h}) + pk(\overline{K}_{r,h} - nrd_{r,h}))$$

$$- \sum_{r,h} \overline{TR}_{r,h} - \overline{BOP}. \tag{A.21}$$

$\overline{BOP}$ denotes the initial balance of payments (deficit).

A.5 Market Clearing Conditions

The system is closed with a set of market clearance equations that determine the equilibrium prices in the different goods and factor markets. The market clearance condition for Armington goods requires that

$$a_{r,i} = \sum_j x_{r,j,i} + \sum_h d_{r,h,i} + i_r \frac{\partial pinv_r}{\partial pa_{r,i}} + g_r \frac{\partial pgov_r}{\partial pa_{r,i}}. \tag{A.22}$$

By Shephard's Lemma, the two last summands in (A.22) represent the investment and government demand for good *i*, respectively. Regional labor markets are in equilibrium if

$$\sum_{r,h} (\overline{L}_{r,h} - leis_{r,h}) = \sum_j ld_{r,j}, \tag{A.23}$$

The integrated U.S. capital market clears if

$$\sum_{r,h} (\overline{RK}_{r,h} + \overline{K}_{r,h}) = \sum_{r,j} kd_{r,j} + \sum_{r,h} rsd_{r,h}, \tag{A.24}$$

and equilibrium on resource markets requires that

$$\sum_{r,h} \overline{F}_{r,h,z} = \sum_{r,j} rd_{r,z,j}. \tag{A.25}$$

Balanced intranational trade for non-energy goods that are traded on a bilateral basis requires that

$$y_{r,i} \frac{\partial p_{r,i}}{\partial pn_{r,i}} = \sum_{rr} a_{rr,i} \frac{\partial pa_{rr,i}}{\partial pn_{r,i}}, \quad i \in ne, \tag{A.26a}$$

balanced domestic trade for nonelectricity energy goods requires that

$$\sum_{r} \left(y_{r,i} \frac{\partial p_{r,i}}{\partial pnn_i} - a_{r,i} \frac{\partial pa_{r,i}}{\partial pnn_i} \right) = 0, \quad i \in e, \tag{A.26b}$$

and regional electricity trade is in equilibrium if

$$\sum_{r \in pool} \left(y_{r,i} \frac{\partial p_{r,i}}{\partial pe_{pool}} - a_{r,i} \frac{\partial pa_{r,i}}{\partial pe_{pool}} \right) = 0, \quad i \in ele. \tag{A.26c}$$

Foreign closure of the model is warranted through a national balance-of-payments (BOP) constraint, which determines the price of foreign exchange:

$$\sum_{r,i} EX_{r,i} + \overline{BOP} = \sum_{r,i} IM_{r,i} \frac{\partial pdfm_{r,i}}{\partial pfx} \tag{A.27}$$

where the level of foreign exports, $EX_{r,i}$, and foreign imports, $IM_{r,i}$, is determined by conditions (A.10) and (A.11).

A.6 Extensions of the Model for Policy Analysis

So far we have described the generic model without explicitly incorporating policy variables and other structural model features that are required for the policy analyses that we carry out in the chapter. This section provides a description of how we implement GHG policies and certain model features specific to the scenarios laid out in the chapter.

Following the MIT EPPA model (Paltsev et al. 2005), we generally introduce greenhouse gas emissions into the nest structure of each production sector as a Leontief input associated with fuel, reflecting the reality that abatement involves using less of the fuel. In most other cases, we introduce greenhouse gases into a top CES nest, and the elasticities of substitution are chosen to match bottom-up estimates of abatement possibilities (Hyman 2001; Hyman et al. 2003).

Note that we tax energy at the point of consumption; that is, imported coal, oil, and natural gas, like domestically produced energy, are subject to GHG taxes. We tax energy associated with a process of energy (i.e., refineries), so it does not matter where energy is consumed, domestically or abroad. Finally, note that we tax energy used in production of exported goods but do not tax energy used in production of imported goods.

In our policy scenarios that consider the auctioning of permits, we impose additional constraints that determine the endogenous level of the active recycling instruments such that (1) the share of government expenditure in GDP remains constant and (2) uniform transfers per household or a uniform change in terms of percentage points of the active recycling instrument are achieved. In the free allocation scenarios, we impose the constraint that the share of government expenditure in GDP is constant and we distribute the revenue (net of the portion needed to keep the share of government fixed) according to the scenario-specific allocation scheme.

In the ELE_SUB scenario we use the value of allowance going to the electricity sector, denoted by AV_r, to subsidize the domestic electricity consumer price, denoted by $psele_r$. We implement this by adding the following pricing equation for the electricity consumer price:

$$psele_r = pa_{r,ele} - sub_r \qquad (A.28)$$

where the endogenous region-specific subsidy rate, sub_r, is determined such that

$$\sum_h sub_r d_{r,h,ele} = AV_r. \qquad (A.29)$$

APPENDIX B: DATA SOURCES

The USREP model is built on state-level economic data from the IMPLAN dataset (Minnesota IMPLAN Group 2008) covering all transactions among businesses, households, and government agents for the base year 2006. Aggregation and reconciliation of IMPLAN state-level economic accounts to generate a benchmark dataset that can be used for model calibration is accomplished using ancillary tools documented in Rausch and Rutherford (2009). The detailed representation of existing taxes captures the effects of tax-base erosion and comprises sector- and region-specific ad-valorem output taxes, payroll taxes, and capital income taxes. IMPLAN data have been augmented by incorporating regional tax data from the NBER tax simulator to represent marginal personal income tax rate by region and income class. The USREP model is built on energy data from the Department of Energy

EIA State Energy Data System (Energy Information Administration 2009) and comprises price and quantity data on energy production, consumption, and trade. For each state, we have replaced all energy data in the economic IMPLAN dataset with assembled price-quantity EIA data and used optimization techniques to reconcile economic and energy data. The integrated dataset is *micro-consistent*, that is, it describes a reference equilibrium and is benchmarked to EIA energy statistics.

Additional data for the greenhouse gas (CO_2, CH_4, N_2O, HFCs, PFCs, and SF_6) emissions are based on the EPA inventory data, including endogenous costing of the abatement of non-CO_2 GHGs (Hyman et al. 2003)). Following the approach outlined in Paltsev et al. (2005), the model incorporates supplemental physical accounts to link economic data in value terms with physical quantities on energy production, consumption, and trade. Furthermore, the USREP model incorporates demographic data on the population and number of households in each region and income class based on U.S. Census Data (U.S. Census Bureau 2006).

APPENDIX C: MODEL CALIBRATION

As customary in applied general equilibrium analysis, we use prices and quantities of the integrated economic-energy dataset for the benchmark year 2006 to calibrate the value share and level parameters in model. Exogenous elasticities determine the free parameters of the functional forms that capture production technologies and consumer preferences. Tables 3.11 and 3.12 provide a list of the elasticity parameters used in the model and the respective values employed in the core scenarios. Whenever possible, we adopt the parameterization of the single U.S. region in the EPPA model (version 4, Paltsev et al. 2005) for all U.S. regions that has been subject to extensive sensitivity analysis in Webster et al. (2002) and Cossa (2004). There are, however, a few elasticity parameters that are specific to the USREP model.

In order to parameterize capital and labor we follow the approach outlined in Babiker et al. (2001) to infer values for elasticities of substitution from data on related supply elasticities and benchmark shares. Based on Paltsev et al. (2005) we assume that the share of leisure time relative to hours worked is 0.25. The elasticity of substitution between leisure and consumption is then calibrated to match an aggregate labor supply elasticity of 0.25 based on Babiker, Reilly, and Viguier (2004). We assume a uniform labor supply elasticity across regions and income groups. In a similar way we calibrate a uniform elasticity of substitution between residential and other investment to match an aggregate capital supply elasticity of 0.3, based on Chirinko, Fazzari, and Meyer (2004). The elasticity of transformation between outputs destined for domestic and international markets is set to 2.0 for all goods. We assume a uniform price elasticity for world export demand and world import supply for all goods and regions, that is, $\gamma_{r,i} = v_{r,i}$.

References

Armington, Paul. 1969. A theory of demand for products distinguished by place of production. *International Monetary Fund Staff Papers* 16: 159–176.

Babiker, Mustafa, John M. Reilly, Monika Mayer, et al. 2001. The MIT Emissions Prediction and Policy Analysis (EPPA) Model: Revisions, Sensitivities, and Comparison of Results. MIT Joint Program on the Science and Policy of Global Change, *Report 71*, Cambridge, MA, http://globalchange.mit.edu/files/document/MITJPSPGC_Rpt73.pdf.

Babiker, Mustafa, Gilbert Metcalf, and John M. Reilly. 2003. Tax distortions and global climate policy. *Journal of Environmental Economics and Management* 46: 269–287.

Babiker, Mustafa, John M. Reilly, and Laurent Viguier. 2004. Is emissions trading always beneficial? *Energy Journal* 25 (2): 33–56.

Bento, Antonio M., Lawrence H. Goulder, Mark R. Jacobsen, et al. 2009. Distributional and efficiency impacts of increased US gasoline taxes. *American Economic Review* 99 (3): 667–699.

Bovenberg A. Lans, and Lawrence H. Goulder. 2001. Neutralizing the adverse industry impacts of CO2 abatement policies: What does it cost? In *Distributional and Behavioral Effects of Environmental Policy*, Carlo Carraro and Gilbert E. Metcalf (eds.), pp. 45–85. Chicago: University of Chicago Press.

Bovenberg A. Lans, Lawrence J. Goulder, and Derek J. Gurney. 2005. Efficiency costs of meeting industry-distributional constraints under environmental permits and taxes. *RAND Journal of Economics* 36 (4): 951–971.

Bull, Nicholas, Kevin Hassett, and Gilbert E. Metcalf. 1994. Who pays broad-based energy taxes? Computing lifetime and regional incidence. *Energy Journal* 15 (3): 145–164.

Burtraw, Dallas, Richard Sweeney, and Margaret Walls. 2009. *The incidence of U.S. climate policy: Alternative uses of revenue from a cap and trade auction.* Washington, D.C.: Resources for the Future.

Burtraw, Dallas, Margaret Walls, and Joshua A. Blonz. 2009. *Distributional Impacts of Carbon Pricing Policies in the Electricity Sector.* Washington, D.C.: American Tax Policy Institute.

Chirinko, R., S. Fazzari, and A. Meyer. 2004. That elusive elasticity: A long-panel approach to estimating the capital-labor substitution elasticity. CESifo Working Paper, Ifo Institute for Economic Research, Munich, Germany.

Congressional Budget Office. 2009a. *Assessment of Potential Budgetary Impacts from the Introduction of Carbon Dioxide Cap-and-Trade Policies.* Washington, D.C.: Congressional Budget Office.

Congressional Budget Office. 2009b. *H.R. 2454 American Clean Energy and Security Act of 2009 Cost Estimate.* Washington, D.C.: Congressional Budget Office.

Cossa, Paul F. 2004. Uncertainty analysis of the cost of climate policies. *Technology and Policy Program.* Cambridge: Massachusetts Institute of Technology.

Davies, James B., France St.-Hilaire, and John Whalley. 1984. Some calculations of lifetime tax incidence. *American Economic Review* 74 (4): 633–649.

Dinan, Terry, and Diane Lim Rogers. 2002. Distributional effects of carbon allowance trading: How government decisions determine winners and losers. *National Tax Journal* 55 (2): 199–221.

Dirkse, S., and M. Ferris. 1993. The PATH solver: A non-monotone stabilization scheme for mixed complementarity problems. Technical Report, Computer Sciences Department, University of Wisconsin-Madison.

Energy Information Administration. 2009. State Energy Data System. Energy Information Administration. Available at http://www.eia.doe.gov/emeu/states/_seds.html. Accessed August 2009.

Friedman, Milton. 1957. *A Theory of the Consumption Function.* Princeton: Princeton University Press.

Fullerton, Don, and Garth Heutel. 2007. The general equilibrium incidence of environmental taxes. *Journal of Public Economics* 91 (3–4): 571–591.

Fullerton, Don, and Diane Lim Rogers. 1993. *Who Bears the Lifetime Tax Burden?* Washington, D.C.: Brookings Institution.

Grainger, Corbett, and Charles D. Kolstad. 2009. *Who pays a price on carbon?* NBER Working Paper No. 15239, Cambridge, MA.

Harberger, Arnold, 1962. The incidence of the corporation income tax. *Journal of Political Economy* 70: 215–240.

Hassett, Kevin, Aparna Mathur, and Gilbert Metcalf. 2009. The incidence of a U.S. carbon tax: A lifetime and regional analysis. *The Energy Journal* 30 (2): 157–179.

Holt, Mark, and Gene Whitney. 2009. *Greenhouse gas legislation: Summary and analysis of H.R. 2454 as passed by the House of Representatives.* Washington, D.C.: Congressional Research Service.

Hyman, Robert C. 2001. A More Cost-Effective Strategy for Reducing Greenhouse Gas Emissions: Modeling the Impact of Methane Abatement Opportunities. *Technology and Policy Program.* Cambridge: Massachusetts Institute of Technology.

Hyman, Robert C., John M. Reilly, Mustafa H. Babiker, et al. 2003. Modeling non-CO_2 greenhouse gas abatement. *Environmental Modeling and Assessment* 8 (3): 175–186.

Lyon, Andrew, and Robert Schwab. 1995. Consumption taxes in a life-cycle framework: Are sin taxes regressive? *Review of Economics and Statistics* 77 (3): 389–406.

Mathiesen, Lars. 1985. Computation of economic equilibria by a sequence of linear complementarity problems. *Mathematical Programming Study* 23: 144–162.

Metcalf, Gilbert. 1999. A distributional analysis of green tax reforms. *National Tax Journal* 52 (4): 655–681.

Metcalf, Gilbert. 2007. A proposal for a U.S. carbon tax swap: An equitable tax reform to address global climate change. In *Hamilton Project Discussion Paper.* Washington, D.C.: Brookings Institution.

Metcalf, Gilbert. 2009. Designing a carbon tax to reduce U.S. greenhouse gas emissions. *Review of Environmental Economics and Policy* 3 (1): 63–83.

Metcalf, Gilbert E., Sergey Paltsev, John M. Reilly, et al. 2008. Analysis of U.S. greenhouse gas proposals. MIT Joint Program on the Science and Policy of Global

Change, *Report 160*, Cambridge, MA, http://globalchang e.mit.edu/files/document/ MITJPSPGC Rpt160.pdf.

Minnesota IMPLAN Group. 2008. State-Level U.S. Data for 2006. Minnesota IMPLAN Group Inc.

Paltsev, Sergey, John M. Reilly, Henry D. Jacoby, et al. 2005. The MIT Emissions Prediction and Policy Analysis (EPPA) Model: Version 4. MIT Joint Program on the Science and Policy of Global Change, *Report 125*, Cambridge, MA, http://globalchange.mit .edu/files/document/MITJPSPGC_Rpt125.pdf/

Parry, Ian. 2004. Are emissions permits regressive? *Journal of Environmental Economics and Management* 47: 364–387.

Pechman, Joseph A. 1985. *Who Paid the Taxes: 1966–85?* Washington, D.C.: Brookings Institution.

Poterba, James. 1989. Lifetime incidence and the distributional burden of excise taxes. *American Economic Review* 79 (2): 325–330.

Poterba, James. 1991. Is the gasoline tax regressive? *Tax Policy and the Economy* 5: 145– 164.

Rausch, Sebastian, Gilbert E. Metcalf, John M. Reilly, et al. In press. Distributional implications of alternative U.S. greenhouse gas control measures. *The B.E. Journal of Economic Analysis & Policy.*

Rausch, Sebastian, and Thomas F. Rutherford. 2009. *Tools for Building National Economic Models Using State-Level IMPLAN Social Accounts. Mimeograph.* Cambridge: Massachusetts Institute of Technology.

Ross, Martin. 2008. Documentation of the Applied Dynamic Analysis of the Global Economy (ADAGE). Working Paper 08–01, Research Triangle Institute.

Rutherford, Thomas F. 1995a. CES Preferences and Technology: A Practical Introduction. Mimeograph.University of Colorado.

Rutherford, Thomas F. 1995b. Extensions of GAMS for complementarity problems arising in applied economic analysis. *Journal of Economic Dynamics and Control* 19 (8): 1299–1324.

Rutherford, Thomas F. 1999. Applied general equilibrium modeling with MPSGE as a GAMS subsystem: An overview of the modeling framework and syntax. *Computational Economics* 14: 1–46.

Tuladhar, S., M. Yuan P. Bernstein, et al. In press. A top-down bottom-up modeling approach to climate change policy analysis. *Energy Economics.*

U.S. Environmental Protection Agency. 2009. *Inventory of U.S. Greenhouse Gas Emissions and Sinks: 1990–2007.* Washington, D.C.: Environmental Protection Agency, EPA 430-R-09–004.

U.S. Census Bureau. 2006. *American Household Community Survey 2006: Household Income in the Past 12 Months.* Washington, D.C.: U.S. Census Bureau.

U.S. Senate Committee on Finance. 2009. Testimony of Dallas Burtraw. Hearing on Climate Change Legislation: Allowance and Revenue Distribution. Washington, D.C.

Webster, M, M. Babiker M. Mayer, et al. 2002. Uncertainty in emissions projections for climate models. *Atmospheric Environment* 36 (22): 3659–3670.

Weisbach, David. 2009. Instrument Choice Is Instrument Design. Washington, D.C.: American Tax Policy Institute.

Comments

Richard D. Morgenstern

As the Washington policy process grinds forward, it is essential to examine the distributional impacts of efforts to put a price on CO_2 emissions. As the authors of this impressive chapter note, questions of "who gets what and who pays" are often more important to legislative victories than the efficiency issues that are traditionally of greatest concern to economists. Rausch and colleagues apply their modeling skills to analyzing the impacts of a national cap-and-trade system of the type contained in the American Clean Energy and Security Act of 2009 (H.R. 2454). They focus on two critical household-level impacts: income class and region.

Most previous analyses have examined distributional effects purely on the basis of the energy expenditures of households. In contrast, Rausch and colleagues employ a general equilibrium framework to trace the effect of a new policy on the cost of all goods and services, and returns to capital and other resources, including labor. The analysis is based on the static MIT U.S. Regional Energy Policy (USREP) model, and represents a first phase toward developing a dynamic model consistent with the MIT's global Emissions Prediction and Policy Analysis (EPPA). This welcome advance offers sectoral detail, production structure, and other key parameters that are similar to EPPA. By restricting their focus to the United States and introducing household heterogeneity in lieu of a representative agent approach, they are able to generate explicit modeling of regions and states within the United States, and multiple household income classes in each region.

The analysis focuses on net distributional impacts, considering the effects of both the newly introduced CO_2 prices and a series of alternative mechanisms for recycling allowance auction proceeds within a revenue neutral framework. Particular attention is paid to the mechanisms for freely distributing a portion of the allowances to LDCs, as specified in H.R. 2454, an innovation that makes this work especially relevant to current policy discussions.

Overall, the analysis confirms and supports previous research findings that virtually all of the costs of a CO_2 pricing policy are passed forward to consumers. Not surprisingly, the modeling suggests that an equal lump-sum payment to households is by far the most progressive allocation scheme when compared to alternatives such as reducing existing taxes on labor or capital, although the latter do involve small efficiency gains. The modest size of the efficiency gains is dictated by the revenue neutrality assumption, because only about half the revenues are available for recycling, with the other half going to cover lost tax revenues.

As regards the free distribution of allowances to LDCs, the authors voice concern that revenues be returned in a manner that is perceived to pass through to ratepayers the higher electricity rates resulting from the cap-and-trade program. The fear is that even if utility bills contain a separate entry (rebate) for the value of the allowances, the consumer might not fully understand that rates have risen. The analysis shows a relatively large welfare cost associated with such consumer misperception. Accordingly, Rausch and colleagues recommend that an equal lump-sum payment be considered rather than one based solely on electricity consumption. This would have the advantage of simplicity and would also increase the chances that the consumer would recognize that electricity prices now include some consideration of carbon damages.

From a regional perspective, Rausch and coauthors find that some politically "blue" states, California, the Pacific Coast, New England, and New York, experience the lowest overall program costs and even receive net benefits under certain redistribution schemes. The principal cause of the interregional differences in burdens is the energy source for electricity generation: regions with heavy reliance on renewables, including hydro, or nuclear fare better than those using coal. Interestingly, regions with the lowest welfare costs tend to be those with higher-than-average prepolicy electricity prices, suggesting that prior action contributes to the lower costs borne by residents of those regions. Not surprisingly, the lump-sum redistribution approach also leads to the smallest cost differences among regions.

As a guide to future model development, I would suggest three areas for further analysis, which are discussed in the sections that follow.

Reconciling Assumptions Relevant to Short-Term and Long-Term Analysis

Rausch and coauthors have chosen to focus on long-term impacts, after households and firms have adjusted by using new energy-efficient technologies and, at least implicitly, after new import patterns have been established. Such a framework, however, fails to capture the short- or medium-term costs that most households or firms will likely experience. Neither a household nor a steel mill suddenly faced with higher energy costs can immediately or costlessly adopt more energy-efficient technologies. Similarly, the path taken to the long-run outcome is clearly important. A carbon control policy that ignores these short- and medium-term impacts will raise concerns about fairness. Further, the desired approach may change over time: a policy that addresses fairness questions in the initial years may not be considered equitable in the future. Accordingly, it is important to consider distributional impacts over different timeframes, including the short term, when firms (and households) have a limited ability to adjust prices; the medium term, when the mix of inputs may be altered but capital cannot be easily replaced; and the long term, when capital may be reallocated and replaced with more energy-efficient technologies.

Although the long-term approach adopted by Rausch and colleagues is eminently reasonable, some of the individual assumptions used in the analysis seem more appropriate for a short- or medium-term framework. For example, in their general equilibrium modeling, the authors have assumed that capital is fully mobile, whereas labor is not able to cross state lines. Recent reports of the exodus of workers from Michigan in the wake of the diminishing job prospects in the auto industry suggest, as do a host of academic studies, that workers can and do move fairly quickly in response to changing labor market conditions. Arguably, the impacts of this labor immobility assumption may be important for a distributional analysis, as changes in state or regional wage levels are likely to be an important element in the adjustment to a new CO_2 pricing regime. As the demand for labor shrinks in some regions, for example, those areas dominated by energy-intensive, trade-sensitive industries, the modeling assumption of labor immobility means that wages may have to fall substantially to achieve a labor market equilibrium in those areas. If, alternatively, workers were able to move outside the hardest-hit areas, overall impacts on wages and incomes would likely be reduced, as would certain regional disparities. Thus, at a minimum, I would recommend relaxing the assumption of labor immobility and introducing an alternative framework.

More Disaggregated Modeling of the Energy-Intensive Industrial Sector

Despite the rich detail on energy production and consumption in USREP, the energy-consuming industries are disaggregated into only five sectors: agriculture, services, energy-intensive industries, other industries, and transportation. This is particularly important for cap and trade or other carbon pricing mechanisms in which increased production costs lead to reduced domestic output, especially in energy-intensive, trade-exposed industries. Clearly, output reduction in these energy-intensive, trade-exposed industries will not be distributed equally across all regions. Further disaggregation of the energy-intensive sector in the USREP model would clearly provide a more accurate picture of the underlying differences in regional impacts. Especially if the authors want to use their model to inform policy debates on fairness, understanding which industries in which states/regions are most vulnerable under a CO_2 pricing regime is critical. Such analysis is also critical to understanding the effect of specific policies designed to mitigate these adverse distributional impacts, as described in the next section.

Modeling of the Use of Output-Based Rebates in Some Industries Rather than Grandfathering

It is widely recognized that a significant portion of the output losses in energy-intensive, trade-exposed industries associated with the uneven international CO_2 pricing policies likely to be adopted, at least in the near term, will be made up by increased foreign production. Estimates of emissions leakage as a percent of reduced emissions of energy-intensive domestic industries range up to 40 percent or more (Fischer 2009).[1] H.R. 2454 addresses at least some of the potential for emissions leakage by introducing an output-based allocation scheme for energy-intensive, trade-exposed industries. Importantly, the per-unit allocation is not based on the firm's emissions, but on a sector-based intensity standard, such as average emissions. Such a system keeps vulnerable industries under the emissions cap while offsetting increases in their production costs. In essence, the CO_2 price remains in place while the allowances/rebates prevent operating costs from rising too high. However, the use of these rebates to reduce competitiveness

---

[1] Also see Ho, Morgenstern, and Shih (2008).

impacts does come at the expense of opportunities to reduce consumption of emissions-intensive goods.

By failing to distinguish trade-exposed from other energy-intensive industries, USREP is unable to model the output-based allocation scheme included in H.R. 2454. An early paper by Fischer and Fox has attempted to capture provisions of this type in the context of a computable general equilibrium model using a representative agent approach (2009). Recent work using an updated version of this model was developed by an interagency group in the U.S. government (EPA 2009). Because an output-based allocation scheme will almost certainly limit the production losses in the energy-intensive, trade-exposed industries, there are clear distributional implications for the policy, as regards different regions of the United States and, quite possibly, for different income classes. Thus, an assessment of the distributional impacts of H.R. 2454 would be enhanced by consideration of such an allocation scheme within the context of a model with household heterogeneity.

Overall, Rausch and colleagues make an important contribution to the literature by developing sophisticated, general equilibrium analyses of distributional issues under a CO_2 pricing regime. As in any modeling effort, choices have to be made on the allocation of scarce resources. My suggestions for future improvements are generally aimed at making the work more relevant to the policy audience the authors seek to inform.

References

Fischer, C., and A.K. Fox. 2009. Output-based allocation of emissions permits for mitigating tax and trade interactions. *Land Economics* 83:575–599.

Ho, Mun S., Richard D. Morgenstern, and Jhih-Shyang Shih. 2008. Impact of carbon price policies on US industry. Discussion Paper 08–37. Washington, D.C.: Resources for the Future.

U.S. EPA. 2009. *The Effects of H.R. 2454 on International Competitiveness and Emission Leakage in Energy-Intensive Trade-Exposed Industries: An Interagency Report Responding to a Request from Senators Bayh, Specter, Stabenow, McCaskill, and Brown*, December (available at http://www.epa.gov/climatechange/economics/pdfs/InteragencyReport_Competitiveness-EmissionLeakage.pdf).

FOUR

Instrument Choice Is Instrument Design

David Weisbach

This chapter analyzes the choice between taxes and cap-and-trade systems as methods of controlling greenhouse gas emissions. It argues that within a single country, commonly discussed differences between the two instruments are due to unjustified assumptions about design. In the climate change context and within a single country there is sufficient design flexibility that these differences can be substantially eliminated. To the extent that there are remaining differences, there should be a modest preference for taxes, but the benefits of taxes are swamped by the benefits of good design; even though the very best tax might be better than the very best quantity restriction, the first order of business is getting the design right.

In the international context, however, taxes dominate more strongly. The design flexibility available within a single country is reduced in the international context because of the problems of coordinating systems across countries and minimizing holdouts. Moreover, the incentives to cheat and the effects of cheating are not equivalent for the two instruments in the international setting. Because climate change will require a global system for emissions, these considerations mean we should favor taxes for controlling greenhouse gas emissions. Nevertheless, the preference should be modest; substantial flexibility remains even internationally, and taxes also have coordination and enforcement problems.

Section 4.1 provides basic definitions. Section 4.2 considers the arguments attributed to Weitzman (1974) that taxes and permit systems are different when the government is uncertain about the marginal costs of abatement. Weitzman's arguments rely on an assumption that taxes are flat, per-unit taxes, permits are a fixed-quantity limitation, and neither taxes nor

I thank Louis Kaplow, Michael Graetz, and Eric Toder, as well as participants at workshops at Yale and Harvard and at the ATPI conference, for comments on an earlier draft.

permits can be changed over time in response to new information. These assumptions are not correct in the climate context. Building on arguments advanced by Kaplow and Shavell (2002), Section 4.2 shows that with flexible design, uncertainty does not affect the choice of instruments.

Section 4.3 discusses seven additional potential differences between taxes and permits in the single-country context. It considers, for example, whether the two instruments have different distributional or revenue consequences, whether tipping points and environmental certainty should alter the choice, whether permit price volatility is a problem, and whether framing effects matter in this context. It concludes that these and other claimed differences are most often a result of unjustified assumptions about design. With flexibility, both systems will be substantially the same along these dimensions.

Section 4.4 considers the implementation of carbon taxes or cap-and-trade systems internationally. Some of the design flexibility in the domestic context is lost once coordination across nations and hold-out problems are considered. In particular, in the international context, it might be hard to adjust the tax rate or the quantity of permits in response to new information, and taxes perform better in the absence of such adjustments. Moreover, the effects of cheating are different for taxes and permits and in general are worse for permits. Therefore, there should be a modest preference for taxes in the international context.

Before turning to the discussion, it is worth a word about intuitions about domestic political institutions. In analyzing the choice of instruments in the single-country context, I am considering a generic, market-based economy rather than any particular country or any particular time period, such as the United States in the early twenty-first century. Political institutions and coalitions will vary across countries and time periods. If it is the case that a given country in a given time period simply will not enact a pricing system with a particular label or feature, there is nothing to analyze – the political system will do what it does (although there is then room for ingenuity in designing good systems that also meet the political constraints). Similarly, if a particular country at a particular time has a regulator or legislative committee that is especially competent or incompetent, that country will want to choose an instrument that takes advantage of this fact. A general analysis of instrument choice cannot take these sorts of local considerations into account; they will vary too much by country and across time. The goal here is instead to analyze the underlying features of different instruments and emphasize constraints that apply across countries, such as information constraints, the effects of uncertainty, and so forth.

4.1 Basic Definitions and Terminology

When individuals or firms emit CO_2 or other greenhouse gases, they impose harm on others.[1] Because the individuals or firms (together, polluters) do not have to consider these harms, they emit too much.

Harm from climate change is a result of the total stock of greenhouse gases in the atmosphere, not the flow. Emissions in a particular year do not matter except to the extent that they add to the stock. Carbon dioxide also mixes in the atmosphere globally; no matter where emissions originate, the harm is the same. Pre-industrial concentrations of CO_2 were about 280 parts per million (ppm). Current concentrations are 380 ppm, increasing by around 2 ppm per year. Doubling pre-industrial concentrations would likely result in global average temperature increases of around 3.5° C, although the estimate is highly uncertain. Most analysts agree that high concentrations, such as 700 ppm or higher, would result in severe harm, and typical targets for climate change proposals are between 400 to 500 ppm.

Control of environmental externalities was traditionally done through command and control regulations, under which the government specified particular technologies or firm-by-firm emissions limitations. Market-based instruments, however, are thought to be able to control externalities far more cheaply because the government does not have the ability to determine which particular technologies are best or which firms should use which technology. Market-based instruments utilize private information about firms' abatement costs to minimize total costs. The two chief market-based instruments are taxes and quantity restrictions.

A tax on greenhouse gases would simply be a charge on emissions. A polluter, considering whether to emit one more unit of pollution should face a cost equal to the harm imposed on others from that additional unit. Polluters, faced with a charge equal to the additional harm imposed on others from another unit of emissions, would adjust their behavior appropriately.

If marginal harm is not flat – a fixed dollar amount per unit of pollution – the tax should vary with marginal harm. For example, if marginal harm increases as pollution increases, so should the optimal tax. Similarly, if the government learns that the marginal harm is different than it first believed, the tax should be changed to reflect the new information.

---

[1] A large number of gases contribute to the greenhouse effect, including CO_2, methane, and nitrous oxide. CO_2 is the most important. I will refer here to all greenhouse cases as CO_2.

Metcalf and Weisbach (2009) consider the design of a carbon tax. They show that a carbon tax in the United States could cover 80 percent of total emissions by taxing less than 2,500 entities. The reason is that emissions from fossil fuels make up about 80 percent of U.S. emissions, and these can be taxed upstream on extraction or refining without a loss of accuracy. Globally, fossil fuel emissions are around 67 percent of total emissions, and a global carbon tax could similarly tax these emissions upstream.

Another 14 percent of global emissions are from agriculture. These emissions would be much more difficult to include in a tax system because they come from a wide variety of disparate sources, many of which are hard to observe. Taxes on inputs, such as nitrogen fertilizer or head of cattle, might be the only way to include these emissions in the tax base. Deforestation is the third largest source of emissions, making up about 12 percent of global emissions. A tax on deforestation would be complex because it would have to be based on deforestation relative to a baseline and because the effects of deforestation depend on many factors, including location, use of the timber, and what replaces the forest. A decision to tax agricultural and forestry emissions will depend on the marginal abatement costs in these industries and whether there is a reasonably accurate and administrable method of including them in the base.

Design considerations can significantly affect the costs and benefits of a tax system. For example, rather than imposing the tax upstream on a small number of firms producing or distributing fossil fuels, the government could impose the tax downstream on emitters. There are almost 250 million automobiles in the United States and no easy way to measure emissions from each vehicle. There are also a large number of homes using natural gas for heating. Attempts to impose a tax downstream would significantly increase administrative costs, reduce the tax base, or both.

Quantity restrictions, also called permits or cap-and-trade systems (I will use these terms interchangeably here), limit the total quantity of emissions. The government issues permits (either by auctioning them or otherwise allocating them) equal to the total amount of emissions it decides is appropriate, usually over a given period. Polluters would be required to have a permit in order to pollute. Holders of the permits would be allowed to sell them, creating a market in permits. Anyone who could reduce emissions for less than the market permit price would do so, and everyone else would buy a permit, thereby equalizing the marginal cost of abatement across all users. If the government issues a quantity of permits so that the permit trading price is equal to the marginal harm from emissions, polluters would, like in a tax, face a price equal to marginal harm and adjust behavior appropriately.

The number of permits does not have to remain fixed in a cap-and-trade system. The government can change the number of permits over time so that their price reflects marginal harm, for example, by buying permits to increase their price or selling additional permits to lower their price. Section 4.2 discusses the reasons and mechanisms for doing this.

Stavins (2008) considers the design of a cap-and-trade system. Implementing a cap-and-trade system raises similar issues to a tax. Issues such as determining what emissions to cover and at what level to impose the permit requirement (e.g., upstream on fossil fuel production or downstream on emitters) are the same for permits as they are for taxes. Quantity restrictions also require a trading market and a method of making the initial allocation of permits.

Taxes and permit systems are equivalent if the government sets the tax rate or the number of permits correctly so that in either case the price faced by polluters is the marginal harm from emissions. They are, in a sense, duals. In a tax, the government sets the price and firms determine quantity subject to that price. In a permit system, the government sets the quantity and firms determine the price given that quantity. So long as the government has sufficient information, it can choose to regulate along either margin, and for every tax, there is an equivalent set of permits and vice versa. Moreover, the core implementation issues – what emissions to cover and at what level to regulate (e.g., upstream or downstream) are the same. For example, a decision to regulate upstream can be equivalently made for taxes and permits. The question in the next two sections is what happens when the assumption that the government correctly picks the price no longer holds or when we consider more subtle implementation issues.

4.2 Equivalence of Taxes and Permits with Uncertainty about Marginal Abatement Costs

Weitzman (1974) argued that the equivalence between tax and quantity restrictions does not hold when there is uncertainty about the marginal cost of abatement because the error costs will be different for taxes and quantity limitations.[2] Depending on the relative slopes of the marginal abatement cost curve and the marginal harm curve, either taxes or permits might be preferred. Virtually every analysis of instrument choice begins with this argument.

---

[2] Similar arguments made contemporaneously by Adar and Griffin (1976), Rose-Ackerman (1973), and Fishelson (1976).

This section argues that Weitzman's arguments rely on assumptions about the design of the systems that are unlikely to hold in the climate change context. In particular, Weitzman assumes that taxes are flat, per-unit taxes and that quantity limits are fixed caps. In addition, Weitzman assumes that neither the tax rate nor the quantity limit is adjusted in response to information showing that they were set in error. Weitzman is explicit about these assumptions and makes arguments that they are appropriate in the single-polluter context he was considering. Nevertheless, these assumptions are rarely mentioned in the literature on climate change that builds on Weitzman's arguments, and as far as I have been able to tell, never been defended in the climate context. I will argue that neither of these assumptions is appropriate in the climate context, and without both, taxes and quantity limits are equivalent.

The arguments here build on and extend to the climate change context arguments made in Kaplow and Shavell (2002). Kaplow and Shavell directly address Weitzman's assumptions that taxes are flat, per-unit taxes, indefinitely fixed, and argue (1) that taxes can be and regularly are nonlinear,[3] and (2) that nonlinear taxes are second-best optimal; errors in estimating marginal abatement costs do not affect the efficiency of well-designed nonlinear taxes. As a result, Kaplow and Shavell argue that nonlinear taxes dominate simple permit systems, such as non-traded permits or traded permits with hard caps. They also address flexible permit designs, focusing on flexible designs such as those introduced by Roberts and Spence (1976). With sufficient design flexibility, they conclude the equivalence between taxes and permits is restored, as is argued here.

Section 4.2.1 briefly reviews Weitzman's argument, which is likely familiar to readers. Section 4.2.2 discusses the assumption of no updating in response to new information, arguing that sufficiently rapid updating would not be difficult in the climate change context. Section 4.2.3 discusses the assumption of flat-rate taxes and fixed quantity limits, arguing that more accurate schedules would not be difficult to implement. Section 4.2.4 considers the possibility of combining complex schedules and adjustments in response to new information.

4.2.1 Weitzman's Argument

Recall that the optimal charge on emissions would be the marginal harm; if marginal harm is nonlinear, so is the optimal tax, and if marginal harm

---

[3] Ireland (1976) makes a similar argument that contingent tax systems are possible and presents an example.

changes, so does the tax. Weitzman makes two assumptions about the government's regulatory options that prevent the government from imposing the optimal charge. He assumes first that the government must impose either a fixed, per-unit tax or a fixed quantity limitation. The tax, for example, must be fixed at a given amount per unit of pollution. The quantity limit must specify the total emissions over time or in a given period.[4] Second, Weitzman assumes that the tax rate or quantity remains fixed; even if the government gains new information about the optimal tax or quantity, the original guess is not changed, at least for some unspecified time period.

Sections 4.2.2 and 4.2.3 discuss whether these assumptions are reasonable for climate change. To demonstrate Weitzman's argument, I assume in this section that they are; the government must pick either a fixed, per-unit tax or a fixed quantity of emissions.

If using a fixed-rate tax, the government should set the tax rate where it estimates the marginal cost of abatement equals the expected marginal harm from another unit of pollution. Firms, knowing their own marginal costs of abatement and faced with this tax, will emit up to the point where the marginal costs of abatement equal the tax rate. If the government estimates marginal harm and marginal costs correctly, firms will emit the optimal amount. If using permits, the government should set the number of permits the same way it sets a tax: where it estimates the marginal cost of abatement equals the expected marginal harm from another unit of pollution. As just discussed, if set this way, permits will trade at the same price as the tax and the result will be the same.

If the government incorrectly calculates the marginal abatement cost, taxes and permits will have different effects. When the government imposes a tax, the firm will set emissions so that the marginal cost of reductions equals the tax rate. The quantity of emissions will adjust. When the government fixes the quantity, polluters will emit that amount and the price will adjust. The deadweight loss from the error will be different because of the different ways the error plays out.

---

[4] Weitzman was considering a pollutant that causes harm in the period emitted – a flow pollutant. CO_2 emitted in one period contributes to the stock of CO_2 in the atmosphere, and it is stock concentrations that cause harm. Hoel and Karp (2002), Newell and Pizer (2003), and Karp and Zhang (2005) discuss how to translate Weitzman's arguments from flow to stock pollutants. These considerations do not change the arguments in the text.

Weitzman was also considering something closer to a command and control regulation than a modern cap-and-trade system. It appears that the system he was considering involved the government imposing quantity restrictions on individual firms. His arguments, however, are now commonly applied to cap-and-trade systems, and I will continue this tradition.

David Weisbach

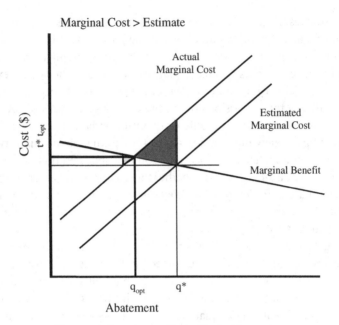

Figure 4.1. Instrument Choice Under Uncertainty.

To determine which instrument is preferred, we must compare quantity flexibility to price flexibility. If the marginal harm is relatively flat relative to the marginal cost of abatement, the costs of getting quantities wrong is low, making taxes preferable. Alternatively, if the marginal harm from changing quantities is steep relative to the marginal cost, the cost of getting the quantity wrong is very high. If an additional unit of pollution causes terrible harm, we may want to simply ban the emission of the additional unit rather than impose a tax on it. Quantity restrictions would be preferable. Weitzman demonstrates these points by using a second-order approximation of the marginal cost and marginal harm curves, and develops a simple formula for instrument choice that relies on the relative slopes of these curves.

To remind readers of the analysis, I reproduce in Figure 4.1 the standard diagrams used to illustrate the issue. The x-axis represents abatement, the reduction in emissions; as we move to the right, emissions go down. The y-axis is dollars. The downward sloping curve is the marginal benefit from abatement (the inverse of marginal harm), and the upward sloping curve is the marginal cost of abatement. The (universal) assumption is that the marginal benefit of abatement goes down as we increase abatement; going from very high CO_2 concentrations to modest concentrations may yield huge benefits, but going from low to very low concentrations may have small benefits. Similarly, marginal costs increase.

Given the government's best guess of the marginal abatement costs and marginal benefits of abatement, the optimal tax is equal to t^*, and the optimal quantity limit is q^*. If set correctly, a tax of t^* would result in a quantity q^* of emissions, and permits traded with quantity limit of q^* would sell for t^*. The two systems would be equivalent.

Suppose, however, that the actual marginal cost turns out to be higher than anticipated. If we use a tax, it will have been set too low. The optimal tax is where the actual marginal cost intersects the marginal benefit curve, t_{opt}. Polluters will emit carbon up to the point where t^* intersects their actual marginal cost. At this level of emissions, the marginal benefit of additional abatement exceeds the marginal cost, creating deadweight losses because of too little abatement. This is represented by the small, lightly shaded triangle. If we use permits, polluters will emit up to the allowed amount, q^*. At this amount, the marginal cost of abating exceeds the marginal benefit and abatement should be reduced. The losses are represented by the large, dark triangle. The instrument that performs better is the one with the smaller loss triangle, in this diagram, the tax.

The relative size of the triangles depends only on the slopes of the marginal cost curve and the marginal benefit curve. As the marginal benefit curves gets shallower and the marginal cost curve steeper, taxes look better. Permits dominate if the relative slopes are reversed. The intuition behind this result is that taxes allow quantities to vary while holding price constant, whereas permits allow prices to vary while holding quantity constant. The question is where is it better to be wrong: the price or the quantity? A shallow marginal benefit curve indicates that getting the quantity wrong does not matter very much, whereas a steep marginal cost curve indicates that getting the price wrong does matter, and vice versa if the slopes of the curves were reversed.[5]

The centrality of these arguments can hardly be overemphasized. They form the core of almost every analysis of instrument choice. Influential reports, such as the *Stern Review*, adopt the Weitzman analysis wholesale (Stern 2007). Almost all of the scholarly literature on instrument choice

---

[5] Uncertainty over marginal harm (as opposed to the marginal costs of abatement) does not affect instrument choice. Although estimates of marginal harm affect the level of taxes or quantities imposed, once they are chosen by the government, firms will optimize without regard to marginal harm; firms will make decisions based on their costs and the costs imposed by the regulatory regime. Therefore, uncertainty over marginal harm does not affect the choice of instruments. Kaplow and Shavell (2002) show that when there is uncertainty over marginal harm, the optimal schedule equals the expected marginal harm.

elaborates on Weitzman's analysis; a Web of Knowledge citation count lists around 400 citations to Weitzman's article, and this is likely substantially incomplete because it does not include many books and edited volumes. (Google Scholar lists 1185 citations as of November 3, 2009.) It is reproduced without criticism in graduate economics textbooks (Mas-Colell, Whinston, and Green 1995). It is described in numerous Handbook chapters on instrument choice (Bovenberg and Goulder 2002; Helfand et al. 2003; Kolstad and Toman 2005). The Congressional Budget Office uses it to analyze congressional proposals and to provide information to members considering legislation (Congressional Budget Office 2008). Research reports by think tanks and environmental nongovernmental organizations, which are designed to inform and influence policy makers, almost always start with this analysis.[6] It is the central analysis of instrument choice.

4.2.2 Responding to New Information, Asymmetry in Information

Weitzman's Assumption

Weitzman's argument is that firms will respond differently to government error when faced with taxes or permits. For this to be true, it has to be the case that firms have different estimates of marginal abatement costs than the government does. Even if wildly erroneous, if firms' estimates and the government's estimates are the same, the effects of taxes and permits will be the same.

In Weitzman's model, the government initially makes an informed guess of marginal abatement costs but ends up with an estimate that differs from private firms' estimates because it does not adjust as new information is revealed. He imagines a regulator engaging in the process of tátonnement, groping toward the optimal tax rate or quantity limit, but eventually stopping the process and fixing a rate or quantity, at least for some period of time. He notes that

[i]n an infinitely flexible control environment where the planners can continually adjust instruments to reflect current understanding of a fluid situation and producers instantaneously respond, the above considerations are irrelevant and the choice of control mode should be made to depend on other factors. (Weitzman 1974, p. 482)

He argues, however, that at some point, the regulator has to stop gathering information and actually implement a plan based on current information.

---

[6] For example, Aldy et al. (2009).

Therefore, he concludes that the right way to model the issue is as if the regulator has set a fixed tax or quantity limit. Laffont (1977) characterizes Weitzman this way: "suppose an iterative scheme is used but is stopped after a few iterations when a decision has to be taken."

An alternative route to differing government and firm estimates of marginal abatement costs is to assume that there is asymmetric information. If the regulator does not have the same information about abatement costs as the firm, the regulator will set the tax or quantity limit in error, and the firm, knowing its actual abatement costs, will respond differently to this error depending on whether the regulator uses taxes or quantity limits.

Weitzman's arguments can rely on either assumption: either there is asymmetric information about abatement costs or the regulator has good information but fails to update. In either case, the price or quantity limit will be set in error, and firms will respond differently to the different forms of regulation.

The assumptions of no updating and asymmetric information are rarely defended or even mentioned. Weitzman himself is careful to note that the regulator might subsequently adjust taxes or quantities and that his model only applies during the interim period. Newell and Pizer (2003) defend the assumption briefly, arguing that, "[a]lthough state-contingent policies could, in principle, be designed to maintain this proposition even under conditions of uncertainty, such policies would be of little if any practical use." Sandmo (2000) argues that "in most cases of interest, a tax or quota has to be fixed *ex ante*, with uncertainty about the exact nature of costs and benefits." Most often, the assumption is not mentioned. For example, at least recent three chapters in the *Handbooks of Economics* discuss the Weitzman argument in some detail; none mention this restriction.[7] The relevant chapter in Mas-Colell, Whinston, and Green (1995), a standard graduate text in microeconomics, does not mention these assumptions.

The question, then, is how rapidly and how well each system can adjust to new information about the marginal cost of abatement. If the adjustment is sufficiently rapid and accurate, the Weitzman-type differences between the systems will be small. If the systems are necessarily rigid, the analysis might have force (although it might not, as discussed in Section 4.2.3). This is a question of design: how can each instrument be designed to respond to new information, and are there differences in their rates of adjustment?

---

[7] Kolstad and Toman (2005), Bovenberg and Goulder (2002), Helfand et al. (2003). Karp and Zhang (2006) is the only paper I have found on learning and instrument choice.

The Extent of Asymmetric Information in the Climate Change Context Generally

Before examining how well taxes and quantities can be adjusted, we should first ask what would be needed in the climate context. Weitzman's model was of a single polluter. If the pollutant is from an individual firm or a modest number of firms, the assumption that the firm or firms have better information about their marginal cost of abatement than the regulator or that the marginal cost of abatement might change quickly may be justified. A single, closely-held invention by a firm might cause the regulator's estimate to have a large error.

Pizer (2002) provides an illustrative example of how the climate change literature incorporates assumptions about information. He calculates that taxes produce benefits that are five times larger than permits. The calculation is based on an assumption that the relevant policy (say, the choice to use a tax and the rate it is set at) remains fixed for 250 years (longer than the existence of the United States and longer than the entire industrial revolution). In an illustrative calculation for 2010, he assumes that the annual standard deviation in marginal abatement costs is $16.43 per ton of carbon.[8] To get a sense of the magnitude of this assumption, he estimates that the marginal abatement costs at the optimum is $7.50 per ton of carbon. In effect, he assumes that the government's best guess ($7.50) is wildly off from the private sector's information, and notwithstanding that, the government's estimate remains fixed basically forever. Pizer's estimates have been used by the Congressional Budget Office to inform Congress about instrument choice (see Congressional Budget Office 2008).

Assumptions of this sort are not appropriate for climate change. Climate change is a global problem, involving thousands (or perhaps millions) of firms and billions of individual polluters. Abatement will require massive changes to the economy. Because of the massive, public scale of the problem, firms are not likely to have a significant information advantage over governments, nor will the information about abatement costs change rapidly. Firms, of course, will know their individual costs better than the government, but the relevant price is the economy-wide marginal cost of abatement, and firms will have no systematic advantage computing this number.

---

[8] Pizer is using carbon rather than CO_2 as his units. CO_2 weighs 44/12 of carbon, so the equivalent tax on CO_2 can be calculated using this ratio.

To elaborate, global carbon emissions come from three basic sources: about 67 percent are from burning fossil fuels, 14 percent are from agriculture, and 12 percent are from deforestation.[9] Estimating the marginal cost of reductions involves estimating the marginal cost of changing these systems. It will involve estimates of abatement technologies that spread across the entire economy, such as the installation economy-wide, new energy systems, or the widespread use of new agricultural methods. Almost all of these abatement methods will be public; the technologies will be readily observable. To the extent there are some private technologies – say, a proprietary, low-emissions method of production – no single or even modest set of private technologies will change overall estimates of abatement costs very much. Firms are unlikely to have an information advantage over regulators in estimating overall marginal abatement costs.[10]

Moreover, estimates of the marginal abatement cost are unlikely to change very rapidly. The energy, forestry, and agriculture sectors are massive, global systems that will be difficult to change. Absent an invention like table-top cold fusion, changes to these systems are incremental. Even important inventions are likely to have only a modest effect on the marginal cost of abatement. For example, a new method of producing solar or wind power, or a new method of raising livestock to reduce methane emissions, will have only a modest effect on overall marginal cost. Moreover, current estimates of the marginal cost of abatement can include expected technological developments. Only surprises matter. It would likely take significant time before current estimates are far off previous estimates.

Taxes

The question is how likely is it that taxes would be set based on estimates of the marginal cost of abatement that are systematically different from firms' estimates because of information problems.[11] As noted, the government is unlikely, in general, to have an information disadvantage in estimating marginal abatement costs in the climate change context. The questions are what type of information would taxes generate to improve the estimates

---

[9] Herzog (2009).

[10] The government will not know any particular firm's abatement costs or the best technology to use, which is why market-based instruments should be preferred.

[11] The political system may, of course, produce suboptimal regulation, but claims about differential political outcomes for taxes and permits are separate from Weitzman-type claims.

and how often could taxes be adjusted to respond to new information. I address each in turn.

Tax collections provide the government with information about private estimates of marginal abatement costs. In a tax system, the regulator would know the tax rate and quantity information. From this information, it can infer polluters' current estimate of marginal abatement costs. For example, suppose that the government set the tax rate at $50 per unit of CO_2 and estimated that at this rate, 100 units should be emitted. If it observes 110 or 90, it can infer that it misestimated the marginal cost curve and adjust. If emissions are 110, marginal cost is higher than it expected and the tax rate should be adjusted downward, and vice versa for emissions of 90. In other words, the quantity of emissions at a given tax rate reveals private information about marginal abatement costs, and the government can use that information to adjust the rate.

Tax returns will necessarily provide this information because quantities are necessary for computing taxes; taxpaying entities would have to report quantity and multiply this by the tax rate to compute their tax. Tax returns could be required at relatively short intervals, at least for fossil fuel emissions because these taxes can be collected upstream on a small number of large entities. Moreover, the regulator can also observe imports, exports, production, and storage of fossil fuels from data already being collected, and infer emissions. The U.S. Energy Information Agency, for example, collects this information on a weekly basis.[12] Similarly, satellites are being developed that can closely monitor forestry changes on short time scales.

It is apparent that by both observing technological and cost changes to the energy, agriculture, and forestry industries directly and by collecting emissions information through the tax or other information reporting systems, there would be little difference in the government's and polluters' information about aggregate marginal abatement costs.

Given this information, the question is how often could the government adjust tax rates? It is possible to have very rapid adjustments simply through

---

[12] The EIA publishes a weekly petroleum report, which has information on supply, imports, exports, total stocks of crude oil, and petroleum products. Similarly, there is a Weekly Natural Gas Storage Report that breas down storage and production of national gas into the east and west regions of the lower forty-eight states. A separate report (Natural Gas Monthly) gives month-to-month import and export data for the entire country. As for coal, there is a Weekly Coal Production Report, which provides estimates for U.S. coal production by state, weekly and cumulatively for the year. Additionally, EIA publishes the Monthly Energy Review, of which coal has its own section, which reports monthly production, consumption, and stocks by sector, as well as imports and exports cumulatively for the United States.

delegation to an expert agency with the authority to make these adjustments. Models include the Federal Reserve in the United States, the EU Central Bank, and the Bank of England, in which legislatures delegated monetary policy decisions to an expert agencies that are largely insulated from political interference. These agencies collect detailed information and are able to respond rapidly when new information dictates. When adjusting interest rates, they are not subject to the normal rule-making constraints, such as notice and comment, which slow down regulation. When new information indicates that there is a dramatic change in circumstances, there is essentially no delay in action. There is no a priori reason a carbon tax rate could not similarly be delegated. This may be unrealistic, because legislatures in a given country and time period may be unwilling to delegate tax rates in this manner. Given that rate adjustments would not be needed very frequently, however, lesser delegations or other methods of adjusting rates would suffice.

Quantities

The analysis is similar for quantity restrictions. The government would still observe overall changes to the energy, agriculture, and forestry markets, and would likely have as good information as polluters about the overall marginal costs of abatement. Moreover, the permit system itself would generate information because permits are traded. The government, knowing the total quantity limitation, would only have to observe price, and it would know this by the second simply by observing the market.

It could also use this information to update the quantity limit. Like with taxes, we can imagine delegation to an expert agency like the Federal Reserve that could react rapidly to changes in information. Given the relatively slow pace of changes in the marginal cost of abatement, lesser delegations and slower changes in quantity limits would also suffice.

Conclusion

Weitzman's argument relies on an assumption of asymmetric information, either because the government does not have as good information as polluters about marginal abatement costs or because it has the information but fails to update the regulatory system because of some bureaucratic flaw. This assumption is untenable in the climate context. If the government has good information about the marginal cost of abatement and can update whenever that information is significantly out of date, there are no differences between taxes and permits.

4.2.3 Complex Schedules

Assumption of Simple Schedules

The second necessary assumption in Weitzman's argument is that the tax is a flat-rate tax –x dollars per unit of pollution – and that the quantity restriction is a simple, fixed quantity. As noted, the optimal system would impose a charge equal to the marginal harm from emissions, which is not likely to match either of these schedules. Weitzman defends this assumption by arguing that it should be "apparent that it is infeasible" to use more complex schedules and that analyzing these systems "is the best way to focus sharply and directly on the essential differences between prices and quantities as planning instruments." (Weitzman 1974). As noted previously, Newell and Pizer (2003) argue that state-contingent schedules are infeasible.[13]

If the government imposes a charge equal to the marginal harm from emissions, it would not have to know marginal abatement costs. Whatever the private estimates of marginal abatement costs, the charge would be correct. Therefore, there would be no Weitzman-type differential error costs from taxes and permits. To illustrate, imagine that the government is unsure whether marginal abatement costs are high or low. If it imposes a schedule equal to estimated marginal harm, firms will face the correct charge regardless.[14] Asymmetric information about the marginal abatement cost or failure to update would, as a result, be irrelevant, and Weitzman's argument would not hold.

How Complicated Would the Schedule Have to Be?

An initial question in determining whether the government could impose a charge equal to the marginal harm from emission is how complex would such schedule be? The answer is that in the climate context, it could be extremely simple and relatively flat, because the marginal harm of climate change is thought to change slowly with emissions

Marginal harm will increase over a broad range of concentrations – the harm from an increment of emissions will likely be higher at 750 parts per million than at 400. But these are changes in marginal harm over an enormous difference in concentrations. Even at current emissions rates,

---

[13] This could refer either to complex schedules or to simple schedules that are adjusted to new information. Pizer (2002) recommends a system with a complex schedule but assumes that policies stay in place for 250 years without adjusting to new information, implying that the quote refers to adjusting to new information.

[14] Figure 4.1 in Kaplow and Shavell (2002) illustrates.

changes of this magnitude would take more than a century. Within any region, the changes are likely minimal. The difference in harm from an increment of emissions at 350, 450, and 550 is likely small enough to be difficult to measure. If the government merely estimated marginal harm over this range of concentrations, sufficient to cover decades of emissions, the marginal harm curve would likely be relatively simple (not simple to estimate, but simple in its shape).

To illustrate, right now CO_2 is increasing at about two parts per million per year. A schedule that used a different marginal harm estimate for each one part per million change in concentrations would only mean a tax rate or quantity limitation that changes every six months. It is doubtful that there are measurable differences in marginal harm at this level of detail. If we could only measure changes in marginal harm for differences of, say, around ten parts per million, a new tax rate or quantity would only have to apply once every five years. Tax rate schedules or quantity restrictions that mimic the marginal harm curve could be extremely simple.

One question is whether the possibility of a tipping point changes this conclusion. Environmental outcomes might be nonlinear, so that we see very little change until carbon concentrations hit some level, at which point we see dramatic and fast changes. For example, as sea-ice melts, it exposes a darker ocean surface that absorbs more heat, amplifying the warming. If this effect is strong enough, sea-ice melting might be self-sustaining once it gets past a given point. Scientists looking at climate history going back millions of years see evidence for very fast changes, which creates real concern about the possibility of a tipping point. Lenton (2008). If there is a tipping point, it would be very important to keep concentrations below that level.

The possibility of a tipping point does not change the conclusion that the expected marginal harm curve would likely look relatively smooth.[15] The optimal charge is equal to the expected marginal harm. We have little information about where such a tipping point might be or how steeply damages would increase at a tipping point. When we average over uncertain schedules, even if some of them have sharp kinks, the expected schedule will still be smooth.

To illustrate, suppose that the likelihood of a kink in the marginal harm curve at 550 ppm, 600 ppm, 650 ppm, and so forth, was some estimated percent, say 1 percent or 2 percent (which, if one thinks about the damages from surpassing a tipping point, is a large number). To determine expected marginal harm, we take the probability-weighted average over all possible

---

[15] Louis Kaplow pointed out this argument to me.

marginal harm curves. At each level of concentration, there is only a small chance of a kink, and the expectation will be relatively flat. The overall expectation will be higher because of the possibility of tipping points (because marginal harm is higher if there are tipping points), but the expectation will still rise smoothly. The possibility of tipping points would not make the schedule substantially more complex.

Taxes

It is clear that a tax schedule could be sufficiently complex to mimic the marginal harm curve. The schedule would only need to list a set of concentrations (or possibly flows of emissions) and the corresponding tax rate. Data on flows and concentrations are computed at least annually under the United Nations Framework Convention on Climate Change. Polluters could simply look up the tax rate applicable to the current concentration or flow of CO_2 and apply it. If rates change over time – for example, in some proposals they go up with the interest rate even absent changes in concentrations – taxpayers would also have to know the date.

This is vastly simpler than the type of schedule currently in use for income taxes around the world. Section 1 of the U.S. Internal Revenue Code includes multiple nonlinear rate schedules. There are phase-outs, limitations, and different rates that apply to specific items. There are uncertainties and judgment calls on how to report many items. Tax rates also change over time; as was done in the recent Bush tax cuts, Congress may apply one set of rates to one year and other sets of rates to another year, and do so differently for different items of income and different types of deductions. Other countries have similarly complex schedules.

In addition, income tax schedules apply to individuals. A carbon tax could be imposed at the firm level.[16] Firms would have a much easier time dealing with complex schedules than individuals. It is hard to think of a defense of the argument that carbon tax rates could not be sufficiently complex to mimic expected marginal harm.

Quantities

It might be slightly more difficult for a quantity schedule to mimic the marginal harm curve because a simple, fixed quantity limit would not be as close to marginal harm as would simple, fixed-rate taxes (because

---

[16] Metcalf and Weisbach (2009).

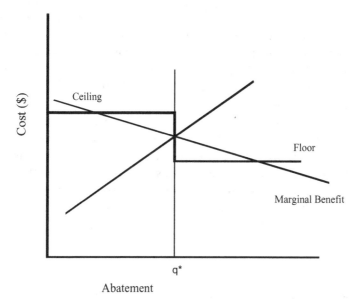

Figure 4.2. Quantity Limit with Price Ceiling and Floor.

the marginal harm from emissions is relatively flat, even the simplest tax schedule would be close to marginal harm). Nevertheless, it is apparent that it is feasible.

One widely discussed possibility is a set of price ceilings and floors: if the traded permit price in a quantity regime exceeds a limit, new permits could be issued automatically, creating a price ceiling. Similarly, if permit prices drop below a floor, the government could repurchase permits.[17]

To illustrate, consider Figure 4.2. In Figure 4.2, the government imposes a quantity restriction in which the estimated marginal harm from emissions equals the estimated marginal cost – the vertical line at q*. The government, however, also includes a price ceiling and floor. If the price goes above a set amount, the government will issue new permits at that price, effectively converting the system into a tax at the ceiling price. Similarly, if the price goes down below a set amount, the government will repurchase permits, ensuring that they do not go below that price. The heavy black line illustrates the net effect. As can be seen, the heavy black line closely matches the marginal benefit curve.

A related alternative, proposed by Roberts and Spence (1976), is having the regulator issue permits with different exercise prices; permits at a given

---

[17] For a discussion of this system, see Jacoby and Ellerman (2004).

exercise price would allow holders to pay the exercise price for the right to emit a set amount. Once all of the permits at a given exercise price are used up, holders would have to use permits with higher exercise prices, and so forth, thereby creating a price schedule that mimics the marginal harm schedule. The system could comes as close to the marginal harm schedule as desired by adding more steps.

Newell, Pizer, and Zhang (2005) consider the possibility of a banking system in which the number of permits issued in each period varies based on information learned in the prior period. They show that this system has the same cost flexibility as a price-based system. Depending on the degree of flexibility desired, various limits could be placed on the regulator, such as a limit on the number of permits it could sell. Pizer (2002) and Murray, Newell, and Pizer (2009) consider additional mechanisms.

Conclusion

It is clear that both taxes and permits can be structured to mimic the marginal harm curve. For taxes, we need merely to publish a schedule of rates. For permits, we need a slightly more elaborate mechanism in which additional permits are bought or sold over time. If the regulatory regime mimics the marginal harm curve, Weitzman's argument about asymmetric information in the marginal cost curve does not apply.

Combining Complex Schedules and Adjustments

The preceding two sections argued that either (1) rate or quantity adjustments while maintaining Weitzman's assumption of flat-rate taxes and simple quantity limits or (2) more complex (yet still relatively simple) schedules would alone be sufficient to make Weitzman's arguments irrelevant in the climate context. The argument, however, is even stronger because complex schedules and adjustments to new information can be combined.

All that matters is that the price faced by polluters equals the best estimate of marginal harm. We can achieve this by dialing in how complex a schedule we want and how often we want to adjust the schedule in response to new information about the marginal abatement cost curve. A schedule that perfectly mimics marginal harm would eliminate the differences between taxes and permits.[18] A schedule that was adjusted to include all new

---

[18] It would, of course, have to be adjusted as we learn new information about marginal harm, but these adjustments do not affect instrument choice.

information about the marginal abatement cost curve would also eliminate the differences. If there are concerns about schedule complexity or frequency of adjustments, systems could combine the two. A schedule of intermediate complexity would need less frequent adjustments than a simple schedule because it would already be closer to marginal harm; when marginal costs of abatement change, the intermediately complex schedule would have some built-in adjustments. Only when these built-in adjustments are not sufficient would the entire schedule have to be changed.

In the climate change context, it is likely that optimal schedules would be relatively simple and would need to be adjusted relatively infrequently. We could have schedules that are as complex as need be and that adjust as frequently as need be. As noted, if a different tax or quantity limit were imposed for every single additional part per million of CO_2 concentrations, we would only need a new tax rate or quantity limit twice per year. Adjustments to the schedule, if necessary, could happen instantaneously as new information is revealed or on a regular basis, such as once every year or every five years. It is hard to imagine that between nonlinear price schedules and adjustments to those schedules that we cannot impose a price that is close to expected marginal harm.

The Artificial Distinction between Prices and Quantities and Modeling Strategies

Weitzman's arguments rely on two assumptions that are untenable in the climate change context: (1) flat-rate tax rates or fixed quantity limitations and (2) no adjustment as new information about the optimal schedule is revealed. Once we consider complex schedules and rate adjustments in response to new information, the difference between taxes and permits begins to dissolve. The goal of market-based climate policy is to force polluters to consider the harm they impose on others. They need to face a set of charges equal to the marginal harm they cause. Flat-rate taxes and fixed quantity limits are just two possible schedules of prices that a regulator can use, and neither is likely to be optimal unless marginal harm happens to take a particular shape. Complex schedules fall between these extremes. A better debate to have than which simple instrument is better is how to best construct a more accurate instrument.

Recent proposals implicitly make this point. Indeed, they almost seemed designed to make fun of the artificial distinction between taxes and permits. One example is the "managed price allowance' approach to permits. Under this approach, put forth most prominently by the Congressional Budget

Office, polluters would be required to purchase a permit, just like in an ordinary quantity restriction regime,[19] but permits would be purchased directly from the government at a preset price and without a restriction in the amount that can be sold. It is simply a tax disguised as a permit system. Under another proposal put forth by Gilbert Metcalf, the government would impose a tax in which the rate would automatically adjust to meet a quantity target.[20] If, in a given period, emissions are too high, the rate would go up in the next period and stay there until emissions are back on the preplanned path. This is a quantity restriction disguised as a tax (and with some features that often go along with taxes, such as no strict per-period emissions limit and flexibility across periods). It is also exactly the sort of state-contingent system that Weitzman (1974) and Newell and Pizer (2003) rule out as infeasible. Once we consider proposals of this sort, it should be clear that the simple endpoints are meaningless.

It is clear that these sorts of complex schedules are feasible. In the climate change context, cap-and-trade proposals with price caps and floors are regularly discussed. Price ceilings have been included in numerous bills. At a minimum, given recent proposals, it is no longer possible to argue that only simple systems are realistic; the bills currently being debated in the U.S. Congress are over one thousand pages long and are unbelievably complex.

Sometimes it is useful to examine endpoints because it helps inform us about the middle; models with extreme assumptions are often useful to illustrate the underlying structure. In this case, however, it is not clear how much, if anything, we learn by examining flat-rate taxes or fixed quantity permits that remain fixed for centuries when both are dominated by feasible intermediate regimes. Doing so frames the debate in a way that causes commentators to focus on the wrong issues, such as which of the extreme systems is preferable, rather than how to design a system that best causes polluters to internalize marginal harm.

4.3 Seven Potential Differences

A large number of other potential differences between taxes and permits have been mentioned in the literature. Brief discussions of seven such potential differences follow.

[19] U.S. House of Representatives Committee on Ways and Means (2009).
[20] Metcalf (2009).

4.3.1 Revenue/Distribution/Transition

One claimed difference between taxes and permits is that they might raise different amounts of revenue and consequently have different distributive effects and secondary effects on the income tax system. The reason is that permits tend to be given away, which means that they would not raise any revenue, unlike a tax.

Taxes and permits are, however, the same in this regard. Auctioned permits would raise the same revenue as a tax imposed at the auction price. Similarly, a tax system with grandfathering for existing emissions or that offered refundable tax credits to the same individuals or firms that would have received free permits would have the same revenue and distributional effects as freely allocated permits.[21]

The basis of the claim that they are different is that as a historical matter, environmental permits, with minor exceptions, have always been given away, whereas new taxes sometimes have grandfathering but often do not. The claim that permits have always been given away is based on a list of environmental cap-and-trade systems, such as the U.S. SO_2 system and the EU CO_2 system. If we look at cases in which the government has created new property rights more broadly, however, there are examples of auctioning. The most significant example is the auctioning of electromagnetic spectrum rights in both the United States and the EU, which, in each case, raised tens of billions of dollars. There are numerous other examples of government allocation of new property rights, such as the allocation of public lands or mineral leases and the distribution of newly public firms in the transition away from communism. Often these property rights are given away, but not always. It is not clear that we can draw general lessons that apply across nations, time periods, and programs.

Suppose it is irresistible for the government to give away permits; the opportunity to pay off favored industries is simply too great. If this is the case, however, taxes will also likely be given away through grandfathering and the like. In other words, the basic problem of building a coalition to pass a carbon pricing regime does not change with the label. If an adversely affected industry can block a bill, they will have to be paid off regardless of which system is enacted. Both taxes and permits offer equal opportunities for graft.

---

[21] Tax credits or similar tax benefits might have to be transferrable or refundable to be equivalent to transferrable but freely allocated permits.

If, notwithstanding these considerations, the two systems are different (e.g., in a given country and time period; permits likely to be given away, taxes not), we have to ask which approach is better: requiring polluters to pay for the initial rights to pollute through a nongrandfathered tax or giving them the right for free through a permit allocation? A complete discussion of this issue would take us afield, but most commentators argue that it is better to collect the revenue by imposing a tax or auctioning permits. The reasons vary, but the most important reason is that grandfathering existing emissions creates bad incentives; the more you polluted in the past, the more valuable emissions permits you will receive. The argument is similar to the arguments made about legal transitions in other contexts.[22] The result is a preference for taxes.

At a minimum, commentators should be clear about their rankings. Rather than basing rankings on the assumption that permits will be given away and taxes will not be grandfathered – and relying on the reader to have these same assumptions – commentators should distinguish four (or more) systems: auctioned permits, taxes, freely allocated permits, and grandfathered taxes (plus combinations, such as 50 percent auctioned permits). The ranking of these four systems will look different than a ranking of just pure flat-rate taxes and fixed quantity restrictions with an implicit assumption about grandfathering.

4.3.2 Complexity

An argument against cap-and-trade systems is that they are more complex to administer than a tax. There are three possible reasons. The first is that a cap-and-trade system needs a market, and markets may be costly to operate. Even in deep and liquid markets, trading costs can add up. A tax system does not need such a market; the regulator simply collects the tax. Note that in both systems, the regulator needs to monitor the quantity of emissions, so monitoring and enforcement costs should be similar. The difference is the costs of creating and operating the market.

A second difference is that cap-and-trade systems tend to have time-stamped permits. Time-stamped permits are permits that can be used only in a specified time period. Time-stamped permits are the default assumption when commentators discuss permits. This is likely because for pollutants where the flow matters, time-stamped permits are necessary; the regulatory system must control emissions in each period because it is emissions per

---

[22] Kaplow (1986), Graetz (1977), Shaviro (2000).

period that cause harm. In the case of a stock pollutant like CO_2, flows do not matter; therefore, we need additional reasons to use time-stamped permits.

One possible reason for using time-stamped permits is that periodic allocations allow the regulator to better control the number of permits issued (and thereby respond to new information). If the regulator is uncertain about the optimal number of permits to issue, it might be best to issue only a limited number in each period so that adjustments can be made more easily. Another reason might be that the government might want to prevent firms from unduly accelerating permit use if the government cannot credibly commit not to issue new permits in the future.[23]

If permits are issued only for fixed periods, however, then the economy loses the flexibility to determine when to reduce emissions.[24] Cap-and-trade systems would potentially create inefficiencies in the allocation of abatement efforts across time. The problem then becomes one of minimizing this inefficiency while not subjecting the government to whatever problems caused it to issue limited-time permits in the first place.

Mechanisms that do this – so-called banking and borrowing provisions – add complexity. Banking systems allow firms to use permits issued for one period in future periods. These are relatively uncontroversial and not very complex to administer. Borrowing systems allow firms to borrow permits from the future to use today. This is more difficult to administer because it requires commitments to future actions by the firms, the government, or both. For example, if permits are freely allocated and firms could borrow, they could simply borrow permits from the future and then hope the government reneges in the future and issues additional permits. If firms depleted future years' permit supplies, the government would face significant pressure to issue more permits to prevent severe dislocations. Mechanisms to control borrowing, therefore, tend to be complex and limited.

The third difference is that cap-and-trade systems may need a larger number of caps, floors, adjustments, and the like than a tax system would. A simple, flat-rate tax might more closely match the marginal harm curve than a simple fixed quantity restriction, so it would need less jury-rigging

---

[23] A third reason might be that periodic allocations provide more opportunities for rent extraction by legislators. With a single permanent allocation, however, the stakes are larger. It is not clear whether legislators would be better off with a single, massive allocation or periodic smaller allocations. If legislators have limited terms in office, they would likely prefer giving away all of the permits relatively quickly. See Fischel and Sykes (1999).

[24] Individual firms could still purchase permits to pollute today in exchange for permits in the future, but in the aggregate, emissions would be fixed in each period.

to improve its accuracy. Caps, floors, and similar adjustment mechanisms add complexity and costs.

Although these arguments demonstrate that a cap-and-trade system is likely to have some additional costs, it is not clear how much. The costs of operating markets, having price ceilings and floors, and having banking and borrowing provisions, may be high, but we do not yet have sufficient evidence to know.

4.3.3 Information Generation

A possible advantage of a cap-and-trade system is that the market for permits generates information. In particular, the set of future prices for permits is information about market participants' views of abatement costs in the future. To consider an extreme example to illustrate the point, imagine that industry but not the government knows that, five years from now, we will have a low carbon technology that will make it free to eliminate emissions (i.e., the price of carbon-free energy will be below the price of fossil fuels). In a cap-and-trade system, industry would borrow permits from the future to use now. The government, not knowing about the technology, would observe low permit prices and high permit usage now. It would also observe low futures prices. The government could draw inferences from this information and could use it to set policy; it would be able to infer that industry expects abatement to be cheap in the future.

With taxes, the government would have a harder time making similar observations. Industry would anticipate very low taxes in the future, but the government would not get any signal indicating this expectation. It would likely see little abatement now but would not know that this is because of anticipated reductions to abatement costs. Instead, it might be because abatement is more costly than expected. The government could observe forward prices in fossil fuels, however, which will give some indication of expected marginal costs. To the extent that permit markets convey better information than commodity markets, permit systems might convey some information to the government that taxes do not.

If the government issues time-stamped permits (and banking and borrowing are limited), however, this advantage for permits would disappear. The key informational advantage of permits in this example was that by giving polluters price and quantity flexibility across years, the government could infer information about expectations for future years. If firms no longer have flexibility across years – and they would not in a time-stamped permit system – the government can no longer make these inferences. It would have no better information that it would get from a tax system.

The information available from the market, moreover, reflects the market's view of future government policy as well as abatement costs; the market in the aforementioned example might think that the government is going to issue more permits in the future. The government, therefore, would have a hard time getting clean interpretations from market data. The only way it could get clean information would be to not act on the information it learns.

Finally, if the information generated by a futures market is truly valuable in setting policy, we can set up an information market within a tax system. The market, for example, could allow participants to place bets on emissions at given dates.

4.3.4 Price Volatility

One common concern with quantity restrictions is volatility in the price of traded permits. The history of existing cap-and-trade systems demonstrates that they tend to have significant price volatility. Nordhaus (2007), for example, computes the price volatility of the U.S. cap-and-trade system for SO_2, showing that it has volatility very close to that of oil and substantially greater than the S&P 500. The concern is that this sort of volatility will hurt investment, reducing the benefit of imposing a carbon price. In addition, Baldursson and von der Fehr (2004) argue that if permit holders are risk-averse, volatility will reduce trading and might result in inefficient patterns of permit ownership.

To evaluate concerns about volatility, we need to ask why it arises. A central reason permit prices may change is new information about marginal abatement costs. If, for example, new information shows that abatement will be less expensive than thought, permit prices will go down, and vice versa if abatement will be more expensive. Price changes in response to new information should be encouraged. Markets are a method of aggregating information held by dispersed parties. They are one of the central advantages of a market system as opposed to centralized planning. Indeed, Section 4.3.3 listed the information gained from the permits market as a *benefit* of permits. The last thing we should want to do is to suppress these sorts of price changes. An analogy is to commodity markets. The earth has scarce resources of various minerals, fossil fuels, and atmosphere. Markets for these commodities serve as a method of conveying information about their relative scarcity, the price of substitutes, and so forth. In fact, the same holds true for markets in almost any product. As a general matter, we do not want to suppress price changes.

A second reason for volatility might be what we might call noise trading effects. A long-standing concern in the stock market, stemming from Shiller (1981), is that stock prices might be excessively volatile. Following Shiller, a number of papers, including Delong et al. (1990) developed models of stock trading by irrational "noise traders" that lead to excess volatility. It is possible that permit markets would exhibit similar effects. After more than 30 years of study, however, we do not know whether, and the extent to which, stock markets are excessively volatile. Researchers disagree (Malkiel 2003). Simply showing that permit markets have been volatile does not show that they are excessively volatile.

If permit markets are excessively volatile owing to noise trading and similar effects, it is not clear what can be done that does not also suppress price changes that convey information. The problem is quite general – it applies to all markets that exhibit excessive volatility – and there are no widely accepted solutions. Stock markets take some measures to reduce volatility, such as circuit breaker rules, short sale restrictions, and the like. These measures are all controversial because they inhibit price discovery and may do little to address the underlying problems of excess volatility. To the extent measures of this sort work, they might be incorporated into permit markets.

A final reason for permit market volatility is bad market design. In the climate context, even if we think we know optimal maximum concentration of CO_2, nobody claims to know the year-by-year optimal flows. Time-stamped permits, however, impose year-by-year limits. Year-by-year limits, by preventing trading across periods, can create excess supply or too little supply of permits in a given period. Going back to the analogy of a commodity market, extraction of commodities can be accelerated or commodities can be stored. Time-stamped permit markets would not be like most commodity markets in this regard. They would look more like the market for raspberries – no storage and no ability to accelerate production once planting is done. The solution to this sort of volatility is good market design. If time stamping is the source of volatility, it will be desirable to reduce time stamping either by not doing it at all or by allowing banking and borrowing.

What about the claim that volatility will reduce investment or alter trading patterns? It is not clear why the effects of volatility in permits markets would be different than volatility in other markets. Individuals deal with volatility through diversification. Although firms, as a result, should be risk-neutral, risk may affect firm behavior in adverse ways. For example, it may make it harder for owners to monitor managers, managers may be risk averse because they have overly concentrated exposure to the firm, and so forth. Firms can diversify to some extent to reduce this risk and can also use hedging techniques to transfer the risk to market participants who can diversify or otherwise bear the risk cheaply.

Note, in addition, that firms will not suboptimally delay investment because of price volatility that is a result of changes to estimates of marginal costs.[25] So long as the trading price is a good estimate of marginal cost, firms will invest optimally, making decisions to delay or accelerate investment just like they do in general. Other than volatility caused by bad permit market design, it is hard to see why volatility is a particular problem of permit markets.

Finally, note that in a tax system, firms must still face the problem of newly arriving information about marginal abatement costs. If the estimated marginal abatement cost shifts around constantly owing to new inventions, studies, and the like, firms will have to make investment decisions in the face of the uncertainty. Tax systems do not face the problem of market design or noise traders, but they do face the same problem of underlying uncertainty about abatement costs.

4.3.5 Framing

A number of potential differences between taxes and permits fall under the rubric of perceptions or framing. Claims about these differences are invariably made casually, so it is difficult to evaluate them. Consider the following three.

One commonly made claim with respect to the choice of instruments in the United States is that the U. S. Congress will not pass anything called a tax on emissions or energy. Many commentators who make this claim say that this is one of the primary reasons they prefer a cap-and-trade system (Keohane 2009). But this is not a rationale for a cap- and-trade system. This is simply a statement that if a tax cannot be enacted, a cap and trade is next best. That the United States Congress will not do something is not an argument that it is not preferred; it is unrelated to the merits. Moreover, it is difficult to predict outcomes of legislative negotiations. To the extent the views of these analysts matter, they hurt the chances of a tax being enacted when they support a cap-and-trade system for political rather than

---

[25] Kaplow and Shavell (2002), footnote 16, make a related point in the context of taxes.

fundamental reasons; if all analysts had a true rank ordering of taxes over permits and if they gave their true rank ordering rather than modifying it to predict what the legislature will do, legislative outcomes might be different.

An example might be the history of tradable permits. When economists first suggested the idea of tradable permits, the idea was not widely accepted. Environmentalists opposed the idea because it allowed people to pay for the right to behave badly. People called it "morally bankrupt" or "a license to kill."[26] Over time, however, as analysts continued to argue the merits of the system, the ideas became acceptable and eventually, some environmental groups accepted it. The U.S. Congress used the system in a major amendment to the Clean Air Act in 1990 and eventually the Europeans accepted the idea for CO_2. It was only because analysts ignored the conventional wisdom that cap-and-trade systems were politically unacceptable that we can tell this history. We cannot know whether there will be a similar evolution for environmental taxes, but analysts can only help by making arguments on the merits rather than guesses about political acceptability.

A second claim, discussed above, is that the legislature is more likely to give away permits than to grandfather existing emissions in a tax. Somehow, the framing of forcing firms to purchase the right to do something they have always done in the past is different than imposing a tax on them for doing it. It is true that legislators in the United States and around the world have often given away permits, although, as mentioned, there are examples of very large auctions. It is, however, just as easy to grandfather existing emissions under a tax by offering "tax relief" to aggrieved taxpayers. If the politics require buying off powerful interests to pass a bill, it is hard to see how those interests go away when the framing is changed, and even harder to see how commentators considering the economics of instrument choice are well positioned to predict political outcomes. Moreover, as noted, if it is true that permits will be given away and taxes will not be grandfathered, commentators should simply be clear about their ranking of the systems with all of their assumed attributed, as suggested previously.

Finally, it may be more likely that we end up with a fixed quantity limit when we use permits than when we use taxes simply because of the language of permits as fixing quantities. Cap-and-trade systems tend to start with hard limits, and then people debate about whether to have a price ceiling and floor. In the current U.S. debate, the price ceiling is referred to as a safety valve and is viewed as a deviation from the basic system rather than an

---

[26] Conniff (2009).

inherent feature that makes the prices faced by polluters better reflect the marginal harm. Taxes tend to start with systems with variable quantities and then there is a debate about how to limit quantities if emissions do not decline fast enough. Perhaps starting at each end, the two meet in the middle at the optimal system, but it is not clear that this would happen. The framing might matter. On the other hand, if the emphasis were switched from instrument choice to instrument design, we might be more likely to arrive at a workable system.

4.3.6 Environmental Certainty, Tipping Points

The most commonly made argument that a quantity limit is preferable to a tax in the climate context is that a quantity limit provides certainty; it avoids the possibility of catastrophic outcomes. Section 4.2.2 argued that such a possibility should have no effect on the choice of instrument, although it will increase the stringency of the system, whichever one is chosen. The basic idea was that even if some possible marginal harm schedules have tipping points, and tipping points might happen at various concentrations, the expected marginal harm will be higher than without this possibility but still smoothly increasing. A marginal increase in concentration at any given point will increase the probability of hitting the tipping point only by a small amount, so expected marginal harm increases only by a small amount. The optimal environmental charge would reflect this smoothly increasing schedule.[27] Both taxes and permits perform equally well in this context.

A related (perhaps the same) claim is that because taxes allow people to pollute as much as they want by paying the tax, taxes do not provide the necessary environmental certainty; they run the risk of carbon concentrations that are dangerously high. Only a fixed cap on emissions ensures that we keep concentrations at a safe level. As two well-known climate analysts put it, "a cap-and-trade system, coupled with adequate enforcement, assures

---

[27] The argument in the text is that Weitzman-type considerations do not apply in the climate context because, even with tipping points, there is sufficient design flexibility to make taxes and permits equivalent. Even if one were to adopt a Weitzman-type analysis, the result is similar. Pizer (2003) used a model based on Weitzman's analysis to analyze the problem of tipping points. He concluded that if we were near a tipping point, the differences between the two instruments are swamped by the shear necessity of putting a stringent regime in place quickly. That is, if we were near a tipping point, it wouldn't matter so much how we reduced emission but that we did so quickly. Moreover, there may be substantial harms from setting policy based on incorrect guesses about a tipping point.

that environmental goals actually would be achieved by a certain date. Given the potential for escalating damages and the urgent need to meet specific emission targets, such certainty is a major advantage."[28]

The environmental certainty claim has a number of problems. Suppose that there was a hard cap on global emissions with strong enforcement measures to ensure compliance so that we knew that carbon concentrations would be limited to a chosen amount. This would create emissions certainty but would not create environmental certainty. The reason is that we have very little understanding of the environmental outcomes for any given level of carbon concentration. The International Panel on Climate Change, for example, puts climate sensitivity (the equilibrium global average temperature increase for a doubling of CO_2 concentrations) between 2° and 4.5° C, a range wide enough to include modest but manageable harms to severe disruption. That is, even if we knew for certain that CO_2 concentrations would at most double, we would have very little idea of the environmental outcome.

Moreover, modest changes in CO_2 concentrations do not substantially change our expectations for the environment. The International Energy Agency compared a hard emissions cap to policies that allowed some flexibility (Philibert 2008). The hard cap cut emissions in half by 2050; the flexible policy had the same goal but put a ceiling and floor on permit prices, so that if, say, permits traded above some amount, polluters could purchase additional permits at that price, effectively converting the cap into a tax. In their model, the hard cap fixed concentrations at 462 parts per million (ppm), whereas the flexible policy produced a range of outcomes between 432 ppm and 506 ppm.[29] The environmental outcomes in the two cases were essentially identical: the median temperature increase was 2.49° C for the hard cap and 2.53° C for the flexible policy; the risk of avoiding a very bad outcome (5° C increase in global average surface temperatures) was 98.5 percent for the hard cap and 98.3 percent for the flexible policy. However, the flexible policy cost less than one-third of the hard cap. The study concluded, "achieving a given concentration level (such as 462 ppm) exactly or on average does not make any real difference to the environmental outcome. The uncertainty introduced by price caps in concentration levels is entirely masked behind the uncertainty on climate sensitivity."

---

[28] Chameides and Oppenheimer (2007).

[29] Parts per million refers to the concentration of CO_2 in the atmosphere. Pre-industrial revolution concentrations were around 280 ppm, and current concentrations are around 380. Commonly discussed goals tend to be around 450 ppm.

The second problem with the environmental certainty claim is that it makes unrealistic assumptions about how taxes and permits would work. It assumes compliance with a cap that remains fixed over time regardless of cost, and it assumes no adjustment to the tax rate if emissions exceed expectations. Once we relax the assumption of a compliance with a cap that does not change, we lose any benefit of certainty that a cap might offer. For example, if costs under a stringent cap turn out to be very high and we therefore loosen the cap, we no longer have certainty over final concentrations. Similarly, once we relax the assumption of a tax that is not adjusted to take its effect on behavior into account, taxes are able to achieve more certain carbon concentrations. Thus, if a given level of tax does not produce the predicted emissions reductions, we can increase the tax rate. Realistically, both caps and taxes will (and should) be adjusted over time as we learn more about climate science and the costs of reducing emissions.

4.3.7 Institutions

A final difference between quantity restrictions and taxes is that they may rely on different administrative apparatus and go through different legislative processes. In the United States, a tax is likely to be administered by the Internal Revenue Service, and the congressional committees with primary jurisdiction are the tax-writing committees. A quantity limit is likely to be administered by the Environmental Protection Agency or perhaps the Energy Department, and the committees with primary jurisdiction are likely committees with responsibility for energy and the environment. These differences will change the results. It might, for example, be much simpler to have the Internal Revenue Service administer the program because of its regular contact with taxpayers and its experience in measuring quantities. Or it might be better to have the Environmental Protection Agency administer the program because of its expertise in climate matters, or the Energy Department because of its expertise on fossil fuels and alternative energy. Other countries may have different considerations.

These considerations mean that individual nations might prefer one system or another because of local contingencies, such as a particularly competent agency, expert legislative committee, and so forth. It says nothing in general about the choice of instruments. Indeed, even with local knowledge, such as knowledge about how the U.S. system works, it is hard to say how these considerations change the balance.[30]

---

[30] See Weisbach and Nussim (2004) for a discussion of this issue.

4.3.8 Conclusion for Domestic Systems

The conclusion from the preceding analysis is that the major differences between quantity restrictions and taxes are all attributable to the design of the systems rather than anything inherent in one or the other system. If we insist on the simple design imagined by Weitzman (a flat-rate tax fixed forever or hard quantity limit, fixed forever), then there are real differences, and taxes likely dominate in the climate context. However, these assumptions are inappropriate in the climate context. With more sophisticated design, the two are substantially equivalent, with differences relating to subtle questions such as political economy and the like.

4.4 International Systems

The discussion so far shows that within a single country, there are few differences between quantity restrictions and taxes because of design flexibility; claimed differences most often simply reflect unstated and incorrect assumptions about design. Climate change, however, is a global problem, and a solution will require all major emitting nations to reduce emissions. The analysis changes for international systems. An internationally harmonized system requires the cooperation of multiple governments, which raises costs of implementation. For example, compliance monitoring gets more expensive as more nations join an agreement. Similarly, hold-out problems in negotiating the agreement may limit the ability to make adjustments to the system later on, which limits flexibility. If the costs of implementation are higher and there is less flexibility in an international system, some of the conclusions in the previous sections may not hold.

Section 4.4.1 discusses the benefits of having an international regime. Section 4.4.2 examines whether the design flexibility available in a domestic regime is equally possible internationally, arguing that there will be less flexibility in international systems.[31] Section 4.4.3 considers the problem of monitoring and enforcement in an international system, arguing that the problem of cheating is worse with permits than with taxes. Section 4.4.4 considers whether distributive issues are more easily solved with a cap-and-trade system.

---

[31] Strand (Chapter 7 in this volume) considers whether taxes and caps differentially affect the ability of a monopolistic fossil fuel supplier to extract rents. The differences between taxes and caps in his model require caps to be fixed rather than flexible and, therefore, depend on considerations similar to those discussed in Section 4.4.2.

Before beginning the discussion, it is worth clarifying what internationally harmonized taxes and quantity limits might look like. In an internationally harmonized carbon tax, nations would have a tax with the same base and rate schedule, and the same or similar enforcement mechanisms. Rate adjustments would have to be coordinated. In an internationally harmonized cap-and-trade system, nations would have to agree to the same base and enforcement mechanism. To ensure a common price, we would need cross-country trading of permits or have some other similar mechanism to achieve price consistency. In addition, we would need an initial global allocation of quantities to nations or polluters.[32]

Another, perhaps more likely, possibility is a set of regional systems with coordination across regions. In such a system, regions would agree to harmonized systems within the region. Across regions, there might be coordination mechanisms, such as allowing credits in one region for reductions in other regions. Value-added taxes and income taxes might be examples in which there is substantial coordination across systems but different rates and bases. The less coordination, the greater the potential will be for missing low-cost abatement opportunities. The following discussion considers the problem of instrument choice when there are a large number of participating nations; this can be taken to be either a global system or a regional system.

4.4.1 The Benefits of Coordination

Although it is possible, and perhaps likely, that nations or regions will have separate systems with perhaps some coordination between them, there are likely significant benefits to a fully harmonized system. In a fully harmonized system, all nations, and all polluters in those nations, would face the same set of prices. A uniform, global price for CO_2 means that the lowest cost abatement opportunities will be pursued regardless of location. If nations or regions have separate systems with differing prices, marginal abatement costs will not be equalized and some higher cost abatement options will be pursued at the expense of lower cost options. Depending on how different the prices are across regions and how different the abatement opportunities in each region are, the efficiency gains to harmonization may be substantial.

---

[32] With taxes, the allocation is implicit – each nation keeps its own tax revenues. The allocation could be made explicit for taxes just like for quantity restrictions by having payments of tax revenue across nations that would mimic the effect of permit allocations.

Analysts have estimated the cost of pursuing climate change using a subset of countries. Zhang (2003), for example, considered the costs of meeting the Kyoto targets with and without trading across nations, in various permutations (i.e., no trading, only trading within Annex I, trading across all countries, etc.). The costs fall dramatically as more nations are included in the trading regime, dropping by more than 93 percent from the "no-trading" case to the "trading across all countries" case. When considering the size of the global restructuring needed to reduce carbon emissions, these savings are large indeed. Other studies have found similar results.[33]

There are similar estimates of gains from allowing trading within a single country or region. Ellerman and Harrison (2003), for example, estimate the abatement cost savings from trading in the U.S. SO_2 system as compared to a regulatory system without trading. Over the thirteen-year period from 1995 to 2007, they estimate that the total savings is 57 percent of the cost without trading – the trading system costs less than half. Similarly, Burtraw and Mansur (1999) find health-related benefits of $124 million in 2005 (in 1995 dollars) from the trading of sulfur permits compared to a no-trading baseline, which is large given the size of the program.

4.4.2 Flexibility

The preceding discussion argued that the Weitzman analysis of the differences between quantity restrictions and taxes inappropriately relied on an assumption of limited flexibility both in adjusting to new information over time and in the complexity of the systems. The question is the extent to which these arguments carry over to the international context. I break the discussion into the same two pieces as in Section 4.2: adjusting to new information and complexity of the schedules.

Adjustments Based on New Information

Taxes. Achieving agreement in the international context is more difficult than in the domestic context because of the hold-out problem. It would not be feasible to renegotiate a climate treaty each time rates needed to be adjusted.

---

[33] Markandya and Halsnaes (2004) looked at the results from sixteen different models, all addressing this question. When trading across regions is not permitted, the costs of meeting the Kyoto requirements range from around $200/ton for the United States to $400/ton for Japan, with the EU in the middle, at $305/ton. When trading is allowed within the developed countries, the average drops to $77/ton. If trading is allowed globally, the average drops to $36/ton. Stevens and Rose (2002) have similar findings.

We can imagine an entity like the IMF, the World Bank, the WTO, or the International Panel on Climate Change being delegated the task of adjusting tax rates. To avoid giving international bureaucrats too much discretion over national policies, the entity could be given a formula to use in making its decisions, so that they would be based on evidence rather than political views. Nations might have opt-out options or provisions to review the adjustments.

Although possible, such a delegation would be an extraordinary change from the current environment. Nations have not regularly agreed to delegate tax rates to international bodies. Even within the EU nations have freedom regarding tax rates. An international body would inevitably have considerable discretion because of the complexity of the task. In addition, nations would have to agree to tax rate adjustments if emissions are higher or lower than expected, which means that they would have to agree that their domestic tax rate would go up if emissions in other countries were higher than expected. Nations may not readily agree to such a system, particularly if cheating is a problem. (Cheating is addressed in Section 4.4.3.)

Permits. Permits present similar problems. Because of the difficulties of negotiation, adjusting the number of permits in response to new information would probably require delegation much like a tax would. It is not clear that the problems would be any different. Nations would still have to delegate fiscal policy to an international body with discretion to make adjustments.

Summary. There is likely to be less flexibility to adjust to new information in the international than in the domestic context. Nations would have to agree to delegating tax rates or quantity restrictions to an international organization. There would be no way to force holdouts to agree to such a delegation. If a major emitter did not want such a delegation, nothing could be done. In the domestic context, legislatures typically have majority rule voting procedures, so holdouts have less power. This is at least one reason we see few examples of substantial delegation of authority in the international context and none like central banks, unlike in the domestic context where they are common. Therefore, it is likely that rate or quantity adjustments would be slower internationally than domestically.

Complex Schedules

Taxes. In principle, there would be no problems with imposing a nonlinear tax in an international, harmonized system. Even if nations are unlikely to delegate the setting of tax rates to an international body, they might agree up front to a tax rate schedule that mimics the expected marginal harm from emissions. There is no reason to believe that the problem of holdouts means simpler schedules; the need to satisfy everyone in a negotiation may lead to more complex schedules or simpler schedules, and it is hard to say in advance which way it cuts.

The only real issue would be the same issue that arises for tax rate adjustments: whether nations would agree to allow their rate to increase because of excess emissions elsewhere. In the case of a pre-set, complex tax schedule, the rate increase would happen automatically under a formula, but the issue would be the same. Excess emissions by one nation force others to raise their rates.

Permits. Nations could just as easily agree to a complex system of quantity restrictions as they could to a complex tax schedule. The problem with complex quantity schedules comes at the implementation stage. Consider a quantity restriction with a cap and a floor on the trading price of the permits. If the permit prices get above a ceiling, new permits would be issued. If they were auctioned, nations would have to agree to the allocation of the revenue. If the permit prices were to go below a floor, the price would have to be supported through a purchase of permits. Nations would have to agree on who would pay for the purchase.

In principle, the allocation of these costs and benefits is no different from the allocation of other costs and benefits in a treaty generally. We can imagine a nation or group of nations setting up an international fund with the role of enforcing a price floor and having the right to sell permits to create a price ceiling. Or, if we use a Roberts and Spence type of mechanism, the entity would buy and sell options on permits. This seems more plausible than an international body using its discretion to set tax rates or quantities based on new information. Nevertheless, caps and floors may be more difficult to implement than in the domestic context. For example, if the price of permits drops because of cheating by a nation or set of nations, other nations might be unwilling to pay to support a price floor.

Yet another alternative is to design self-adjusting permits. Given emissions in the prior period, permits would adjust to allow a different amount of emissions in the current period based on a formula designed to keep the price near the marginal benefit of abatment.

Summary. Complex schedules are not as easy to implement in the international context as domestically. Nevertheless, complex schedules seem more feasible internationally than frequent tax rate or quantity adjustments based on new information.

Conclusion

Flexibility will be somewhat more difficult in the international context than domestically. Delegation to an agency with discretion seems unlikely, but complex rate or quantity schedules may be feasible. Nevertheless, the optimal schedule may be relatively simple and the optimal timing of adjustments infrequent. It is not clear that a well-designed international regime would not have sufficient flexibility to make the Weitzman-type differences between taxes and quantity restrictions second order.

4.4.3 Rogue Regimes

Nordhaus (2007) argues that the problem of rogue countries is a strong reason for favoring taxes. The argument is that in a cap-and-trade regime, countries have an incentive to cheat by not monitoring domestic emissions and selling their allocation of permits in the international markets. Nordhaus gives the example of Nigeria, which Nordhaus puts as having emissions of around 100 million tons per year.[34] If it were allocated permits equal to its recent emissions – 100 million tons – and could sell them for $20 per ton, Nigeria would receive $2 billion of foreign currency per year, which is more than three times the size of its non-oil exports. Taxes, Nordhaus argues, would create less of an incentive to cheat because countries cheating on carbon taxes would be giving up revenue. This section compares the problem of cheating under taxes and permits.

As discussed by Hovi and Holtsmark (2006), the sale of the permits by a rogue country would increase total emissions. The rogue country would have business-as-usual emissions instead of the capped amount. In addition, the rest of the world would have an increase in the number of permits equal to those allocated to the rogue country. The net would be an increase in global emissions (above the agreed cap) equal to the business-as-usual emissions in the rogue country (there would be permits equal to the agreed amount plus the additional business-as-usual emissions in the

---

[34] This estimate appears to be low. According to the World Resources Institute database of emissions, Nigeria has just under 300 million tons of emissions, making it the twenty-fifth highest emitting country. See www.cait.wri.org. At $20 per ton, Nigeria would receive $6 billion per year in cash by selling the permits.

rogue country). So, in the case of Nigeria, there would be 100 million tons of additional emissions above whatever had been agreed to.

The problem of rogue countries is different in a tax regime. With permits, the rogue country exploits the rest of the world by failing to enforce. With taxes, if the rogue country does not enforce the rules, it loses tax revenue. To be sure, there is a net gain for failing to enforce a tax. Taxing emissions reduces the externality that domestic polluters impose on the world; failing to enforce the tax allows domestic polluters to impose that externality, producing a local gain. However, the gain is smaller than with permits, because with permits the rogue country gets hard currency in addition to imposing an externality on the rest of the world.

Similarly, the increase in emissions is lower with rogue countries under a tax than under a quantity restriction. The increase will only be equal to the difference between emissions with a tax and without in the rogue country. Emissions in the rest of the world are unaffected (leaving aside the problem of carbon leakage).

The extent of the advantage for taxes because of this problem depends on the ability to monitor emissions and enforce agreed-upon caps. If there were sufficient ability to monitor the regimes and flexibility to adjust the regimes once cheating is detected, the two systems would be equivalent. This follows in a straightforward way from the discussion in the domestic context: if cheating causes emissions or permit prices to vary from expected amounts, the system can be adjusted to keep the price close to the marginal benefit of abatement. As long as there is sufficient flexibility in making adjustments, the two systems are functionally the same.

We do not have experience with a similar system to know how well monitoring will work; to some extent, it depends on technology. For nations that do not produce substantial amounts of fossil fuels, we may be able to monitor imports of fossil fuels and infer compliance. If states produce fossil fuels, we would have to be able to measure production (as well as imports and exports) to determine compliance. This may be possible, but if permit prices were high, incentives to cheat would also be high. Finally, satellites may soon be able to monitor local emissions, providing a method of monitoring that might be difficult to evade.[35]

We also would need to design an enforcement mechanism once a cheater is caught. For some countries, trade sanctions or similar measures may work; for others this may not be sufficient or, because they export an important product, may be unlikely to be imposed. Victor (2001) and Keohane and

---

[35] See http://www.economist.com/sciencetechnology/displayStory.cfm?story_id=13097822.

Raustiala (2008) argue that buyer liability – a system in which buyers cannot use permits if the seller is found to be in violation – works because it creates a market-based enforcement incentive. Such a system, however, would still ultimately rely on ex post political enforcement against rogue countries to declare the permits invalid. A related alternative is to prohibit the future use of rogue country permits, thereby limiting the effects of cheating to a single or perhaps small number of periods.

Taxes have their own monitoring problems. As Victor (2001) has argued, to determine compliance with an internationally harmonized tax system, we would have to be able to look at a country's entire set of taxes and subsidies to see whether the tax is offset elsewhere in the system with subsidies; that is, a country could have a nominal tax but elsewhere offer an offsetting subsidy so that there is no net tax. Reporting of all net taxes and subsidies to an international body would be required. Emissions monitoring through satellite technology – a potentially promising approach for quantity targets – would not be helpful.

Enforcement problems once a cheater is caught might be more difficult in a tax system. With a cap-and-trade system, use of rogue country permits can be prohibited. There is no similar option for taxes.

To summarize, the incentives to cheat are greater and the effects of cheating are worse in a cap-and-trade regime than in a tax regime. If good monitoring systems are available, such as accurate accounting for fossil fuel consumption or satellite tracking of emissions, the problems of cap-and-trade systems relative to taxes are reduced because enforcement might be easier in a cap-and-trade system than in a tax.

4.4.4 Baselines, Distribution

Nordhaus (2007) also argues that a disadvantage of a cap-and-trade system is that it will likely require a set of baselines to determine targets, such as 20 percent of emissions in 1990 by 2050. Establishing baselines, he argues, will be complex and controversial. In a tax system, all we need is the rate structure, making a tax system easier to establish. It is not clear that this argument is correct.

Establishing baselines is the same as determining total emissions by each country: y percent of a given year's emissions by a target date can be translated into x million tons of CO_2 by the same target date. So long as the percentages of the baseline can be varied, the baseline year itself does not matter, and vice versa. All that really matters is the total emissions allowed for each country in each year or over the set period. Because emissions permits would be traded internationally, the initial allocation does not have direct efficiency effects;[36] the allocation primarily determines the distributional effects of the system.

Tax systems, or at least tax systems in which each country keeps its own tax receipts, have an assumed distributional effect. It is equivalent to one in which permits are allocated based on business-as-usual emissions. Tax systems do not avoid distributional problems. If countries object to the implicit distribution in a tax system, they will demand side payments or the like to agree to a treaty. Whatever problems there are in determining who gets what in a cap-and-trade system will not go away because of a change in the method of regulating emissions.

The alternative view is that permits help with distributional issues because it will be easier to buy off nations with permits than to make the same side payments directly. Commentators such as Stewart and Wiener (2003) argue that a treaty is, therefore, more likely with permits than with taxes. The problem with this argument is the same as the problem with the Nordhaus argument in reverse. Whatever the distributional problems, they do not change because of the choice of instruments. Moreover, the massive distributional issues cannot be hidden through the choice of instruments. Nations will easily be able to determine who is paying what regardless of which instrument is chosen.

One possibility, similar to the framing discussion, is that the explicit allocation of permits will appear different to negotiators and their home country constituents than the implicit allocation in a tax. Many people have an intuition that emissions permits should be allocated to all individuals in the world on a per capita basis (based on the idea that all people have an equal right to the atmosphere) but at the same time have an intuition that countries get to keep the taxes that they raise. These two intuitions are inconsistent. Because of these inconsistent intuitions, the end result of purely distributional bargaining might be different in the two systems. Framing might matter. Nevertheless, given the size of the issue, it seems unlikely that anyone would be fooled. At the end of the day, there are enormous distributional issues in a climate treaty, and they cannot be avoided through the choice of regulatory instruments.

---

[36] There may be efficiency effects related to the transition between regimes. These transition issues should not be minimized. If permits are allocated based on business-as-usual projections, countries will have an incentive to increase emissions prior to the treaty. See Kaplow (2008) for a discussion.

4.5 Conclusion

Discussions of instrument choice almost always have strong assumptions about design. Taxes are normally taken to be fixed, per-unit charges and cap-and-trade systems are taken to have annual, hard caps on emissions, perhaps sometimes with limited additional flexibility, such as banking and limited borrowing or a safety valve. These assumptions are not justified in the climate context. Other differences, such as distributional or revenue differences, are also based on assumptions about design that are unlikely to hold in the domestic context.

Rather than focus on instrument choice, it is better to focus on the design of whichever instrument is chosen. A casual glance at existing or proposed climate change regimes indicates that much work needs to be done. The EU cap-and-trade system, for example, covers only a modest fraction of emissions, has freely allocated permits, and includes an unadministrable offset program. Most proposals seriously considered by the U. S. Congress have similar problems have massive command and control regulations embedded within them. The gains from improving the design of these systems likely massively outweigh the gains from the choice of instruments.

References

Adar, Zvi, and James M. Griffin. 1976. Uncertainty and the choice of pollution control instruments. *Journal of Environmental Economics and Management* 3: 178–188.

Aldy, Joseph E., Alan J. Krupnick, Richard G. Newell, et al. 2009. Designing climate mitigation policy. Discussion Paper 08-16. Washington, D.C.: Resources for the Future.

Baldursson, Fridrik M., and Nils-Henrik M. von der Fehr. 2004. Price volatility and risk exposure: On market-based environmental policy instruments. *Journal of Environmental Economics and Management* 48 (1): 682–704.

Bovenberg, A. Lans, and Lawrence H. Goulder. 2002. Environmental taxation and regulation. In *Handbook of Public Economics*, A.J. Auerbach and M. Feldstein (eds.). Amsterdam: Elsevier Science.

Burtraw, D., and Erin Mansur. 1999. Environmental effects of SO2 trading and banking. *Environmental Science & Technology* 33 (20): 3489–3494.

Chameides, William, and Michael Oppenheimer. 2007. Carbon trading over taxes. *Science* 315: 1670.

Congressional Budget Office. 2008. *Policy Options for Reducing CO2 Emissions.* Washington, D.C.: Congressional Budget Office.

Conniff, Richard. 2009. The political history of cap and trade. *Smithsonian Magazine*, August. http://www.smithsonianmag.com/science-nature/Presence-of-Mind-Blue-Sky-Thinking.html.

Delong, J. Bradford, Andrei Shleifer, Lawrence H. Summers, et al. 1990. Noise trader risk in financial markets. *Journal of Political Economy* 98 (4): 703–738.

Ellerman, A. Denny, and David Harrison, Jr. 2003. Emissions trading in the U.S.: Experience, lessons, and considerations for greenhouse gases. Pew Center on Global Climate Change.

Fischel, D. R., and A. O. Sykes. 1999. Governmental liability for breach of contract. *American Law Economic Review* 1 (1): 313–385.

Fishelson, Gideon. 1976. Emission control policies under uncertainty. *Journal of Environmental Economics and Management* 3: 189–198.

Graetz, Michael. 1977. Legal transitions: The case of retroactivity in income tax revision. *University of Pennsylvania Law Review* 126: 47.

Helfand, Gloria, Peter Berck, Tim Maullet, et al. 2003. The theory of pollution policy. In *Handbook of Environmental Economics*, vol 1., K. -G. Maler and J. R. Vincent (eds.), pp. 249–303. Amsterdam: Elsevier Science.

Herzog, Tim. 2009. World greenhouse gas emissions in 2005. World Resources Institute.

Hoel, Michael, and Larry Karp. 2002. Taxes versus quotas for a stock pollutant. *Resource and Energy Economics* 24: 367–384.

Hovi, Jon, and Bjart Holtsmark. 2006. Cap-and-trade or carbon taxes? The feasibility of enforcement and the effects of non-compliance. *International Environmental Agreements: Politics, Law and Economics* 6 (2): 137–155.

Ireland, N.J. 1976. Ideal prices vs. prices vs. quantities. *Review of Economic Studies* 44 (1): 183–186.

Jacoby, H. D., and A. D. Ellerman. 2004. The safety valve and climate policy. *Energy Policy* 32 (4): 481–491.

Kaplow, Louis. 1986. An economic analysis of legal transitions. *Harvard Law Review* 99: 509–617.

Kaplow, Louis. 2008. Capital levies and transition to a consumption tax. In *Institutional Foundations of Public Finance, Economic and Legal Perspectives*, A. J. Auerbach and D. Shaviro (eds.), pp. 112–146. Cambridge: Harvard University Press.

Kaplow, Louis, and Steven Shavell. 2002. On the superiority of corrective taxes to quantity regulation. *American Law and Economics Review* 4 (1): 1–17.

Karp, Larry, and Jiangfeng Zhang. 2005. Regulation of stock externalities with correlated abatement cost. *Environmental & Resource Economics* 32 (2): 273–299.

Karp, Larry, and Jiangfeng Zhang. 2006. Regulation with anticipated learning about environmental damages. *Journal of Environmental Economics and Management* 51 (3): 259–279.

Keohane, Nathaniel O., and Kal Raustiala. 2008. Toward a post-Kyoto climate change architecture: A political analysis. *The Harvard Project on International Climate Agreements*. Harvard Kennedy School, Cambridge, MA.

Keohane, Nathaniel O. 2009. Cap and trade, rehabilitated: Using tradable permits to control U.S. greenhouse gases. *Review of Environmental Economics and Policy* 3 (1): 42–62.

Kolstad, Charles D., and Michael Toman. 2005. The economics of climate policy. In *Handbook of Enviromental Economics*, vol. 3, no. 30. K. -G. Mäler and J. R. Vincent (eds.), pp. 1561–1618. Amsterdam: Elsevier Science.

Laffont, Jean Jacques. 1977. More on prices vs. quantities. *Review of Economic Studies* 44 (1): 177–182.

Lenton, Timothy. 2008. Tipping elements in the earth's climate system. *Proceedings of the National Academy of Sciences* 105: 1786.

Malkiel, Burton, G. 2003. The efficient market hypothesis and its critics. *Journal of Economic Perspectives* 17(1): 59–82.

Markandya, Anil, and Kirsten Halsnaes. 2004. Developing countries and climate change. In *The Economics of Climate Change*, A. Owen and N. Hanley (eds.), pp. 239–258. New York: Routledge.

Mas-Colell, Andreu, Michael D. Whinston, and Jerry R. Green. 1995. *Microeconomic Theory*. New York: Oxford University Press.

Metcalf, Gilbert E. 2009. Reaction to greenhouse gas emissions: A carbon tax to meet mission targets. Medford, MA: Tufts University.

Metcalf, Gilbert E., and David A. Weisbach. 2009. The design of a carbon tax. *Harvard Environmental Law Review* 33 (2): 499–556.

Murray, Brian C., Richard G. Newell, and William A. Pizerl. 2009. Balancing cost and emissions certainty: An allowance reserve for cap-and-trade. *Review of Environmental Economics and Policy* 3 (1): 84–103.

Newell, Richard G., and William A. Pizer. 2003. Regulating stock externalities under uncertainty. *Journal of Environmental Economics and Management* 45: 416–432.

Newell, Richard G., William A. Pizer, and Jiangfeng Zhang. 2005. Managing permit markets to stabilize prices. *Environmental and Resource Economics* 31: 133–157.

Nordhaus, William D. 2007. To tax or not to tax: Alternative approaches to slowing global warming. *Review of Environmental Economics and Policy* 1(1): 26–44.

Philibert, Cedric. 2008. Price caps and price floors in climate policy: A quantitative assessment. OECD and the International Energy Agency.

Pizer, William A. 2002. Combining price and quantity controls to mitigate global climate change. *Journal of Public Economics* 85 (3): 409–434.

Pizer, William A. 2003. *Climate Change Catastrophes*. Washington, D.C.: Resources for the Future.

Roberts, Marc J., and Michael Spence. 1976. Effluent charges and licenses under uncertainty. *Journal of Public Economics* 5 (3–4): 193–208.

Rose-Ackerman, Susan. 1973. Effluent charges: A critique. *Canadian Journal of Economics* 6:512–527.

Sandmo, Agnar. 2000. *The Public Economics of the Environment*. New York: Oxford University Press.

Shaviro, Daniel. 2000. *When Rules Change: An Economic and Political Analysis of Transition Relief and Retroactivity*. Chicago: University of Chicago Press.

Shiller, Robert, J. 1981. Do stock prices move too much to be justified by subsequent changes in dividends. *American Economic Review* 71 (3): 421–436.

Shiller, Robert, J. 2003. From efficient markets theory to behavioral finance. *Journal of Economic Perspectives* 17 (1): 83–104.

Stavins, Robert, N. 2008. Addressing climate change with a comprehensive US cap-and-trade system. *Oxford Review of Economic Policy* 24 (2): 298–321.

Stern, Nicholas. 2007. *The Economics of Climate Change: The Stern Review*. Cambridge, UK: Cambridge University Press.

Stevens, Brandt, and Adam Rose. 2002. A dynamic analysis of the marketable permits approach to global warming policy: A comparison of spatial and temporal flexibility. *Journal of Environmental Economics and Management* 44 (1): 45–69.

Stewart, Richard B., and Jonathan B. Wiener. 2003. *Reconstructing Climate Policy*. Washington, D.C.: AEI Press.

Strand, Jon. 2010. Taxes and caps as climate policy instruments with domestic and imported fuels. Chapter 7. In *U.S. Energy Tax Policy*, Gilbert E. Metcalf (ed.). Cambridge, UK: Cambridge University Press.

U.S. House of Representatives, Committee on Ways and Means. 2009. Testimony of Douglas W. Elmendorf on the Timing of Emission Reductions under a Cap-and-Trade Program. Washington, D.C.: Congressional Budget Office.

Victor, David. 2001. *The Collapse of the Kyoto Protocol and the Struggle to Slow Global Warming*. Princeton: Princeton University Press.

Weisbach, David A., and Jacob Nussim. 2004. The integration of tax and spending programs. *Yale Law Journal* 113: 995.

Weitzman, Martin L. 1974. Prices vs quantities. *Review of Economic Studies* 41 (128): 477–491.

Zhang, Z. X. 2003. Meeting the Kyoto targets: The importance of developing country participation. Paper presented at the International Conference on Reconstructing Climate Policy after Marrakech, Honolulu, HI, Elsevier Science.

Comments

Eric Toder

Introduction

David Weisbach addresses one of the most widely debated issues among policy analysts in the climate policy debate: Is the best way to reduce greenhouse gas emissions to impose an excise tax on carbon emissions (carbon tax) or to allocate a fixed amount of emission permits, which firms may then be permitted to trade (tradable permits)? This debate occurs within a broad consensus among economists that free market mechanisms that allow firms and households faced with higher energy prices to choose how best to reduce emissions are superior to alternative approaches. These alternatives include command and control regulations that mandate how emissions should be reduced and subsidies that encourage the use of specified investments in renewable energy and conservation.

This academic debate on how best to use a market mechanism to reduce emissions is occurring within a larger political debate on whether to enact any form of market-based limits on carbon emissions in the United States. Politicians and commentators opposed to overall limits on carbon emissions are refusing to accept the broad scientific consensus that man-made carbon emissions are causing global climate change, and public opinion polls also reflect growing skepticism of the scientific consensus and the need for action (Pew Research 2009). The U.S. House of Representatives enacted legislation in 2009 establishing a system of tradable permits, but the legislation faces uncertain prospects in the U.S. Senate. Although the tradable permits bill appears stalled, Congress in the past year has extended and expanded subsidies for conservation and renewable energy, and the

---

These comments were prepared in response to an earlier version of the Weisbach paper. The published version in this volume addresses most of the issues I raise.

Environmental Protection Agency is considering imposing new limits on carbon emissions.

Given the uncertain prospects for any form of market-based carbon emissions limits, the choice between "tax" and "cap and trade" may appear less important than making the case for any market-based approach. But a major theme of Weisbach's paper is that the debate between tax and cap and trade may also be intellectually arid because carbon taxes and tradable permits can be designed with exactly the same features. Carbon taxes are thought to fix prices instead of quantities, but a tradable permit system can also limit price movements (with an associated expansion or contraction of quantities), if the government establishes ceiling and floor prices at which it will issue or buy back additional permits. Carbon taxes are thought to raise revenue that can be returned to workers and companies through income or payroll tax cuts, but a tradable permit system could collect the same revenue if the permits are auctioned off instead of being allocated to firms based on current emissions or other criteria. And carbon taxes can mimic the free allocation of permits that is often a feature of cap-and-trade systems if tax credits or exemptions are provided based on current emission levels. Weisbach concludes that these detailed design issues are what matters, not the choice between carbon taxes and tradable permits itself. As he states, "The gains from improving the design of these systems likely massively outweigh the gains from choice of instrument."

I agree with this conclusion, but it only begins the policy discussion. In these comments, I focus on three of the many issues that Weisbach discusses in his chapter: (1) targeting prices vs. targeting quantities, (2) taxing or limiting production versus taxing or limiting consumption, and (3) considerations of technical purity versus political economy in the choice of instrument.

Targeting Prices versus Targeting Quantities

A key choice in designing a market-based system for reducing carbon emissions is whether to target prices or target quantities. As Weisbach notes, the choice between targeting prices and targeting quantities is not the same as the choice between a carbon tax and a system of tradable permits. Tradable permits with price floors and ceilings could function much like a carbon tax.

That still leaves us with the core question, however, of whether there should be price targeting, quantity targeting, or a combination of the two. Given the reactions of producers and consumers to higher prices, any price of permits, P*, will be associated with a quantity of emissions, Q*, and vice versa. But because exact behavioral responses can only be estimated imprecisely, policy makers do not know in advance the value of Q* for any given P* or the value of P* for any given Q*.[1]

In principle, as Weisbach points out, the policy objective is to reduce emissions up to the point where the marginal abatement cost equals the marginal social benefit of lower emissions. Profit- and utility-maximizing private agents will reduce emissions until their marginal abatement costs equals P*, so that the level of P* will determine the short-run economic cost to society of reducing carbon emissions without the need for policy makers to know the technological parameters of emissions reduction (relative costs of alternative abatement technologies; substitutability among energy sources in power generation, industrial production, and transportation; substitutability in consumption between energy-intensive goods and other goods).

However, private agents have no way of assessing the marginal social benefit from reducing emissions, and government has no way of exactly forecasting the Q* that would result from reducing emissions. Beyond this, accepting the scientific consensus that carbon emissions are producing harmful climate changes still leaves huge uncertainty about the marginal benefit of additional emissions reduction at any level of Q*.

So that leaves us with the question of how to define policy objectives and the relationship between instruments and objectives. Typically, policy works through changing inputs (i.e., economic resources allocated to particular activities). These inputs can often be linked to outputs, such as quantities produced or consumed. But the real objectives might be outcomes, such as increased economic growth, a better environment, or improved public health. One can think of climate policy in this framework (Table 4.1).

The policy debate Weisbach addresses is focused on the choice between fixing the price of emissions, which directly raises energy prices and is expected to cause agents to reduce the quantity of emissions, or fixing the amount of CO_2 emissions of domestic energy producers (refiners and

---

[1] Arguments about whether to target price or quantity are pervasive in discussions of economic policy making. For example, in monetary policy, it has long been debated whether the Federal Reserve Board, in seeking to promote the outcomes of price stability and full employment, should in the short run target some measure of the growth of the quantity of money or interest rates. Designers of government spending programs face the choice of designing them as rules-based entitlements that establish formulas for benefit eligibility and amounts (creating a risk that the programs will cost too much) or as fixed budgetary allotments (creating a risk that funding will be inadequate to achieve program goals).

Table 4.1. *Measures of success: Climate policy*

Target	Climate goals	Costs
Inputs	Reduced CO_2 emissions	Higher energy prices
Outputs	Reduced stock of atmospheric CO_2	Reduced energy consumption
Outcomes	Slower rate of climate change; economic disruptions avoided; improved health.	Short-term loss in economic growth and efficiency; distributional effects

utilities), which will cause prices of carbon-intensive energy sources to rise. Fixing the price instead of the quantity reduces the uncertainty in predicting economic costs. Reasonable estimates can be generated about the effects of higher energy prices on energy use and (with less precision) on wider outcomes such as economic efficiency losses (from distorted prices), slower GDP growth, and changes in income distribution, with the latter depending how any revenues are used to households hurt by higher energy prices (see Chapter 3).

Outputs and outcomes from changes in inputs are harder to measure on the benefit side. Reducing the annual flow of CO_2 emissions will over time affect the growth of the stock of atmospheric CO_2, but the emissions that policy regulates (either through ceilings or legislated increases in permit prices) are not the only contributors to atmospheric CO_2. The stock of CO_2 will also be affected by emissions from non-regulated sources (methane gas from sheep and cattle; deforestation) and uncontrolled regulated sources (energy producers in countries outside any agreement). Published estimates have established a strong link between climate change and broader measures of economic performance, environmental quality, and public health and estimated costs of climate change (Stern 2007), but considerable uncertainty surrounds these estimates.

Moreover, in the short-to-medium term, the benefits of emissions limits will be less visible to the public than the costs, making it hard to sustain a policy that imposes costs without apparent results. This suggests that some form of short-term price targeting is almost certainly necessary for a policy to be acceptable and sustainable, whether this is accomplished by using a tax as the chosen instrument or by including some form of "ceiling" price trigger within any cap-and-trade system.

More generally, criteria for choosing between price and quantity targets are discussed in the sections that follow:

Elasticity of Loss Function

The traditional argument for fixing prices instead of quantities is that, over any short time period, the marginal benefit curve from emission reduction is much flatter than the marginal cost curve for emission abatement (Weitzman, 1974) because the marginal benefit depends on the stock of emissions, which varies by only a small percentage with changes in one year's emissions, whereas the marginal costs rise rapidly with restrictions on the annual flow of emissions. Weisbach rejects this argument, claiming that it relies on an assumption of asymmetric information that is "untenable in the climate context."[2] Weisbach then asserts nonetheless that "all that matters is that the price faced by polluters equals the marginal harm," suggesting that fixing the price is the best policy after all, although it can be done within a modified cap-and-trade system and therefore does not require using a carbon tax as the policy instrument.

Flexibility of Targets

Another criterion for choosing between price and quantity targets is which target is easier to change if there are forecast errors. If a price target is set too low to generate enough emissions reduction, will it be easy to raise the price later? Or if the quantity target is set so low that it generates too high a permit price, will be it be possible to relax the quantity targets in a future year?

By this criterion, quantity targets look better than price targets. Raising the price on emissions will always be difficult, and having absorbed an initial price increase, those interests opposed to limits will be expected to resist further increases even more strongly. If the quantity limits are too restrictive to begin with, however, the problem will be one of preventing *too much adjustment*, as industries and energy consumers clamor for lower prices, than of not increasing them at all, although there also will be some resistance from current holders of tradable permits to anything that reduces permit prices.

---

[2] Weisbach claims that the government can forecast the overall costs of marginal abatement as well as the "polluters" (e.g., private producers). This may be true in the sense that government analysts can forecast the aggregate effects on prices of quantity restrictions as well as private analysts and better than analysts in specific firms, but it is irrelevant. What is relevant is that private producers know better than government their own abatement costs, and it is the sum of all their responses that will generate the aggregate price effect of quantity restrictions.

Quantifying Success

Quantity targets look better on this criterion, as policy makers will be able to claim that they "reduced" emissions actively, not that they undertook a policy that could reduce emissions. The benefits of the policy will be measurable in reduced greenhouse gas emissions, not the higher energy prices or taxes that brought them about. Nonetheless, as noted, it will be very hard to quantify real success in terms of avoiding the costs of the greater damage from climate changes absent the policy. Even a successful policy may appear a failure if damages from climate change are visible, regardless of any improvement relative to a "no intervention" baseline.

Targeting "Goods" versus "Bads"

Most policies involve trade-offs; people have to sacrifice some goals in order to achieve others. Policies that raise energy prices are almost uniformly unpopular, but reducing greenhouse gas emissions is widely thought to be a good thing. It is much easier to sell a policy by promoting its benefits instead of its costs, which is why it should not be a mystery that congressional sponsors of market-based approaches to pollution control are much more interested in policies that restrict emissions (even if the result is to push prices up) than in new taxes on energy (even if the result would be to reduce emissions).[3]

Efficiency versus Cost-Effectiveness

Weisbach concludes that efficiency in greenhouse gas emissions implies targeting prices, with the price of permits set equal to the marginal external social benefit of reducing emissions; however, this implies that we can measure the marginal social benefit of emissions reductions. Failing that,

---

[3] A similar dynamic characterized the development and eventual enactment of the Tax Reform Act of 1986, one of the most successful and complex legislative accomplishments of the past quarter century. The goal of tax reform was to broaden the tax base, eliminating tax preferences so that tax rates could be lowered without sacrificing revenue. The original Treasury proposal in 1984 started with an effort to design an ideal tax base, with the rates set at the end of the process to reach revenue targets. But Congress adopted the reverse approach – they started with Treasury's reduced rates (the benefits) first, which then made it necessary to reduce preferences (the costs to private taxpayer groups) to meet the rate and revenue goals (Birnbaum and Murray 1988). When the effort seemed stalled in the Senate, Senator Packwood went to the Joint Tax Committee and asked them to find a way to pay for *even lower* rates. It was the emphasis on the benefits of sharply lower rates that enabled proponents to push the legislation through.

we may simply seek to achieve a set (and somewhat) arbitrary reduction in the quantity of emissions. Dinan (2009) argues, however, that if one starts with a pre-specified reduction in the quantity of emissions, the least-cost way of achieving that may involve a combination of price and quantity targets.

Limiting Production or Consumption

Much of the literature (including chapters in this volume) discusses the problem of emissions reduction in the context of a closed economy. Most of the Weisbach chapter is also written in the context of a closed economy, with a short section at the end discussing issues of international coordination. This might be relevant if what was being considered was global legislation to restrict emissions, but the legislation now under consideration in the U.S. Senate would limit U.S. emissions unilaterally.

In an open economy, production does not necessarily equal consumption in any jurisdiction. For one country acting unilaterally, reducing the greenhouse gas emissions attributable to its consumers is the relevant target. However, reducing greenhouse gas emissions by U.S. energy producers and raising their costs of emissions alone would accomplish little, other than to damage U.S. producers, if U.S. consumers substituted imports for domestic production and foreign consumers imported less from the United States.[4]

Because any tax or permit system would, for administrative reasons, be imposed on producers instead of final consumers, there would be a need for border adjustments, as in European-style value-added taxes, to convert an "origin-based" to a "destination-based" system. As McLure (see Chapter 6) discusses in great detail, the technical issues and legal issues that need to be confronted in designing such a system are complex and formidable. Nonetheless, the issues of how best to design a tax or permit system that raises prices of greenhouse gas consumption to U.S. consumers instead of domestic producers is too central to be swept under the rug.

Technical Purity or Political Economy

Commentators in the debate between carbon tax and tradable permit systems often interchangeably mix purely technical and political arguments to

---

[4] A reduction in U.S. output of carbon-intensive fuels would have some benefit if it increased world energy prices, but if supplies from other countries are relatively elastic, the effects on world prices would be small.

advance their positions. Weisbach takes a strong position on this, asserting that "Analysts can only help by making arguments on the merits rather than guessing about political acceptability" This view of the role of the analyst is clear and straightforward. Technicians (lawyers, economists, climate scientists) design optimal policies for their country or the world. They then try to sell them to policy makers.

Those of us technicians who have spent our careers in a political environment find it hard to accept this framework, no matter how superficially attractive. Insisting on technical purity puts us at risk of being irrelevant to the policy discussion, but going too far towards accepting political reality puts us at risk of rationalizing everything politicians do and using our analytical skills only for narrow tasks, such as drafting legislation or estimating the effects on government receipt of policies that others design.

Where to locate oneself on this spectrum, so that one can make a useful contribution to policy development, while avoiding the problems of becoming either an irrelevant theorizer or an enabler to politicians, is challenging. If one is to provide useful policy advice, it is impossible to avoid making some judgments about both political and economic trade-offs, and this seems nowhere more apparent than in the debate between carbon taxes and cap and trade. As Weisbach so persuasively argues, the same critical policy design choices can be accommodated within both broad policy instruments. So when an analyst argues that carbon taxes are superior to cap and trade because the government, instead of the polluters, gets the revenue, he is really saying that the "political" process is more likely to buy off the polluters under cap and trade than under a carbon tax. When an analyst argues that carbon taxes are superior to cap and trade because the loss from getting the wrong quantity is smaller than the loss from setting the wrong price, he is really making implicit assumptions about what price ceilings may or may not be included in a cap-and-trade system and how quickly the political system will react if forecasts prove erroneous. These implicit political judgments may be right or wrong, but they are political judgments nonetheless and are central to most analysts' views on whether a carbon tax or cap-and-trade system is superior.

Conclusions

Formulating climate change policy is an unusually challenging problem. As yet there are few visible costs of damage from greenhouse emissions, and those who deny evidence of a human role in global climate change wield strong political influence in the United States. Any policies that are enacted can at best forestall future costs, not produce visible benefits.

Given the widespread view among experts that the costs of inaction are very high, it is important to assess policies based on the likelihood of their acceptability. Can the gains from climate policy be made visible? Will any short-term economic harm, either real or perceived, cause climate control polities to be scrapped or watered down after they are enacted?

Given the potential interchangeability between carbon tax and cap-and-trade systems, the attention given to the debate about which instrument is better seems misplaced. Instead, it would be useful to focus more attention to the specific details within each policy instrument, accepting that either market-based system is superior to alternatives. Should permits be auctioned or given away? What are the best ways to design price ceilings and/or floors? Under a cap-and-trade system, what banking rules for future credits, if any, are necessary? Should there be an automatic process of adjusting allowances (or tax rates) over time and upon what should it be based? How can border adjustments be designed to place the incidence on consumers instead of domestic producers and stay within international trading norms?

Weisbach's chapter is a useful contribution to thinking about these important design issues for either a carbon tax or cap-and-trade carbon limitations.

References

Birnbaum, Jeffrey, and Alan Murray. 1988. *Showdown at Gucci Gulch – Lawmakers, Lobbyists, and the Unlikely Triumph of Tax Reform*. New York: Vintage Books.

Dinan, Terry. 2009. Carbon taxes and carbon cap-and-trade programs: A comparison. *National Tax Journal* 62: 3.

Pew Research. 2009. Fewer Americans see solid evidence of global warming. http://people-press.org/report/556/global-warming, October 22.

Stern, Nicholas. 2007. *The Economics of Climate Change: The Stern Review*. Cambridge, UK: Cambridge University Press.

Weitzman, M.L. 1974. Prices vs. quantities. *Review of Economic Studies* 41 (128): 477–491.

FIVE

Taxes, Permits, and Climate Change

Louis Kaplow

5.1 Introduction

Kaplow and Shavell (2002) offer a systematic critique of the view associated
with Weitzman (1974) that the choice between corrective taxes and quantity
targets is highly contingent in a world of uncertainty.[1] They emphasize that
this conventional understanding, heavily represented in texts and surveys
on environmental economics as well as in more general textbooks, rests on
a poorly appreciated and dubious set of assumptions.

First, in the Weitzman story, taxes are constrained to be linear, even
though marginal harm is taken to be nonlinear (typically, rising in the
quantity of emissions), so the Weitzman tax instrument violates the basic
Pigouvian prescription that the marginal tax rate equal marginal harm. Second, taxes are taken to be fixed for all time, even though any error in setting
the (constrained-to-be-linear) tax rate would become immediately apparent to the government. Relaxing *either* assumption restores the superiority
of taxes over quantity regulation. Moreover, neither assumption was well
motivated by Weitzman or in the subsequent literature. Nonlinear taxes are
simple to state in many settings, and tax rates (really prices) of all sorts –
whether set by government or the market – are routinely adjusted in response
to changed circumstances.

Second, Kaplow and Shavell (2002) extend their analysis to permit
schemes. On one hand, this instrument has the familiar and important
advantage over command-and-control quantity regulation that a given

---

[1] In addition to Weitzman (1974), see also Adar and Griffin (1976), Fishelson (1976), Roberts
and Spence (1976), and Rose-Ackerman (1973).

I am grateful to the John M. Olin Center for Law, Economics, and Business at Harvard
University for financial support.

quantity target is achieved at minimum cost.[2] On the other hand, like familiar schemes, the quantity is set by fiat, once and for all. Kaplow and Shavell emphasize, however, that this latter defect is not inherent in permit schemes because, unlike command-and-control regulation, permit markets generate a price. Hence, the government learns whether firms' marginal costs (which in equilibrium equal the market price for permits) exceed or fall short of the marginal benefit of emissions reductions at the current targets. Drawing on prior literature, they describe a number of ways that the permit quantity could be adjusted to achieve the (same) second-best optimum produced by taxes (that are either explicitly nonlinear or adjustable). They point out that there is an underlying duality between properly designed tax and permit schemes: the former constitutes a quantity-dependent price, whereas the latter is a price-dependent quantity. In both cases, firms' information about their control costs is harnessed, so that each firm's marginal cost is equated to marginal benefits.

Weisbach (see Chapter 4) devotes the first half of his fine chapter to applying and elaborating Kaplow and Shavell's (2002) critique of Weitzman (1974) in the context of controlling greenhouse gas emissions. His motivation is that, sadly, just as the limitations of Weitzman were underappreciated a decade ago, the same holds true today, and such misunderstanding may lead to the design of regulatory schemes that are substantially and needlessly inefficient. Given the high stakes, such an outcome would be unfortunate for the United States and the rest of the world. In addition to economic waste, on a potentially vast scale, there is also the concern that one may control too little despite possibly catastrophic consequences.

This chapter seeks mainly to reinforce and further extend the argument that the standard Weitzman assumptions should carry far less, if any, significant weight in instrument choice and design, particularly in the context of combating greenhouse gases. Section 5.2, by way of background, articulates Weitzman's (1974) assumptions and why they matter and then relates that framework to optimal policy. Section 5.3 analyzes nonlinear taxes, Section 5.4 considers permit schemes, and Section 5.5 brings the analysis of the two side by side to consider the underlying similarities, political appeal, and also some important complications in the climate control context. Section 5.6 notes two important additional considerations: the impact of uncertainty

---

[2] This traditional advantage of permits (or taxes) is, unfortunately, getting far too little attention, notably in the United States, where aggressive fuel economy standards, biofuels mandates, and other requirements may well be imposing huge costs relative to potential benefits, a waste in itself and a phenomenon that may reduce the political will to pursue further control through taxes or permit schemes.

about future "prices" (whether tax rates or permit prices) on innovation and the importance of transition issues (notably, grandfathering based on prior emissions). Finally, Section 5.7 addresses concerns about distribution, which are central in a number of the other chapters in this volume as well.

5.2 Background

5.2.1 Weitzman Framework

Weitzman (1974) compares quantity regulation and taxation in a world of uncertainty. Firms' marginal control costs are taken to be known by firms themselves but not observable by the government.[3] Realistically, we can think of this gap as capturing the government's residual uncertainty: that is, the government may have significant knowledge of control costs, but not as much as do individual firms. Regarding the control of greenhouse gas emissions, where the magnitude of marginal control costs in the future is of central importance, we are also concerned about the quality of firms' projections relative to those of the government.[4]

Marginal harm is likewise subject to uncertainty, a point of undoubted significance in the present setting. A further point, also quite pertinent, is that total marginal harm is not taken to be constant, but rather rising with the level of emissions, an uncontroversial and important factor with regard to climate change.

Weitzman's instruments are quite simple: a quantity regulation specifies the quantity of emissions that firms may produce, whereas a tax instrument (which he calls a price) specifies a single, fixed price per unit of emissions.

---

[3] Strictly speaking, the Weitzman scenario envisions a single firm, and Kaplow and Shavell (2002) devote considerable attention to differences that may arise in considering settings with multiple firms. Given the nature of the climate change problem, the focus throughout this chapter is on the case in which there are a large number of firms.

[4] One view would be that, at any point in time, the government's knowledge of the economy-wide marginal control cost would be as good as firms' knowledge. In this case, both linear taxes and permit schemes could hit the second-best price target perfectly, without any further adjustment. However, because marginal control costs (especially in the future) can depend on technological change, learning curve effects, and other subtle phenomena, significant asymmetric information may remain. Following the standard approach, the remainder of the discussion here assumes that the government is at an informational disadvantage, although it should be noted that much of what is stated would be applicable if the government's knowledge of private control costs was as good as firms'. (Note that with both taxes and permit schemes, all that is relevant is the economy-wide marginal control cost in equilibrium, not any particular firm's marginal control cost schedule.)

Given that the government is uncertain about both marginal control costs and marginal harm, it is easy to see that neither instrument will hit the optimum except by chance. The optimal quantity is that for which marginal control costs equal the marginal benefits of limiting emissions. If the government picks quantity, it may choose one that is too high or too low. Similarly, if it picks a tax rate, the quantity thereby induced (by firms that each equate their marginal costs to the tax rate) may be too high or too low. A priori, either approach might do better, and Weitzman shows that, under some particular assumptions, taxes are better when marginal control cost curves are steeper than the marginal harm schedule, and quantity regulation is preferable in the converse case.[5]

5.2.2 Optimal Policy

It is generally understood that the Pigouvian ideal can be achieved by setting an emissions tax equal to marginal harm. Crucially, even if the government does not know firms' marginal control costs, this instrument is sufficient. Faced with a tax (price) equal to marginal external harm, the externality is internalized and firms' quantity decisions will be optimal. The fact that a tax instrument harnesses firms' information about control costs is their central virtue, as economists have long appreciated.

One complication is that the government may have uncertainty about marginal harm, a point that is of obvious relevance to climate change. Although many economists seem to believe (or act as if they believe) that uncertainty about harm tends to favor a quantity instrument, this view is mistaken. Another section of Kaplow and Shavell (2002) offers a simple proof that the second-best optimal scheme involves setting the tax rate equal to the *expected* marginal harm, and this result holds for all manner of distributions of uncertainty about marginal harm.[6]

---

[5] To suggest the intuition, suppose first that marginal harm was constant (so the marginal harm curve is horizontal); then a single, linear, fixed-for-all-time tax would achieve the second-best optimum. If instead the marginal harm curve is vertical (marginal harm goes from zero to infinity at a threshold quantity), then it is obvious that a quantity regime (setting the quantity at the threshold) would achieve the second-best optimum.

[6] As shown in Weitzman (1974) and Stavins (1996) in the setting with Weitzman's assumptions, correlation between marginal control costs and marginal harm affects optimal instrument choice. A nonlinear tax nevertheless continues to dominate quantity regulation, but the optimal nonlinear tax would no longer equal marginal harm. (Firms' quantity choices given a tax rate convey information on control costs, which, because they are now taken to be correlated with marginal harm, bear on the optimal marginal tax rate.) However, in many settings, this complication seems essentially irrelevant. Uncertainty about marginal harm derives from uncertainty in climate models, the effects of

It is worth noting, moreover, that this logic extends to any shape of the marginal harm schedule, including the possibility of thresholds or tipping points. If there was a tipping point at a known quantity level, the tax rate would jump infinitely at that point. More relevant for the present setting, consider the case of a stock pollutant and significant uncertainty about the location of any such tipping point – to which, one might add, no one really believes that there is a literal tipping point, at which another molecule will trigger catastrophe. In this scenario, marginal harm may be thought to rise more steeply as the size of the stock passes some given point. However, that point is uncertain; moreover, there is uncertainty about the likelihood that an additional unit today will lead the stock to cross such a threshold at a distant future time. Taken together, the expected marginal harm schedule will be a probability-weighted sum (integral) over myriad possible scenarios. Even with fairly sharp thresholds in some or many scenarios, the expected value of all such schedules will undoubtedly be a smooth expected marginal harm schedule.

Therefore, with uncertainty about harm and firms' control costs, the optimal scheme is a tax that imposes a charge on firms equal to the expected marginal harm from emissions. Because marginal harm is taken to be rising with the level of emissions, the optimal tax schedule is nonlinear, likewise increasing with quantity. As Weisbach (see Chapter 4) properly emphasizes, with a stock pollutant, as in the present context, this schedule is nevertheless locally pretty flat: a few percentage points more or less of emissions in a given month or year will (relatively) have a far smaller effect on the size of the present and future level of the stock and thus little effect on marginal harm and, accordingly, on the optimal marginal tax rate.

By contrast, charging a significantly wrong tax rate for extended periods of time will have high social costs. If the tax rate is much too low for a decade, there will be substantial buildup of greenhouse gases that will cause long-lasting harm. Even if one could control more later (and to a degree one can and should), the cost of doing so will be greater than it would have been if the proper tax rate had been charged earlier, inducing firms to undertake reductions for which the marginal control cost was below expected harm. Likewise, if the price is much too high for an extended period, costs significantly in excess of any marginal benefit will be incurred.

warming on agriculture, and myriad other factors that for the most part have little to do with control costs (e.g., the future cost of alternative energy sources or of carbon capture). For an important qualification, see the discussion of the second further complication in Section 5.5.3.

5.3 Nonlinear and Adjustable Taxes

The basic Pigouvian principle is that, ideally, the tax rate at any moment in time should equal the current best estimate of the expected marginal harm from emissions. With a slowly evolving stock pollutant like greenhouse gases, as just explained, the expected marginal harm from incremental emissions is not a rapidly moving target. Even if, say, emissions were to jump by many percentage points above expectation in a given year, the long-run impact on the level of the stock would be a very small fraction of the short-run change in the flow. Accordingly, even in the original formulation in Weitzman (1974), a single, constant, fixed tax rate will be nearly optimal over short time horizons (where *short* should be interpreted as a few years, not a few days).

However, the evolution of the stock over longer time periods exhibits considerably more uncertainty, due primarily to uncertainty in control costs. Current control costs may not be well understood; imposing a new regime designed to reduce emissions below the baseline path will move actors (both firms and consumers) to new portions of their control schedules, about which even less may be known; and technological change further contributes to uncertainty over longer periods. Accordingly, the degree of control in the future, in response to a given tax rate, could be substantially more or less than may have been anticipated. In turn, the marginal benefits of control could be less or more (respectively) than predicted, so the future optimal tax rate would be lower or higher, to a degree determined by the then-existing stock level and, of course, the marginal damage schedule. This is the reason that an optimal tax regime consists of a nonlinear schedule rather than a single tax rate, fixed for all time.

Weitzman (1974), as mentioned, restricts the tax regime to be linear (i.e., for there to be a single, quantity-independent tax rate), and he does not allow adjustment of the tax rate in light of the observed quantities. (Note that the quantities must be observed to apply even a constant tax rate.) In other words, the tax schedule is stipulated to be nonoptimal and to be immune from correction in light of the information that inevitably flows in. Kaplow and Shavell (2002) as well as Weisbach (see Chapter 4) emphasize that Weitzman offers minimal practical justification for these assumptions and that subsequent literature does little more; worse, both fail to emphasize or sometimes even to mention the role that these restrictive assumptions play. This state of affairs is all the more surprising because most expositions purport to be generic, institution-independent analyses of the regulation of externalities. Finally, it should be mentioned that it is hardly clear that Weitzman himself has a strong, broad belief in the applicability of the assumptions in his 1974 paper. Indeed, in a subsequent publication (Weitzman 1978), he unapologetically assumes that the pertinent tax is nonlinear, and proceeds to examine its implications in a different model.

In the present context, a nonlinear schedule – itself an instrument less complicated than is sometimes supposed – would take an even simpler form. As explained, the need for a nonlinear schedule is to allow the marginal tax rate that firms' face in a given time period to reflect the level of marginal harm implied by the current level of the stock of greenhouse gases. Accordingly, it would not even be necessary for individual firms to face a nonlinear schedule. All that is required is for the current period's (fixed, linear) tax rate to be read off the previously announced marginal harm schedule.[7]

By analogy, consider the fact that some tax rates (or nonlinear tax schedules, such as with an income tax) may have predetermined paths: for example, a scheduled rate increase may be phased in over a number of years, according to a stated formula or table promulgated at the outset. Likewise, it is not uncommon for some taxes (again, notably, income taxes) to have automatic inflation adjustments of tax brackets. A given inflation index level from one year may mechanically determine the bracket (or exemption or other) levels for the next. What these examples have in common is that features of a tax system can change over time in essentially automatic ways based on predetermined intentions. Furthermore, these adjustments can be made a function of conditions as they unfold over time.

It is obvious that the described scheme – one with carbon tax rates, say, in a given year to be set based on stock levels observed as of the preceding year – is exceedingly simple administratively. Nor is it the case that nonlinear taxes would strike citizens and politicians as odd. Many have lived with nonlinear income taxes for their entire lives. There are other, familiar uses of nonlinear pricing as well. Quantity discounts (prices that fall with quantity) are commonplace in numerous settings, some utilities charge nonlinear rates, and the legal system sometimes employs nonlinear sanctions (sentencing guidelines determine fines and prison terms in sometimes complex ways that may depend nonlinearity on, say, the magnitude of a theft or fraud,

---

[7] Actually, nonlinear taxes with more complexity are themselves quite straightforward. The personal income tax in the United States and in many other jurisdictions applies a nonlinear schedule to each individual taxpayer, even individuals of highly limited sophistication. They might look up their tax obligations on a simple table (which does the computations for them) or go to the expense of purchasing tax preparation software or paying a tax preparer. Even if it were thought to be helpful, therefore, to employ nonlinear schedules for greenhouse gas emissions on a firm-by-firm basis, within a single period, it is hard to see why this challenge is thought to be other than trivial, much less prohibitive.

and speeding tickets sometimes involve nonlinear charges depending on the extent by which the driver exceeded the stated limit).

Furthermore, nonlinear taxes make intuitive sense in the context of regulating greenhouse gases. Consider the nonlinear schedule for tax rates that is stated in advance, but with a fixed (linear) tax imposed on all emissions in a given time period. Suppose it turns out that, in the previous period, the stock rose more quickly than the implicit benchmark rate. All would readily appreciate that there was some need to catch up. Hence, the imposition, according to the predetermined nonlinear tax schedule, of a correspondingly higher tax rate in the subsequent period would seem entirely natural. Indeed, the failure to undertake any self-correction would seem strange. Note that this simpleminded intuition is roughly in accord with the core logic of optimal Pigouvian taxation. Being behind in control of the stock means that the expected marginal damage caused by incremental subsequent emissions is higher than otherwise, making a higher tax optimal. The higher tax, in turn, induces firms to be willing to spend more at the margin to curtail emissions – up to the point that their marginal control costs are equated to the now-higher tax rate.

Likewise, if it turned out that the stock was below the expected level – the prior taxes resulted in more reductions than anticipated – we would be ahead of the game and it would seem natural to ease off somewhat. Of course, in this scenario, emissions are less costly at the margin, so a lower tax rate, leading to somewhat less effort at control, is optimal. In sum, in both situations, the nonlinear prescription is not only quite simple administratively, but it also is not at all difficult to rationalize, even to the uninitiated.

In the foregoing analysis, no interim political decisions or international renegotiations are required at any point. All that has been described follows from an initial determination, which needs to set a marginal tax rate *schedule* – which is identical to the expected marginal harm schedule – as a function of the level of the stock at various future time periods. This schedule is automatically responsive to control costs being higher or lower than expected. As Kaplow and Shavell (2002) explain, there is built-in feedback with tax schemes. Levels must be observed in order to impose the tax in the first place (and, note, this information requirement is no different from what is required under a quantity scheme, like permits). And those levels provide exactly the feedback that is necessary to implement the nonlinear schedule. Accordingly, so-called regulatory stickiness is beside the point.

One can take the analogy to inflation adjustments in an income tax or welfare programs. If the adjustment is made on a discretionary basis, requiring new legislation, we might imagine all manner of political complications that could lead to something other than smooth adjustments. On the other hand, if we (as is now done in many settings) state an adjustment rule, the changes are made annually and almost effortlessly. There is no agency engaging in elaborate deliberations and no lobbying. A statistical agency publishes the index, and it is automatically used by low-level bureaucrats to compute the new schedules, which are then published. The notion that employing nonlinear schemes, or regularly adjusting linear tax rates, is subject to all sorts of political problems so as to render it highly impracticable or unreliable seems to be without foundation.

There is, however, another important channel that would require some sort of deliberative process: new information about expected marginal harm. As explained in Section 5.2.2, the optimal nonlinear tax schedule should be set equal to the expected marginal harm schedule. This approach achieves the second best. In the case of climate change, however, we anticipate that our knowledge of expected marginal harm will evolve, possibly quite significantly, over time as a result of new information and better models. It follows, therefore, that it would be optimal to change the schedule itself. For example, if we learn that warming is occurring more rapidly, we should impose higher taxes, whereas if ways to mitigate harm develop more quickly than anticipated, the tax schedule should be lowered.

How this challenge should best be met is an important problem, and one worth more thought up front. Short of a full global renegotiation, it might be possible to delegate the task to an agency. In any case, when the control instrument is a tax schedule, the nature of the required adjustments are transparent and straightforward (i.e., given the highly complex new information on marginal harm). Furthermore, it might be possible to build even some of this flexibility into an original schedule. For example, there could be a formula for how the schedule should be adjusted based on new findings about, say, how much warming is associated with various levels of greenhouse gas concentrations, so all the agency or negotiating group would have to determine would be that new relationship. Of course, such reassessments would naturally become the occasion for attempts to renegotiate a previous deal, a problem that seems inevitable under any approach to the problem of climate change.

5.4 Permits and Quantity Adjustment

As explained in Section 5.2, it has long been understood that setting quantity targets tends to be inefficient when the regulator is uncertain about firms' control costs. Except by chance, the quantity will be set too high (when marginal control costs are less than expected marginal harm, the externality will be excessive relative to its optimal level), or it will be set too low (in which case non–cost-justified control will be undertaken). Moreover, as mentioned previously, there may exist substantial uncertainty about firms' control costs, especially when setting quantity targets well into the future. If technological progress in reducing costs is more rapid than anticipated, valuable control opportunities will be forgone under a quantity target, whereas if projected breakthroughs do not occur, huge costs may inefficiently be borne.

This deficiency of quantity targets was traditionally associated with command-and-control regulation but is equally applicable to permit schemes set to meet hard targets. This point is equally true if those targets are changing over time, such as by becoming stricter over time in anticipation of cost reductions. It remains true that the target is determined by regulators' preconceived estimates of what firms' costs will be over time rather than being based on what those costs actually turn out to be.

Ever since Roberts and Spence's (1976) important paper, however, it has been appreciated by some theorists of environmental regulation that this need not be so. As Kaplow and Shavell (2002) explore more broadly, permit schemes have a highly attractive feature, in addition to their well-known ability to minimize control costs across firms for a given quantity target. The key point is that the market price of permits not only coordinates control efforts efficiently, wherein each firm equates its marginal cost to the common market price, thus ensuring that all firms' marginal control costs are equated to each others', the condition for cost-minimization. This price also signals to the public regulatory authority the value of the current level of firms' marginal control costs, which is precisely the piece of information that the regulator initially lacked, making it have to guess at the optimal quantity. (Note that command-and-control regulation, by contrast, does not yield such a price, and thus no matter how badly off is the quantity target, the regulator will not learn the magnitude or even the direction of its error from firms' behavior.)

Armed with knowledge of the permit price, the regulator can adjust the quantity of permits so as to achieve the second best, under which firms' marginal control costs are equated to expected marginal harm – just as is true under the nonlinear tax. Doing this is, in principle, straightforward: The regulator merely looks up the current quantity on the marginal harm schedule and sees what the marginal harm at that quantity is. With the nonlinear tax scheme, the regulator then announced that figure as the tax rate. With a permit scheme, the regulator merely has to compare this figure to the current permit price. If the price is below the tax rate, it should be raised, and this is accomplished by reducing the quantity of permits. If the price is above the desired tax rate, it should be lowered, which is done by increasing the number of permits. Although the regulator may not hit the target precisely and immediately – that is, the point at which the permit market price equals the ideal tax rate at the given quantity (here, the level of the stock) – it seems plausible that the regulator could come close fairly quickly.[8]

There are many methods of permit quantity adjustment, a number of which are described in prior theoretical papers (many of which are discussed in Kaplow and Shavell [2002] as well as in Chapter 4, by Weisbach). If permits were perpetual, one could sell additional ones or buy some back if the quantity was too low or too high (i.e., if the market equilibrium permit price was too high or too low).[9] More likely, permits would be issued and reissued annually or over some other period of moderate duration. In that case, the next period's issuance would be determined, as it would in any case, by some preexisting schedule or mechanism. The foregoing analysis indicates that such a scheme should adjust the number of permits in light of the previous equilibrium permit price so that the quantity going forward will more closely equate the market permit price with the expected marginal harm at the appropriate quantity.[10]

---

[8] Note further that permit schemes that adjust quantities to maintain target permit market prices are like nonlinear taxes in most other respects. For example, the central result of Strand (see Chapter 7 in this volume), that exporters behave strategically differently, to importers' disadvantage, under permits compared to under taxes presumes that the permit regime has hard quantity targets. If instead price targets were employed, this difference (and disadvantage of permit schemes) would vanish.

[9] Alternatively, one could redesignate the units of existing permits. For example, instead of selling additional permits to raise the total by 2 percent, one might make prior permits worth (in terms of emissions or units of carbon) 1.02 times as much as before. A benefit (compared to sales and repurchases) is that, by leaving undiluted or uninflated the value of prior permits, permit prices would not be as directly influenced by the anticipation of subsequent expected permit purchases or issues. All perpetual schemes (and some others) face the challenges that firms with market power may have incentives to seek to manipulate permit prices to influence subsequent government policy. However, if permits are widely dispersed, as inevitably they may need to be, this problem may not arise. (A further complication is that a firm may seek to accumulate a large market share of permits, leasing their use to firms that actually need them; this practice might accordingly be prohibited or limited.)

[10] Another clever variation – first suggested by Roberts and Spence (1976, appendix) and also examined by Collinge and Oates (1982) and Laffont and Tirole (1996) – is to issue permits with different exercise prices, with those prices set to simulate the marginal damages

Reflecting on such permit schemes with quantities that are adjusted in one manner or another over time, it seems clear that one can accomplish essentially the same outcome as with a second-best nonlinear tax schedule that equates the tax rate to expected marginal harm at the stated quantity. The up-front requirements are the same: this harm schedule must be determined, as best as can be done. Then, each period, instead of using the schedule to determine that period's tax rate, as a function of the observed quantity (projected forward to the next period), one would attempt to induce a market equilibrium permit price at the same level by selecting an appropriate quantity of permits.

Such adjustments could be largely automatic and formulaic, rather than the product of discretionary, regular reconsideration. Also as with nonlinear taxes, if new information comes in regarding the expected marginal harm schedule, some reanalysis (such as by an agency delegated to perform such a process) or renegotiation would be required.

Furthermore, note that these permit quantity adjustments should appear entirely natural to unsophisticated onlookers. If permit prices are much lower than expected, it will be clear that control costs are lower than anticipated, so it is sensible to lower the target quantity (i.e., to aim for stronger emissions control), which is precisely what the permit quantity adjustment does in this situation. Likewise, unexpectedly high prices signal that costs are greater than imagined, calling for some relaxation of the target.

5.5 On the Comparison of Taxes and Permits

5.5.1 Tax and Permit Duality

One of the important observations in Kaplow and Shavell (2002) is that nonlinear taxes and adjustable-quantity permit schemes can be viewed as duals to each other. A nonlinear tax of the sort described in Section 5.3 is one in which the price (tax rate) depends on the quantity. An adjustable permit scheme as described in Section 5.4 is one in which the quantity depends on the price (in the permit market). Moreover, it is not simply that one is a quantity-dependant price and the other is a price-dependant quantity.

schedule. The exercise price of the ith permit would be the marginal harm of the ith unit of emissions. In that way, the lowest numbered permits would be used first, permits would be used until the marginal permit in use had an exercise price just equal to firms' marginal costs in equilibrium, and each permit would trade for the exercise price of that marginal permit minus the particular permit's exercise price.

It is further true that the second function is simply the inverse of the first function. It's the same curve, just flipping the x- and y-axes.

In addition, this theoretical equivalence is borne out by the particular analysis of practical mechanics in Sections 5.3 and 5.4. Nearly every feature examined in Section 5.3, for nonlinear taxes, has a close analogue in Section 5.4, for permits, and conversely. That is, the close conceptual linkage is also reflected to a great degree in administrative aspects of implementation. There are obviously limits to this latter claim, some of which are explored in Weisbach (see Chapter 4), but the central point, in harmony with Weisbach's theme, is that there is far more in common than meets the eye. Indeed, for purposes of analysis, it is a good starting hypothesis that properly constructed tax and permit schemes are equivalent; differences need to be demonstrated, with an explanation of why features deemed unique to one of the approaches are not or cannot be replicated in the other. On reflection, given the underlying, abstract similarities – one might say near identity – this conclusion should not be surprising.

5.5.2 Political Appeal

This chapter and this author's expertise do not extend to political considerations; however, some brief observations are in order. First, as already explained with regard to both nonlinear taxes and adjustable-quantity permit schemes, the nature of the price or quantity adjustments over time is in strong accord with common sense. Hence, there is not an obvious problem with technical economics producing a complex, subtle, or counterintuitive policy prescription that must be somehow explained to or snuck past legislators and citizens.

Second, there seems to exist some direct appeal to certain factions in the climate control debate, and these sorts of control schemes may actually facilitate compromise in light of actual (or feigned) disagreements on important facts. For example, strong environmentalists often advance the view that control costs – especially in the long run, once a serious regime becomes a reality, making technological advance highly profitable – will become much lower than fearmongers assert. If these proponents really believe this to be true, then nonlinear taxes or adjustable-quantity permit schemes should be highly attractive. If costs indeed will be low, the resulting level of control will be high – in particular, higher than would result from pre-established quantity targets that reflected a compromise between differing views (rather than the environmentalists' views being vindicated).

Likewise, to those worried about the effect of stringent controls on the standard of living – either for rich or for developing countries – both nonlinear taxes and adjustable-quantity permit schemes have a built-in safety valve. If control costs do remain high, the stringency of the controls automatically loosens.

Notice that there is a close connection between these observations and the original theoretical justification for using (nonlinear) taxes rather than hard quantity targets (originally understood to be implemented by command-and-control regulation). The problem with the latter is that the government learns nothing about firms' control costs and thus is unable to adjust targets accordingly over time. The beauty of taxes is that they harness firms' information about control costs. Permit schemes, through the market equilibrium permit price, do the same. Both types of systems – nonlinear taxes and adjustable-quantity permit schemes – use this information, implicitly or explicitly, to adjust quantity targets in light of the information thereby revealed, producing the second-best optimum (or a reasonable approximation thereof).

Uncertainty about control costs, which becomes greater the longer one projects into the future, is not only a problem for a benevolent, all-powerful regulator, but also serves as an obstacle to reaching political consensus. It appears that the magic of nonlinear pricing, through taxes or adjustable-quantity permit schemes, may allow us to elide some of the political problem as well. Opponents in the debate about the likely levels of future control costs can agree to disagree. All that needs to be set is the expected marginal harm schedule, and the market does the rest. Of course, there is also substantial disagreement (to say the least) about future harm. Accordingly, these schemes are no political panacea. However, given the huge magnitude of the political challenges in achieving consensus, the process can use all the help it can get.

5.5.3 Complications[11]

One complication, the largest political challenge, concerns the inevitably international scope of the climate change problem. The coordination (free-rider) problem is massive. As a consequence, the task is even more complex and of more doubtful efficacy if constant renegotiation is required. This

---

[11] Obviously, there are myriad additional complications, some of which are addressed in Weisbach (see Chapter 4). This chapter examines two that are closely related to the foregoing discussion.

difficulty is one reason why it is thought to be important to strike a deal that reaches far into the future. However, a major challenge in so doing is that the future is highly uncertain, so any long-term deal is likely to become substantially suboptimal as time unfolds, above and beyond sacrifices to political expediency.

Nonlinear taxes and adjustable-quantity permit schemes address this problem in part. A central need for adjustment concerns ex ante uncertainty about future control costs, where more information will be revealed by marketplace activity over time. As already explained, these schemes have built-in, automatically adjusting flexibility in this regard. Thus, their efficiency advantage may also be a political advantage in yet another respect. As noted, however, this benefit does not extend to new information about marginal expected harm. To some extent, one might build some such information, perhaps as interpreted by a predesignated expert agency, into the nonlinear tax or permit price schedule, but there are probably political limits on the extent to which this can be done.

A second complication concerns the stock nature of the greenhouse gas problem. As already noted, this is an advantage in one important respect: because the stock changes very slowly relative to possibly unexpected short-term fluctuations in the flow, the optimal tax rate or permit price also changes very slowly, so there is little efficiency loss in a regime that adjusts taxes or permit quantities even with a substantial lag. (Fairly rapid adjustment would be feasible; the point is that, in the present setting, it does not seem to be very important.)

One problem, however, is that the stock nature of the pollutant greatly complicates the problem of estimating the marginal harm from a given current unit of emissions. In addition to all of the problems of climate change modeling and other aspects of ascertaining marginal damages, there is the point that the marginal harm of a current unit of emissions depends in significant part on estimates of future marginal control costs (an interdependency that is absent with a flow pollutant). For example, if future costs turn out to be lower than anticipated, the self-adjusting system will generate a lower future stock, and this in turn will reduce the expected marginal harm of *current* emissions. Therefore, estimates of contemporaneous expected marginal harm will in part reflect expectations about future control costs. Despite this complication, it remains true that the optimal present tax rate or permit price equals the best estimate of expected marginal harm (taking this interdependency into account). The current point is that determining this magnitude will be even harder than the daunting task one envisions considering only the harm side of the calculus.

5.6 Additional Considerations

5.6.1 Future Price Uncertainty and Innovation

It is sometimes feared that uncertainty about future prices, whether future tax rates under a nonlinear tax scheme or future permit prices under an adjustable-quantity permit system, will inhibit innovation (and otherwise impose social costs). As a first approximation, it seems that this is a nonissue in the following sense. Markets generate investments based on expected future payoffs. If there is genuine future risk – climate change has a substantial enough magnitude to contribute to systematic risk, which even in theory cannot be fully diversified – ex ante investments will take this uncertainty into account. However, that investments reflect future uncertainty tends to be socially optimal. Market risks are real. They cannot be wished away by government or anyone else, and, given their presence, decisions should be optimized in light thereof.[12]

The situation with regard to investments that pertain to climate change seems like that for all manner of investments in a market economy.[13] Especially in recent decades, during which massive investments have been undertaken in technology sectors – computer chips, communications, the Internet, software – it is clear that the market operates tolerably well in light of massive uncertainty. The market is hardly perfect. One particular concern is innovation spillovers, which cannot be fully captured and thus lead to inadequate investment, particularly in basic research. Even optimal and well-enforced intellectual property rights regimes involve distortion, and determining the optimal regime is no easy task. Accordingly, there may be a substantial role for government support of basic research and for international cooperation along this dimension as well. However, just as it probably would have been a poor (if not disastrous) alternative to have the government pick winning and losing technologies in high-tech industries – and substantially problematic for the government, say, to peg computer chip or broadband prices in the distant future – so too government should not interfere with permit market prices, that is, except to equate them to best

---

[12] There will inevitably be mechanisms to allocate risks to some degree (investors hold diversified portfolios; futures markets may allow some risks to be hedged), but whatever is the residual risk, it reflects real uncertainty about economic activity and hence should be taken into account by private actors.

[13] The analysis is closely related to the core argument against transition relief (considered in the next subsection) that its anticipation distorts ex ante investment incentives. See, for example, Kaplow (1992, 2003) and Shaviro (2000).

estimates of expected marginal harm. Likewise, tax rates should be set with regard to the estimated magnitude of the externality, not tinkered with in order to provide a more stable investment environment.

The importance of this point can be made more concrete by considering the actual impact of future price uncertainty. Suppose, for example, that there is a ten percent probability that future prices will be much higher than standard estimates, perhaps because it is possible that certain cost-reducing technologies will confront unanticipated hurdles. In that case, it is important for investors to be unsheltered from this risk. The prospect of such high prices will induce greater ex ante efforts toward alternative means of reducing emissions, whether through the development of alternative technologies or through more aggressive conservation. Similarly, if there is a serious prospect that prices might be much lower than consensus predictions, perhaps as a result of the possibility of major breakthroughs, then the dampening effect of this prospect, which is to reduce the incentive to pursue other means of emissions control, is optimal to that extent. Granted, bubbles and other phenomena can render markets (sometimes highly) imperfect guides, and it is desirable to minimize such pricing defects where possible. However, a general policy of arbitrarily dampening the range of tax or permit price movement is a blunt instrument that would likely cause avoidable inefficiencies. Even worse would be to move more toward command-and-control alternatives that eschew the benefits of the price mechanism to an even greater degree in the misguided pursuit of predictability.

5.6.2 Transition, Grandfathering, and Ex Ante Incentives

The transition problem is substantial for the regulation of greenhouse gases, and this issue, viewed generally, has received sustained attention in some of my own prior work (e.g., Kaplow 1992, 2003, 2008b) and that of other scholars (e.g., Shaviro 2000). For the present, it is useful to emphasize one teaching: the importance of accounting for ex ante investment incentives, particularly when a substantial transition is anticipated for a long period of time. With climate change, it is likely that major agreements still may be many years off, and the prospect of a substantial, global regulatory regime has been under serious consideration for an extended period of time. Moreover, whatever national legislation may be enacted in the immediate future or global agreement may be ratified in the near term, it seems likely that significant alterations will be ever on the horizon, making ex ante concerns relevant well into the future.

If firms (and countries) anticipate substantial grandfathering, great inefficiency can arise. One particular concern is misdirected investment that is counterproductive in combating climate change. One form of grandfathering would involve distributing free permits based on pre-enactment emissions. Another would be granting analogous preferences under a tax scheme (e.g., exemptions for pre-enactment quantities of emissions might be provided).[14] To the extent that any such relief is based on prior investment, firms and countries have inadequate ex ante incentives to begin bringing their investments and policies into line with the anticipated new regime, and they may even behave counterproductively in order to secure greater preferences upon enactment. As just one illustration, if such grandfathering is long anticipated, China may build thousands more dirty coal plants than they would if their permit allotment had to be purchased or was distributed, say, based on their population or some other factors (i.e., factors independent of how much annual greenhouse gases they manage to be pumping into the atmosphere before a deal is struck).

Granting free permits or otherwise providing relief to costly, preexisting sources is often viewed as a trade-off between equity and political feasibility. However, the world may well be currently incurring a tremendous cost by following a course in which firms and countries expect to be rewarded for increasing rather than reducing emissions in the interim, and this process has been going on for over a decade and may continue for quite some time. Likewise, if subsequent renegotiations are expected to favor those who have done the worst job complying with a new regime, any agreement is much less likely to be successful going forward. Accordingly, any moves that can be made now to signal credibly that such transition relief will not be provided (or will be less generous than currently anticipated) could have a substantial social payoff – the more, the sooner, the better.

5.7 Distribution

Both tax and permit schemes raise serious concerns – normative and political – about their impact on the overall distribution of income.[15] The subject

---

[14] A difference would arise if the free permits were tradable, whereas the tax preferences were not (i.e., firms could not directly or indirectly transfer their units of exempt emissions to other firms with greater control costs). On one hand, free transferability ex post is more efficient because those receiving the relief may have lower marginal control costs than do other firms. On the other hand, the prospect of transferability, by raising the value of relief, worsens the ex ante incentives discussed in the text.

[15] There are other dimensions of distribution, such as geographic incidence, that may have political relevance but are set to the side here (see Chapter 2). Note, however, that protecting the preexisting distribution on such dimensions based on pre-enactment emissions

comes up in Weisbach (Chapter 4), receives greater attention in a number of other chapters in this volume, notably those by Burtraw, Walls, and Blonz (Chapter 2) and Rausch et al. (Chapter 3), and plays an important implicit role in chapters by de Gorter and Just (Chapter 10) and Parry (Chapter 8). A number of powerful lessons are important to keep in mind.

First, it is often supposed that one must design the climate change interventions themselves to meet distributive objectives. For example, free permits or other leeway might be given to the poor or to people who drive in order to mitigate the regressive distributive incidence of gasoline price increases. This view, however, is fundamentally mistaken, and it tends to confuse analysis and generate policies that are less efficient than available alternatives. The most straightforward and (approximately) best approach is to design an optimal environmental control scheme that fully allows price increases, such as in the price of gasoline, to occur in order to induce all manner of efficient behavior (driving less, purchasing more fuel-efficient vehicles), and then achieve distributive objectives through the income tax and transfer system. In other words, rather than contort environmental policy, we can implement it efficiently and adjust the general distributive apparatus of the economy to provide any desired offsets.

One particular means of doing so, which is a central focus of my recent book (Kaplow 2008a), as well as of my writing on optimal environmental policy and regulation specifically (Kaplow 2004, 2006), is to adjust the income tax and transfer system so that the combined scheme is distribution neutral. For example, if a carbon tax or permit scheme raises the price of gasoline, which is consumed disproportionately by the poor, one might lower taxes (or raise an earned income tax credit and/or adjust other transfer programs) to make up the difference. If environmental benefits are disproportionately concentrated on the rich, their income taxes might be raised in an offsetting manner.

This simple prescription follows from familiar economic principles. It is generally best to use a separate instrument to address each distinct problem;

---

patterns can both produce the sorts of inefficiencies discussed in Section 5.6.2 and also (if design provides long-term, ongoing compensation) perpetuate or even increase inefficiencies in subsequent behavior. For example, if energy usage is much higher in some climates, and in light of the greenhouse gas problem the true total social cost of energy is much higher than previously thought, then a part of long-run efficient adjustment involves a different geographic distribution of the population. Over the pertinent time horizons in climate change debates (covering decades, or even a century or more), margins of this sort can be quite significant: population distribution will be much different in 2050 than it is today, and it is important that the incentives guiding such movement reflect the true social costs of living in different regions.

moreover, for each problem, it tends to be desirable to employ the instrument that addresses it most directly. Use emissions taxes or permit schemes to get the carbon price right (which will induce efficient behavior on all margins related to the environmental challenge), and use the income tax and transfer scheme to produce the desired distribution. (The distribution-neutral approach need not be optimal, of course, because the preexisting distribution need not be optimal, but its availability suggests the ability to separate the two problems.)

Another often overlooked feature of distribution-neutral implementation is that it not only neutralizes distributive effects (by definition) but is also, as a crude first approximation, neutral with regard to labor supply. (The assumption that generates this result is that labor is weakly separable in utility from other features of the problem, notably, different forms of consumption and environmental effects.[16]) The basic intuition is that, with distribution-neutral implementation, there is the same marginal return to earning more income after the reform as there was before, all things considered, so individuals would be induced to choose the same level of labor effort.

These ideas are also pertinent to the common practice of comparing the implications of different means of implementation regarding the collection and distribution of revenues. Auctioned permits raise revenues compared to free distribution; likewise, tax schemes add funds to the treasury. Differences in revenue raised are thus seen by some to be important distinctions among permit schemes and between permits and taxes. Moreover, it is common for economic analyses to compare different means of distributing these collections. Revenue might be rebated lump sum (equal per capita), by proportionally reducing labor income taxes, or otherwise. Indeed, some of the aforementioned chapters in this volume devote substantial attention to these comparisons.

In light of the foregoing discussion, however, one can see that such analyses are often incomplete and, as a consequence, misleading. Sometimes different revenue treatments (on the collection and the disbursement side) are compared in terms of their efficiency costs, without regard to distribution. However, the differential efficiency cost of different revenue treatments is largely or fully a consequence of differences in redistribution,

---

[16] For formal analysis, see Kaplow (2006). If, instead, gasoline is, say, a leisure complement, as indicated by West and Williams (2007), then it is optimal to set the corrective tax wedge on gasoline above the Pigouvian level (because doing so will further reduce gasoline use, which under the maintained assumption will also reduce leisure, which is distorted upward by the income tax and transfer system).

as emphasized in Kaplow (2004, 2006, 2008a). Should we be surprised that distributing funds lump sum has a higher efficiency cost than using them to reduce marginal tax rates? After all, comparing these two approaches, the environmental intervention is held constant, and the only difference is that the former, by comparison to the latter, has higher marginal tax rates to finance a more generous lump-sum transfer. This is a quintessential increase in redistribution through the tax system that really has nothing to do with regulating greenhouse gases. Should we be surprised that this redistributive difference is associated with greater overall distortion? As explained, a distribution-neutral implementation would wash out this efficiency consequence (the distortionary effect of redistribution on labor supply) and the distributive difference, leaving just the intrinsic effects of the environmental regulation under consideration.

Some other analyses do attend to distributive effects but, as mentioned, tend to see them as tied to particular means of deploying various regulatory instruments. Because, as explained, one can adjust the tax and transfer system so as to achieve distribution neutrality – or any other desired distribution, for that matter – distribution (and labor supply distortion associated therewith) should be seen as a largely separable problem from that of addressing climate change. Moreover, if academic analysis is to usefully and clearly guide the political process, which is concerned with distributive matters, it seems best to present versions of implementation that are explicitly distribution neutral – to which analysts might append other distributive scenarios, clearly described, with accompanying distributional tables or diagrams. The distribution-neutral case is a useful analytical and political benchmark that facilitates communication and clarifies thinking.

Observe further that there is a potentially important political advantage of distribution-neutral policy packages. Part of the difficulty of reaching agreement, whether within a single country's legislature or in an international multilateral bargain, concerns such distributive effects.[17] Indeed, they may be one of the greatest obstacles. Note, however, that a feature of an efficient policy change that is implemented in a distribution-neutral fashion is that it tends to result in a Pareto improvement. Enhanced efficiency

[17] In the domestic context, the income tax and transfer programs are the core instruments to adjust distribution. Internationally, using similar logic, it tends to be best to use explicit transfer payments precisely because indirect means tend to involve additional, avoidable inefficiencies. In the present setting, it is familiar that one of the greatest sources of efficiency from an optimal international agreement is the potential to achieve cost-minimization across countries, with more control taking place in often poorer countries where opportunities for cheap reductions may be large, which effort may be induced by appropriate side-payments.

means a larger pie, and distribution neutrality means that this expanded pie is divided among parties the same way that it was before. Therefore, everyone's slice is larger. Although this depiction of political deal making is highly oversimplified, it seems plausible that this factor should carry some weight.

5.8 Conclusion

The principal conclusion of this chapter is that there exists a strong duality between nonlinear tax schemes and adjustable-quantity permit schemes. Moreover, both possess a significant advantage over fixed-quantity permit schemes because the level of control of greenhouse gases under the latter could readily be much too great or too lenient, especially in the long run. The Pigouvian dictum that polluters should face a tax or price equal to the marginal expected damage that they cause is the appropriate benchmark for thinking about policies that regulate externalities, including greenhouse gas emissions.

Weitzman's (1974) framework, which compares a fixed quantity regulation to a fixed, linear tax scheme, is substantially misleading and inapt with regard to climate control. In regulating a stock pollutant, the level of which evolves quite slowly, the second-best optimal nonlinear tax can be very closely approximated in administratively straightforward ways using both taxes and permits. Moreover, the adjustments over time that are necessary in light of the resolution of uncertainty about control costs – which is substantial when considering projections decades into the future – can be done in an essentially automatic, nondiscretionary manner. Unfortunately, any type of scheme will need discretionary adjustment, and possibly political renegotiation, as more is learned about the level of expected social harm due to greenhouse gases.

Furthermore, the built-in adjustment process in a nonlinear scheme, whether implemented through taxes or permits, is fairly intuitive and thus does not in itself present an obvious political barrier. Indeed, as explained, these adjustments seem so natural that it actually may appear more surprising not to make them (such as would be the case under fixed-rate tax or hard-target quantity schemes).

Some additional considerations are also addressed. One often overlooked problem concerns transition, in particular that giving away permits or providing tax exclusions on the basis of existing emission levels provides perverse incentives for control prior to enactment. This problem is likely to be substantial in light of the fact that truly tough limitations are unlikely to become binding for quite some time, making it far more attractive for both individual sources within countries and many nations to expand activities that will cause additional interim damage and make more daunting the achievement of future emissions reductions.

Another dimension – addressed by many of the chapters in this volume, but often analyzed incompletely and misleadingly – concerns distributive effects, particularly with regard to the overall distribution of income within and between countries. The central point to keep in mind is that the tax and transfer system (including transfers between countries) typically offers the most efficient means of addressing distributive concerns. In particular, distribution-neutral implementation – combining an efficient greenhouse gas regulatory scheme with tax and transfer adjustments that, taken together, keep the overall distribution constant – is quite appealing as an analytical construct. It clarifies thinking, for example, by distinguishing distortions due to increased redistribution from distortions related to externality regulation. Furthermore, distribution-neutral systems may be easier to communicate to policy makers (who could also have non–distribution-neutral proposals compared side-by-side to clarify distributive effects), and they also have some pragmatic appeal, for efficient (pie-expanding) regulatory schemes that are also distribution-neutral will make all groups better off.

In closing, it is useful to emphasize that basic economic principles – like setting prices for externalities that equal marginal harm and carefully distinguishing the task of externality correction from that of redistribution – are important to keep in mind and to disseminate, even amidst ongoing, intense political debate and negotiation about practical problems. In the short run, better policies can be designed and implemented, whether they take the form of taxes or permit schemes.

Also important is the long run, especially because the greenhouse gas problem, unfortunately, is likely to be with us for generations, and further regulation and modification are inevitable in the mid and distant future. Many will recall that, only a few decades ago, economists' advocacy of permit schemes as superior to command-and-control regulation was often viewed as evil because such an approach entailed approval of paying to kill people. Had proponents of permits given up the battle then, existing environmental regulation would almost certainly be more costly and less effective, and the prospects for addressing climate change would be even more grim.[18]

---

[18] Even after the introduction of the first SO_2 trading system in the early 1990s, media responses (including a prominent cartoon) portrayed permits as legalized certificates to kill people.

Pushing the point that optimal control is cost-effective control, which entails not only cost minimization in achieving a given target but the choice (and modification) of targets that reflect an equation of marginal control costs and marginal benefits, both of which may change substantially over time from current estimates, is of first-order importance. No final, definitive, international regime for addressing greenhouse gases will be in place any time soon, and whatever arrangements are adopted, there will be continuing pressure to modify them. Hence, even ideas that cannot fully and persuasively be presented in the short run are worth advancing for the long run.

References

Adar, Zvi, and James M. Griffin. 1976. Uncertainty and the choice of pollution control instruments. *Journal of Environmental Economics and Management* 3:178–188.

Burtraw, Dallas, Margaret Walls, and Joshua Blonz. 2011. Distributional impacts of carbon pricing policies in the electricity sector. Chapter 2. In *U.S. Energy Tax Policy*, Gilbert E. Metcalf (ed.). Cambridge, UK: Cambridge University Press.

Collinge, Robert A., and Wallace E. Oates. 1982. Efficiency in pollution control in the short and long runs: A system of rental emission permits. *Canadian Journal of Economics* 15:346–354.

de Gorter, Harry, and David R. Just. 2011. The social costs and benefits of U.S. biofuel policies with preexisting distortions. Chapter 10. In *U.S. Energy Tax Policy*, Gilbert E. Metcalf (ed.). Cambridge, UK: Cambridge University Press.

Fishelson, Gideon. 1976. Emission control policies under uncertainty. *Journal of Environmental Economics and Management* 3:189–198.

Kaplow, Louis. 1992. Government relief for risk associated with government action. *Scandinavian Journal of Economics* 94:525–541.

Kaplow, Louis. 2003. Transition policy: a conceptual framework. *Journal of Contemporary Legal Issues* 13:161–209.

Kaplow, Louis. 2004. On the (ir)relevance of distribution and labor supply distortion to government policy. *Journal of Economic Perspectives* 18 (4):159–175.

Kaplow, Louis. 2006. *Optimal control of externalities in the presence of income taxation.* NBER Working Paper No. 12339, Cambridge, MA.

Kaplow, Louis. 2008a. *The Theory of Taxation and Public Economics.* Princeton: Princeton University Press.

Kaplow, Louis. 2008b. Capital levies and transition to a consumption tax. In *Institutional Foundations of Public Finance: Economic and Legal Perspectives*, Alan Auerbach and Daniel Shaviro (eds.), pp. 112–146. Cambridge: Harvard University Press.

Kaplow, Louis, and Steven Shavell. 2002. On the superiority of corrective taxes to quantity regulation. *American Law and Economics Review* 4:1–17.

Laffont, Jean-Jacques, and Jean Tirole. 1996. Pollution permits and environmental innovation. *Journal of Public Economics* 62:127–140.

Parry, Ian W.H. 2011. How much should highway fuels be taxed? Chapter 8. In *U.S. Energy Tax Policy*, Gilbert E. Metcalf (ed.). Cambridge, UK: Cambridge University Press.

Rausch, Sebastian, Gilbert E. Metcalf, John M. Reilly, et al. 2011. Distributional impacts of a U.S. greenhouse gas policy: A general equilibrium analysis of carbon pricing. Chapter 3. In *U.S. Energy Tax Policy*, Gilbert E. Metcalf (ed.). Cambridge, UK: Cambridge University Press.

Roberts, Marc J., and Michael Spence. 1976. Effluent charges and licenses under uncertainty. *Journal of Public Economics* 5:193–208.

Rose-Ackerman, Susan. 1973. Effluent charges: A critique. *Canadian Journal of Economics* 6:512–527.

Shaviro, Daniel. 2000. *When Rules Change: An Economic and Political Analysis of Transition Relief and Retroactivity*. Chicago: University of Chicago Press.

Stavins, Robert N. 1996. Correlated uncertainty and policy instrument choice. *Journal of Environmental Economics and Management* 30:218–232.

Strand, Jon. 2011. Taxes and caps as climate policy instruments with domestic and imported fuels. Chapter 7. In *U.S. Energy Tax Policy*, Gilbert E. Metcalf (ed.). Cambridge, UK: Cambridge University Press.

Weisbach, David. 2011. Instrument choice is instrument design. Chapter 4. In *U.S. Energy Tax Policy*, Gilbert E. Metcalf (ed.). Cambridge, UK: Cambridge University Press.

Weitzman, Martin L. 1974. Prices vs. quantities. *Review of Economic Studies* 41: 477–491.

Weitzman, Martin L.1978. Optimal rewards for economic regulation. *American Economic Review* 68:683–691.

West, Sarah, and Roberton C. Williams. 2007. Optimal taxation and cross-price effects on labor supply: Estimates of the optimal gas tax. *Journal of Public Economics* 91:593–617.

SIX

Border Adjustments for Carbon Taxes and the Cost of Emissions Permits

Economic, Administrative, and Legal Issues

Charles E. McLure, Jr.

6.1 Introduction

Under the Kyoto Protocol, most advanced countries other than the United States committed to reduce emissions of CO_2 occurring within their boundaries, on average, to 95 percent of their 1990 levels between 2008 and 2012. By comparison, the protocol exempted developing countries from the requirement to reduce CO_2 emissions. Although the protocol does not prescribe the means to be employed to achieve this target, it is anticipated that either carbon taxes or cap-and-trade systems – hereafter referred to as carbon pricing – will play an important role. The first carbon pricing systems to be implemented rely on what, in the tax literature, would be called *origin-based* systems for pricing carbon embedded in internationally traded products.[1]

For example, under the European Union's Emissions Trading System (ETS), by far the most important extant system for pricing carbon, emissions permits are required to engage in *production* in a member state that entails *emissions* of CO_2. Exports are not exempt from the requirement to hold permits, and the cost of permits for carbon emissions embedded in the cost of exports is not rebated when products are exported. Conversely, it is not necessary to hold CO_2 emissions permits of EU members of destination to import into the EU products that would be subject to the requirement for emissions permits if produced within the EU. The first column of Table 6.1 describes the treatment of international trade under an origin-based system, for both carbon taxes and a cap-and-trade system.

---

[1] Two conventions are followed here, as in much other literature. In both cases, meaning should be clear from context. First, because of the technological relationship between the amount of carbon consumed in combustion and the quantity of CO_2 emitted, *carbon* and CO_2 are sometimes used interchangeably. Second, carbon that causes global warming is said to be "embedded" in products, although it is emitted as part of the emission of CO_2.

Table 6.1. *Alternative trade regimes for carbon taxes and cap-and-trade systems*

	Trade regime			
	Global participation		Nonparticipation/exemption for developing countries	
	Pure origin (No BAs) (1)	Pure destination (BAs on all imports and exports) (2)	Mixed *Symmetrical*: origin for trade with "white list" countries; BAs for other trade *Asymmetrical*: origin for imports from "white list" countries and for exports; BAs for other imports (3)	Import BAs, with credit for origin-country tax or cost of permits (4)
Border Adjustments for Carbon Taxes				
Imports	Exempt	Taxed	From "white list" countries: exempt From other countries: BTAs	BTAs, with credit
Exports	Taxed	Exempt, with rebate of embedded tax	*Symmetrical* To "white list" countries: taxed To other countries: exempt, with rebate of embedded prior-stage tax *Asymmetrical*: taxed	Taxed
Border Adjustments for Cap-and-Trade Systems				
Imports	Permits not required	Permits required	From "white list" countries: permits not required From other countries: permits required	Permits required; credit for embedded cost of origin-country permits
Exports	Permits required	Permits not required, with rebate of embedded cost of prior-stage permits	*Symmetrical* To "white list" countries: permits required To other countries: permits not required, with rebate of embedded cost of prior-stage permits *Asymmetrical*: permits required	Permits required

The origin- (or production/emissions-) based system for pricing carbon has adverse consequences that are now well recognized, in part because not all nations "participate" in the Kyoto Protocol coalition, in the sense of agreeing to reduce emissions of carbon.[2] The list of nonparticipating nations includes the United States, which refused to ratify the Kyoto treaty, as well as China, India, and other developing countries. First, firms that produce carbon-intensive products in participating countries are placed at a competitive disadvantage, in both domestic and export markets, relative to those that produce in nonparticipating countries.[3]

Second, there is an incentive for nations to be "free riders," by not participating in the Kyoto coalition, in order to retain a competitive advantage for their producers. Because global warming involves transnational external costs, these nations enjoy the benefits of preventing it.

Third, partial coverage can lead to "carbon leakage," as production, including that associated with new investments, shifts from participating countries to nonparticipating countries, impeding the reduction of global emissions.[4] Even if the United Sates decides to participate, as long as China and India do not curtail emissions, there is little hope of meeting global targets for stabilizing the concentration of CO_2 in the atmosphere at a level that many believe is necessary to avoid serious risk of irreversible and potentially catastrophic global warming.

Fourth, even if the Kyoto targets were to be realized, if some countries of origin impose a price on emissions and some do not, worldwide economic efficiency suffers, because the reduction of emissions does not occur where it is cheapest. The first column of Table 6.2 summarizes these four problems. (The table also describes other key characteristics of several systems of pricing carbon that are described in the sections that follow.)

---

[2] Strictly speaking, developing countries that signed the Kyoto Protocol participate in the Protocol. The term *participating* is used here to refer only to countries in the Kyoto coalition that have undertaken commitments to reduce emissions. Other countries are treated as not participating.

[3] As stressed in other literature, competitiveness should be defined at the sectoral or perhaps firm level, not the level of an entire economy.

[4] It is important to distinguish two types of carbon leakage. In what follows the term *leakage* is reserved for a drop in domestic production of CO_2 that exceeds the fall in domestic consumption of embedded CO_2 resulting from pricing carbon. It occurs because of the change in the relative cost of using carbon-based energy in participating and nonparticipating countries induced by carbon pricing. Computer models reveal that a quantitatively more important form of leakage occurs because carbon pricing depresses the demand for energy in countries that adopt such policies. As a result, the price of energy falls and more of it is used, especially in nonparticipating countries. See, for example, McKibben and Wilcoxen (2009).

Table 6.2. *Implications of alternative trade regimes for a carbon tax*

Features compared	Trade regime in country taxing carbon		
	Without global participation		Nonparticipation/developing country exemption
	Pure origin (No BAs)	Pure destination (BAs on all imports and exports)	Mixed *Symmetrical*: origin for "white list" trade; BTAs for other trade *Asymmetrical*: origin for "white list" imports and for exports; BTAs for other imports
General Descriptive Features			
Marginal tax rate on traded goods	Origin	Destination	"White list" trade: origin *Asymmetrical*: Imports from nonparticipants: destination Exports to nonparticipants: origin
Country receiving revenues	Origin	Destination	"White list" trade: origin *Asymmetrical*: Imports from nonparticipants: destination Exports to nonparticipants: origin
Carbon leakage?	Yes	No	*Symmetrical*: No *Asymmetrical*: Yes
Free-rider problem	Yes: Aids producers	Yes: Aids consumers	*Symmetrical*: No *Asymmetrical*: Yes
Economic efficiency?	No	No	*Symmetrical*: Yes (if uniform carbon price) *Asymmetrical*: No
Additional administrative requirements	Baseline: no	Institute BTAs	BTAs for trade with countries not on "white list" Definition of "white list"
Implied meaning of "polluter pays"	Where CO_2 is emitted	Where embedded CO_2 is consumed	Logically consistent interpretation is difficult
Perspective of a Developed Country Choosing the Regime			
Competitiveness problem	Yes	No	*Symmetrical*: No *Asymmetrical*: Imports: No Exports: Yes

This origin/production/emissions-based system for pricing carbon stands in marked contrast to the way value-added taxes (VATs) are commonly levied. In the standard *destination-based* VAT, imports are subject to the same tax as domestic products, and exports enter world markets tax-free. In short, the tax applies to *consumption*, rather than to production. The application of VAT to imports and the exemption from, and rebate of, tax on exports required to achieve destination-based taxation are commonly called *border tax adjustments* (BTAs).

Not surprisingly, the outcomes under a destination-based tax are very different from those under an origin-based tax.[5] There is no competitive advantage to producing in a country that does not have such a tax, the tax does not distort choices of where to produce, and free riding is not an issue.

The same reasoning applies to destination-based systems for pricing carbon.[6] Unlike origin-based pricing, destination- (or consumption-) based carbon prices would not affect competition between producers in countries that do and do not price carbon. Moreover, policy-induced leakages of carbon emissions would take a different and less pernicious form, and incentives for countries to be free riders by eschewing carbon pricing would be muted. In particular, if the community of nations decided to impose a destination-based price on carbon, some countries might choose not to do so, to avoid burdening their *consumers*. The mitigation of emissions would be less than if carbon pricing were universal, and these countries could be described as free riders in the effort to reduce global warming. However, the environmental and free-rider effects would be less harmful than under an

---

[5] An old theorem says that taxes that apply to all production or to all consumption are equivalent in their economic effects, because differences will wash out in movements in exchange rates or price levels. This theorem has limited applicability to real-world VATs, which are not levied on all consumption and presumably would not be levied on all production, if the origin principle were chosen. See Feldstein and Krugman (1990).

[6] The theorem cited in the previous footnote has even less relevance to carbon prices, which have quite different impacts on different sectors, than to real-world VATs. Thus, Hufbauer and Kim (2009, p. 3, notes 3 and 4) write the following in successive paragraphs:

"When the profile of VAT across traded sectors is jagged – some very high rates, some very low rates – the similarity begins to fade between the impact of origin and destination BTAs. Origin BTAs will not adequately shield the highly taxed sectors from foreign competition, even after the exchange rate adjusts."

For a different view, see Lockwood and Whalley (2008) and Whalley (2009), which emphasize the possibility that carbon prices might be reflected in wage rates and returns to other factors that are sector-specific, rather than affecting product prices. Although labor and other factors may be specific to certain sectors in the short run, specificity is much less in the long run. More to the point, it is precisely the short-run impacts on specific sectors and factors employed therein that motivate much of the concern about competitiveness.

origin-based system, in which free-riding countries avoid burdening their *producers*. The second column of Table 6.2 summarizes these benefits (and other characteristics and effects) of a destination-based carbon tax. (The results for a cap-and-trade system, with obvious reinterpretations, are the same, except that administrative requirements differ and revenue accrues to the country issuing permits. The latter, in turn, is determined by the international allocation of authority to issue permits.)

As with a VAT, implementation of a destination-based system of pricing carbon would require border adjustments, or BAs. (The term *border adjustments* is equally applicable to carbon taxes and cap-and-trade systems; the acronym BTAs is reserved here for *border adjustments for taxes*.) In the case of a carbon tax, taxes would be levied on carbon embedded in imports, exports would be exempt, and embedded carbon tax paid before the export stage would be rebated. Under a cap-and-trade system, permits (or the payment of a tax) would be required for imports, based on their embedded carbon content, but not for exports, and the embedded cost of permits incurred before the export stage would be rebated. The second column of Table 6.1 describes destination-based systems for pricing carbon.

Responding to concerns about competitiveness, carbon leakage, and free-rider problems, a number of public officials in the EU have suggested that imports from nations that do not participate in the Kyoto Protocol (most notably those from the United States) should be subject to BAs, and draft legislation for carbon taxes and cap-and-trade systems introduced in the U.S. Congress includes such provisions.[7] Proposals for BAs on exports to nonparticipating countries are less common, presumably because unfair competition in domestic markets is seen to be a greater threat than unfair competition in export markets. Most examinations of BAs for carbon prices envisage grafting destination-based features onto what is fundamentally an origin-based system, rather than creating a conceptually coherent, universally applicable destination-based system. Thus, BAs might be applied only to trade with countries that do not have "comparable" origin-based programs to curtail emissions, creating what Section 6.3 calls a *mixed system*.[8]

Despite the advantages described earlier, the case for destination-based carbon pricing is easily overstated. First, implementing such a scheme must overcome daunting technological and administrative challenges. Second, there may be legal barriers to implementing a destination-based system

---

[7] See McLure (2010a) for references.

[8] See, for example, Aldy, Orszag, and Stiglitz (2001), Biermann and Brohm (2005a), and Metcalf and Weisbach (2009).

for pricing carbon, especially a mixed system, under the rules that govern international trade, principally the General Agreement on Tariffs and Trade (GATT) and the Agreement on Subsidies and Countervailing Measures (ASCM). Third, whether it makes sense to attempt to implement destination-based pricing depends on the magnitude and nature of the distortions, effects on competitiveness, carbon leakages, and incentives for free riding that would exist if some countries do not price carbon. Finally, because of the strong opposition by developing countries to the use of BAs by developed countries, there is widespread concern that unilateral introduction of BAs could set off trade wars, especially given the uncertainty of the legality of such measures under the international trade rules. This hung like a dark cloud over the Copenhagen negotiations that began in early December 2009. It would, in principle, be both possible and desirable to revise those rules to allow explicitly for BAs for carbon prices, but revision would not occur quickly – and it might never occur – because of political resistance to revision.

This next section describes the economic equivalence of three comprehensive harmonized systems of pricing carbon and suggests criteria for choosing among them. Section 6.3 considers, at a conceptual level, alternative ways of achieving the benefits of destination-based pricing of carbon in a world of origin-based carbon pricing, including a zero price for carbon set by countries not participating in the Kyoto Protocol. Section 6.4 examines technological and administrative issues related to implementation of BAs, and Section 6.5 summarizes the discussion of the GATT legality of BTAs for carbon taxes and of BAs for the cost of emissions permits. Section 6.6 summarizes and concludes.

In order to concentrate on the issues at hand, several limitations are placed on the analysis. First, CO_2 is the only greenhouse gas considered, but much of what is said here would, with some modifications, be applicable to a more comprehensive scheme that included pricing of other greenhouse gases. Second, only emissions of CO_2 arising from the combustion of fossil fuels are considered explicitly; thus, for example, CO_2 released in the burning of forests is not considered, but the same reasoning could be applied to some other emission-intensive activities, including the production of cement. Third, the chapter generally does not consider the need to make allowances for the physical embodiment of carbon in some products (e.g., in chemicals, steel, and asphalt). Fourth, there is no attempt to compare the efficacy of BAs and other proposed ways to deal with competitiveness and leakage, such as free allowances and output-based rebates. Finally, this analysis pertains specifically to trade between nations. The international trade rules are, of course, of no relevance for determining the legality of BAs for state carbon pricing related to interstate trade.

6.2 The First-Best Solution: Globally Comprehensive Harmonized Carbon Pricing

From an economic point of view, the ideal way to price carbon is via a harmonized system that achieves *carbon price equivalency* – the same price for carbon, wherever carbon combustion or consumption of embedded carbon occurs. With a uniform price for carbon, mitigation of emissions would occur where most cost-effective, because the marginal cost of reducing emissions would equal the uniform price for carbon in all countries, and penalties for emitting CO_2 would not depend on where products that embody CO_2 are produced or consumed. There would be no carbon leakages and no competitive advantages and disadvantages in a harmonized global system. By assumption, there would be no free riders.

The simplest such system to understand, and perhaps to implement, would be a globally uniform carbon tax, but a cap-and-trade system with international trading of emission permits could, in theory, also produce a globally uniform price for carbon. (In the absence of international trading, there is no reason to expect carbon price equivalency.)

This section describes three prototypical (or stylized) ways to achieve carbon price equivalency, examines criteria for choosing among them, and discusses the effects of nonparticipation, including exemptions for developing countries, under origin- and destination-based systems.

6.2.1 Three Globally Comprehensive Harmonized Systems for Pricing Carbon

In the three prototypical systems for pricing carbon, the price is imposed on the *severance* of fossil fuels, on the *emission* of CO_2, or on the *consumption* of embedded carbon. (The same country could, of course, be the source of fuel, the origin of emissions, and/or the destination of embedded carbon.) For reasons described in this section, the community of nations is not likely to choose the first and it may not be cost-effective to implement either of the others – especially a destination-based system – in their pure forms.

- In a *severance-based system*, countries where fossil fuels come out of the ground (i.e., where coal mines and gas and oil wells are located) would require payment of taxes or royalties for permission to extract

Table 6.3. *Comprehensive harmonized systems for taxing carbon, based on the severance of fossil fuels, the origin of CO_2 emissions, and the consumption of embedded carbon*

Economic activity	Basis for taxation		
	Severance of fuel	Emissions of CO_2/ combustion of fuel (Origin/emissions)	Consumption of "carbon" (fuel and embedded carbon) (Destination/ consumption)
	Taxation of carbon		
Severance of fuels	Taxed	Not applicable; taxed by source country	
Emission of CO_2/ combustion of fuel	Not applicable	Taxed, without BTAs for embedded carbon; see below	Taxed, with BTAs for embedded carbon; see below
	Treatment of international trade		
Import of fossil fuel	Not applicable	Taxed	
Export of fossil fuel	Not taxed as such; taxed at severance	Not taxed; rebates if taxed upon import	
BTAs for import of embedded carbon	Not applicable	No	Yes
BTAs for export of embedded carbon		No	Yes

the fuels. This is inherently an origin-based system, but one based on the *origin of fuels,* not the origin of emissions.

- In an *origin- (or emissions-) based system,* jurisdictions where CO_2 is emitted would impose a price on all combustion of carbon or on all emissions occurring on their territory. Because imported fuel would be subject to tax (or permits), but exported fuel would not be, it could be said that such fuels are subject to BAs.
- In a *destination- (or consumption-) based system,* jurisdictions where households consume embedded carbon (including electricity, residential heating oil, and motor fuel, as well as manufactured products and services) would levy taxes on (or require permits for) the consumption of embedded carbon occurring within their borders. Thus, BAs would be allowed for carbon taxes embedded in the prices of imports and exports, including imports and exports of fossils fuels.

Table 6.3 describes the crucial structural differences between these three systems.

6.2.2 Choosing among Globally Comprehensive Harmonized Systems

In thinking about the choice between the three systems described in the preceding section, it will be useful to distinguish between considerations that are invalid or irrelevant in the present context, those that are likely to be controlling, and others that should be kept in mind. The discussion of the first two sets of considerations assumes that the systems would be implemented as described, in particular, that there would be full participation and no cheating by countries.

Invalid or Irrelevant Considerations

Several arguments that may be offered in favor of the origin or the destination principle are either invalid or irrelevant in the present context of establishing a globally comprehensive harmonized system for pricing carbon. (They will be reexamined in the next section, in a context in which they are both valid and relevant.) For now the fact that revenues would be distributed very differently is ignored.

Economic Effects. Some may think that effects on production, employment, consumption, prices, mitigation of emissions, carbon leakage, or economic efficiency would be different under the three systems. This is, however, clearly wrong. Because the three approaches have identical impacts on the price of carbon, *the economic and environmental effects of a global harmonized system of pricing carbon do not depend on which approach is employed.*

Incidence. There may also be a tendency to think that the three ways of pricing carbon would have different effects on the distribution of income among people (commonly called *incidence* in the tax literature) – for example, that consumers would bear relatively more of the burden of a destination-based system and producers more of the burden of an origin-based system.[9] Again, this is false. Because the three systems affect prices identically, their incidence would be identical.

The "Polluter Pays" Principle. Finally, some may believe that the "polluter pays" principle points toward origin-based taxation, because the firms that

---

[9] For expositional convenience, the comparison in the text is limited to these two systems. Like other economic effects, the incidence of a severance-based tax would, of course, be the same as that of the other two systems. As emphasized below, the distribution of revenues is quite different under the three systems.

emit carbon are the ones doing the polluting and thus should pay. By comparison, others may believe that the principle dictates destination-based pricing, because pollution occurs on behalf of consumers of embedded carbon. In fact, the principle offers no guidance; no matter whether the tax is severance-, origin-, or destination-based, the same people ultimately "pay."

Controlling Considerations

The origin/emission-based system clearly dominates both the severance- and consumption-based systems, but for quite different reasons.

Distribution of Revenues. The distribution of revenues from carbon taxes (or the sale of emissions permits) among nations would be markedly different under the three alternatives. Under a severance-based system, revenues would flow to the members of OPEC, non-OPEC producers of oil and gas, and nations where coal is mined. Although included for completeness, this alternative does not seem to be relevant, as a practical matter. It is not likely that the community of nations would choose to encourage and facilitate the expansion and strengthening of the OPEC cartel as a way to slow global warming. The discussion in the remainder of this chapter thus focuses on origin- and destination-based systems, including systems that are neither comprehensive nor pure.

The choice between these two systems also has implications for the distribution of revenues. Under a destination-based carbon *tax,* the distribution of revenues among nations is determined by the distribution of consumption, under an origin-based system by the distribution of emissions.[10] Because developed countries are responsible for more consumption of carbon than for carbon emissions, more of the revenues would flow to them under a destination-based system than under an origin-based system.

By comparison, under a *cap-and-trade system* with international trading of permits, the distribution of revenues would be determined by the distribution of authority to issue permits, but it would probably resemble the distribution of tax revenues. In any event, compared to differences in costs of compliance and administration, the distribution of revenues is likely to be a

---

[10] In principle, international revenue sharing, side payments, or even a supranational taxing (or cap and trade) authority could exist. Those possibilities are not considered here, as they are secondary to the present purpose of examining international trade regimes for pricing carbon. See, however, Seidman and Lewis (2009).

secondary consideration in the choice between comprehensive harmonized origin- and destination-based systems.

Costs of Compliance and Administration. Of the three prototypical systems for pricing carbon, the severance-based system would almost certainly be the simplest to implement. Countries where fuels originate could impose a price on the carbon content of fossil fuels as the fuels come out of the ground (e.g., at the wellhead in the case of oil and gas and at the mine mouth in the case of coal) or at various "choke points" (e.g., at gas processing plants or refineries or at export) (see Metcalf and Weisbach 2009, pp. 522–527). Even so, this system is unlikely to be chosen.

The origin-based system would require monitoring of either combustion of carbon (most easily achieved by monitoring domestic production, imports, and exports of fossil fuels) or the amount of CO_2 emissions. It would be the next easiest to implement, especially if imposed upstream, rather than on the emission of CO_2.[11]

Implementation would be particularly difficult in the case of a globally comprehensive destination-based system. In addition to the administrative and compliance requirements of an origin-based system, destination-based carbon pricing would require knowing the embedded carbon content of all non-fuel exports and imports, in order to calculate the appropriate BAs. As explained in Section 6.4, this would be an overwhelming task. It would be senseless to incur these costs, because the same environmental effects could be achieved under an origin-based system. (Moreover, it might be necessary to renegotiate the rules of international trade, but that would presumably occur if there were an international consensus to adopt this approach.)

To reduce costs of compliance and administration and thereby increase cost-effectiveness, it is virtually certain that carbon pricing would be subject to limits, even if imposed on a globally comprehensive and harmonized manner. This is especially true under a destination-based system. For example, carbon pricing might be limited to certain sectors and not extend

---

[11] Emissions could not be measured by the amount of fuel purchased in those instances in which CO_2 is captured and sequestered or in which carbon is incorporated in products, as in the case of chemicals, rubber, plastic, steel, and asphalt. Given the variation of the carbon content of fuels, especially coal, it may be easier and cheaper, for a given level of accuracy, to measure emissions than to measure the carbon content of fuel inputs used by particular installations. But it may be easier and cheaper still to measure the carbon content of fuels upstream.

beyond certain points in the production-distribution chain. Moreover, BAs would probably be limited to carbon- and trade-intensive products (see Section 6.4).

Other Considerations

As in many cases in which globally comprehensive harmonized systems are preferable from the viewpoint of society, there would be incentives for countries not to participate in the systems described and to cheat. The incentives would be different under the various systems.

Incentives for Nonparticipation. The benefits of not participating in an origin-based system – the world of the Kyoto Protocol – are increased competitiveness for domestic firms in energy-intensive sectors. The cost of nonparticipation that is internalized by the nonparticipating country (in contrast to the unfair competition that is experienced elsewhere and the damage to the environment associated with carbon leakage) would be the foregone revenues from taxation or the sale of permits. However, nonparticipation could generate substantially increased revenues from other sources, including greater income tax receipts. The trade-off between costs and benefits would depend on the shapes of the supply and demand curves for products that embody carbon. Given that the demand curve for the carbon-intensive products of a single country is likely to be highly elastic, the net incentives for nonparticipation may be substantial – a conclusion that is borne out by experience in negotiating the Kyoto Protocol and in the Copenhagen negotiations.

Nonparticipation in a destination-based system reduces the prices consumers in nonparticipating countries pay for carbon-intensive products. As with an origin-based system, weighing against tendencies not to participate (or to cheat) is the possibility that pricing carbon may be the most attractive means for a country, especially a developing one, to raise revenue. However, implementing a destination-based system is likely to be especially difficult for developing countries. Perhaps the strongest motivation for nonparticipation in a destination-based system is the desire to maintain the status quo.

Incentives to Cheat. There would also be incentives for countries (as well as for firms) to cheat under all three systems; indeed, these incentives and their effects would resemble those for nonparticipation. Under origin- and destination-based systems, cheating would take the form of lax administration – undercharging for the emission or consumption of CO_2.[12]

Like undercharging under an origin-based system, excessive BAs under a destination-based system (i.e., excessive charges for carbon embedded in imports and excessive rebates for carbon embedded in exports) would artificially increase the competitiveness of producers in the cheating nation and induce carbon leakage into the cheating nation. This is one of the concerns that have been expressed about allowing BAs for carbon prices.

6.2.3 Effects of Nonparticipation in a Less than Globally Comprehensive Destination-Based System

In negotiations leading up to the Kyoto Protocol, developing countries argued successfully that they should not be required to reduce emissions, because developed countries are responsible for the vast majority of the current overhang of CO_2 in the atmosphere and because reducing CO_2 emission would seriously undermine their opportunities to develop and achieve a higher standard of living. Moreover, the United States refused to sign the protocol, because of the fear of loss of competitiveness to exempted developing countries. This section discusses the implications of nonparticipation in a destination-based system, focusing on the exemption of developing countries.

The implications of exemptions for developing countries under an otherwise globally harmonized destination-based system of pricing carbon are quite different from those under a similarly harmonized origin-based system. (In this context, *exemption* is interpreted to mean that developing countries would not be required to price carbon embedded in production for the domestic market or in imports. It does not mean that developed countries would not apply BAs to imports from developing countries. In short, consumption in developing countries would benefit from the exemption, but production for export would not.) China, India, and other developing countries would not be able to emit CO_2 with impunity, without fear of undermining the competitiveness of their energy-intensive industries, as

---

[12] A problem related to cheating is the provision of subsidies, including tax exemptions, that offset the intended effects of carbon pricing, for example, in an origin-based system imposed by countries where emissions occur. Given the plethora of taxes and subsidies that impinge on the production and combustion of carbon and the consumption of carbon embedded in non-fuel products, it may be difficult to agree on the baseline for the measurement of compliance with any system.

Table 6.4. *Pricing of consumption of carbon, under origin- and destination-based treatment of international trade, with and without exemptions for developing countries*

	Origin-based system		Destination-based system	
	No	Yes	No	Yes
Exemptions for developing countries?	(1)	(2)	(3)	(4)
Pricing of carbon embedded in consumption in developed countries				
Domestic products	Yes	Yes	Yes	Yes
Imports from other developed countries	Yes: X	Yes: X	Yes: M	Yes: M
Imports from developing countries	Yes: X	**No**	Yes: M	Yes: M
Pricing of carbon embedded in consumption in developing countries				
Domestic products	Yes	**No**	Yes	**No**
Imports from developed countries	Yes: X	Yes: X	Yes: M	**No**
Imports from other developing countries	Yes: X	**No**	Yes: M	**No**

"Yes: M" and "Yes: X" mean that embedded carbon is priced in the importing or exporting country, respectively. Bold type indicates implications of exemptions for developing countries.

their exports to developed countries would be subject to BAs. On the other hand, their imports from developed countries would not be burdened with carbon prices, as they would under either a comprehensive destination-based system or an origin-based system.

Table 6.4 shows the results of exemptions for developing countries under otherwise harmonized origin- and destination-based systems. The first and third columns show that if there are no exemptions for developing countries, consumption of carbon is priced in both developed and developing countries under both origin-and destination-based pricing systems; the only issue (assuming a harmonized carbon price) is whether the country of origin or of destination receives the revenues. In an origin-based system in which developing countries are exempt from the requirement to curb emissions, as in the second column, consumption of carbon is priced in developed countries if it is embedded in domestic products or imports from other developed countries, but not (as indicated in bold) if it is embedded in imports from developing countries. On the other hand, carbon consumed in developing countries is priced if it is embedded in imports from developed countries, but not if it is embedded in domestic products or imports from other developing countries (also indicated in bold). This column illustrates the competitiveness concerns and the potential for carbon leakage inherent in this system. Finally, the fourth column shows that exemption of developing countries under a destination-based system does not distort the choice of where to produce, as all carbon embedded in consumption in a given country is treated the same, whether in a developed country (where it is taxed) or in a developing country (exempt, shown in bold), whether production occurs domestically, in other developing countries, or in developed countries.

Much has been made of the role that BAs, the topic of this chapter, might play in leveling the competitive playing field, preventing carbon leakage, and reducing the incentive for free riding. Table 6.4 helps to highlight a glaring limitation that is inherent in an attempt to use BAs to achieve the more ambitious and arguably much more important goal of reducing global emissions of CO_2. Under either origin- or destination-based pricing of carbon, combustion of fossil fuels or emission of CO_2 related to production for domestic consumption in developing countries would be taxed or subject to permits, as long as such countries are not exempt. On the other hand, if these countries are exempt, carbon combusted or released in production for domestic markets would not be priced, regardless of which system is chosen. Given the overwhelming relative importance of production for domestic consumption in even the most export-driven developing country, this suggests that BAs are not likely to be very effective in reducing global emissions. Either developing countries must not be exempted or alternative techniques must be found to induce them to reduce emissions of CO_2. Examining the efficacy of such techniques is well beyond the scope of this chapter.

6.2.4 Economic Efficiency, Incidence, and "Polluter Pays" Reconsidered

Once it is recognized that participation may not be universal, it is necessary to reconsider economic efficiency, incidence, and the "polluter pays" principle, issues that were argued in the preceding section to be irrelevant under a globally comprehensive harmonized system. Indeed, the first two issues have already been considered implicitly in the discussions of nonparticipation and exemptions for developing countries and need not be discussed much further, beyond the following observations. Destination-based pricing of carbon has clear advantages over origin-based pricing from the point of economic efficiency in a world of less than universal participation. This consideration is, however, likely to be outweighed by the difficulties of implementing a destination-based system.

Incidence. If an origin-based system for pricing carbon is not universally applied, whether producers of products containing embedded carbon can recover the cost of carbon pricing from customers depends on conditions of supply and demand, especially the elasticity of demand. Because demand for the products of a particular country is generally likely to be rather elastic, the possibilities of shifting the cost of carbon pricing forward are limited; thus, owners, employees (via lower wages or lower employment), and suppliers of the polluting firm, and not those who consume embedded carbon, are likely to bear the burden of a geographically limited origin-based carbon-pricing system.

The situation is quite different in the case of a geographically limited destination-based system for pricing carbon. Because the supply curve facing consumers in a given country tends to be quite flat, the burden of a destination-based system is likely to be borne by those who consume the embedded carbon. Even if the aggregate burden on residents of a participating country is as great under a destination-based system as under an origin-based system, burdens are less concentrated. Fear of concentrated burdens under origin-based carbon pricing underlies concerns about lost competitiveness.

"Polluter Pays" Principle. The "polluter pays" principle is not meaningless in the context of carbon pricing that is not globally comprehensive. Whether it implies origin- or destination-based pricing of carbon seems to boil down to a matter of philosophy and interpretation: Is it those who emit carbon or those who consume embedded carbon who should pay?

To gain insight, it may be useful to quote Principle 16 of the Rio Declaration on Environment and Development, which states, regarding internalization of environmental costs:

National authorities should endeavour to promote the internalization of environmental costs and the use of economic instruments, taking into account the approach that the polluter should, in principle, bear the cost of pollution, with due regard to the public interest and *without distorting international trade and investment* [emphasis added].

The first part of this statement seems consistent with either origin- or destination-based charging, because both internalize environmental costs of carbon emissions. However, only destination-based charging satisfies the italicized requirement.

6.2.5 Summary Appraisal of Options

Because of the concentration of revenues in nations in which fossil fuels are produced, severance-based pricing of carbon does not deserve – and is not likely to receive – serious consideration. Of the remaining two options, if carbon pricing is not universal, destination-based pricing seems preferable to origin-based pricing on economic grounds. It avoids adverse effects on competitiveness and economic efficiency, it is arguably better suited to implement the "polluter pays" principle, it is likely less vulnerable to cheating and nonparticipation, it better tolerates exemptions for developing countries, and carbon leakage and incentives for free riding are less pernicious. It does, however, raise crucial – and perhaps controlling – questions of implementation and compatibility with international trade law. These questions are considered in Sections 6.4 and 6.5.

6.3 Achieving Destination-Based Carbon Pricing in an Origin-Based World

Origin- and destination-based systems of pricing carbon differ enormously in their complexity. Section 6.4 shows that the BAs required to implement the destination principle accurately on all the trade of a participating country would be extremely difficult, if not impossible, to calculate. It thus seems appropriate, as well as likely, that origin-based carbon prices will be the primary market-based instruments of choice in the battle against greenhouse gases. However, it is neither appropriate nor likely that countries that adopt origin-based systems will eschew measures to combat what they see as unfair competition from, carbon leakage to, and free riding by countries that do not take measures to reduce carbon emissions. This section describes two ways countries concerned with competitiveness, carbon leakage, or free riding – or merely seeking negotiating leverage – could, in principle, implement destination-based charging in a world of origin-based charges. (For expositional convenience, carbon pricing is the only means of controlling carbon that is considered. It is assumed initially that the carbon intensity of production is the same in all countries and that all participating countries impose the same price on carbon. Given this simplifying assumption, the only question is whether carbon pricing is imposed by the country of origin or that of destination.)

6.3.1 A "Mixed" Origin/Destination System

Under the mixed system, trade with countries that have "comparable" systems for pricing carbon would be origin-based and thus not subject to BAs. By comparison, imports from other countries would be destination-based, and thus subject to adjustments. Exports to these countries would also be subject to BAs under the symmetrical mixed system described in this section, but not under an asymmetrical system. Of course, carbon embedded in trade between countries that do not price carbon would go unpriced. (It is assumed for now that trade falls neatly into these boxes – that it does not contain components originating in both countries that price carbon and those that do not. This issue is discussed further in Section 6.4.)

This system could be applied broadly or narrowly, to only specific carbon-intensive products. The Waxman-Markey bill passed by the U.S House of Representatives in June 2009 contains a list of covered industries. Moreover, a country might be treated differently for different products. Thus, BAs would presumably apply only if the trading partner did not apply carbon pricing to the sector in question. Similarly, if the United States were to adopt a system with broader coverage than the ETS, only U.S. imports from the EU that are subject to carbon pricing under ETS would be exempt from BAs in the United States.[13] Of course, countries would not make BAs for products containing embedded carbon not subject to pricing.

The third column of both Tables 6.1 and 6.2 describes a "mixed" system from the perspective of a particular country that prices carbon,[14] differentiating between a "symmetrical" system and an "asymmetrical" system. (To save space, Table 6.2 considers only carbon taxes. The analogous implications for a cap-and-trade system are obvious.)

Symmetrical and Asymmetrical Border Adjustments

There are several reasons to distinguish between symmetrical and asymmetrical mixed systems. First, as a practical matter, most attention in public

---

[13] In the first stage, the ETS caps on emissions apply only to energy activities (electric power, oil refineries, coke ovens), production and processing of ferrous metals (metal ore and steel), mineral industry (cement kilns, glass, ceramics), and industrial plants that produce paper and pulp.

[14] Border adjustments should, of course, be allowed for trade with countries that employ destination-based systems to price carbon; otherwise, carbon embedded in exports to such countries would be priced twice, and import from them would not be priced. It is thus assumed in what follows that BAs under a mixed system would be applied to such trade, as well as to trade with countries that do not price carbon. Because pure destination-based systems do not exist – and are not likely to be created – this qualification may be of little practical importance.

policy debates on BAs has focused on imports. Second, many believe that BAs for carbon prices would fail to pass muster under the basic rules of the GATT, that adjustments for imports could be saved, if at all, under one of the general exceptions provided under Article XX of the GATT, but that adjustments for exports could not be salvaged in this way (see Section 6.5). In short, an asymmetrical mixed system might be GATT legal, but a symmetrical system that included BAs for exports would not be. Third, BAs for exports would arguably impede the achievement of several of the policy objectives behind carbon pricing. This last argument is worth examining at the outset.

In the case of the VAT, the economic argument for BTAs for exports is as strong as that for import BTAs; both are needed to implement the destination principle and assure that VAT is applied to all consumption (including imports), and not to production for export. If importing countries choose not to impose a VAT, no issues of global public policy arise. This reasoning arguably does not carry over to BAs for carbon taxes.

Application of BAs to carbon embedded in imports from nonparticipating countries has the benefits posited, but, except for competitiveness benefits, the analogous conclusion does not hold for BAs on carbon embedded in exports to nonparticipating countries, which essentially allow exports to occur free of carbon prices. Border adjustments for imports prevent competitive effects, and thus carbon leakage, by leveling the playing field so that the same carbon price must be paid for imports as for domestic products. By comparison, allowing BAs for exports to nonparticipating countries levels the playing field by eliminating the carbon price embedded in exports. Although there may be no incentive for carbon leakage if BAs were applied to exports, there is also no incentive for exporting sectors to reduce domestic emissions of CO_2. Rather than reducing the incentive to be a free rider, BAs for exports increase such incentives, by putting competitive pressures on those producing for the domestic market in importing countries that do not price carbon. Finally, economic neutrality suffers, in that exports are favored over production for the domestic market of the country that prices carbon. For all these reasons, it may make sense to concentrate on BAs for imports. The last column of Table 6.2 describes the effects of symmetrical and asymmetrical BAs in a mixed system.

What Is a Comparable System?

If there is an otherwise uniform worldwide tax on carbon or international trading of emissions permits, in which a country either participates or does not, it is clear whether the country has a comparable system for pricing carbon. In other contexts it may be difficult to know in particular instances whether a country's system for pricing carbon is "comparable" to another's. How similar must carbon prices be for systems to be deemed comparable? Moreover, carbon pricing is not the only way to meet targets for emissions reductions; inter alia, regulations could be used. Examination of how comparability might be defined is beyond the scope of this chapter. It should be noted, however, that application of BAs to trade with countries that use non-price methods to reduce emissions may not pass muster under Article XX, as discussed in the following section.

6.3.2 Border Adjustments with Credit for Origin-Based Carbon Prices

The fourth column of Tables 6.1 and 6.2 shows another option. Under this option, the importing country would apply BAs to all imports, but allow credits on imports for taxes or the cost of permits incurred in the exporting country, up to the level of BA in the importing country.[15] (Exports could be either subject to BAs or not.) Exporting countries would have an incentive to impose origin-based carbon prices up to the level of carbon prices imposed by importing countries in order not to lose the revenue that would otherwise go to the importing country. Like the mixed system, this system could be applied broadly or narrowly.

This approach seems markedly inferior to the mixed system described in the preceding section, because it is significantly more complicated. It would require calculation of the amount of carbon embedded in imports from both participating and nonparticipating countries (needed to calculate both the before-credit BA on imports and the credit for the carbon price paid in the exporting country). By comparison, in the first instance, the mixed system described earlier would require only a determination of whether a particular trading partner has a comparable system for charging for CO_2 emissions related to a particular product. If so, the imports or exports in question are not subject to BA, and the investigation goes no further. Only in the case of trade (in a particular product) with a country that does not price carbon is it necessary to calculate and apply BAs. Although the burden of compliance and administration under the mixed system should not be underestimated, it would be far smaller than under a destination-based system with credits for origin-based carbon prices embedded in imports. This alternative deserves no further consideration.

---

[15] The analogy to the operation of foreign tax credits for income taxes should be obvious.

Table 6.5. *Transactions assumed in illustration of BTAS for VAT and turnover tax*

Purchasing sector	Fuel	Transport	Electricity	Aluminum	Automotive	Total
			Selling sector			
Transport	50					50
Electricity	100	50				150
Aluminum	50	50	200			300
Automotive	50	50		150		250
Consumers					300	300
Exports				200	100	300
Total	250	150	200	350	400	1350

6.4 Technical and Administrative Issues

At best, the technical and administrative challenges involved in implementing BAs for carbon prices would be daunting, as it would be necessary to determine the carbon content embedded in the cost of exports (so that carbon taxes or the cost of emissions permits could be rebated) and – even more challenging – of imports (so that carbon taxes or permit fees could be collected). These problems would be alleviated to the extent that the pricing of carbon is limited to a small number of energy-intensive sectors or that BAs are limited to carbon- and trade-intensive products.

This section uses a simple numerical example to contrast the simplicity of BTAs under a VAT and the difficulty of making accurate BTAs under either a turnover tax (called a prior-stage cumulative indirect tax in the ASCM) or a carbon tax. The analysis is equally applicable to a cap-and-trade system. Table 6.5 provides the basic transactions data assumed to underlie the example. It considers five productive activities: sales of refined fossil fuel, transportation, generation of electric power, production of aluminum, and automotive manufacturing, which can be considered a proxy for all manufactured goods that are either bought by households or exported. Several extreme assumptions are made to simplify the analysis and allow concentration on key issues. First, it is assumed that each sector makes sales only to purchasers listed below it in the table. Second, it is assumed that there are no exemptions under the VAT and the turnover tax (except for exports, in the latter case). Third, only the automotive sector makes sales to consumers, and only it and the aluminum sector export. Fourth, all refined fuel is assumed to be imported. Fifth, imports of fuel are not subject to VAT at the border; although this assumption is generally unrealistic, it has no ultimate effect and is made to simplify the presentation. By comparison, imported fuel is assumed to be subject to the turnover tax. Finally, it is assumed that units of carbon and the carbon tax rate are chosen so that the amount of carbon combusted in each sector and the tax thereon both equal the monetary value of fuels purchased by that sector. It should be emphasized that the numbers used in the example are not intended to reflect accurately the energy intensity of various activities or the importance of inputs to the various sectors.

Value-Added Tax. Table 6.6 describes the calculation of VAT in each sector, BTAs for VAT, turnover tax, and embedded carbon. The first three columns describe each sector's total sales, gross tax liabilities under a 10 percent VAT, and liabilities under a 2 percent turnover tax; the two taxes are assumed to be paid only on domestic sales, as under the destination principle. (These two tax rates would not necessarily yield the same amount of revenue; indeed, whether they would do so depends on the assumptions regarding BTAs for the turnover tax. That is not important for present purposes, which is to understand the mechanics of BTAs for the two taxes.) Significantly, no VAT is collected directly on exports of aluminum and automotive goods, which are zero-rated. Figures in the column for turnover tax will be discussed in the next section.

The fourth column shows total purchases subject to VAT and the breakdown thereof, according to the sector making the sales. The first entry reflects the assumption that the 250 of imports of fuel (shown in the first column) are not subject to VAT at the border. The fifth column shows the total amount of credit allowed for VAT on purchased inputs. The next two columns show value added, as calculated under the destination principle and subtraction method (the difference between domestic sales and purchases) and net VAT liability, as calculated under the credit method (the difference between tax on domestic sales and tax on purchases). Because exports of aluminum and automotive goods are zero-rated, credit is allowed for VAT on all purchased inputs. In the former case, because tax paid on purchases exceeds tax due on domestic sales, net VAT liability is negative, implying refund of some of the VAT paid on inputs. The entries for consumers and exports, enclosed in brackets to indicate that they are different in kind from the other numbers in the table, indicate that VAT paid by consumers exactly equals the VAT on domestic automotive

Table 6.6. Illustration of calculation of value-added tax, BTAs for VAT, turnover tax, and embedded carbon

Sector making sales	Sales; taxes			Purchases; VAT input credit		Value added; Net VAT		Carbon embedded in sales (8)
	Sales (1)	VAT on domestic sales (2)	Turnover tax on domestic sales (3)	Taxed purchases (4)	VAT input credit (5)	Value added (6)	Net VAT (7)	
Fossil fuel	250	25	5	0	0	250	25	50 (fuel)
Transport	150	15	3	50 (fuel)	5	100	10	117
Electricity	200	20	4	150 100 (fuel) 50 (trans)	15	50	5	100 (fuel) 17 (trans)
Aluminum	350	15	3	300 50 (fuel) 200 (elect) 50 (trans)	30	−150	−15	183 50 (fuel) 117 (elect) 17 (trans)
Automotive	400	30	6	250 50 (fuel) 50 (trans) 150 (alum)	25	50	5	145 50 (fuel) 17 (trans) 78 (alum)
Consumers				300 (auto)			[30]	109 (auto)
Exports				300 200 (alum) 100 (auto)			[0]	141 105 (alum) 36 (auto)
Total	1350	105			75	300	30	250

216

sales – the only sales to households – and that no net VAT is paid on exports.

Significantly, because of the way the input credit system works, it does not matter that fuel imports are assumed not to be taxed at the border; because there is no tax on purchases, there is no input credit, and all products sold to households for which fuel is an input bear the full 10 percent tax.[16] Of course, it is common for imports to be subject to tax – the import BTA, which is eligible for input credit.

Turnover Tax. It is extremely difficult to calculate accurate BTAs for a turnover tax, which is applied to gross receipts from domestic sales every time a product is sold, or "turns over" (and to imports but not exports). Tax paid by consumers includes turnover tax paid at earlier stages and embedded in the prices of automotive products – what are called *taxes occultes* (hidden taxes) in the literature on BTAs under the GATT – as well as the tax levied directly on those products. Accurate BTAs for imports of consumer goods would ideally reflect the cascading of turnover tax on domestic products. (Note that, in contrast to the analogous situation with regard to carbon taxes, there is no reason that BTAs on imports should differ from the amount of turnover tax paid on domestic products to reflect a different degree of foreign cascading.) This is not something that is readily known, although in this simple example it could be calculated from the information provided in Table 6.5.

Of course, cascading is not limited to products sold to consumers; turnover tax is also embedded in the prices of goods destined for export. Thus, it is not enough simply to exempt exports of aluminum and automotive products, as that would result in no compensation for turnover tax paid at prior stages of the production-distribution process – in this example, the tax on domestic sales of fuel, transport services, electricity, and aluminum. Nor is it sufficient to allow automotive producers BTAs only for turnover tax paid directly on purchases of aluminum, the only input that is physically incorporated in automotive products, as that would leave the tax embedded

---

[16] It is worth noting that, in theory, it would be possible to implement a sales tax as a retail sales tax (RST) – one levied only on sales to households. Thus, a 10 percent tax on the 300 of sales of automotive goods to households would yield the same amount of revenue as the 10 percent VAT. BTAs would not be necessary under an RST (except in the case of imports made directly by consumers, not considered here), because both imports and exports occur before the tax is levied at the retail stage. In fact, the RST is administratively inferior to the VAT, because of the need for retailers to distinguish between exempt sales to registered traders and taxable sales to households and for administrators to monitor this aspect of compliance.

in the cost of other inputs uncompensated. Given the importance of electricity used to produce aluminum, it would be desirable at least to allow for turnover tax paid on electricity in calculating BTAs for exports of aluminum and perhaps those for automotive products made from aluminum; however, this would leave uncompensated the turnover tax paid on imports of fossil fuels and transportation. Unless BTAs reflect all embedded turnover taxes, exports will not occur tax-free, as under the VAT.

The relative ease of tracing embedded turnover taxes through to sales to consumers and to exports in this simple example belies the difficulty of calculating BTAs that would exactly eliminate the tax embedded in exports and impose on imports the same burden borne by domestic products. The calculation would be rendered substantially more difficult by the inclusion of more sectors selling taxed inputs and more stages in the production-distribution process. Moreover, the real world does not obey the simplifying assumption that sales are made only to purchasers further down the list in Table 6.5, which implies, inter alia, that the transportation sector does not purchase any of the output of the automotive sector, that the electric power sector does not purchase anything made of aluminum, and so on. Of course, at the level of aggregation in this example, this complication could be handled by the straightforward application of input-output analysis. In the real world, however, GATT-legal BTAs cannot be applied to sectors; they must be applied to individual products (e.g., to automobiles, trucks, and various types of spare parts, rather than "automotive" products) – a level of disaggregation well beyond even the most sophisticated input-output analysis. The difficulty of calculating accurate BTAs for turnover taxes is one of the reasons that the six member states of the European Common Market, the forerunner of the EU, decided in the early 1960s to shift to the VAT.

Carbon Tax. Table 6.7 illustrates the difficulty of calculating accurate BTAs for a carbon tax, which resembles in some ways that of calculating BTAs for turnover taxes and stands in sharp contrast to the ease of BTAs under the VAT (and the fact that BTAs are not required under a retail sales tax).[17] As noted earlier, it is assumed that the amount of carbon combusted in each sector (shown in the first column) and the tax thereon both equal the monetary value of fuels purchased by that sector (shown in the first

---

[17] McLure (forthcoming) analyzes, and finds wanting, proposals to overcome this difficulty by using a "carbon added tax" patterned after the credit-method VAT.

Table 6.7. *Illustration of calculation of embedded carbon*

| | Direct | First level: Tax on combusted fuel embedded in cost of: | | | | Second level: First-level indirect cost of carbon tax embedded in: | | | | | Third level: Second-level indirect cost of fuel embedded in: | | | Fourth level | Total |
| | | | | | | Cost of transport embedded in cost of: | | | Cost of electricity embedded in cost of: | Cost of aluminum embedded in cost of: | Transport cost embedded in electricity cost embedded in: | Transport cost embedded in aluminum cost embedded in: | Electricity cost embedded in aluminum costs in: | Transport costs in electricity costs in aluminum costs in: | |
		Tran	Elec	Alum	Auto	Elec	Alum	Auto	Alum	Auto	Alum	Auto	Auto	Auto	Total
Trans	50														50
Elect	100	16.7													116.7
Alum	50	16.7	100			16.7									183.3
Auto	50	16.7		21.4			7.1								145.2
Cons					37.5			12.5	42.9	16.1	7.1	5.4	32.1	5.4	108.9
Exp				28.6	12.5		9.5	4.2	57.1	5.4	9.5	1.8	10.7	1.8	141.1
Total	250	50	100	50	50	16.7	9.5	16.7	100	21.4	16.7	7.1	42.9	7.1	250

column of Table 6.5). In this example, it does not matter whether carbon pricing is achieved through a tax paid on (the carbon content of) imported fuel, on purchases of fuel, or on CO_2 emissions. Moreover, the same analysis would be applicable to the cost of emissions permits.

As with the turnover tax, the cost of the carbon tax paid initially by the transport and electricity sectors are embedded in the cost of aluminum, and the tax embedded in the costs of those three sectors are embedded in the cost of the automotive sector. The problem, then, is to calculate BTAs for exports of aluminum and automotive products that would relieve exports of the cost of carbon taxes, including those embedded in the cost of inputs. It is not adequate to allow BTAs only for carbon taxes paid directly, to the neglect of embedded taxes.

The "direct" costs of the carbon tax on fuel are shown in the first column. "Indirect" costs of the tax embedded in the prices of non-fuel products and total (direct and indirect costs) are shown in the remainder of the table. (The preceding terminology is based on the assumption that the carbon tax is imposed on the purchase or combustion of fuel or on emissions of CO_2; if, instead, the tax were paid at import it would be embedded in the cost of fuel.) Thus, the second set of columns allocates the "first-level indirect costs" of carbon tax initially borne by each sector among the other sectors buying its products, consumers, and exports. Of course, as shown in the third set of columns, except where the tax is embedded in sales to consumers and exports, there are "second-level indirect costs" of the tax; for example, the cost to the tax on fuel used to produce electric power is embedded in the cost of aluminum, which is either sold to the automotive industry or exported. By the same token there are third- and fourth-level indirect costs. (In the latter case, the chain of embedded costs is from fuel to transportation, to aluminum, to automotive, to consumer sales and exports.) The last column of Table 6.6 summarizes these calculations, with prior indirect effects being consolidated and traced through to the point that they are embedded in the cost of the sectors listed.

The bottom three entries in the "total" column indicate the ultimate allocation of direct and indirect costs among consumer sales and exports. The objective of export BTAs is to rebate the entire amount of carbon tax embedded in the price of exports, but, as with turnover taxes, calculating the appropriate rebate is a formidable task. Not only are many of the same problems encountered; there are additional ones. (At least it is not necessary to take account of the degree of cascading, as multiple taxation of the same carbon does not occur under a well-structured carbon tax.) For example, if (contrary to the assumptions underlying this example) electricity is produced using both carbon-intensive and "clean" technologies, but sold at a uniform price, producers of aluminum have an incentive to use (or claim that they use) electricity generated in the carbon-intensive manner to produce exports, in order to maximize export rebates. There is no analogous problem in the VAT. Of course, under the asymmetrical system described earlier, which does not include export BTAs, these problems would not arise.

The calculation of import BTAs would be even more problematic, as it should reflect the carbon content of production in the exporting country. Obtaining the requisite information may be extremely difficult, especially in developing countries. Compounding the difficulty is the fact that imports, including those from countries that price carbon, may contain components produced in several countries, including the importing country. It would be necessary to have rules of origin and methodologies for calculating the appropriate BTAs in such cases.[18] (Analogous problems would occur on the export side. No similar issues arise under the VAT or the turnover tax, as BTAs do not depend on the taxation in the country of origin.) Finally, the two methodologies for calculating import BTAs that are assumed to be legally "fail-safe" – predominant method of production in the importing country and best available technology – would presumably need to be applied at each stage of the production-distribution process to calculate the acceptable level of import BTAs, further greatly complicating the calculation. These methodologies are discussed in Section 6.5.6.

Limiting BAs. The difficulty of making accurate BAs suggests that, as a practical matter, the effort to do so is likely to be limited in several ways. First, BAs are likely to be applied only in the most energy- and trade-intensive sectors (e.g., aluminum, iron and steel products, pulp and paper, and chemicals).[19] This might be called the *sectoral breadth* of BAs. Second, whereas combustion of carbon directly related to production would almost

---

[18] Ismer and Neuhoff (2007, p. 152) raise the specter of re-export by countries that price carbon of products originating in countries that do not, perhaps after enough modification to satisfy rules of origin, and the need for antiabuse rules. Cosbey (2008, p. 5) provides examples of possible diversion of trade through countries that price carbon.

[19] The Waxman-Markey bill foresees the possibility that importers of energy-intensive and trade-sensitive goods such as chemicals, iron and steel, cement, glass, lime, some pulp and paper products, and nonferrous metals such as aluminum and copper might be required to purchase "international reserve allowances." The earlier Warner-Lieberman bill contained similar provisions.

certainly be considered in calculating BAs, energy combusted for most other purposes (e.g., in heating offices and perhaps even transportation) probably would not be. This could be described as limiting the *intrasectoral breadth* of BAs. Third, although some indirect effects (most prominently, the pricing of carbon combusted in generating power used by the aluminum industry), as well as direct effects, might be considered, it seems highly unlikely that compensation for higher-order indirect effects, which would involve an expansion of the sectoral breadth of BAs, would be attempted. This could be described as a limit on the *vertical depth* of BAs. It is illustrated by the question of whether to provide BTAs for taxes on energy used in transporting inputs and outputs of the trading sector, including energy itself, but not for taxes on energy used to transport inputs of suppliers of that sector.

The upshot of such limitations is that BAs are likely to fall short of those theoretically needed to maintain competitive balance and prevent carbon leakage. How important this is, as a practical matter, depends on the coverage of the carbon pricing for which BAs are sought, as well as the breadth and depth of BAs. If carbon taxes (or their equivalents) are imposed only on the same sectors for which BAs are allowed, and BAs are allowed for a high percentage of the total direct and indirect costs of carbon pricing in those sectors, these differences would be relatively insignificant. If, on the other hand, the application of carbon taxes was substantially broader than that of BAs or if BAs were allowed for only a relatively small share of total costs of carbon pricing in the sectors where applied, the effects would be more serious.

6.5 The GATT Legality of BAs

Under the GATT and the ASCM – the multilateral treaties that specify the rules for international trade of most relevance for present purposes – BAs are allowed for only certain types of taxes. The World Trade Organization (WTO) oversees compliance with the GATT and the ASCM. Even if the WTO finds that a measure contravenes the basic or substantive trade rules, it may find that it qualifies for one of the general exceptions provided by Article XX of the GATT. Unfortunately, as the Organisation for Economic Co-operation and Development (2006, p. 92) has stated, and many others have confirmed, "The application of BTAs to energy taxes under the GATT/WHO rules is clouded with uncertainty." Whether the WTO would allow BAs for the cost of emissions permits is even less certain, especially if permits are distributed free of charge or bought on the secondary market.

This section examines the GATT legality of BAs for both carbon taxes and the cost of emissions permits under a cap-and-trade system.[20] Because the GATT rules were formulated to deal with border *tax* adjustments – albeit not with BTAs for carbon (or other environmental) taxes, BTAs for carbon taxes are examined first, and in greatest detail.

There are many subsidiary questions within the overarching question that is the focus of this section. Among them are whether the same rules apply to BAs for imports and exports; whether carbon taxes are direct taxes; whether carbon taxes are "prior-stage cumulative indirect taxes," a concept to be explained later; whether carbon taxes are levied on *products*; whether they are levied on *like* products; whether BTAs for carbon taxes would qualify for one of the general exceptions of GATT Article XX, even if found to violate the basic GATT/ASCM rules – a question that has still further questions nested within it; whether the legality of BAs for the cost of auctioned emissions permits can be deduced from conclusions regarding the legality of BTAs for carbon taxes; and whether BAs would be allowed for entities that have not purchased permits from a government.

6.5.1 Rules for Imports and Exports

Although economists may think of BAs as a package that should be applied symmetrically to imports and exports, as they commonly are in the case of the VAT, that is not the way they are treated in WTO law and the literature thereon. Moreover, and perhaps of vital importance, it seems unlikely that an Article XX exception would be allowed for export BAs, even if one is available for import BAs.

The basic GATT rules that determine the GATT legality of BAs for imports are those that specify national treatment and most-favored-nation treatment. Under the first, imports cannot be taxed more heavily than like domestic products; under the second, discriminatory treatment of imports from different GATT signatories is outlawed. The rules that are relevant for exports are primarily those in the GATT and the ASCM pertaining to subsidies, which treat exemption from, and rebate of, taxes in excess of those borne by like products as an export subsidy. Demaret and Stewardson (1994, p. 30) summarize the situation: "GATT contains different provisions,

---

[20] The discussion of this section is based on McLure (2010a), which provides a much more detailed and nuanced discussion, as well as references to much of the voluminous literature on this topic. See also, inter alia, Hufbauer, Charnowitz, and Kim (2009).

formulated differently, in respect of imports and exports, and no explicit statement as to whether those respective provisions should be implemented in symmetric fashion."

One of the keys to gaining an exception under Article XX of the GATT is that a trade measure must either be necessary to the protection of health or relate to the conservation of exhaustible natural resources. As explained in the following section, given the likely economic effects of BAs for exports described earlier, it seems unlikely that an exception for export BAs would be forthcoming. This compounds the case for treating BAs for imports and exports differently and is one of the reasons for considering asymmetrical BAs under the mixed system examined earlier.

6.5.2 The Nature of Carbon Taxes

Before turning to the crucial question of whether carbon taxes are levied on "like products," for which the answer is unclear and controversial, it will be useful to dispose of two others that arguably have clear answers. First, are carbon taxes direct taxes, for which BTAs are per se not allowed? If not, are they prior-stage cumulative indirect (PSCI) taxes, for which the GATT explicitly allows BTAs?

The GATT does not provide a satisfactory answer to the first question. It merely states that BTAs are allowed for taxes "in respect to like domestic products," leaving to be inferred the type of taxes for which BTAs are not allowed. By comparison, the ASCM states explicitly that BTAs are allowed for indirect taxes, but not for direct taxes, and includes a definition of direct taxes that most tax experts would recognize ("...taxes on wages, profits ... and other forms of income ..."). Although the view is not unanimous, the preponderance of opinion seems to be that carbon taxes are not direct taxes and that BTAs for them are thus not per se illegal.

The ASCM provides specifically that BTAs are allowed for PSCI taxes on inputs consumed in production, including explicitly energy, fuels, and oils. Some believe that this means that BTAs would be allowed for carbon taxes, but this view seems to be based on a misunderstanding of the nature of PSCI taxes. Coined at a time that countries were beginning to adopt VATs, for which BTAs were explicitly allowed, the term *prior-stage cumulative indirect taxes* was intended to describe the turnover (gross receipts) taxes that still existed in some countries. The rule regarding the legality of PSCI taxes thus seems to be irrelevant in the present context.

6.5.3 Are Carbon Taxes Levied on "Like Products"?

Whether carbon taxes are levied on "like products" involves three inter-related issues: whether such taxes are levied on products, rather than on process and production methods (PPMs); whether taxes based on PPMs are adjustable; and whether differences in carbon intensity make products unlike, so that BTAs on imports can exceed the carbon tax paid on production of otherwise identical products for the domestic market.

Products versus PPMs

The GATT refers to taxes that are "applied, directly or indirectly, to like domestic products." Carbon taxes levied directly on fossil fuels are thus clearly adjustable, as are taxes on inputs that are physically incorporated in traded goods. But what about carbon taxes embedded in the prices of products? Carbon that is emitted is clearly not incorporated in products. In earlier discussions of the legality of BTAs, indirect taxes not levied directly on products or inputs physically incorporated therein were called "taxes occultes" (hidden taxes). Now they are commonly described as relating to PPMs, rather than being levied on products.

BTAs Based on PPMs

Although opinions on the adjustability of taxes related to PPMs are divided, the WTO (2004, p. 21) makes the following nearly categorical statement:

Under existing GATT rules and jurisprudence, "product" taxes and charges can be adjusted at the border, but "process" taxes and charges by and large cannot. For example, ... tax on the energy consumed in producing a ton of steel cannot be applied to imported steel.

Whether this view would prevail if BTAs for a carbon tax were challenged is unclear. In the *Superfund* case, a WTO panel sustained the legality of BTAs for imported chemicals intended to compensate for the domestic U.S. tax on feedstocks used in the domestic production of such chemicals. Unfortunately, the panel did not indicate whether the feedstocks were physically incorporated in the domestically produced chemicals or whether it mattered – issues that could be crucial for the appraisal of the legality of BTAs for carbon taxes. (If the feedstocks were not physically incorporated, it could be argued that the domestic U.S. tax for which the BTAs compensated was based on PPMs.)

The BTAs that accompanied the U.S. tax on ozone-depleting chemicals (ODCs) was clearly based on PPMs, as they were imposed on products manufactured with ODCs, but not containing them, as well as imports of ODCs and products incorporating them. That these BTAs have never been challenged before the WTO leads some to believe that BTAs for PPMs would be found GATT legal, but there is no way of knowing how the WTO would have ruled, had it been asked to decide the legality of the BTAs for the ODC tax.

What many believe to be the most relevant WTO case did not even involve taxes. In the *Shrimp-Turtle* case, the WTO Appellate Body ruled that the United States could restrict imports of shrimp caught using nets that lacked turtle-exclusion devices. Although this case involved an Article XX exception, it has been interpreted as suggesting that the WTO might sustain BTAs based on PPMs under the basic GATT rules, as well as under Article XX. It should be noted, however, that WTO decisions are not governed by *stare decisis*.

Energy Intensity and "Like Products"

If BTAs for carbon taxes are to level the playing field between imports and domestic goods, they must reflect the energy intensity of imports; but BTAs cannot exceed the tax on "like" domestic products. This raises the question of whether physically identical products are "like," if they differ in energy intensity. If they are "like," BTAs cannot be based on the energy intensity of imports.

"Likeness" involves the competitive relationship between products. Because identical products generally are competitive, they seem likely to be found to be "like." Although the WTO Appellate Body has found that likeness may depend on consumers' tastes and habits, as well as the product's end-use, properties, nature, quality, and tariff classification, this qualification is not likely to matter much for the industrial inputs that figure most prominently in the debate over BAs for carbon prices, including steel, aluminum, wood and paper, and chemicals.

Although the aforementioned considerations would almost certainly be important for appraising the GATT legality of BTAs under the basic rules (national treatment and most-favored-nation treatment), it is unclear whether they would be dispositive with regards to an Article XX exception.

6.5.4 Mixed Systems and Most-Favored-Nation Treatment

Whether BTAs would pass muster under the national treatment and subsidy provisions of the GATT and the ASCM, is unclear. On the other hand, it seems virtually certain that a mixed system that applied BTAs only to imports from countries that are not pricing carbon (and perhaps exports to such countries) would be found to violate the most-favored-nation clause of the GATT.

6.5.5 The Article XX Exceptions

If one assumes that the preceding analysis is correct, could BTAs for carbon taxes, including those under a mixed system, be rescued by the general exceptions of Article XX, which come into play only if the basic rules are violated? The answer involves passing a two-tier test to be applied sequentially: first, consistency with one of the general exceptions, and then acceptability under the chapeau (headnote), which is concerned with how a measure is applied and is intended to balance the rights and duties of the nation seeking the exception and of those protesting the measure in question.

The Article XX exceptions that are most relevant are those for measures

(b) necessary to protect human, animal or plant life or health; or

(g) relating to the conservation of exhaustible natural resources if such measures are made effective in conjunction with restrictions on domestic production or consumption.

Although some believe that BTAs for carbon taxes would qualify under paragraph (b), the more common belief is that qualification under paragraph (g) is more likely.

Based on the decision of the WTO Appellate Body in the *Shrimp-Turtle* case, it is reasonable to believe that BTAs for imports would be found to satisfy paragraph (g), as they relate directly to conservation of the atmosphere, which the Appellate Body has previously determined to be an exhaustible natural resource, and would be implemented in conjunction with a domestic carbon tax. Significantly, the Appellate Body stated in the *Shrimp-Turtle* decision that the words "conservation of exhaustible natural resources" in exception (g) of Article XX must be read "in light of contemporary concerns of the community of nations about the protection and conservation of the environment." The United Nations Framework Convention on Climate Change (UNFCCC) and the Kyoto Protocol reflect such concerns. By comparison, it seems difficult to argue that BTAs for exports would relate to conservation of clean air, as they effectively remove a disincentive for emission of CO_2. It is thus assumed in what follows that export BTAs for carbon taxes would not be allowed.

It is not enough for a measure to satisfy paragraph (b) or (g); it must also satisfy the chapeau, which requires that the measure in question not be "... applied in a manner which would constitute a means of arbitrary or unjustifiable discrimination between countries where the same conditions prevail, or a disguised restriction on international trade...."

Border tax adjustments on imports from countries that employ origin-based carbon taxes (or other means to reduce emissions) arguably would not be allowed, as that would entail double taxation (or its functional equivalent). On the other hand, developed countries might well be allowed to impose BTAs on imports from "renegade" developed countries that do not adopt such policies (e.g., the United States), as in the mixed system. Qualifying this conclusion is the need to have engaged in good-faith negotiations (such as those preceding and following the adoption of the Kyoto Protocol) and respect for due process and fairness.

The legality of BTAs imposed on imports from developing countries seems to be less certain. Developed countries would contend that BTAs should be allowed because the same conditions – the lack of carbon pricing, as well as the state of development – do not prevail in developing countries. Perhaps more important, developing countries could note the logical inconsistency of exempting them from the requirement to reduce emissions in the Kyoto Protocol and then imposing BTAs on their exports. Although the United States could counter that it had not ratified the Kyoto Protocol, it was a party to the UNFCCC, which acknowledged that nations have "common but differentiated responsibilities and respective capabilities" in addressing climate change.

6.5.6 Calculating BTAs

If BTAs are found to be GATT legal, but physically identical products are found to be "like," BTAs for imports could not exceed the tax on carbon embedded in like domestic products. The WTO, in the *Superfund* case, condoned use of the "predominant method of production" (PMP) in the importing country in calculating the maximum BTA that could be applied to imports of chemicals. (The same method was used to calculate BTAs for the tax on ODCs.) It is presumed that the same methodology could be employed to calculate the maximum allowable BTAs for carbon taxes. If, however, a foreign producer could demonstrate that its products were less carbon-intensive than domestic products, it could pay BTAs based on actual carbon content. The Superfund and ODC legislation also provided this option. By comparison, it is presumed that BTAs for exports, if allowed, would reflect the actual carbon content of exports.

Another method for calculating BTAs on imports that has been suggested is "best available technology" (BAT), which its primary proponents define as "for example, the most effective and advanced stage in the development of activities and their methods of operations which indicate the practical suitability for providing in principle the basis for emission limit values designed to prevent and, where that is not practicable, generally to reduce emission and the impact on the environment as a whole. . . . " (Ismer and Neuhoff 2007, p. 147). Although these authors say that implementing BAT would be "relatively simple," they have identified (pp. 154–158) a number of issues that would need to be resolved, including the definition of product classes, variations of energy-intensity within product classes, identification of the technology that should be labeled BAT, and the choice of fuel used to calculate the carbon content of traded goods – an especially troubling issue in the case of electricity, because the options range from zero-emissions alternatives (wind, hydro, and nuclear) to medium carbon-intensity alternatives (oil and gas) to high carbon-intensity coal-fired generation. See also the discussion of technical and administrative issues in Section 6.4.

Use of either PMP or BAT would not level the playing field between highly energy-intensive imports and less energy-intensive domestic products. That would require basing BTAs on the actual carbon content of imports, which, of course, would be GATT legal only if identical products were not found to be "like" or if this methodology were approved in response to a request for an Article XX exception. Implementing this approach would be especially daunting, as it would require knowledge of the carbon content of imports. Estimates of carbon content must pertain to particular products produced by specific firms (or perhaps even specific plants); they could not be based on country or sectoral averages, provided, for example, by the use of input-output analysis. Leaving aside problems of calculating carbon content, especially in developing countries, verification would pose an enormous challenge. Also, if a firm uses technologies that differ in energy intensity, they can be expected to export (or say they export) products made using the technology with the highest carbon intensity, in order to maximize export BTAs. This issue could be addressed by basing BTAs on the average energy intensity of a firm's products, but it is not clear that that approach would be GATT legal.

6.5.7 BAs for the Cost of Emission Permits

The GATT legality of BAs for the cost of emissions permits must be inferred from provisions originally written to deal with other issues, namely, those dealing with BTAs for taxes and other charges and perhaps those dealing with regulations, a possibility that is not considered here. Thus, the uncertainty of the GATT legality of BTAs for carbon taxes is compounded by uncertainty as to how those provisions would be applied to the cost of permits.

The OECD has defined taxes as "compulsory, unrequited payments to general government."[21] It seems reasonable to see the cost of permits bought from governments as a compulsory, unrequited payment, in which case the GATT legality of BAs for such costs should logically be governed by the same considerations as the GATT legality of BTAs for carbon taxes. However, there is no way of knowing whether the WTO would share that view.

It may be important, moreover, that permits are not only acquired by making payments to governments. In particular, they may be distributed free of charge and may be bought on the secondary market. To overcome the problems of competitiveness, carbon leakage, and free riding identified earlier, it is necessary to allow BAs for the cost of permits acquired in these ways. The reasoning is simple. The free allocation of permits can best be seen as a lump-sum transfer. Permits have value, and thus an opportunity cost, whether bought from a government, received free of charge, or purchased on the secondary market. These opportunity costs will be reflected in prices – at least if the agencies regulating electric utilities allow it. Unless they are also reflected in BAs, they will reduce competitiveness and induce carbon leakage and free riding.[22] Although this reasoning may be logically impeccable to economists – and may actually describe how things play out in the real world – it may not be persuasive to the WTO, especially in the case of freely allocated permits. After all, it implies that BAs should be allowed for costs not actually incurred, in direct contrast to the wording of the GATT and the ASCM. There seems to be general agreement that BAs would be limited to the fraction of permits that are not allocated freely.

Whether the cost of acquiring auctioned permits on the secondary market would be considered a tax for which adjustments would be appropriate would seem to depend on where one placed the emphasis in the OECD definition of a tax as a "compulsory, unrequited payments to general government." The holding of permits for emissions would be compulsory and arguably unrequited, but payment would not be made to a government, at least not directly. Acquisition on the secondary market of permits originally granted without charge compounds the uncertainty.

---

[21] OECD, "Note on the Definition of Taxes by the Chairman of the Negotiating Group on the Multilateral Agreement on Investment (MAI)" (DAFFE/MAI/EG2(96)3, 19 April 1996), at 1, visited September 3, 2009, cited in de Cendra (2006, p. 135, n. 44).

[22] See, for example, Frankel (2009, p. 14.)

6.6 Summary and Conclusions

The possibility that BAs for carbon taxes and the cost of emissions permits will be introduced raises serious economic, administrative, and legal issues, and threatens to inflame protectionist tendencies. Border adjustments are likely to be grafted onto what is – and should be – essentially origin-based systems for pricing carbon and applied only to trade with countries that do not have comparable regimes for reducing emissions, in order to ameliorate competitive disadvantages for energy-intensive industries and carbon leakage and to induce carbon pricing. They are thus almost certain to be found to violate the most-favored-nation treatment provision of the GATT; being imposed on PPMs rather than products, they may also be found to violate the requirement of national treatment. It seems quite possible that import BAs would be granted an exception under GATT Article XX, but it is unlikely that export BAs would be. It is not certain whether import BAs could be based on the carbon content of imports, as would be required to level the playing field between imports and domestic products, rather than on that of production of comparable products in the importing country or on best available technology. In any event, calculating the appropriate BAs would be extremely complicated. It is thus likely that BAs would be limited in both breadth and scope –that is, that they would be applied to only a relatively small number of energy-intensive products, might compensate only for direct and indirect (embedded) carbon prices incurred in production, and would not reach very far upstream in their inclusion of indirect carbon prices, as it would probably not be cost-effective to go beyond that. Thus limited, BAs are unlikely to compensate fully for all carbon prices embedded in international trade, but they would compensate for the most important costs.

References

Aldy, Joseph E., Peter R. Orszag, and Joseph E. Stiglitz. 2001. Climate change: An agenda for global collective action. Paper prepared for a conference on the timing of climate change policies, Pew Center on Global Climate Change, 2001.

Biermann, Frank, and Rainer Brohm. 2005. Implementing the Kyoto protocol without the USA: The strategic role of energy tax adjustments at the border. *Climate Policy* 4:289–302.

Cosbey, Aaron. Border carbon adjustment. Paper presented at the Trade and Climate Change Seminar, Copenhagen, June 18–20, 2008.

de Cendra, Javier. 2006. Can emissions trading schemes be coupled with border tax adjustments? an analysis vis-à-vis WTO law. *RECIEL* 15 (2): 131–145.

Demaret, Paul, and Raoul Stewardson. 1994. Border tax adjustments under GATT and EC law and general implications for environmental taxes. *Journal of World Trade* 28 (4): 5–65.

Frankel, Jeffrey. 2008. Global environment and trade policy. In *Post-Kyoto International Climate Policy* Joseph E. Aldy and Robert N. Stavins (eds.). New York: Cambridge University Press.

Hufbauer, Gary Clyde, and Jisun Kim. 2009. Climate policy options and the World Trade Organization. *Economics, the open access-open assessment e-journal* 3:2009–2029.

Hufbauer, Gary Clyde, Steve Charnowitz, and Jisun Kim. 2009. *Global Warming and the World Trading System.* Washington, D.C.: Peterson Institute for International Economics.

Ismer, R., and K. Neuhoff. 2007. Border tax adjustment: A feasible way to support stringent emission trading. *European Journal of Law and Economics* 24:137–164.

Lockwood, Ben, and John Whalley. 2008. Carbon motivated border tax adjustment: Old wine in green bottles. Working Paper No. 14025, NBER, Cambridge MA.

McKibbin, Warwick J., and Peter J. Wilcoxen. 2009. The economic and environmental effects of border tax adjustments for climate change policy, In *Climate Change, Trade and Competitiveness: Is a Collision Inevitable?* Lael Brainard and Isaac Sorkin (eds.). Washington, D.C.: Brookings Institution Press.

McLure, Charles E., Jr. 2010a. The GATT-legality of border adjustments for carbon taxes and the cost of emissions permits: A riddle wrapped in a mystery, inside an enigma. Mimeograph, Hoover Institution, Stanford, CA.

McLure, Charles E., Jr. forthcoming, Carbon-added taxes: An idea whose time should never come. *Carbon and Climate Law Review.*

Metcalf, Gilbert E., and David Weisbach. 2009. The design of a carbon tax. *Harvard Environmental Law Review* 33 (2):499–556.

Organisation for Economic Co-operation and Development. Environment Directorate. 2006. *The Political Economy of Environmentally Related Taxes.* Paris: OECD.

Peterson, Everett B., and Joachim Schleich. 2007. Economic and environmental effects of border tax adjustments. Fraunhofer Institute for Systems Innovation Research, Hannover, Germany.

Seidman, Laurence, and Kenneth Lewis. 2009. Compensations and contributions under an international carbon treaty. *Journal of Policy Modeling* 31:341–350.

van Asselt, Harro, and Thomas Brewer. 2010. Addressing competitiveness and leakage concerns in climate policy: An analysis of border adjustment measures in the US and the EU. *Energy Policy* 38:52–51.

Whalley, John. 2009. On the effectiveness of carbon-motivated border tax adjustments. Working Paper No. 63, Asia-Pacific Research and Training Network on Trade Working Paper Series.

World Trade Organization. 2004. *Trade and Environment at the WTO.*

SEVEN

Taxes and Caps as Climate Policy Instruments with Domestic and Imported Fuels

Jon Strand

7.1 Introduction

Most economists and policy makers today seem to find few fundamental differences between setting an emissions tax and setting a cap on total emissions with free trade of emissions rights among emitters, as an effective policy tool for reducing global carbon emissions.[1] This chapter demonstrates that such a view is generally incorrect. The two climate policy instruments are not (and are often far from) equivalent when different groups of countries have antagonistic interests in fuel markets. I will make the assumption, considered realistic, that these markets and policies are dominated by two groups of countries, with clashing interests: one group that consumes most fossil fuels, and that defines and implements climate policy; and another group that produces fossil fuels. Importantly, both producer and consumer countries tend, as groups, when their within-group policies are coordinated, to behave noncompetitively in the fossil fuels markets. I then show that tax solutions typically dominate cap-and-trade solutions, as the most efficient and effective climate policy instruments from the point of view of fuel-consuming countries.

I consider a highly stylized set-up in which the world economy is divided into two blocs. The first bloc, called region A, consumes all fossil fuels and defines and implements a climate policy. I assume that region A consumes two fuels: fuel 1, imported entirely from the other region (think of oil), and

[1] In this presentation, we ignore all climate gases other than carbon, which represents about 80 percent of the climate effect of all greenhouse gases. Concerning our two sets of policy instruments, any differences are generally considered to exist only under uncertainty, or in terms of distribution between government and the private sector, depending, for example, on whether emissions rights are given away or auctioned off by governments. Differences resulting from noncompetitive behavior of policy makers is much less recognized.

233

fuel 2, produced in its entirety within region A itself (interpreted alternatively as coal, natural gas, or renewables). Region B is assumed to produce all of fuel 1, but nothing of fuel 2, and it consumes no fuel itself. The two regions have antagonistic interests in the sense that a higher importer (exporter) tax on fuel 1 lowers maximal welfare for the exporting region B (the importing region A). I assume, accordingly, that *the two regions do not cooperate* in setting fuel or carbon taxes, or cap policies. Instead, each bloc sets its policy optimally, given the policy of the other bloc. The natural equilibrium concept invoked is then the noncooperative Nash Equilibrium (NE).

I also assume that *policies are fully coordinated among all countries within each bloc,* so that the bloc acts as a single decision maker. In terms of climate policy, such an ideal is easy to conceptualize: an optimal climate policy for carbon emitters must be one that coordinates all emitters' strategies optimally. Region A, which sets climate policy, can be thought of as the entire OECD, plus most of Asia, Latin America, and Africa (apart from a small number of countries). These countries are overwhelmingly fuel importers, and together comprise almost 90 percent of both global energy consumption and population. These are also the countries that appear to be preoccupied with limiting greenhouse gas emissions. Region B, which consists of fuel exporters, is a much smaller group of countries, comprising principally OPEC and Russia. The view that fuel exporters coordinate their export strategies is, we argue, not far-fetched, particularly with reference to OPEC as a global force in the oil market. Our assumption that this block has no energy consumption of its own, and little basic interest in controlling climate change, is also realistic: the block represents no more than about 10 percent of global population and energy consumption.

In addition to fuel 1 (oil), which is produced entirely by exporters and consumed entirely by importers, we assume that there exists a fuel 2, which is produced and consumed exclusively by the importing bloc. The existence of this second fuel turns out to make a great difference for the analysis. Its main significance is to increase the choice set for the fuel-importing region (A) in the case in which region A chooses a cap-and-trade policy to limit carbon emissions. With an additional fuel (in addition to oil), the importing bloc has two fuels, instead of just one, by which the overall carbon cap can be adjusted or fulfilled. This turns out to improve the strategic position of region A versus the exporting region B, under a cap policy.

The analysis focuses, as already mentioned, on two alternative paradigms for controlling carbon emissions – namely, fuel or carbon taxes versus a cap-and-trade solution – that also represent the two main competing paradigms used at this time for addressing mitigation of climate gases. This chapter extends a paper (Strand 2009a) in which I considered a similar model with two world regions, but with only one fuel (oil) instead of two fuels. I then showed that the NE aggregate fuel (and carbon) tax exceeds the Pigou level. I also showed that selecting an optimal cap-and-trade solution is less advantageous for the importer than setting a tax. Intuitively, when the importer sets a cap, the exporter is free to extract more of the rent from the fuel market, compared to when the importer sets a tax. In the NE solution to that game, the exporter strategically adjusts its tax so as to extract maximum rent from the importer, at the given (exogenous) cap, leading to a zero equilibrium value for tradable emissions quotas in the importer region.

In this chapter, I consider three different models, which are discussed in Sections 7.3 through 7.5. In all cases, region B (the fuel exporter) sets an optimal export tax (which can equally be interpreted as a domestic tax on fuel production within region B). The models differ in terms of the behavior of region A. Under model 1, I assume *NE in tax setting, with region A optimally differentiating between fuels 1 and 2*, thus setting one consumption tax for fuel 1 and another tax for fuel 2.

Under model 2, I assume that region A sets *a common carbon tax for both fuels*. This is to recognize that when taxes are differentiated between two fuels, the tax on fuel 1 could, conceivably, be interpreted not as an emissions tax, but instead as a strategic import tax, which could be difficult to defend in view of WTO regulations. A common tax per unit of carbon emissions, which also applies to a domestically produced and consumed fuel, is likely to be much harder to oppose on such grounds.

Model 3 implies that region A, instead of setting a tax, selects *a cap-and-trade solution*, fixing the level of carbon emissions from the region's consumption of the two fossil fuels combined. Region A is assumed to be in the position to set, and enforce, a global carbon emissions cap, as the only region that consumes fossil fuels. Region B cannot directly control the amount of carbon emitted, but we assume that it still sets an export tax on fuel 1.

Although the strategic games in the two tax-setting cases (under models 1 and 2) are similar, and parallel to the equivalent game in the one-fuel case, the strategic game in the cap-and-trade case (model 3) is quite different. The exporting region B now sets its tax optimally, taking *the schedule of trade-offs between consumption of the two fuels in region A* as given, facing a preset cap on carbon emissions. The importing region can here be viewed as setting an emissions quota price (dual to the cap, given that a common quota price is set for both fuels, and given that region A faces a given export tax on fuel 1 set by region B). By contrast, in my previous paper on the topic (Strand 2009a; with only one fossil fuel), setting an emissions cap was tantamount to selecting a given amount of fuel 1 imports. This strategic difference turns out to have substantial impact on the equilibrium solution, at least in some cases. This is illustrated numerically in Tables 7.2, 7.3, and 7.4. In the limit when fuel 2 has no carbon content (and fuel 2 is interpreted as renewables), the two models turn out to be equivalent.

Section 7.6 provides numerical illustrations, and Section 7.7 concludes.

To reiterate, two major weaknesses of my previous paper are remedied here, which should make this chapter far more realistic and relevant to policy. These remedies are both related to the feature that there are two fuels instead of one. First, a second fuel 2 serves as a substitute, albeit an imperfect one, for fuel 1 in region A. Secondly, the fuel-consuming region now also produces fuels; it is the only producer (and consumer) of fuel 2. Fuel 1 can be considered as oil throughout (the main internationally traded fuel). I have three alternative interpretations in mind for fuel 2. Under two of these, fuel 2 is fossil, either coal or natural gas. When fuel 2 is coal (natural gas), emissions per energy unit are higher (lower) than for fuel 1. In the third alternative, fuel 2 is renewable energy. Some renewables are likely to have emissions properties similar to those of gas; but some are also likely to have much lower (perhaps negligible) emissions. Interestingly, the model turns out to yield distinctly different, and illuminating, results under these three alternative interpretations. The outcomes under a cap-and-trade solution for the importer now differ substantially according to the characteristics of fuel 2, as illustrated in the simulations reported in Tables 7.2, 7.3, and 7.4. The paper thus yields a set of empirically relevant predictions, in particular concerning the optimal strategy of the fuel exporter in meeting an importer-determined emissions cap.

The literature dealing with the topics of this paper is limited. A previous companion paper (Strand 2009a) considers a similar (static) model, but one with only one fuel. In that paper, I showed that fuel importers gain from a tax policy instead of a cap for limiting their fuel consumption, whereas exporting countries always wish to set a positive fuel tax. With strategy coordination within each country bloc (but not across blocs), the sum of exporter and importer fuel taxes exceeds the Pigou level, reflecting two separate motives for taxation: externality correction (due to the climate impact of emissions), and a strategic rent-extraction (which, for the importer, may be justified as an "energy security" motive).

Some of the other related literature is explicitly dynamic, but it ignores the two new key issues here, by focusing on one fuel and on taxes only. An early but influential paper by Bergstrom (1982) considered strategic tax setting by independent oil-importing countries that face either a competitive oil supply or a monopoly oil exporter, but it ignored environmental costs. The full burden of an importer excise tax was here shown to generally fall on the exporter.[2] Similar results were found by Karp and Newbery (1991) and Amundsen and Schöb (1999); in the latter paper the strategic and environmental tax motivations were combined, and some conclusions are similar to ours (e.g., that rent-capture arguments may lead fuel importers to set fuel taxes in excess of Pigou levels). More recently, Rubio (2005) considered quantitative versus price mechanisms (as we do in Section 7.6) in which the exporter (and not, as in our model, the importer) sets a quantity. Liski and Tahvonen (2004) studied a dynamic model in which only importers tax fossil fuels; their conclusions were similar to ours, in particular, that the importer tax may be set in excess of the Pigou level when the environmental externality is "small" but lower than the Pigou level when the externality is "great." More recently, Wei (2009) has studied a dynamic "end game" (for extraction of a given fossil fuel resource) between a block that consumes and imports fossil fuels (oil) and a second block that exports it; this is similar to the model discussed in Liski and Tahvonen (2004), but in this case the exporter has no extraction costs and consumes part of the fuel itself. Results are similar to those under tax solutions in our paper: the importer sets a tax in excess of the Pigou level, and the exporter sets a positive export tax to extract part of the potential producer surplus. This analysis confirms that fuel or carbon taxation is advantageous for the importer also in a dynamic context, and then perhaps even more so than in a short-run model such as ours.[3] A further contribution is Keutiben (2010), who extends the dynamic one-fuel model to cases in which the importer produces some of the fuel, and the exporter consumes some of it. It is then shown that greater own-production facilitates importer rent capture, while greater exporter fuel consumption makes importer rent capture more difficult.

---

[2] This result rests on assumptions of exhaustibility of the fossil-fuel resource and zero extraction cost, which leads to a shift in the equilibrium future price path for the resource when an importer tax is imposed. Note that Bergstrom's assumption of no extraction cost is restrictive, and makes his results somewhat difficult to generalize. In our formulation, extraction costs play a key role, while exhaustibility is ignored.

[3] Wei (2009) shows that the exporter generally gains from selling some of its fuel less expensively on the home market, thus explaining the propensity of fuel exporters to subsidize domestically sold fuels. See also Strand (2009b) for a similar result.

Recently, Sinn (2008) has argued that a "green paradox" may arise in the context of importer fuel or carbon taxation; this implies an extreme case of rent-shifting whereby the exporter price can be reduced so much that overall fossil fuel extraction, and emissions, in fact increase.[4] Eichner and Pethig (2009) have considered the possibility of such a "green paradox" given that cap policies are used, in a dynamic model with three regions: fuel exporters, fuel importers with a climate policy (implementing a carbon price through a cap-and-trade scheme), and fuel importers without any policy. A stricter cap among climate-policy makers can lead to excessive "leakage" to the region without a policy. They find that this occurs only in very special cases, and more likely when a cap policy is executed only in the first of two periods. Note that this paper does not study (strategic) taxation by exporters, which is a main feature here.

None of the cited papers deals with what I consider the two main topics of this chapter – namely, optimal or equilibrium climate policy when fuel importers and consumers have their own fossil fuel production, and the choice between tax and cap-and-trade solutions in climate policy.

7.2 Basics

Consider a world with two fossil fuels, both of which are consumed only in one region (A). Fuel 1 (identified as oil) is produced in its entirety in region B, whereas fuel 2 is produced (*and* consumed) in its entirety in region A.[5] Fuel 2 can be identified with either coal, natural gas, or renewables. All demand and supply functions are assumed to be linear.[6]

Global externalities (from carbon emissions when fossil fuels are burnt) are $(1 + \alpha)(c_1 R_1 + c_2 R_2)$, where R_1 and R_2 are global consumption levels

---

[4] Strand (2007) shows that policies to support the development of alternative energies can lead to a "green paradox," at least in the short run, by forward-shifting fossil fuel extraction. Ploeg and Withagen (2009) and Kalkuhl and Edenhofer (2010) study the conditions under which a longer-run "green paradox" can arise, and find them to be limited and, in particular, dependent on the nature of the backstop technology that may ultimately replace fossil fuels.

[5] To fix ideas, region A can be thought of as the OECD, most of South and East Asia, and much of Africa and Latin America; region B is OPEC and Russia. Important characteristics of the regions are that region A cares about climate change and region B cares much less; region A has the bulk of population and fuel consumption; and region B has high oil output but much less output of other fuels (an exception is Russia's natural gas output).

[6] Quadratic utility and production functions, which lead to linear demand and supply functions, can be viewed as second-order Taylor approximations to the respective "true" functions. This is not a serious limitation on functional form as long as the changes in variables under consideration are small.

for fuels 1 and 2, and c_1 and c_2 represent carbon emissions per unit of fuel for the two fuels. Normalizing the externality cost per unit of emissions for region A to one, these are also the externalities per fuel unit felt by the population in region A, whereas αc_1 and αc_2 are externalities felt by the population in region B. α is a coefficient indicating region B's valuation of carbon emissions, relative to that of region A.[7] We assume that $\alpha < 1$, so that "most" of the (willingness to avoid) climate damage occurs in region A. When fuel 1 is oil and fuel 2 is coal, we can assume that c_2 is substantially greater than c_1. When fuel 2 is natural gas or renewables, c_2 can be presumed to be smaller than c_1.

The utility of the public in region A related to fuel consumption (not counting externality values) is assumed to be given by[8]

$$V(A) = a_1 R_1 - \frac{1}{2}\gamma_1 R_1^2 + a_2 R_2 - \frac{1}{2}\gamma_2 R_2^2$$
$$- \theta R_1 R_2 - (p_1 + t_1)R_1 - (p_2 + t_2)R_2 \qquad (7.1)$$

where p_1 and p_2 are producer prices of fuels 1 and 2, and t_1 and t_2 are fuel taxes imposed by country A. Equation (7.1) implies a simple quadratic form for the utility functions related to each of the two fuels, apart from the interaction term with θ, which indicates a negative demand dependency whereby the two fuels are assumed to be substitutes in consumption for region A. Maximizing $V(A)$ with respect to R_1 and R_2 yields the first-order conditions

$$\frac{dV(A)}{dR_1} = a_1 - \gamma_1 R_1 - \theta R_2 - (p_1 + t_1) = 0 \qquad (7.2)$$

$$\frac{dV(A)}{dR_2} = a_2 - \gamma_2 R_2 - \theta R_1 - (p_2 + t_2) = 0. \qquad (7.3)$$

Fuel 1 is produced by region B (but consumed entirely in region A), by competitive firms with collective profit function

$$\Pi_1(P) = (p_1 - s)R_1 - p_{01}R_1 - \frac{1}{2}\phi_1 R_1^2 \qquad (7.4)$$

yielding the first-order condition

$$p_1 - s - p_{01} - \phi_1 R_1 = 0. \qquad (7.5)$$

---

[7] Throughout, we abstract from local externalities due to fuel consumption.

[8] Individual private actors here have no incentive to take the emission externalities into consideration in determining their demand; thus, these externality terms can be dropped when determining demands.

Producers of fuel 2 are located in region A, and pay no additional fuel taxes (consumer countries are already taxing consumption of this fuel). Their profit function is assumed to take the following quadratic form:

$$\Pi_2 = p_2 R_2 - p_{02} R_2 - \frac{1}{2} \phi_2 R_2^2. \tag{7.6}$$

Their first-order condition for producers of fuel 2 is

$$p_2 - p_{02} - \phi_2 R_2 = 0. \tag{7.7}$$

We now solve for p_1 and p_2, together with R_1 and R_2, from (7.2), (7.3), (7.7), and (A.2, in the Appendix).[9] The full derivation is given in the Appendix. We find that consumption (and production) of one fuel is affected negatively by higher taxes on this fuel, and affected positively by higher taxes on the other fuel. The latter follows from demand substitutability. Because higher taxes on one fuel reduce consumption of the same fuel, the marginal consumption value of the other fuel is increased, and its demand is increased. The direct response of production of any fuel to its own taxes (t_1 and s for fuel 1, and t_2 for fuel 2) is greater than in the case of a single fuel. This follows from the negative cross-demand effect: when the tax on a given fuel (say, fuel 1) increases, region A substitutes more of the opposite fuel (7.2), which at the same time reduces the demand for fuel 1.

7.3 Nash Equilibrium Taxes with Separate Fuel Taxes

7.3.1 NE Taxes for Region A

We now turn to deriving Nash Equilibrium (NE) levels of t_1 and t_2, set by the consuming country, and a "tax" on fuel 1, s, set by the producing country.[10]

---

[9] All formulas in the Technical Appendix that are not stated in the main text are numbered as (A.1), (A.2), and so forth.

[10] We need not necessarily interpret s as a "fuel tax" on fuel 1 set by the exporter. This may equally well be a production tax, charged to all fuel producers in the exporting block. It may also, in principle, be interpreted as a scheme for supplying fuels from publicly owned fuel companies where a part of revenue per fuel unit is retained in exporting countries' treasuries and individual countries' fuel supplies respond to prices as assumed. Such alternative interpretations are highly relevant in practice, particularly because an explicit export tax may be difficult to maintain formally, in view of WTP rules.

Define the objective function of the importing countries' governments as follows:

$$W(A) = a_1 R_1 - \frac{1}{2}\gamma_1 R_1^2 + a_2 R_2 - \frac{1}{2}\gamma_2 R_2^2 - \theta R_1 R_2$$

$$- p_1 R_1 - p_{02} R_2 - \frac{1}{2}\phi_2 R_2^2 - c_1 R_1 - c_2 R_2. \qquad (7.8)$$

Equation (7.8) simply mirrors the public utility function (7.1) plus firms' objective (7.6), corrected for government tax receipts. R_1, R_2, p_1 and p_2 are determined simultaneously by t_1, t_2, and s, the two former of which are set by region A, and the latter by region B. Nash Equilibrium tax setting in region A implies that s is taken as given when setting the t_i. The first-order conditions for optimal t_1 and t_2 for given s, by region A are derived in the Appendix. Define $t_1^* = t_1 - c_1$, $t_2^* = t_2 - c_2$. We find the following solutions for t_1^* and t_2^* in terms of R_1:

$$t_1^* = \phi_1 R_1 \qquad (7.9)$$

$$t_2^* = 0. \qquad (7.10)$$

Using (7.5), (7.9) can alternatively be written as

$$t_1^* = p_1 - p_{01} - s. \qquad (7.9a)$$

Equation (7.9) has the same basic form as in the one-fuel case, from Strand (2009a). Obviously, $t_1^* > 0$. The optimal tax on the foreign-produced fossil fuel, set by the importer, then *exceeds* its marginal environmental damage cost for the importer. Moreover, introducing an additional, domestically produced and consumed fuel does not alter the basic tax-setting rule by the consuming region (A), for the internationally traded fuel involving strategic tax setting, given that the fuel importer is able to optimally differentiate the taxes on the two fuels. This is the case regardless of the substitution relationship between the two fuels (represented by the degree of substitutability parameter θ).

For fuel 2, produced and consumed domestically by region A, the NE tax equals marginal environmental damage cost for the region ($t_2^* = 0$ implies the Pigou rule $t_2 = c_2$). The intuition is simple: region A behaves strategically when taxing the foreign-produced fuel 1 only. Fuel 2 is domestically produced and consumed and invokes no strategic response in the "first-best" solution for this region.

7.3.2 NE Taxes for Region B

For a unified region B government, policy is limited to setting an excise tax s per unit of the exported fuel, assuming as before that this government faces a competitive supply from independent producers; and that the fuel is wholly exported (region B has no independent fuel demand). The objective function of region B can be expressed as

$$W(B) = p_1 R_1 - p_{01} R_1 - \frac{1}{2}\phi_1 R_1^2 - \alpha c_1 R_1 - \alpha c_2 R_2. \qquad (7.11)$$

The first-order condition for the regional government in region B, derived in the Appendix, is

$$s^* = \left(\gamma_1 - \frac{\theta^2}{\gamma_2 + \phi_2}\right) R_1 - \frac{\theta}{\gamma_2 + \phi_2}\alpha c_2, \qquad (7.12)$$

where $s^* = s - \alpha c_1$ is the unit export tax on fuel 1 in excess of the externality per unit of fuel 1 consumption as valued by the exporter.

To interpret (7.12), note first that the exporter tax rule can then be said to be Pigouvian if $s^* = 0$. The expression for s^* has one positive term (the first main term on the right-hand side) and one negative term (the second main term).[11] Both terms have straightforward interpretations. The first is a *strategic trade term*: s is set high (above the Pigou level) in order for the exporter of fuel 1 to extract more rent than otherwise from consumers of fuel 1, who all reside in region A. This is similar to the result in Strand (2009a), except that there the export tax took the simpler form $s^* = \gamma_1 R_1$. This expression is now modified downward by the second term inside the bracket on the right-hand side of (7.12). The modification is due to a strategic trade effect for region B, which in turn is due to the presence of an additional fuel 2, produced and consumed by region A. The existence of fuel 2 makes region A "less dependent" on fuel 1, as this additional fuel to some degree substitutes fuel 2 for fuel 1 when the price of fuel 1 increases. This effect is stronger when the degree of fuel substitution, represented by the substitution parameter θ, is greater. This effect to some degree deters exporter taxation of fuel 1.

The second, negative, term on the right-hand side of (7.12) is new. It represents the effect of taxation of fuel 1 by region B, on welfare in the same region, through the effect on production and consumption of fuel 2 in region A. When s increases, region A substitutes fuel 2 for fuel 1, and

---

[11] Note that, from our basic assumption $\gamma_1 \gamma_2 - \theta^2 > 0$, the first bracket on the right-hand side of (12) must be positive.

thus increases its consumption of fuel 2. This increase results in increased carbon emissions. This is an externality for region B, of size αc_B per unit increase in fuel 2 consumption, because region B has no direct control over the consumption of fuel 2. This effect discourages taxation of the home-produced fuel in region B.

Arguably, these additional effects are small. First, the correction of the first term depends on θ (representing the degree of substitutability of the two fuels in region A), which could be small.[12] More significantly, the marginal climate damage effect αc_2 for region B is likely to be small. As argued previously, the coefficient α (representing marginal climate damage caused to region B, relative to that caused to region A) is reasonably small for two reasons: first, because the population of region B is much smaller than that of region A (and thus the valuation of climate damages, when aggregated over all individuals in a region, is much smaller for region B given equal valuation by each individual), and second, because the preference for avoiding climate damages per individual, as expressed through the political process, could be weaker in region B.

7.3.3 Overall NE Tax Setting

We now derive the overall equilibrium tax levels t_1 and s, given $t_2^* = 0$ from (7.10), jointly with the solution for R_1. In the Appendix, we show that the solutions for t_1 and s are

$$t_1 = \frac{[(2\gamma_1 + \phi_1)(\gamma_2 + \phi_2) - 2\theta^2]c_1 + \phi_1(\gamma_2 + \phi_2)(a_1 - p_{01} - \alpha c_1) - \phi_1\theta(a_2 - p_{02} - c_2)}{2[(\gamma_1 + \phi_1)(\gamma_2 + \phi_2) - \theta^2]}$$

(7.13)

$$s = \frac{[(\gamma_1 + 2\phi_1)(\gamma_2 + \phi_2) - \theta^2]\alpha c_1 + [\gamma_1(\gamma_2 + \phi_2) - \theta^2]\left(a_1 - p_{01} - c_1 - \dfrac{\theta}{\gamma_2 + \phi_2}(a_2 - p_{02} - c_2)\right)}{2[(\gamma_1 + \phi_1)(\gamma_2 + \phi_2) - \theta^2]}$$

$$- \frac{\theta}{\gamma_2 + \phi_2}\alpha c_2.$$

(7.14)

[12] This may be reasonable, at least when fuel 2 is interpreted as coal or natural gas, where the substitution possibilities against oil (used mainly in transport) are moderate. When fuel 2 is renewable (in particular, biofuels), however, our assumption here could be less realistic. A recent meta study by Stern (2009) indicates that, while highly uncertain and variable, there is generally a high degree of substitutability between fuel types at the macro level. Average typical substitution elasticities, between oil and coal, and between oil and natural gas, are around unity; although there are many examples of estimated elasticities close to or even below zero.

For the aggregate (consumer plus producer) tax, $z_1 = t_1 + s$, on fuel 1, we find the simpler expression

$$z_1 = \frac{1}{2}(c_1 + \alpha c_1 + a_1 - p_{01}) - \frac{1}{2}\frac{\theta}{\gamma_2 + \phi_2}(a_2 - p_{02} - c_2) - \frac{\theta}{\gamma_2 + \phi_2}\alpha c_2.$$
$$(7.15)$$

The aggregate tax on fuel 1 is reduced when θ increases (when there is a higher degree of substitutability between the two fuels), for two reasons. The first effect, identified by the second main term on the right-hand side of (7.15), is for substitutability of fuel 2 for fuel 1. Higher interfuel substitutability leads to a greater demand response for fuel 1 to own taxation (as a greater part of demand is replaced by the other fuel). In response, both t_1 and s are optimally reduced. The second, represented by the last main term in (7.15), is the externality impact on welfare in region B of increased substitution of fuel 2 for fuel 1 by region A (which is the only fuel-consuming region). As we have remarked, region B has an interest in avoiding consumption of fuel 2 in region A, due to a negative "consumption externality" αc_2 (which represents the negative climate effect of this consumption) on region B. Holding back on s induces more consumption of fuel 1, and thus less consumption of fuel 2, and less of an externality for region B.

In conclusion, the second fuel in region A reduces somewhat the power of region B to manipulate the price of its exported fuel 1 (oil), and leads to more rent being transferred to region A. This is seen directly from expression (7.12) for the optimal s. In addition, exporter taxing power is eroded also by the externality caused by carbon emissions from the domestic sector 2 in the importing region (A). The exporter controls this effect only indirectly, through the export price on fuel 1, which is in consequence set lower.

Another new effect is that this latter effect is stronger, the greater the coefficient c_2 is; in other words, the "dirtier" the second fuel is (since, we recall, c_2/c_1 is the relative carbon content of fuels 2 and 1). The point is that when region A has a "dirty" fuel with which to substitute out fuel 1 (oil) when the tax on the latter is increased, emissions are increased "a lot" when such substitution takes place. This is disliked by region B, and serves to reduce region B's export tax. We, however, stress that this effect could be weak, because region B might have little general concern for climate effects of emissions.

Overall, the total tax on fuel 1 is lower here than in the one-fuel case, independent of the carbon intensity of fuel 2.

For comparison with other cases, we consider the special case in which fuel demands are independent ($\theta = 0$; we will concentrate on this in the following sections).[13] t_1 and s then have simplified forms, as follows:

$$t_1^* = t_1 - c_1 = \frac{1}{2}\phi_1^*(a_1 - p_{01} - c_1 - \alpha c_1) \qquad (7.13a)$$

$$s^* = s - \alpha c_1 = \frac{1}{2}\gamma_1^*(a_1 - p_{01} - c_1 - \alpha c_1), \qquad (7.14a)$$

where we have defined $\gamma_1^* = \frac{\gamma_1}{\gamma_1 + \phi_1}$, $\phi_1^* = \frac{\phi_1}{\gamma_1 + \phi_1}$, so that $\gamma_1^* + \phi_1^* = 1$.
The sum of taxes on fuel 1, in excess of the Pigou level, is in this case[14]

$$z_1^* = t_1^* + s^* = \frac{1}{2}(a_1 - p_{01} - c_1 - \alpha c_1). \qquad (7.16)$$

z_1^* is here always positive. Optimal NE taxation, by two antagonistic blocks as shown here, thus always leads to overall taxation in excess of the Pigou level.[15]

7.4 Nash Equilibrium Taxation with a Common Emissions Tax in Region A

7.4.1 Introduction

The previous section was based on the assumption that region A could differentiate its "emissions tax" optimally between the two sectors. It might then be inappropriate to call the resulting tax on fuel 1 an "emissions tax"; it might be better instead to consider it a combination of an emissions tax for both fuels and a specific import tax for fuel 1. This could be problematic, because it may clash with WTO rules. Thus, in this section we will consider

---

[13] When fuel 2 is coal or natural gas, the degree of substitutability of fuel 2 for fuel 1 is arguably low, at least in the short run. Oil is today mainly a transportation fuel, while coal and natural gas are used mainly for heating and electricity generation.

[14] Note here that t_1^* and s^* are defined relative to the respective regional externalities, the sum of which comprise global externalities from consuming fuel 1. Accordingly, z_1^* is defined as the tax in excess of the global externality caused by fuel 1.

[15] It should be noted that this is not a fully general result; it follows, in particular, from the assumption that all functional forms, for demand and supply functions, are linear. See, for example, Liski and Tahvonen (2004) for a discussion.

an alternative case in which region A is confined to setting a common emissions tax for both sectors: This can more easily be defended as a "pure" emissions tax, and thus more difficult to attach on WTO grounds. Overall revenue T to region A from such a tax is

$$T = (c_1 R_1 + c_2 R_2)q \qquad (7.17)$$

where q is a common tax rate per unit of carbon emissions set by fuel consumers and c_1 and c_2 are still the carbon contents per fuel unit of fuels 1 and 2. The tax rate per unit of output is then $c_1 q$ for fuel 1, and $c_2 q$ for fuel 2. The expressions for the R_i and p_i are derived in the Appendix.

7.4.2 NE Taxes for Regions A and B

To derive NE tax setting in this case, we again start by considering region A, which now only sets one tax, namely, the common rate q per unit of carbon emissions. For region B the situation is simple: the same analysis as in Section 7.3 applies, and the basic formula (7.12) still applies. Analytical derivations are also given in the Appendix. The most important features of this solution, and how it deviates from the differentiated-tax solution in Section 7.3, can be discussed for a simplified case with no demand interaction ($\theta = 0$), on which we focus from now on. The solutions for q and s are as follows (as shown in the Appendix):

$$c_1 q = \frac{c_{r1}\phi_1^*(a_1 - p_{01} - \alpha c_1) + (2 - \phi_1^*)c_1}{2 - \phi_1^*(1 - c_{r1})} \qquad (7.18)$$

$$s = \frac{(1 - \phi_1^*)(a_1 - p_{01} - c_1) + (1 + c_{r1}\phi_1^*)\alpha c_1}{2 - \phi_1^*(1 - c_{r1})}. \qquad (7.19)$$

$c_1 q^*$ (the importer tax per unit of fuel 1 in excess of the Pigou level), although still positive, is smaller in (7.18) than the equivalent tax t_1^* in model 1, from (7.13a). s^* (the exporter tax in excess of the Pigou level) is, however, greater in (7.19) than in model 1, from (7.14a). Region A now sets the emissions tax as a compromise between the two individual-fuel taxes (one of which, for fuel 2, was Pigouvian in the individual-tax case), which implies a lower tax for fuel 1 than when taxes are set individually. Region B reacts to this (in Stackelberg fashion) by setting the export tax on good 1 higher. Thus, in this way, setting an optimal "compromise" emissions tax transfers some market power from region A to region B, which the latter region exploits by upping its own export tax.

The aggregate tax on fuel 1 is in this case

$$z_1 = c_1 q + s = \frac{[1 - \phi_1^*(1 - c_{r1})](a_1 - p_{01}) + c_1 + \alpha c_1}{2 - \phi_1^*(1 - c_{r1})}. \tag{7.20}$$

z_1 is lower in (7.20) than in (7.16) when region A sets optimal sector-differentiated taxes (model 1).[16] The reason is that although region B, as a (Stackelberg) follower, increases its tax in response to the reduced tax on fuel 1, this increase is less than the original reduction in t_1.

7.5 Cap Policy in Region A

In this section, I study the case in which region A imposes a cap on overall carbon emissions, in aggregate for the two fuels. (Region B is in no position to impose an overall emissions cap, because it has no command of fuel 2; it has no fossil-fuel consumption whatsoever.) This is a case of particular interest as it corresponds to a mitigation policy recommended by many observers and analysts. The given cap on total carbon emissions can be defined by C, as follows:

$$C = c_1 R_1 + c_2 R_2. \tag{7.21}$$

With a common quota price per unit of emissions, quotas (assumed to be fully auctioned away by the government in region A, and traded freely among emitters) will in total be worth T given by (7.17). The quota price per unit of fuel will be $q_1 = c_1 q$ for fuel 1, and $q_2 = c_2 q$ for fuel 2, equivalent to the tax on fuel 1 in Section 7.4.

Consider each of the two regions separately, as in the tax-setting case. The only difference from Sections 7.3 and 7.4, in terms of actual policy, is that region A now sets a cap on overall GHG emissions, instead of setting a tax as in Section 7.4 (or a set of taxes as in Section 7.3). I assume, as noted, that any cap solution is implemented within region A through a system of freely tradable emissions quotas that must be purchased from the government. Within region A, this defines a common price on emissions from the two fuels (fuel 1 and fuel 2; the price per unit of fuel will vary with emissions intensity).

Under NE behavior, region A chooses an optimal cap given the tax s set by region B. Region B chooses an optimal tax s given a cap set (optimally) by region A. From the point of view of region A, the quantity and price

---

[16] This follows readily from our assumption that $a_1 - p_{10} > c_1 + \alpha c_1$ (which must hold for production of fuel 1 to be at all socially efficient).

setting are dual problems. As a consequence, for region A the problem of choosing a quantity limit is strategically equivalent to that of choosing an emissions price q implementing the same given emissions level for given s.[17] This implies that the maximization problem for region A can be formulated as one of choosing an internal trading price q for emissions quotas within the region.

As a consequence, the problem for region A can, analytically, be set up as one of maximizing the regional objective function (7.8) with respect to q, and taking s as exogenous, in the same way as the problem solved in Section 7.4. The analysis for region A in that section also applies here.

For region B, the strategic situation is now quite different from the previous two models. This region can now be viewed as facing the constraint (7.21), whereby R_1 and R_2 are related, with given C. Region B correspondingly maximizes $W(B)$ with respect to s, subject to a constant C from (7.21). It can be shown (in Appendix) that this gives rise to the following price response for the fuel importer, when the exporter tax is increased:

$$\frac{dp_1}{ds} = 1 - \phi_1^*(1 - c_{r1}). \tag{7.22}$$

Equation (7.22) reveals that p_1 is more sensitive to changes in s here than under a carbon tax (model 2 in Section 7.4); in the latter case (from expression (A.10) in the Appendix), $dp_1/ds = \gamma_1^*$. Moreover, this sensitivity is greater, the greater is c_{r1} (and thus the greater is c_1 relative to c_2). (A low c_2 implies little scope for substitution of good 2 for good 1 when s increases for a given cap on overall GHG emissions; the effect of a higher s is then mainly to reduce the quota price q.) Correspondingly, p_1 is less sensitive to changes in s when c_2 is high; a relatively small substitution out of sector 1 and into sector 2 is then required to retain the carbon emissions constraint when the exporter tax s is increased (leading to reduced demand for good 1).

The problem can now be formulated as maximizing (7.11) with respect to s, under the constraint (7.21), with C as given (this exercise is presented in the Appendix). Because a cap solution is chosen by region A, region B takes overall emissions, C, as given in its own optimization. From the point of view of region B, then, its own tax policy has no influence on carbon

---

[17] One way to see this is to realize that a given cap with cap and trade and full auctioning can, with full certainty and perfect competition in the quota market, be implemented by the importer in two ways: by setting the cap directly and auctioning the corresponding emissions rights, thus inducing a given and a priory known quota price; or by setting the same quota price directly and letting agents purchase emissions rights freely at this given price, thus inducing quota sales equivalent to the given cap.

emissions. In consequence, the two last terms in (7.11) then drop out. The solutions for the price of emissions quotas per unit of fuel 1, $c_1 q^*$ ($= c_1(q - 1)$), and the exporter tax on fuel 1, s^* ($= s - \alpha c_1$) are found (in the Appendix) as

$$c_1 q^* = \phi_1^* c_{r1} \frac{1 - c_{r1}}{2 - c_{r1} - \phi_1^*(1 - c_{r1})^2}(a_1 - c_1 - p_{01}) \qquad (7.23)$$

$$s^* = \frac{1 - \phi_1^*(1 - c_{r1})}{2 - c_{r1} - \phi_1^*(1 - c_{r1})^2}(a_1 - c_1 - p_{01}) - \alpha c_1. \qquad (7.24)$$

For the sum of the exporter tax and the quota price per unit of fuel 1 in the importing block (which, together, comprise the effective "tax" on fuel 1), we find

$$z_1^* = c_1 q^* + s^* = \frac{1 - \phi_1^*(1 - c_{r1})^2}{2 - c_{r1} - \phi_1^*(1 - c_{r1})^2}(a_1 - p_{01} - c_1) - \alpha c_1. \qquad (7.25)$$

We may study the expressions (7.23) through (7.25) under different parametric assumptions. Consider then the case in which α is negligible: this is the case in which region B puts a negligible value on damage caused by carbon emissions. In this case, the overall effective net "tax" (in excess of the Pigou level; as the sum of the exporter tax and the equilibrium emissions quota price in region A) from (7.25) is then always greater than the equivalent sum from (7.20) in the case of a common emissions tax in region A. If we compare it to the sum of fuel 1 taxes in the case of optimal tax differentiation, from (7.16) in Section 7.3, we find that this sum is greater from (7.25) than from (7.16), given that

$$c_{r1} > \phi_1^*(1 - c_{r1})^2 \qquad (7.26)$$

which holds whenever c_{r1} is not too small (e.g., when $\phi_1^* = \frac{1}{2}$, (7.26) holds for all c_{r1} greater than approximately 1/4. c_{r1} here is less than one-half when the carbon content per value unit is lower for fuel 1 than for fuel 2 (as would be the case when fuel 1 is oil and fuel 2 is coal). In this case, the trade-off between fuel for the importer, for a given emissions budget, implies that demand for the traded fuel (oil) is highly elastic, which for the exporter translates into a relatively low market power, resulting in a moderate optimal exporter tax.

For small α, $c_1 q^*$ is always lower in (7.23) than in (7.18), whereas s^* is always greater, in (7.24) than in (7.19). Thus, when the exporter has low aversion to carbon emissions, the exporter of fuel 1 will be more aggressive in its export price policy when the importer sets a carbon cap, than when the importer sets a common emissions tax. To understand why, note that the only reason why the export tax would be higher in the tax case than in the cap case, is that the exporter has great aversion against increased carbon emissions; consequently, when α is high.[18]

Remember that α represents region B's marginal valuation of damages due to GHG emissions. When this valuation is high, it has an appreciable impact on the export tax in the tax-setting cases of Sections 7.3 and 7.4, as the export tax is then set higher to limit emissions and thus damages, as felt by region B. When region A sets a cap, by contrast, region B faces a level of emissions that is independent of its own tax, and its export tax is perceived as having no influence whatsoever on emissions. Thus, region B does not consider climate damages in setting s. This factor contributes to a lower export tax in the cap case. In principle, this could lead to a higher exporter tax in the case in which the importer also sets a tax instead of a cap.

For the importer (region A), the situation is opposite: this region has no intrinsic preference attached to the term containing α, and takes this term into consideration only indirectly, through its effect on the tax set by the exporter. As noted, however, a high α increases the exporter tax in the importer tax case as compared to the importer cap case; the importer reacts to this in an opposite manner (because its optimal reaction in terms of own tax is a falling function of the other side's tax; importer and exporter taxes are strategic substitutes). This factor contributes to a higher importer "tax" (carbon trading price) when it uses a cap, than when it uses a tax, in such particular cases.

One clear result here is that region A loses from a cap solution relative to a tax solution, apart from exceptional and unrealistic cases (particularly cases in which region B has a very high degree of aversion to carbon emissions). This is simply a consequence of the fact that the region B tax on fuel 1 is higher in the cap case, and that optimized region A welfare is a decreasing function of the region B tax on fuel 1.

7.6 Numerical Illustrations

This section provides numerical illustrations of the various cases and models, for equilibrium taxes t_1 (alternatively, carbon trading prices, $c_1 q^*$) and s, and their sum z_1. Throughout we consider a very simplified example where all γ and ϕ coefficients are identical (all demand and supply curves have

---

[18] We argued that this case is implausible, as the exporter's population must be small and because of practical political factors (actually today, major fuel exporters do not seem to worry much about the prospect of climate change).

Table 7.1. *Numerical illustrations of taxes on fuel 1 in model 1, different values of α and θ*

	Tax parameter	$\theta = 0$		$\theta = 0.1$		$\theta = 0.25$	
		$\alpha = 0$	$\alpha = 0.5$	$\alpha = 0$	$\alpha = 0.5$	$\alpha = 0$	$\alpha = 0.5$
Fuel 2 is coal ($c_2 = 2c_1$)	t_1	1.5	1.38	1.48	1.35	1.47	1.34
	s	0.5	0.88	0.47	0.72	0.41	0.54
	z_1	2	2.25	1.95	2.07	1.88	1.88
Fuel 2 is gas ($c_2 = c_1/2$)	t_1	1.5	1.38	1.44	1.32	1.37	1.23
	s	0.5	0.88	0.44	0.75	0.32	0.65
	z_1	2	2.25	1.88	2.07	1.69	1.88
Fuel 2 is renewables	t_1	1.5	1.38	1.43	1.30	1.34	1.20
($c_2 = 0$)	s	0.5	0.88	0.42	0.77	0.31	0.68
	z_1	2	2.25	1.85	2.07	1.63	1.88
Global Pigou tax, fuel 1	z_1	1	1.5	1	1.5	1	1.5

equal slopes). We consider two different values for region B's valuation of environmental damage (relative to the valuation of region A, and represented by the parameter α): either a "low" value, $\alpha = 0$, or a "high" value, $\alpha = 1/2$.[19] We also consider three alternative values for c_2 relative to c_1, to represent our three prototype fuel categories, as follows:

$c_2 = 2c_1$. The carbon content per energy (and economic value) unit of this fuel is twice that of oil. This is a reasonable description of the average properties of coal; correspondingly, we in this case identify fuel 2 with coal.

$c_2 = 1/2\, c_1$. The carbon content per value and energy unit for fuel 2 is now half of that of oil. This is a realistic description of average properties of natural gas, with which fuel 2 is identified in this case.

$c_2 = 0$. There are now no net carbon emissions arising from the consumption of fuel 2. We associate fuel 2 with renewable energy in this case (realizing, of course, that zero carbon emissions are practically unrealistic for many types of renewable energy).

Table 7.1 deals with model 1 only, where we assume that region A sets individual taxes for each fuel. We consider three alternative values for the demand dependence parameter θ, namely, $\theta = 0$ (demand independence), $\theta = 0.1$ ("weak" demand dependence), and $\theta = 0.25$ ("stronger" demand dependence).

In Table 7.1, the overall tax z_1 ($= t_1 + s$) in all cases exceeds the respective Pigou levels (either 1 for $\alpha = 0$, or 1.5 for $\alpha = 0.5$), but is generally lower

[19] Arguably, $\alpha = 1/2$ is an "extreme upper-end" case, particularly because the population of region B is only a fraction of that in region A.

Table 7.2. *Numerical examples of taxes for models 1through 3, for $\theta = 0$ and $c_2 = 2c_1$ (fuel 2 is coal)*

	Model 1: Region A differentiates sectoral taxes optimally		Model 2: Region A selects a single carbon tax		Model 3: Region A selects cap-and-trade solution for emissions	
Variable	$\alpha = 0$	$\alpha = 0.5$	$\alpha = 0$	$\alpha = 0.5$	$\alpha = 0$	$\alpha = 0.5$
t_1	1.5	1.375	1.13	1.09	1.11	1.11
s	0.5	0.875	0.63	1	0.81	0.81
z_1	2	2.25	1.76	2.09	1.92	1.92
Global Pigou tax, fuel 1	1	1.5	1	1.5	1	1.5
t_2	2	2	2.25	2.18	2.22	2.22
Global Pigou tax, fuel 2	2	3	2	3	2	3

when θ is larger. A noticeable feature is that all taxes are reduced when θ is increased, but s more so than t_1. Interestingly, when fuel 2 has a lower carbon content (as when fuel 2 is renewables), the tax rate for fuel 1 is reduced by more when θ increases. This is, from (7.15), related to the overall social value of fuel 2, which is greater when the marginal carbon externality it causes is smaller; this value is induced by the substitution of fuel 2 for fuel 1 when $\theta > 0$ and as a result deters high taxation of fuel 1. Another observation to be made is that, for the range of parameter values chosen, the variation in tax rates is rather moderate.

Tables 7.2 through 7.4 compare models 1,2, and 3. In all these cases we assume demand independence between the two fuel sectors ($\theta = 0$, which is the only case studied in Sections 7.4 and 7.5). In Tables 7.2 through 7.4, results do not differ between the three tables for model 1 (individual tax setting for the two fuels in region A), as there is no interaction between the two fuels in this case. Such interaction, however, occurs under models 2 and 3. In all cases, z_1 *exceeds* its Pigou level: there is *too much* taxation of fuel 1 at the respective NE. Correspondingly, output of fuel 1 is inefficiently low. This results from our strong assumption with respect to coordination of regional strategies, and the fact that a strategic tax motive adds to an externality-correcting motive. Note also that although tax rates differ according to α (region B's valuation of climate damages) under tax-setting solutions for region A (models 1 and 2), they are independent of such valuation under a cap-and-trade solution (model 3). The reason, as pointed out, is that region B, in facing a cap-and-trade solution, takes overall emissions as given, and is not influenced by any climate implications in setting its sector 1 tax, s.

When region A sets a tax or taxes, by contrast, region B in general perceives such an influence, as overall carbon emissions will then be a function of the exporter tax, s, set by region B.

Table 7.2 compares the three models when $c_2 = 2c_1$, where fuel 2 is interpreted as coal (remember that fuel 1 is interpreted as oil throughout). We find in Table 7.2 that taxes on fuel 1 are generally more moderate under models 2 and 3 than under model 1 (where region A differentiates the taxes on fuels 1 and 2 optimally). The fuel 1 tax is more moderate in model 2 than in model 1, as the tax rate set by region A in model 2 is a common carbon tax for both fuels, which is in this case influenced heavily by the tax on the emissions-intensive fuel 2 (interpreted as coal), and this reduces the tax on fuel 1 in the direction of the Pigou level (while still remaining above this level). Correspondingly, the fuel 2 tax is higher under models 2 and 3 than under model 1 (when the tax on fuel 2 is "Pigouvian" for region A).

For fuel 2 the tax situation differs from that for fuel 1 when region B values damages negatively ($\alpha = \frac{1}{2}$); the region B tax t_2 on fuel 2 is then everywhere below the (global) Pigou level ($= 3$). This result would, however, clearly be overturned for α values closer to zero.[20]

An interesting feature of equilibrium when fuel 2 has a high carbon content (and interpreted as coal) is that the "overall tax" (the sum of the exporter taxes and the cap-and-trade quota price in importer countries) does not differ much under the cap-and-trade solution (model 3) from the case of a unified carbon tax (model 2). The exporter (region B) is, in this case, restrained in its tax setting owing to the importer's (region A's) extensive substitution possibilities for a given cap facing the fuel importer. In addition, remember that under the cap-and-trade solution region B does not consider any effects of overall carbon emissions from its fuel-pricing decision; thus, its tax setting is in no way affected by climate considerations. This factor moderates tax setting in the cap-and-trade case, and makes it more favorable to the importing block (region A), which, of course, prefers a lower region B tax on fuel 1. In fact, from Table 7.2, when region B has a "high" aversion to carbon emissions ($\alpha = \frac{1}{2}$), this tax-moderating factor outweighs the monopoly-enhancing effect of the cap-and-trade scheme on region B taxation, and makes the tax t_2 *less aggressive* (lower) in the cap-and-trade case, model 3, than in the tax-setting case (model 2). In this particular

---

[20] Arguably, one half is a very high value for α to take. Remember that, in our model, region B consumes no fuel; logically this must imply that its population is very small (fuel exports are concentrated to a narrow population group globally). If marginal climate damage valuations were equal across populations globally, the total marginal valuation by region B, relative to region A, will simply equal the ratio of the two populations.

Table 7.3. *Numerical examples of NE taxes for models 1 through 3, $\theta = 0$ and $c_2 = \frac{1}{2} c_1$ (fuel 2 is gas)*

Variable	Model 1: Region A differentiates sectoral taxes		Model 2: Region A selects a single carbon tax		Model 3: Region A selects cap-and-trade solution for emissions	
	$\alpha = 0$	$\alpha = 0.5$	$\alpha = 0$	$\alpha = 0.5$	$\alpha = 0$	$\alpha = 0.5$
t_1	1.5	1.375	1.42	1.31	1.14	1.14
s	0.5	0.875	0.53	0.90	1.52	1.52
z_1	2	2.25	1.95	2.21	2.66	2.66
Global Pigou tax, fuel 1	1	1.5	1	1.5	1	1.5
t_2	0.5	0.5	0.71	0.66	0.57	0.57
Global Pigou tax, fuel 2	0.5	0.75	0.5	0.75	0.5	0.75

case, the importing block favors setting a cap instead of a tax. This, however, is the only case in which this result arises; it is arguably unrealistic, as the value of α (region B's aversion to additional carbon emissions, relative to that of region A) is unrealistically high in this case.

Table 7.3 deals with cases in which fuel 2 has a positive but low carbon content, ($c_2 = \frac{1}{2} c_1$), with fuel 2 interpreted as natural gas. The main difference from the numerical examples in Table 7.2 is that the exporter is now much more aggressive in its tax setting in the cap-and-trade case (model 3). The reason is, as noted, that region A's trade-off between the two fuels (for any chosen carbon cap) is now much more favorable for region B, because the demand for fuel 1 is now much less responsive to an ex post increase in the price of this fuel. This leads to more aggressive taxation by region B. In response, the NE tax (or, rather, carbon quota price) for fuel 1 in region A is then lower in the cap-and-trade case (model 3) than in the carbon tax case (model 2). The overall tax is also found to be higher in the cap-and-trade case, and fuel consumption and emissions are lower. In this case, the cap-and-trade solution is far less favorable than a carbon tax solution for region A, owing to the much higher tax set by region B (which, as a result, extracts a much greater share of the rent). The difference between the two solutions is found to be greater when region A has no value of carbon emissions reductions ($\alpha = 0$) than when it has such value ($\alpha = \frac{1}{2}$), as s is lower in the former case under model 2.

Table 7.4 deals with the case in which fuel 2 consumption leads to no carbon emissions (and fuel 2 is interpreted as a noncarbon renewable energy source). Here the contrast between models 2 and 3 is even more stark than

Table 7.4. *Numerical examples of NE taxes for models 1 through 3, $\theta = 0$ and $c_2 = 0$*
(fuel 2 is renewables)

Variable	Model 1: Region A differentiates sectoral taxes		Model 2: Region A selects a single carbon tax		Model 3: Region A selects cap-and-trade solution for emissions	
	$\alpha = 0$	$\alpha = 0.5$	$\alpha = 0$	$\alpha = 0.5$	$\alpha = 0$	$\alpha = 0.5$
t_1	1.5	1.375	1.5	1.375	0	0
s	0.5	0.875	0.5	0.875	2	2
z_1	2	2.25	2	2.25	2	2
Pigou tax, fuel 1	1	1.5	1	1.5	1	1.5
t_2	0	0	0	0	0	0
Pigou tax, fuel 2	0	0	0	0	0	0

in Table 7.3. Region A, in setting its carbon cap, must now achieve the given cap fully on the basis of fuel 1 (oil) consumption, and no ex post fuel substitution is possible. This gives region B maximum monopoly power in setting the tax s on its exported fuel. This tax is now set to eliminate any value of traded quotas in region A, which is zero in consequence. In this case also, models 1 and 2 collapse to one as setting a carbon tax is the same as setting a tax on fuel 1 only, given that this fuel is the only source of carbon emissions; in either case, the effective tax set by region A on fuel 2 is zero.[21]

7.7 Conclusions

I have in this chapter considered a modeling framework in which two fuels are produced and consumed in the world market, and the world is divided into two main regions (A and B). Region A consumes all fuels, and produces one of them (fuel 2), whereas region B produces all of fuel 1. The two regions are involved in three alternative NE games, analyzed in models 1, 2, and 3, corresponding to alternative ways in which climate policy is conducted. In models 1 and 2, the fuel exporter and importer both set taxes. In model 1, the fuel-importing region (A) sets two taxes, one for each fuel; in model 2, region A sets one common carbon tax. The former is the preferable strategy for region A. We, however, also consider model 2, particularly because a carbon tax may, less than individual fuel taxes, be subject to WTO (or other retaliatory) sanctions. In model 3 the importer sets a carbon emissions cap. In all three models, the fuel exporter (region B) is assumed to select an

---

[21] This result can be interpreted as a limit result as c_2 tends to zero. It then replicates, and generalizes, a parallel result in Strand (2009a), for a similar one-fuel model.

optimal export (or domestic producer) tax on fuel 1.[22] We assume a negative demand dependence between the two fuels for region A (represented by a positive interaction parameter θ); this feature is explicitly considered only in the context of model 1 (in our discussion of models 2 and 3, we abstract from demand dependence and assume $\theta = 0$).

Under model 1, the importer (A) *sets two taxes, one for each fuel*, taking the exporter tax on fuel 1 as given. The tax on the imported fuel, t_1, is motivated by two factors: an externality effect due to carbon emissions, and an import-strategic motive. This tax is set above the Pigou level (echoing corresponding results in other papers, including Amundsen and Schöb (2000), Liski and Tahvonen (2004), and a companion paper to the current one, Strand (2009a)). For fuel 2, which is both produced and consumed by region A, there is no strategic motive in tax setting; region A sets this tax at the Pigou level.

For the exporting region, the optimal (NE) export tax in model 1 is adjusted down relative to the level found in Strand (2009a), where only one fuel was assumed. First, the presence of fuel 2 in region A puts that region in a more powerful strategic position relative to region B, as consumption of fuel 2 can be substituted for fuel 1 in region A in response to a higher import price on fuel 1, given a negative demand dependence between fuels (the interaction parameter θ is positive). This factor tends to discourage fuel taxation by region B. The second new factor relative to the one-fuel case is the externality imposed on region B, when carbon emissions from fuel 2 are increased in response to the export tax on fuel 1. This factor reduces the optimal fuel 1 tax set by region B. Overall, relative to the one-fuel case in Strand (2009a), the exporter fuel tax is reduced. The region A tax may, in response, be either higher or lower than in the one-fuel case, but most likely it will be lower.

In model 2 (considered in Section 7.4) region A sets *a carbon tax common for both fuels*. Region B sets, as before, an export tax on fuel 1. The carbon tax is now set as a "best compromise" for both fuels jointly. It is a weighted sum of the individually optimal taxes under model 1 (where, we note, the optimal tax on fuel 1 exceeds the Pigou level, whereas the optimal tax on fuel 2 is at the Pigou level). The optimal exporter tax on fuel 1, as a best response to the importer tax, is now somewhat higher than under model 1, whereas the sum of (export and import) taxes on fuel 1 is lower than under model 1.

---

[22] Note again that these two taxes are equivalent, as region B's entire output of fuel 1 is exported.

Model 3 deals with a fundamentally different type of climate policy. Region 1 now sets an *overall cap on carbon emissions* from both fuels combined, and implements the cap within the region through a unified emissions quota price for both fuels. The main strategic difference from models 1 and 2 lies in the behavior of region B, which now faces a cap-and-trade scheme instead of a tax or set of taxes, as under models 1 and 2. For region B, the strategic situation is altered in two ways, relative to the tax case. First, region B is now strategically more powerful as it recognizes that a reduction in demand for fuel 1, prompted by an increase in the exporter tax on this fuel, must be met through an increased consumption of fuel 2, and thus a substitution of fuel 2 for fuel 1, which may be ex post expensive for region A. This factor *increases* the optimal tax set by region B. Secondly, region B now has no incentive to consider adverse effects of changes in carbon emissions, as the cap ascertains that the emissions level is a constant. Under tax setting in region A, by contrast, this second factor usually leads region B to set a higher export tax on fuel 1, in order to limit region A's consumption of fuel 1, and thus on carbon emissions.[23] The absence of such a factor in the cap-and-trade case then tends to make the optimal region B tax lower, when region A selects a cap-and-trade policy.

The exact nature of this trade-off turns out to be important for the overall tax-setting behavior of region B. In particular, the greater the carbon content that fuel 2 has relative to that of fuel 1, the more elastic the demand for fuel 1 will be in response to an export tax from region B, and the less powerful will region B be when region A sets an emissions cap. The first factor noticed (which serves to raise the region B tax) is then weaker. Conversely, when fuel 1 has a high carbon content relative to that of fuel 2, and a given emissions tax is set, the strategic position of region B is very powerful. For the second factor (tending to reduce the optimal region B tax in the cap-and-trade case), the situation is opposite: when fuel 2 has a high (low) carbon content, this factor matters a lot (little) for the region B tax setting. Consequently, for a "low carbon content" fuel 2, the tax set by region B is increased a lot in the cap-and-trade case relative to the tax cases; for a "high carbon content" fuel 2 the region B tax is increased less or perhaps not at all.

These principles are illustrated in the numerical calculations in Tables 7.2, 7.3, and 7.4, by considering three possible levels for the carbon content of fuel 2 relative to that of fuel 1 (oil): high-carbon (coal); low-carbon (natural

---

[23] Note, however, that when the interaction effect in fuel demand, represented by the interaction coefficient θ, is sufficiently strong, this effect is weakened, or even eliminated, as consumption of fuel 2 increases in response to the higher export tax on fuel 1.

gas); and zero-carbon (renewable energy). These numerical examples verify the theoretical results in showing that the exporter is more powerful, and sets its export tax more aggressively, when fuel 2 has a lower carbon content. In the limit case as the carbon content of fuel 2 goes to zero, the cap-and-trade solution approaches unity, with maximal monopoly power in tax setting to region B and no power to region A (where, in the limit, the carbon quota price is zero).

To recapitulate, the cap-and-trade solution is, in almost all cases, less attractive to the importing (and climate policy–defining) block than either of the tax solutions. This leads the fuel importer (and main consumer) to prefer tax solutions over a cap-and-trade solution in climate policy, in a wide set of circumstances. The only exceptions are found to be when ex post substitution possibilities under a cap solution are "very good" for the importer (when fuel 2 has a "very high" carbon content) and the fuel exporter at the same time has high aversion (perhaps unrealistically high) to carbon emissions.

The immediate policy conclusion is that major fuel-importing and fuel-consuming countries should, on balance, choose tax solutions over cap solutions. The main problem with choosing a cap-and-trade solution, as it appears from my model, is that it leaves them more vulnerable to adverse strategic manipulation of fuel prices by monopolistic exporters. Other implications may be less obvious. One might in particular be tempted to conclude that it is advantageous for the importing block to maintain a substantial output of high-carbon fuel (coal), so as to diminish the strategic pricing power of fuel exporters, thus making a cap-and-trade solution "optimal." However, this would also have unwanted side effects, including an increase in overall carbon emissions. A further analysis of such cases is clearly warranted for future work.

This chapter takes my previous analysis of tax and cap behavior by major fuel-consuming and fuel-exporting blocks, in Strand (2009a), several steps forward. Many issues, however, are left unaddressed. First, the model is rigid in its sharp separation between fuel consumers and exporters; and in assuming full cooperation within each block of countries and no cooperation across blocks. My initial conjecture is that relaxing these assumptions need not alter the model fundamentally; in particular, it should not alter the derived balance between tax and cap solutions.[24] Without full policy

---

[24] One extension has already been addressed in another companion paper (Strand 2009b), where I assume that the exporter consumes part of its own fuel production. This is shown to not lead to substantial changes in the model, given that the exporter is allowed to differentiate the fuel tax between exports and domestic consumption. The own-consumption tax is then Pigouvian, and the export tax takes the same basic form as derived in the current

coordination, however, NE tax and cap solutions will be affected when these assumptions are altered. In particular, equilibrium taxes will be set lower, which is more realistic and potentially also globally more efficient (when overall fuel taxes exceed the Pigou level, as here, they are globally excessive, and unrealistically so). A further step toward realism would entail importer countries themselves producing some of fuel 1 (oil). I conjecture that such extensions would have fewer fundamental implications, although it remains to be studied.

More crucial, perhaps, is the assumption of a static model. Dynamism can be introduced in at least two ways: through an intertemporal budget constraint of exporters, who have a fixed total amount of fossil fuels to be sold; and through an intertemporal carbon emissions constraint, whereby a given emissions cap is assumed to be valid for an extended period of time. As noted in the introduction, some of the related literature is dynamic: first there was the seminal Bergstrom (1982) paper, and later, work by Rubio and Escriche (2001), Salo and Tahvonen (2001), Liski and Tahvonen (2004), and Wei (2009). Generally, these papers consider dynamic games of rent extraction between unified exporting and importing blocks, for a given amount of fuel (typically interpreted as oil) to be extracted in finite time. The general conclusion from these papers is that importer taxes are highly efficient in extracting exporter rents, and more than in a static context. Wei's (2009) model contains an extension to a case in which the exporter sells part of its fuel in its own domestic market. He finds that an optimal strategy for the exporter, in response to an optimal importer tax, is to induce excessive domestic fuel consumption (through a lower domestic fuel price), in order to optimally increase the fuel export price.[25] Keutiben (2010) similarly studies both own production of a single fuel by the importer, and own consumption by the exporter, and finds that the former leads to greater rent capture possibilities for the importer through importer fuel taxation, while the latter weakens these possibilities.

These existing papers, which deal with dynamic aspects, do not study the two main new issues treated in this chapter – namely, the inclusion of a second fuel, and analysis of a cap-and-trade policy for the fuel importer. An obvious topic for future research is to embed these two extensions into a dynamic framework. Without fully prejudging results, I conjecture that the main result here, that taxes are preferable over cap-and-trade solutions

---

paper. When the exporter cannot differentiate its own tax on a given fuel, the solution will be affected more fundamentally, as the exporter will then set the tax on fuel exports lower than otherwise. This could be of significance, particularly when the importer chooses a cap-and-trade solution; a more complete analysis will be left for future work.

[25] See Strand (2009b) for a related static model formulation.

for fuel importers, survives; there seems immediately to be no way for the importing block to effectively extract producer rent when a cap-and-trade solution is chosen, even in a dynamic context.

Several features related to the strategic model setup could also conceivably be altered in future work. One would be to assume that the fuel importer (here, region A) maintains a cap on overall carbon emissions and sets a tax on imported fuels so as to extract part of the producer surplus.[26] Then, however, the fuel tax becomes a very visible strategic import tax, and its objective becomes clear, namely, as a device for rent extraction; this could for obvious reasons clash with WTO rules.[27] Another setup would be to consider the exporter as a Stackelberg leader in the tax-setting game (as is common when one thinks of OPEC as the main strategic fuel exporter), and let the importer react by setting either a (set of) tax(es) or a carbon cap. Alternatively, OPEC could be given further strategic powers by being allowed to set both export price and quantity independently; this is not totally unrealistic, when most of OPEC's output stems from state-owned oil companies. Results are then different: Strand (2009a), in particular, shows that more of the rent can then be extracted by the exporter. More realistically, parts of the supply of fuel 1 ought in such cases to be modeled as coming from a competitive fringe, which would generally weaken the strategic exporter's market power.

Another relevant extension would be to assume, as done by Eichner and Pethig (2009) among others, that the entire world is not covered by either emissions taxes or caps; thus, not all global emissions are covered. This would open up discussions about policy-relevant issues such as interregional carbon leakage and the scope for offset policies, within my basic model framework.

TECHNICAL APPENDIX: ANALYTICS

A.1 Basics

Utility for region A related to fuel consumption, not counting externality values, is given by

$$V(A) = a_1 R_1 - \frac{1}{2}\gamma_1 R_1^2 + a_2 R_2 - \frac{1}{2}\gamma_2 R_2^2 - \theta R_1 R_2$$
$$-(p_1 + t_1)R_1 - (p_2 + t_2)R_2 \tag{1}$$

---

[26] This point was suggested to me by Michael Toman.

[27] One could, of course, argue that the import tax simply retaliates against the export tax and thus cannot itself be sanctioned. One problem is that the export tax may be hidden via producer taxes or other exporter rent-extraction schemes, which may make it difficult to verify by outside observers.

where p_1 and p_2 are producer prices of fuels 1 and 2, and t_1 and t_2 are taxes on these fuels imposed by country A. Maximizing $V(A)$ with respect to R_1 and R_2 yields the following set of first-order conditions:

$$\frac{dV(A)}{dR_1} = a_1 - \gamma_1 R_1 - \theta R_2 - (p_1 + t_1) = 0 \tag{2}$$

$$\frac{dV(A)}{dR_2} = a_2 - \gamma_2 R_2 - \theta R_1 - (p_2 + t_2) = 0. \tag{3}$$

Equations (2) and (3) lead to the following solutions for R_1 and R_2 in terms of the p_i and t_i:

$$R_1 = \frac{1}{\gamma_1 \gamma_2 - \theta^2} [\gamma_2 (a_1 - p_1 - t_1) - \theta (a_2 - p_2 - t_2)] \tag{A.1}$$

$$R_2 = \frac{1}{\gamma_1 \gamma_2 - \theta^2} [\gamma_1 (a_2 - p_2 - t_2) - \theta (a_1 - p_1 - t_1)]. \tag{A.2}$$

A basic stability condition is $\gamma_1 \gamma_2 - \theta^2 > 0$, which amounts to the interaction term in (1) not dominating direct quadratic terms.

Fuel 1 is produced by region B (but consumed entirely in region A), by competitive firms with the collective profit function

$$\Pi_1(P) = (p_1 - s)R_1 - p_{01} R_1 - \frac{1}{2} \phi_1 R_1^2. \tag{4}$$

Maximizing (4) with respect to R_1 yields the first-order condition

$$p_1 - s - p_{01} - \phi_1 R_1 = 0. \tag{5}$$

Producers of fuel 2 are located in region A, and are assumed to pay no fuel taxes (all taxation of this fuel is on consumption). Their collective profit function takes the form

$$\Pi_2 = p_2 R_2 - p_{02} R_2 - \frac{1}{2} \phi_2 R_2^2. \tag{6}$$

Their first-order condition is maximizing Π_2 with respect to R_2:

$$p_2 - p_{02} - \phi_2 R_2 = 0. \tag{7}$$

We now solve for p_1 from (A.1) and (5), and for p_2 from (A.2) and (7). We then arrive at the following two-equation system, which solves for R_1 and R_2:

$$(\gamma_1\gamma_2 + \gamma_2\phi_1 - \theta^2)R_1 - \theta\phi_2 R_2 = \gamma_2(a_1 - s - t_1 - p_{01}) - \theta(a_2 - t_2 - p_{02})$$
(A.3)

$$(\gamma_1\gamma_2 + \gamma_1\phi_2 - \theta^2)R_2 - \theta\phi_1 R_1 = \gamma_1(a_2 - t_2 - p_{02}) - \theta(a_1 - s - t_1 - p_{01})$$
(A.4)

We find the following solutions:

$$R_1 = \frac{(\gamma_2 + \phi_2)(a_1 - s - t_1 - p_{01}) - \theta(a_2 - t_2 - p_{02})}{(\gamma_1 + \phi_1)(\gamma_2 + \phi_2) - \theta^2}$$
(A.5)

$$R_2 = \frac{(\gamma_1 + \phi_1)(a_2 - t_2 - p_{02}) - \theta(a_1 - s - t_1 - p_{01})}{(\gamma_1 + \phi_1)(\gamma_2 + \phi_2) - \theta^2},$$
(A.6)

as well as the following derivatives:

$$\frac{dR_1}{dt_1} = \frac{dR_1}{ds} = -\frac{\gamma_2 + \phi_2}{(\gamma_1 + \phi_1)(\gamma_2 + \phi_2) - \theta^2}$$
(A.7)

$$\frac{dR_1}{dt_2} = \frac{dR_2}{dt_1} = \frac{dR_2}{ds} = \frac{\theta}{(\gamma_1 + \phi_1)(\gamma_2 + \phi_2) - \theta^2}$$
(A.8)

$$\frac{dR_2}{dt_2} = -\frac{\gamma_1 + \phi_1}{(\gamma_1 + \phi_1)(\gamma_2 + \phi_2) - \theta^2}.$$
(A.9)

Producer prices are found, from (5), (7), (A.6), and (A.7), as follows (noting that consumer prices are given by $p_i + t_i$):

$$p_1 = \frac{(\gamma_2 + \phi_2)\phi_1(a_1 - t_1) + [\gamma_1(\gamma_2 + \phi_2) - \theta^2](s + p_{01}) - \phi_1\theta(a_2 - t_2 - p_{02})}{(\gamma_1 + \phi_1)(\gamma_2 + \phi_2) - \theta^2}$$
(A.10)

$$p_2 = \frac{-\phi_2\theta(a_1 - s - t_1 - p_{01}) + (\gamma_1 + \phi_1)\phi_2(a_2 - t_2) + [\gamma_2(\gamma_1 + \phi_1) - \theta^2]p_{02}}{(\gamma_1 + \phi_1)(\gamma_2 + \phi_2) - \theta^2}.$$
(A.11)

A.2 Nash Equilibrium Taxes for Region A

Define the objective function of region

$$W(A) = a_1 R_1 - \frac{1}{2}\gamma_1 R_1^2 + a_2 R_2 - \frac{1}{2}\gamma_2 R_2^2 - \theta R_1 R_2 - p_1 R_1$$

$$- p_{02}R_2 - \frac{1}{2}\phi_2 R_2^2 - c_1 R_1 - c_2 R_2.$$
(8)

Region A here takes s as given in setting the t_i to maximize $W(A)$. The two resulting first-order conditions for region A have the forms:

$$\frac{dW(A)}{dR_1}\frac{dR_1}{dt_i} + \frac{dW(A)}{dR_2}\frac{dR_2}{dt_i} + \frac{dW(A)}{dp_1}\frac{dp_1}{dt_i} + \frac{dW(A)}{dp_2}\frac{dp_2}{dt_i} = 0; i = 1, 2.$$

(A.12)

Using (2), (3), and (7), we find the following partial derivatives of $W(A)$:

$$\frac{dW(A)}{dR_1} = t_1 - c_1; \quad \frac{dW(A)}{dR_2} = t_2 - c_2; \quad \frac{dW(A)}{dp_1} = -R_1; \quad \frac{dW(A)}{dp_2} = 0.$$

(A.13)

The two relations (A.12) give rise to the two-equation system

$$-(t_1 - c_1)(\gamma_2 + \phi_2) + (t_2 - c_2)\theta + R_1\phi_1(\gamma_2 + \phi_2) = 0 \quad \text{(A.14)}$$
$$(t_1 - c_1)\theta - (t_2 - c_2)(\gamma_1 + \phi_1) - R_1\phi_1\theta = 0. \quad \text{(A.15)}$$

Define $t_1^* = t_1 - c_1$, $t_2^* = t_2 - c_2$. Equations (A.14) and (A.15) now solve for t_1^* and t_2^* in terms of R_1 as follows:

$$t_1^* = \phi_1 R_1 \tag{9}$$
$$t_2^* = 0. \tag{10}$$

Using (5), (9) can be written as

$$t_1^* = p_1 - p_{01} - s. \tag{9a}$$

A.3 Nash Equilibrium Tax for Region B

The objective function of region B is

$$W(B) = p_1 R_1 - p_{01} R_1 - \frac{1}{2}\phi_1 R_1^2 - \alpha c_1 R_1 - \alpha c_2 R_2. \tag{11}$$

The first-order condition for the region B with respect to s has the form

$$\frac{dW(B)}{dR_1}\frac{dR_1}{ds} + \frac{dW(B)}{dR_2}\frac{dR_2}{ds} + \frac{dW(B)}{dp_1}\frac{dp_1}{ds} + \frac{dW(B)}{dp_2}\frac{dp_2}{ds}, \tag{A.16}$$

where, using (5)

$$\frac{dV(B)}{dR_1} = s - \alpha c_1; \quad \frac{dV(B)}{dR_2} = -\alpha c_2; \quad \frac{dV(B)}{dp_1} = R_1; \quad \frac{dV(B)}{dp_2} = 0.$$

(A.17)

From (A.7)–(A.8), (A.10)–(A.11), and (A.16)–(A.17),

$$s^* = \left(\gamma_1 - \frac{\theta^2}{\gamma_2 + \phi_2}\right) R_1 - \frac{\theta}{\gamma_2 + \phi_2}\alpha c_2. \tag{12}$$

A.4 Overall NE Tax Setting in Model 1

The overall equilibrium tax levels t_1 and s (recognizing that $t_2^* = 0$) are determined jointly with R_1 from (A.5), (9), and (12). We find:

$$R_1 = \frac{1}{2} \frac{(\gamma_2 + \phi_2)(a_1 - p_{01} - c_1 - \alpha c_1) - \theta(a_2 - p_{02} - c_2)}{(\gamma_1 + \phi_1)(\gamma_2 + \phi_2) - \theta^2} \quad (A.18)$$

$$t_1 = \frac{[(2\gamma_1 + \phi_1)(\gamma_2 + \phi_2) - 2\theta^2]c_1 + \phi_1(\gamma_2 + \phi_2)(a_1 - p_{01} - \alpha c_1) - \phi_1\theta(a_2 - p_{02} - c_2)}{2[(\gamma_1 + \phi_1)(\gamma_2 + \phi_2) - \theta^2]} \quad (13)$$

$$s = \frac{[(\gamma_1 + 2\phi_1)(\gamma_2 + \phi_2) - \theta^2]\alpha c_1 + [\gamma_1(\gamma_2 + \phi_2) - \theta^2]\left(a_1 - p_{01} - c_1 - \frac{\theta}{\gamma_2 + \phi_2}(a_2 - p_{02} - c_2)\right)}{2[(\gamma_1 + \phi_1)(\gamma_2 + \phi_2) - \theta^2]}$$

$$- \frac{\theta}{\gamma_2 + \phi_2}\alpha c_2. \quad (14)$$

For the aggregate tax $z_1 = t_1 + s$ we find

$$z_1 = \frac{1}{2}(c_1 + \alpha c_1 + a_1 - p_{01}) - \frac{1}{2}\frac{\theta}{\gamma_2 + \phi_2}(a_2 - p_{02} - c_2) - \frac{\theta}{\gamma_2 + \phi_2}\alpha c_2. \quad (15)$$

Nash Equilibrium Taxation with a Common Carbon Tax in Region A (Model 2)

The general expressions for the R_i and p_i are in this case

$$R_1 = \frac{-[(\gamma_2 + \phi_2)c_1 - \theta c_2]q + (\gamma_2 + \phi_2)(a_1 - s - p_{01}) - \theta(a_2 - p_{02})}{(\gamma_1 + \phi_1)(\gamma_2 + \phi_2) - \theta^2} \quad (A.19)$$

$$R_2 = \frac{-[(\gamma_1 + \phi_1)c_2 - \theta c_1]q + (\gamma_1 + \phi_1)(a_2 - p_{02}) - \theta(a_1 - s - p_{01})}{(\gamma_1 + \phi_1)(\gamma_2 + \phi_2) - \theta^2} \quad (A.20)$$

$$p_1 = \frac{-[(\gamma_2 + \phi_2)c_1 - \theta c_2]\phi_1 q + (\gamma_2 + \phi_2)\phi_1 a_1 - \phi_1\theta(a_2 - p_{02}) + [\gamma_1(\gamma_2 + \phi_2) - \theta^2](s + p_{01})}{(\gamma_1 + \phi_1)(\gamma_2 + \phi_2) - \theta^2} \quad (A.21)$$

$$p_2 = \frac{-[(\gamma_1 + \phi_1)c_2 - \theta c_1]\phi_2 q - \phi_2\theta(a_1 - s - p_{01}) + (\gamma_1 + \phi_1)\phi_2 a_2 + [\gamma_2(\gamma_1 + \phi_1) - \theta^2]p_{02}}{(\gamma_1 + \phi_1)(\gamma_2 + \phi_2) - \theta^2}. \quad (A.22)$$

Effects of changes in the common region A emissions tax q, valid for both sectors, are

$$\frac{dR_1}{dq} = -\frac{(\gamma_2 + \phi_2)c_1 - \theta c_2}{(\gamma_1 + \phi_1)(\gamma_2 + \phi_2) - \theta^2} \quad (A.23)$$

$$\frac{dR_2}{dq} = -\frac{(\gamma_1 + \phi_1)c_2 - \theta c_1}{(\gamma_1 + \phi_1)(\gamma_2 + \phi_2) - \theta^2} \tag{A.24}$$

$$\frac{dp_1}{dq} = -\frac{[(\gamma_2 + \phi_2)c_1 - \theta c_2]\phi_1}{(\gamma_1 + \phi_1)(\gamma_2 + \phi_2) - \theta^2} \tag{A.25}$$

$$\frac{dp_2}{dq} = -\frac{[(\gamma_1 + \phi_1)c_2 - \theta c_1]\phi_2}{(\gamma_1 + \phi_1)(\gamma_2 + \phi_2) - \theta^2}. \tag{A.26}$$

To study tax setting, start with region A, which now sets one common tax rate q per unit of carbon emissions. $W(A)$ is given by (8), whereas the first-order condition has the form

$$\frac{dW(A)}{dR_1}\frac{dR_1}{dq} + \frac{dW(A)}{dR_2}\frac{dR_2}{dq} + \frac{dW(A)}{dp_1}\frac{dp_1}{dq} + \frac{dW(A)}{dp_2}\frac{dp_2}{dq} = 0. \tag{A.27}$$

In this case,

$$\frac{dW(A)}{dR_1} = c_1 q - c_1; \frac{dW(A)}{dR_2} = c_2 q - c_2; \frac{dW(A)}{dp_1} = -R_1; \frac{dW(A)}{dp_2} = 0. \tag{A.28}$$

The first-order condition for region A can now be found as

$$(-c_1 q^* + R_1)[(\gamma_2 + \phi_2)c_1 - \theta c_2] - c_2 q^*[(\gamma_1 + \phi_1)c_2 - \theta c_1] = 0, \tag{A.29}$$

where $q^* = q - 1$ is the tax per unit of emissions in excess of the Pigou level of unity.

Consider in the continuation the simplified case with no demand interaction ($\theta = 0$). The two equations solving for q and s then simplify to

$$(1 + \phi_1^* c_{r1})c_1 q + \phi_1^* c_{r1} s = \phi_1^* c_{r1}(a_1 - c_1 - p_{01}) + c_1 \tag{A.30}$$

$$(1 - \phi_1^*)c_1 q + (2 - \phi_1^*)s = (1 - \phi_1^*)(a_1 - c_1 - p_{01}) + \alpha c_1, \tag{A.31}$$

where we have defined $c_{r1} = \frac{c_1 c_1^*}{c_1 c_1^* + c_2 c_2^*}$, with $c_i^* = \frac{c_i}{\gamma_i + \phi_i}$, for $i = 1, 2$.
The solutions for q and s are

$$c_1 q = \frac{c_{r1}\phi_1^*(a_1 - p_{01} - \alpha c_1) + (2 - \phi_1^*)c_1}{2 - \phi_1^*(1 - c_{r1})} \tag{18}$$

$$s = \frac{(1 - \phi_1^*)(a_1 - p_{01} - c_1) + (1 + c_{r1}\phi_1^*)\alpha c_1}{2 - \phi_1^*(1 - c_{r1})}. \tag{19}$$

The aggregate tax on fuel 1 is in this case

$$z_1 = c_1 q + s = \frac{[1 - \phi_1^*(1 - c_{r1})](a_1 - p_{01}) + c_1 + \alpha c_1}{2 - \phi_1^*(1 - c_{r1})}. \qquad (20)$$

A.5 Nash Equilibrium with Cap Policy in Region A

Region B can, in this case, be viewed as facing the constraint

$$C = c_1 R_1 + c_2 R_2 \qquad (21)$$

whereby R_1 and R_2 are related, for given C. Region B maximizes $W(B)$ with respect to s, subject to (21), facing a constant C. Equation (21) takes the form

$$c_1 \frac{a_1 - s - c_1 q - p_{01}}{\gamma_1 + \phi_1} + c_2 \frac{a_2 - c_2 q - p_{02}}{\gamma_2 + \phi_2} = C. \qquad (A.32)$$

Differentiating (A.32) with respect to s yields

$$\frac{dc_1 q}{ds} = -c_{r1}. \qquad (A.33)$$

We now find, using (A.33):

$$\frac{dR_1}{ds} = -\frac{1}{\gamma_1 + \phi_1}(1 - c_{r1}), \quad \frac{dR_2}{ds} = \frac{1}{\gamma_2 + \phi_2} \frac{c_2}{c_1} c_{r1} \qquad (A.34)$$

(A.10) in this case (with $\theta = 0$) takes the form

$$p_1 = \frac{\phi_1(a_1 - c_1 q) + \gamma_1(s + p_{01})}{(\gamma_1 + \phi_1)}. \qquad (A.10a)$$

Differentiating (A.10a) yields

$$\frac{dp_1}{ds} = 1 - \phi_1^*(1 - c_{r1}). \qquad (22)$$

Maximizing (11) with respect to s now yields

$$-(p_1 - p_{01} - \phi_1 R_1)\frac{1}{\gamma_1 + \phi_1}(1 - c_{r1}) + R_1 \frac{dp_1}{ds} = 0. \qquad (A.35)$$

Since the cap C on emissions is chosen by region A, region B takes C as a constant in its own optimization. Thus, region B's policy has no influence on carbon emissions. The two last terms in (11) then drop out. We derive the following condition:

$$\begin{aligned}[1 - \phi_1^*(1 - c_{r1})]\, c_1 q^* + [1 + (1 - \phi_1^*)(1 - c_{r1})]\, s \\ = [1 - \phi_1^*(1 - c_{r1})]\, (a_1 - c_1 - p_{01}).\end{aligned} \qquad (A.36)$$

(A.30) and (A.36) now solve for $c_1 q^*$ $(= c_1(q\text{-}1))$ and s^* $(= s - \alpha c_1)$, as follows:

$$c_1 q^* = \phi_1^* c_{r1} \frac{1 - c_{r1}}{2 - c_{r1} - \phi_1^*(1 - c_{r1})^2}(a_1 - c_1 - p_{01}) \qquad (23)$$

$$s^* = \frac{1 - \phi_1^*(1 - c_{r1})}{2 - c_{r1} - \phi_1^*(1 - c_{r1})^2}(a_1 - c_1 - p_{01}) - \alpha c_1. \qquad (24)$$

The sum of the exporter tax and the importer quota price (the "effective tax" on fuel 1) is

$$z_1^* = c_1 q^* + s^* = \frac{1 - \phi_1^*(1 - c_{r1})^2}{2 - c_{r1} - \phi_1^*(1 - c_{r1})^2}(a_1 - p_{01} - c_1) - \alpha c_1. \qquad (25)$$

References

Amundsen, Eirik S., and Schöb, Ronnie. 2000. Environmental taxes on exhaustible resources. *European Journal of Political Economy* 15:311–329.

Bergstrom, Theodore C. 1982. On capturing oil rent with a national excise tax. *American Economic Review* 72:194–201.

Eichner, Thomas, and Pethig, Rüdiger. 2009. Carbon leakage, the green paradox, and perfect future markets. CESifo Working Paper No. 2542. Ifo Institute for Economic Research, Munich, Germany.

Kalkuhl, Matthias and Edenhofer, Ottmar. 2010. Prices Versus Quantities and the Intertemporal Dynamics of the Climate Rent. CESifo Working Paper No. 3044. Munich: CESifo.

Karp, Larry, and Newbery, David M. 1991. OPEC and the U.S. oil import tariffs. *Economic Journal Supplement* 101:303–313.

Keutiben, Octave N. 2010. On capturing foreign oil rents. Working Paper, Department of Economics, Université de Montréal.

Liski, Matti, and Tahvonen, Olli. 2004. Can carbon tax eat OPEC's rents? *Journal of Environmental Economics and Management* 47:1–12.

Newbery, David M. 2005. Why tax energy? Towards a more rational policy. *The Energy Journal* 26:1–40.

Ploeg, Frederick v. d. and Withagen, Cees. 2009. Is there really a green paradox? CESifo Working Paper No. 2963. Munich: CESifo.

Rubio, Santiago J. 2005. Tariff agreements and non-renewable resource international monopolies: Prices versus quantities. Discussion Paper No. 2005–10, Department of Economic Analysis, University of Valencia, Madrid.

Rubio, Santiago J., and Escriche, Luisa. 2001. Strategic Pigouvian taxation, stock externalities and polluting non-renewable resources. *Journal of Public Economics* 79:297–313.

Salo, Seppo, and Tahvonen, Olli. 2001. Oligopoly equilibrium in nonrenewable resource markets. *Journal of Dynamic Optimization and Control* 25:671–702.

Sinn, Hans-Werner. 2008. Public policies against global warming. *International Tax and Public Finance* 15:360–394.

Stern, David I. 2009. Interfuel substitution: A meta-analysis. MPRA Working Paper No. 15792, Arndt-Corden Division of Economics, Research School of Pacific and Asian Studies, Australian National University.

Strand, Jon. 2007. Technology treaties and fossil-fuels extraction. *The Energy Journal* 28:169–181.

Strand, Jon. 2009a. Who gains and who loses by fossil-fuel taxes and caps: Importers versus exporters. World Bank.

Strand, Jon. 2009b. *Why do fossil fuel exporters subsidize their own fuel consumption?* World Bank.

Wei, Jiegen. 2009. Fossil Endgame? Strategic Pricing and Taxation of Oil in a World of Climate Change. PhD thesis, Department of Economics, University of Gothenburg, Sweden.

EIGHT

How Much Should Highway Fuels Be Taxed?

Ian W. H. Parry

8.1 Introduction

The United States imposes, at the federal and state levels, excise taxes of about 40 cents/gallon on gasoline and 45 cents/gallon on diesel for heavy trucks. The federal tax on these fuels is currently 18.4 and 24.4 cents/gallon, respectively (FHWA 2007, Tables 8.2.1 and 8.2.3). The U.S. tax rates are low by international standards; for example, in many European countries gasoline taxes exceed $2/gallon, although the United States is somewhat unusual in taxing diesel more heavily than gasoline, albeit only slightly (Figure 8.1).

Traditionally, the level of fuel taxes in the United States has been governed by highway spending needs; fuel tax revenues account for about two-thirds of the approximately $100 billion in revenues raised from all highway user fees.[1] However, there is growing debate about both the appropriate level of federal fuel taxes and their status as a dedicated revenue source.

One reason is the weakening link between fuel taxes and highway spending. A rising portion of this spending has been financed through nonhighway revenues (e.g., local sales and property taxes), and some fuel tax revenues have been diverted for other purposes (e.g., transit projects). Moreover, there is concern about the erosion of real fuel tax revenues per vehicle mile, especially with the recent tightening of fuel economy regulations, and the failure of nominal tax rates to rise with inflation (federal gasoline and diesel taxes were last increased in 1993). However, whether revenues are

---

[1] Transportation Research Board (2006). Other revenue comes from vehicle license and registration fees, tolls, and various taxes on commercial trucks.

I am grateful to Dan Greenbaum and Roberton Williams for very helpful comments on an earlier draft.

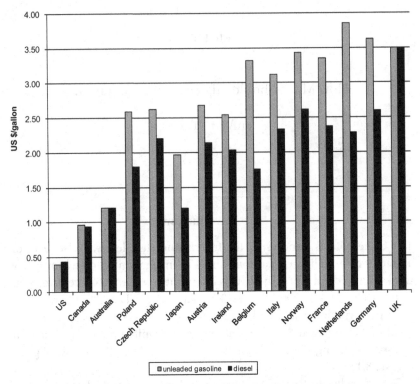

Figure 8.1. Taxation of Motor Fuels: Selected Countries (for 2008). *Source:* OECD (2009).

earmarked or not, the key (though poorly understood) economic issue is what level of fuel taxation is warranted on fiscal grounds.

Another reason for interest in fuel taxes is the increasingly apparent disparity – due to inadequate taxation – between the societal cost of automobile trips and the private cost borne by motorists. These broader costs reflect the global warming potential of CO_2 emissions and, possibly, consequences from the economy's dependence on a volatile world oil market under the influence of unstable suppliers.

Gasoline and (truck) diesel fuel accounted for 20 percent and 6 percent, respectively, of nationwide carbon emissions in 2008, and for 46 percent and 13 percent, respectively, of oil use.[2]

Meanwhile. there is ever-worsening road congestion, as the relentlessly expanding demand for highway travel outpaces capacity growth (Figure 8.2). The average motorist in very large urban areas in the United States

---

[2] From www.eia.gov and Bureau of Transportation Statistics (2009), Tables 4.13 and 4.14.

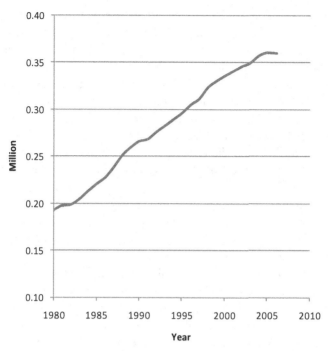

Figure 8.2. Vehicle Miles of Travel per Lane Mile of Capacity, 1980–2007. *Source:* FHWA (2007), Table 4.2.1. *Note:* Figure includes mileage from light and heavy vehicles.

lost 54 hours to traffic delays in 2005; this is up from 21 hours in 1982 (BTS 2009, Table 1.63). Traffic accidents are yet another major externality. About 40,000 people have been killed on U.S. highways each year for the past 25 years (BTS 2009, Table 2.18).

Finally, recent and prospective developments in related policies have implications for efficient fuel taxation, including the new fuel economy regulations and the possibility of a nationwide greenhouse gas cap-and-trade program. Furthermore, advances in electronic metering technology, and experience with area pricing in London, have raised the prospects for vehicle mileage tolls in the United States, which are a far better tool for congestion management than fuel taxes (Santos and Fraser 2006). Similarly, there is growing interest in pay-as-you-drive automobile insurance as a way to internalize accident externalities (Bordhoff and Noel 2008; Greenberg 2009).

It is therefore an opportune time for an updated assessment of the appropriate role of fuel taxes. Here we focus largely on efficiency considerations, that is, what the ideal tax system should look like from a purely economic perspective. The conceptual framework for optimal fuel taxes has been developed previously. Moreover, there is substantial empirical literature on highway externalities in the United States and behavioral responses to fuel prices, though in some cases (e.g., global warming damages) the literature remains highly unsettled. This chapter pulls together prior analytical studies, updates parameter values, and provides some new findings. The latter relate to the implications of recent policy developments and of alternative revenue recycling options. The chapter also provides a comparison of optimal gasoline and diesel taxes for the United States, using consistent methodology and assumptions. We summarize some key points as follows.

In our baseline assessment, the corrective gasoline tax is $1.23/gallon, with congestion and accidents together accounting for about three-quarters of this tax. This estimate might be viewed as a lower bound, as we use conservative values for global warming and perhaps for oil-dependence externalities, both of which are highly contentious. However, if a binding, nationwide cap-and-trade program were introduced, there would be no global warming benefit, as emissions are fixed. On the other hand, the corrective tax may rise to $2/gallon in the presence of (pervasively binding) fuel economy regulations. In this case, more of a given, tax-induced gasoline reduction must come from reduced driving (and less from fuel economy improvements), which magnifies the congestion and accident benefits per gallon of fuel reduction. Conversely, pricing of congestion and other externalities through mileage tolls would dramatically lower the corrective gasoline tax, conceivably even below its current level, although such comprehensive tolling is likely a long way off.

However, an unbiased assessment of fuel taxes must account for how they interact with distortions in the economy created by the broader fiscal system. In fact, the optimal gasoline tax is extremely sensitive to alternative revenue uses. Conceivably, it could rise to $3/gallon if revenues are recycled in highly efficient ways, most notably by cuts in income taxes that distort factor markets and create a bias towards tax-favored spending. On the other hand, if recycling does not increase efficiency, the case for higher gasoline taxes appears to be reversed. This is because efficiency gains from externality mitigation are counteracted by efficiency losses in the labor market, as higher fuel prices drive up transportation prices relative to the price of leisure.

Under baseline parameters, we put the corrective diesel tax at $1.15/gallon, though underlying determinants are different than for the corrective gasoline tax. Road damage plays a significant role in the corrective diesel tax. Congestion and accidents are less important (even though trucks take up more road space), because a given tax-induced reduction in diesel saves only about a third as many vehicle miles as the same reduction in gasoline, owing to the fact that heavy trucks get lower miles per gallon. Again, however, when we account for interactions with the broader fiscal system, the optimal tax is highly dependent on revenue use and varies between essentially zero, when revenues are returned lump sum, and $3.00 per gallon, when revenues finance income tax reductions.

Our optimal tax estimates should not be taken too literally, because we are relying on parameter evidence that is tentative in some cases, if not highly speculative (e.g., for oil-dependence externalities). No doubt fuel tax assessments will evolve over time, perhaps even radically, as valuation methodologies are refined, transportation characteristics change (e.g., emission rates, congestion levels), and with related policy developments (e.g., the spread of congestion pricing).

The rest of the chapter is organized as follows. Section 8.2 provides conceptual details on the corrective gasoline tax. Section 8.3 presents calculations of this tax. Section 8.4 discusses linkages between fuel taxes and the broader fiscal system. Section 8.5 discusses optimal diesel taxes. A final section offers concluding remarks and briefly discusses some caveats, including distributional concerns, feasibility, and the role of induced innovation.

8.2 Corrective Gasoline Tax: Analytical Underpinnings

Currently, for the United States, it is reasonable to assume gasoline and diesel are used exclusively by passenger vehicles and heavy trucks, respectively. Therefore, we can focus on passenger vehicle externalities when assessing gasoline taxes and heavy truck externalities when assessing diesel taxes (with one caveat, noted later).[3]

Consider, based on a modified version of Parry and Small (2005), a long-run, static model in which the representative household solves the following optimization problem:

$$\underset{m,v,g,X}{Max} \; u(v, m, X, E_G(\overline{G}), E_M(\overline{M}))$$

$$+ \lambda \{I + GOV - [(p_G + t_G)gm + t_M m + c(g)]v - p_X X\} \quad (8.1a)$$

$$G = gM, \quad M = vm \quad (8.1b)$$

---

[3] In many European countries a substantial portion of the car fleet runs on diesel. In this case the corrective diesel tax will reflect a weighted average of externalities from passenger vehicles and heavy trucks, while substitution among gasoline and diesel passenger vehicles would affect the corrective gasoline tax.

All variables are in per capita terms, and a bar denotes an economy-wide variable perceived as exogenous by individuals.

v denotes the vehicle stock (vehicle choice is a continuous variable, as we are averaging over many households), m is miles driven per vehicle, and g is gasoline consumption per mile driven, or the inverse of fuel economy. G and M are therefore aggregate gasoline consumption and miles driven, respectively. X is a general consumption good. $E_G(.)$ and $E_M(.)$ are externalities that vary in proportion with gasoline and mileage, respectively (see below). I denotes (fixed) household income, and GOV is a government transfer, to capture the recycling of fuel tax revenues (alternative revenue uses are discussed later). $c(g)$ is the fixed cost of vehicle ownership, which is higher for more fuel-efficient vehicles, reflecting the added production costs of incorporating fuel-saving technologies. p_G and p_X denote the fixed producer prices for gasoline and the general good, whereas t_G is the (nationwide average) gasoline excise tax. t_M is a unit tax on vehicle mileage. Households choose v, m, g, and X to maximize utility $u(.)$ subject to a budget constraint equating income with spending on gasoline, mileage taxes, vehicles, and other goods (λ is a Lagrange multiplier).[4]

$E_G(.)$ includes greenhouse gases and possible energy security externalities associated with dependence on oil. $E_M(.)$ includes accident risk and road congestion. Local tailpipe emissions are also included in $E_M(.)$, given that all new passenger vehicles must meet the same emissions-per-mile standards, regardless of their fuel economy, and that (owing to the durability of emissions control systems as well as emissions inspection programs) emission rates now show relatively modest deterioration as vehicles age (Fischer, Harrington, and Parry 2007).[5] Road wear and tear and noise are ignored, as they are primarily caused by heavy trucks (Small et al., 1989; FWHA 2000).

The corrective gasoline tax, denoted t_G^C, is (see Appendix):

$$t_G^C = e_G + \beta \cdot (e_M - t_M)/g \tag{8.2a}$$

$$e_G = -u_{E_G} E_G'/\lambda, \quad e_M = -u_{E_M} E_M'/\lambda \tag{8.2b}$$

$$\beta = \frac{g \cdot dM/dt_G}{dG/dt_G} \tag{8.2c}$$

---

[4] Our analysis abstracts from the possibility of a market failure associated with consumer undervaluation of fuel economy. Whether and to what extent there is such a market failure remains an unsettled issue in the empirical literature.

[5] Besides tailpipe emissions, local pollutants are also released upstream during oil shipping, refining, and fuel distribution. However, partly due to tight regulations, the resulting environmental damages are relatively small, about 2 cents/gallon according to the National Research Council (2002).

e_G and e_M denote the marginal external costs (or monetized disutility) from gasoline use and mileage in dollars per gallon and dollars per mile, respectively.

The corrective tax in (8.2a) consists of the marginal external cost from greenhouse gases and from oil dependence. It also includes combined marginal external costs from congestion, accidents, and local emissions, net of any internalization through mileage taxes, and scaled by two factors. The first factor is miles per gallon $(1/g)$, to convert costs into dollars per gallon. However, miles per gallon is endogenous and will rise as higher fuel prices raise the demand for more fuel-efficient vehicles. In turn, this multiplies the contribution of mileage-related externalities to the corrective tax, because an incremental reduction in gasoline use is now associated with a larger reduction in vehicle miles. The second factor, denoted β and defined in (8.2b), is the fraction of the incremental reduction in gasoline use that comes from reduced mileage, as opposed to improved fuel economy. The smaller is β, the smaller the contribution of mileage-related externalities to the corrective gasoline tax. In fact, if all of the incremental fuel reduction came from improved fuel economy, and none from reduced driving, then $\beta = 0$ and congestion, accidents, and local pollution would not affect the corrective tax.

We adopt the following functional forms:

$$\frac{M}{M^0} = \left(\frac{p_G + t_G}{p_G + t_G^0}\right)^{\eta_M}, \quad \frac{g}{g^0} = \left(\frac{p_G + t_G}{p_G + t_G^0}\right)^{\eta_g} \tag{8.3}$$

η_M and η_g denote, respectively, the elasticity of vehicle mileage and gasoline per mile with respect to gasoline prices, and 0 denotes an initial value. The gasoline demand elasticity η_G is the sum of these two elasticities. We take all elasticities as constant (a common assumption), which implies β is also constant.

The welfare gain (W_G) from raising the gasoline tax from its current level to the corrective level is (see Appendix):

$$W_G = \int_{t_G^0}^{t_G^C} (t_G^C - t_G) \frac{dG}{dt_G} dt_G. \tag{8.4}$$

Thus, W_G is given by the shaded triangle in Figure 8.3.

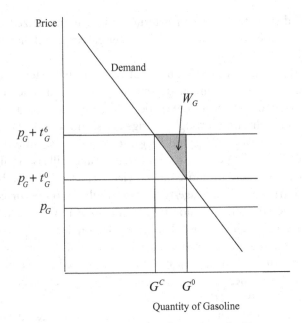

Figure 8.3. Welfare Gain from Corrective Tax

8.3 Computing the Corrective Gasoline Tax

In this section, we discuss the corrective tax under benchmark parameter assumptions and alterative scenarios. Benchmark parameters are representative of year 2007 or thereabouts.

8.3.1 Global Warming Externalities

A gallon of gasoline produces 0.0088 tons of CO_2. Some studies (e.g., Nordhaus 2008) put the marginal damage from current CO_2 emissions at about \$10/ton, whereas others value it at about \$80/ton (e.g., Stern 2007), implying damages of \$0.09 or \$0.70/gallon.[6] To be conservative, we use the former for our benchmark case and the latter for sensitivity analysis.

One reason for the different estimates is that, as a result of long atmospheric residence times and the gradual adjustment of the climate system, today's emissions have intergenerational impacts, and the present value of their damages is highly sensitive to assumed discount rates. Some analysts (e.g., Heal 2009) argue for using low rates to discount intergenerational

---

[6] Marginal damages in Stern (2007) are substantially reduced if future global climate is rapidly stabilized through aggressive mitigation policies.

impacts on ethical grounds (i.e., to avoid discriminating against people just because they are born in the future). Others (e.g., Nordhaus 2007) view market discounting as essential for meaningful policy analysis (i.e., to avoid perverse policy implications in other contexts).

A second reason for different CO_2 damage assessments (though not between Nordhaus and Stern) has to do with the treatment of extreme catastrophic risks. In particular, it is possible that the marginal damages from CO_2 emissions are arbitrarily large if the probability distribution over future climate damages has "fat tails"; that is, the probability of increasingly catastrophic outcomes falls more slowly than marginal utility rises (with diminished consumption) in those outcomes (Weitzman 2009). This reflects the possibility of unstable feedback mechanisms in the climate system, such as a warming-induced release of underground methane (itself a greenhouse gas) leading to a truly catastrophic warming. Others (e.g., Nordhaus 2009) have critiqued the fat tails hypothesis on the grounds that we can head off a future catastrophic outcome by radical mitigation measures and deployment of last-resort technologies (e.g., for atmospheric removal of carbon, or deflection of incoming sunlight through scattering particulates in the atmosphere) in response to future learning about the seriousness of climate change.

For our purposes, these controversies would be redundant if a binding cap-and-trade system is imposed on nationwide CO_2 emissions. In this case, any CO_2 reductions from higher gasoline taxes would be offset by higher emissions in other sectors. In contrast, under an economy-wide CO_2 tax, higher gasoline taxes would reduce nationwide emissions, though benefits per ton would be net of the CO_2 tax.

8.3.2 Oil Dependence

One possible externality from oil dependence is macroeconomic disruption costs from the risk of oil price shocks. However, to what extent private markets adequately internalize these risks in inventory decisions, financial hedging, purchase of high fuel economy vehicles, and so forth, is much disputed. The most widely cited study is by Leiby (2007), who puts the uninternalized macroeconomic disruption cost at about $0.10/gallon for 2004 (Brown and Huntington [2009] reach similar conclusions). Some analysts also suggest that a gasoline tax can proxy for an oil import tariff, which could increase U.S. welfare given its monopsony power in the world oil market. However, whether this component should factor into fuel tax assessments is unclear, given that an oil import tariff would reduce welfare from a global, as opposed to a U.S., perspective, and could even reduce U.S. welfare if other countries can retaliate with trade protection measures.

Oil dependence may also constrain U.S. foreign policy, for example, by making U.S. governments reluctant to press for human rights and democratic freedoms in oil-exporting nations. Oil revenue flows may also help to fund terrorist activities and unsavory governments. However, valuing these types of geo-political costs is extremely difficult. Moreover, even if U.S. oil consumption were significantly curtailed, the proportionate reduction in these petrodollar flows would be relatively small, unless other major oil-consuming countries followed suit.

We assume $0.10/gallon for oil-dependence externalities, though this might be viewed as a (probably conservative) "placeholder" until we have a better handle on externality valuation.

8.3.3 Other Externalities

There is reasonable consensus on local pollution damages from automobiles. We follow Small and Verhoef (2007, pp. 104–105) and assume damages of $0.01/mile nationwide. Mortality effects (caused primarily by particulates rather than ozone) account for the vast bulk of damages. Small and Verhoef assume the value of a statistical life (VSL) for quantifying mortality is $4.15 million, after accounting for discounting of the time lag between pollution exposure and mortality, and the smaller VSL for seniors who are most at risk. Local pollution damages will likely continue their downward trend over time, as the fleet turns over and a greater share of vehicles will have been subject to recently tightened new-vehicle emissions standards.[7]

Parry and Small (2005) assumed marginal congestion costs of $0.035/mile. This is based on an assessment, by FHWA (2000), that averages over marginal congestion costs for representative road classes across urban and rural areas and time of day. Marginal traffic delays are inferred from traffic speed/traffic flow curves and are monetized assuming the value of travel time is half the market wage. The $0.035/mile figure includes an adjustment for the relatively weaker sensitivity of congested, peak-period driving (which is dominated by commuting) to fuel prices, compared with off-peak driving. We use an updated value of $0.045/mile, given that nominal wages grew about 22 percent between 2000 and 2007, whereas congestion delays

---

[7] The "Tier Two" standards imply emission rates for new vehicles of just 0.8 to 5.0 percent of pre-1970 rates.

increased by about 8 percent (CEA 2009, Table B 47; Schrank and Lomax 2009, Table 4).[8]

For accidents, Parry and Small (2005) assumed a marginal external cost of $0.03/mile. External costs include injury risks to pedestrians, a large portion of medical and property damage costs borne by third parties, and the tax-revenue component of injury-induced workplace productivity losses (other accident costs, such as injury risks in single-vehicle collisions, and foregone take-home wages from productivity losses, are assumed internal).[9] We use a value of $0.035/mile for the marginal externality, after updating for a VSL of $5.8 million, now used by U.S. Department of Transportation (this VSL is higher than for pollution deaths, because people killed on roads are typically younger and die quickly rather than with a long lag).[10]

8.3.4 Elasticities and Other Data

We assume the pre-tax fuel price p_G is $2.30/gallon, the combined federal and state gasoline tax is $0.40/gallon, and initial gasoline consumption is 140 billion gallons.[11] For the benchmark case, we assume initial on-road fuel economy $(1/g)$ is 22 mpg (BTS 2008, Table 4.23). The long-run gasoline demand elasticity is assumed to be −0.4, with half of the response coming from improved fuel economy and half from reduced mileage (some combination of reduced vehicle demand and reduced miles per vehicle). Thus, $\eta_g = -0.2$, $\eta_M = -0.2$ and $\beta = 0.5$. These assumptions are based largely on Small and Van Dender (2006).[12]

---

[8] We view the congestion cost figure as conservative. For example, based on extrapolating congestion costs nationwide from a network model of the Washington, D.C., road network, Fischer et al. (2007) put marginal congestion costs at $0.065/mile.

[9] Whether, and to what extent, external costs should also include injury risk to other vehicle occupants in multivehicle collisions is unsettled. All else the same, the presence of one extra vehicle on the road raises the collision risk for all other vehicles (as they have less road space); however, an offsetting factor is that people may drive slower or more carefully in heavier traffic.

[10] To the extent that higher fuel taxes encourage consumers to purchase cars instead of light trucks there may be an added externality gain that our figure does not capture. This is because accident externalities appear to be larger for light trucks (e.g., Li 2009, White 2004).

[11] From Parry and Small (2005) and www.eia.gov.

[12] The estimated magnitude of gasoline demand elasticities has declined over time, reflecting the declining share of fuel costs in total (i.e., time plus money) travel costs. In addition, the relatively low-cost technological opportunities for improving vehicle fuel economy have been progressively exploited.

As a result of legislation in 2007 and administrative action begun in 2009, fuel economy standards were fully integrated with new targets for reducing CO_2 emissions per mile for new automobiles. Manufacturers will be required to meet standards equivalent to 39 mpg for the average fuel economy of their new car fleets, and 30 mpg for their light-truck fleets, by 2016 (prior standards were 27.5 mpg for cars and 24.0 mpg for light trucks). To the extent that these regulations will be binding on all, as opposed to a subset, of auto manufacturers, the gasoline/mile elasticity will be substantially reduced, implying a much smaller β. In fact, the regulations will likely be binding, even if fuel prices were to increase by over \$2/gallon, though there will still be some price responsiveness because motorists can substitute new cars for new light trucks and use existing high-mpg vehicles more intensively (Small 2009). In the sensitivity analysis, we consider a case in which the fuel economy elasticity is 0.1 (based approximately on Small 2009), implying $\beta = 0.67$. For this case, we set initial (on-road) fuel economy for passenger vehicles at 29 mpg (on-road fuel economy is lower than certified fuel economy for new vehicles by about 15 percent).

Finally, we set $t_M = 0$ in the benchmark case, as the nationwide revenue from automobile tolls is very small relative to gasoline tax revenues. In sensitivity analysis, we consider full internalization of mileage-related externalities through mileage tolls $(t_M = e_M)$.[13]

8.3.5 Optimal Tax Estimates

Table 8.1 summarizes the corrective gasoline tax (in year 2007 dollars), and its impacts, under our benchmark parameters, and various sensitivity analyses in which parameters are varied one at a time.

Under benchmark parameters, the corrective tax is \$1.23/gallon. Congestion and accidents contribute most to the corrective tax, \$0.52 and \$0.41/gallon, respectively. Global warming, oil dependence, and local pollution each contribute about the same, \$0.09 to \$0.12/gallon. Increasing the tax from the current rate of \$0.40/gallon to the corrective level moderately increases fuel economy to 23.2 mpg and reduces overall gasoline use by 10 percent. The resulting welfare gain is \$5.9 billion, and tax revenues increase by 180 percent from \$56 billion to \$157 billion.

In the high global warming case, the optimal gasoline tax rises to \$1.88/gallon, and welfare gains are almost three times as large (as both the height

---

[13] For the cases with preexisting fuel economy standards and preexisting mileage taxes, we scale back initial gasoline use accordingly using (3), and with the mileage tax converted to its fuel tax equivalent.

Table 8.1. *Calculations of the corrective gasoline tax (Year 2007 Dollars)*

Benchmark case	**1.23**
Corrective tax, $/gallon	
Contribution from	
global warming	0.09
oil dependence	0.10
local pollution	0.12
congestion	0.52
accidents	0.41
Miles/gallon at corrective tax	23.2
Proportionate reduction in gasoline use	0.10
Welfare gain, $ billion[a]	5.9
Proportionate increase in tax revenue	2.8
High global warming damages	
Corrective tax, $/gallon	**1.88**
Miles/gallon at corrective tax	24.0
Proportionate reduction in gasoline use	0.16
Welfare gain, $ billion[a]	16.6
With preexisting climate policy	
Corrective tax, $/gallon	**1.14**
Binding fuel economy regulations	
Corrective tax, $/gallon	**2.01**
Miles/gallon at corrective tax	30.4
Proportionate reduction in gasoline use	0.17
Welfare gain, $ billion[a]	12.3
With preexisting corrective mileage tax	
Corrective tax, $/gallon	**0.19**
Proportionate reduction in gasoline use	−0.03
Welfare gain, $ billion[a]	0.43

[a] Ignores welfare effects from broader fiscal linkages.
Source: See discussion in text.

and the base of the shaded triangle in Figure 8.3 increase). However, the corrective tax *falls* to $1.14/gallon if there is a preexisting CO_2 cap-and-trade policy (or Pigouvian CO_2 tax that fully internalizes global warming damages).

In the (future) case with (binding) preexisting fuel economy regulations, the corrective tax rises to $2.01/gallon. Here the mileage-related externalities – local pollution, congestion, and accidents – each contribute about 80 percent more to the corrective tax than they do in the benchmark case. This is because the reduction in mileage associated with a given reduction in gasoline use is now higher, and for two reasons. First, an assumed 67 percent (rather than 50 percent) of the marginal reduction in fuel use comes from reduced driving. Second, the distance travelled per gallon of gasoline is about a third higher than in the benchmark case.

Finally, with a preexisting tax that fully corrects all of the mileage-related externalities, the corrective gasoline tax falls dramatically to \$0.19/gallon, or about half its current rate. In this case, the tax reflects global warming and oil-dependence externalities only.

8.4 The Fiscal Rationale for Gasoline Taxes

Gasoline taxes (or any corrective tax or regulation for that matter) interact with distortions in the economy created by the broader tax system, and these interactions should be taken into account to obtain an unbiased assessment of the welfare effects, and optimal level, of the tax. Here we represent the broader tax system by collapsing it into a single tax of t_L on labor income, which reflects the wedge between the gross wage (which we normalize to unity) and the net wage received by households. The gross wage reflects the value marginal product of labor, whereas the net wage reflects the marginal cost of labor supply in terms of foregone time in nonmarket activities. Changes in labor supply induced by fuel taxes therefore induce welfare effects equal to the change multiplied by t_L. We first discuss adjustments to the corrective gasoline tax to account for broader fiscal interactions and then provide some sense of the empirical importance of these adjustments.

8.4.1 Fiscal Adjustments to the Corrective Gasoline Tax

As discussed in the literature on environmental tax shifts (e.g., Goulder 1995), broader fiscal interactions take two forms.

First is the *tax interaction effect*. This is the efficiency loss in the labor market that results when a new product tax drives up the general consumer price level, thereby reducing the real household wage and discouraging labor supply. Of course, the proportionate impact of the product tax on economy-wide labor supply will be extremely small. However, the resulting efficiency loss may still substantially change the overall welfare effect of the tax, given the huge size of the labor market in the economy, and the large wedge that results from federal and state income taxes, payroll taxes, and sales taxes.[14]

Second is the *revenue-recycling effect*. Usually in the literature this is taken to reflect the efficiency gain from recycling environmental tax revenues in broader income tax reductions. Alternatively however, revenues from higher

---

[14] That is, the welfare change rectangle in the labor market has a small base but a large height.

fuel taxes might be used to fund highway spending or, more generally, public goods, transfer payments, or deficit reduction.

There is no need to repeat here the derivations for fiscal adjustments to corrective taxes from other papers that integrate models of externalities into general equilibrium models with prior tax distortions. Instead, we simply start with the following formula derived in Parry, Laxminarayan, and West (2009):

$$
t_G^* = t_G^C + \delta \left\{ G \left(-\frac{dt_G}{dG} \right) - t_G^* \right\} - (1 + \delta) t_L \frac{\partial L}{\partial p_G} \left(-\frac{dt_G}{dG} \right) \tag{8.5}
$$

In this expression, δ is the efficiency gain associated with an extra dollar of government revenue (see below) and $*$ denotes an optimal (as opposed to corrective) tax.

In equation (8.5), the first adjustment to the corrective tax is the revenue-recycling effect. It equals the product of δ and the extra revenue per gallon reduction in gasoline induced by the higher fuel tax. The second adjustment is the tax-interaction effect. This includes the change in labor supply from a marginal increase in the gasoline price, multiplied by the increase in gasoline tax, per gallon reduction in gasoline. This labor supply change is multiplied by the labor tax wedge, and also by $1 + \delta$, to account for the efficiency cost of lost labor tax revenues.

Some manipulation gives, after decomposing the labor supply effect using the Slutsky equation, and using the Slutsky symmetry property (Parry, Laxminarayan, and West 2009)

$$
t_G^* = t_G^C + \delta \left\{ \frac{p_G + t_G^*}{(-\eta_G)} - t_G^* \right\} - \frac{(1 + \delta) t_L (p_G + t_G^*) \left(\eta_{GI}^{comp} + \eta_{LI} \right)}{(1 - t_L)(-\eta_G)} \tag{8.6}
$$

η_{GI}^{comp} is the (compensated) cross-price elasticity of gasoline use with respect to the household wage or price of leisure, and $\eta_{LI} < 0$ is the income elasticity of labor supply.

Suppose for now that extra revenues are used to cut labor taxes. In this case, δ is the efficiency cost of raising an extra dollar of revenue through labor taxes, or the efficiency cost from an incremental increase in t_L divided by the marginal increase in revenue. Thus,

$$
\delta = \frac{-t_L \dfrac{\partial L}{\partial t_L}}{\dfrac{\partial (t_L L)}{\partial t_L}} = \frac{\dfrac{t_L}{1 - t_L} \varepsilon_L}{1 - \dfrac{t_L}{1 - t_L} \varepsilon_L}, \qquad \varepsilon_L = \frac{\partial L}{\partial (1 - t_L)} \frac{1 - t_L}{L} = \varepsilon_L^{comp} + \eta_{LI}
$$

$$
\tag{8.7}
$$

where ε_L is the uncompensated labor supply elasticity. This is related to the compensated labor supply elasticity, ε_L^{comp}, and the income elasticity of labor supply, via the Slutsky equation.

8.4.2 Quantitative Importance of Fiscal Linkages

Although there is considerable dispersion in empirical estimates, a plausible benchmark assumption is that $\varepsilon_L = 0.2$ (e.g., Blundell and Macurdy 1999). This value represents an average over labor supply responses due to changes in average hours worked per employee, and labor force participation rates, across male and female workers. We use a standard value of 0.4 for the labor tax wedge, representing a compromise between the average tax rate (which affects the participation margin) and the marginal tax rate (which affects the hours on the job margin). Our values imply $\delta = \$0.15$. This corresponds to a value of 1.15 for the *marginal cost of public funds* (equal to $1 + \delta$). Note that δ is defined here relative to when revenue is not recycled, and therefore the behavioral responses underlying δ are uncompensated. In contrast, for example, if we were raising income taxes and returning revenue in lump-sum transfers to households, efficiency effects would depend in part on the compensated labor supply elasticity, implying a larger value for δ. This larger value corresponds to the *marginal excess burden of taxation*, as commonly defined.

If gasoline exhibits the same degree of substitution with leisure as consumption goods in general, then $\eta_{GI}^{comp} = \varepsilon_L^{comp}$, that is, gasoline changes in the same proportion to aggregate consumption, or labor supply, following a compensated increase in the price of leisure (Parry, Laxminarayan, and West 2009). From manipulating (8.6) and (8.7), we can easily show $t_G^* = t_G^C/(1 + \delta)$. In this case, using our value for δ, the optimal tax is about 15 percent smaller than the corrective tax. This downward adjustment reflects the balance between the externality benefit per gallon of gasoline reduced, and the efficiency cost per gallon reduced, where the latter is the tax per gallon, times $1 + \delta$, to account for the erosion of the base of the gasoline tax (which must be offset by higher labor taxes).

If all auto passenger travel were work-related, it might be reasonable to assume gasoline is an average substitute for leisure, as travel would change in rough proportion to hours worked (or total consumption) following a change in the price of leisure. However, evidence in West and Williams (2007) suggests that gasoline is a relatively weak substitute for leisure (i.e., $\eta_{GI}^{comp} < \varepsilon_L^{comp}$), a plausible explanation being that a large portion of passenger-vehicle trips are leisure-related rather than work-related. Based on West and Williams (2007), we set $\eta_{GI}^{comp} + \eta_{LI} = 0.1$. With this assumption, the optimal gasoline tax rises to $1.71/gallon or about 40 percent more than the corrective tax (from equations (8.6) and (8.7) and the benchmark value for t_G^C).

However, the U.S. fiscal system distorts not only factor markets, but also the allocation of spending across ordinary consumption and tax-favored goods, like owner-occupied housing and employer-provided medical insurance. Although the tax-favored sector is small in size relative to the labor market, it is relatively more responsive to income tax changes than labor supply. This means that the efficiency costs of higher income taxes caused by exacerbating distortions in the pattern of spending can still be significant relative to efficiency costs in factor markets. Based on empirical evidence, Parry (2002) suggests that the efficiency gain from recycling a dollar of revenue in income tax reductions (relative to not recycling the dollar) might be in the order of $0.30 rather than $0.15. If so, the optimal gasoline tax rises dramatically, because the revenue-recycling effect is doubled. As indicated in Figure 8.4, which is obtained from equation (8.6) with alternative values for δ in both the revenue-recycling and tax-interaction components, the optimal gasoline tax rises to over $3/gallon.

On the other hand, additional fuel tax revenue might be used to fund highway maintenance and expansion projects. It is difficult to put a general figure on the marginal value of highway spending, given that it will be highly project-specific and that transportation agencies do not routinely conduct economic valuations of projects. In fact, a long-standing concern has been the lack of pressure for efficient allocation of highway spending, given that federal grants to states (which account for more than half of federal highway spending) are largely allocated in proportion to vehicle miles rather than degree of congestion or road quality. Empirical estimates of the social rate of return to highway spending are typically within a range of 0 to 30 percent (TRB 2006, chapter 3). If the social discount rate is 5 percent, this would imply δ is between about -0.05 and 0.25 for highway spending.[15] As indicated in Figure 8.4, this would imply an optimal gasoline tax of anywhere between about $0.50 and $2.50/gallon.

More generally, extra revenues might fund (non–transport-related) public spending or deficit reduction, although without more specifics, it is difficult to know how efficiency gains would compare with those from cutting distortionary taxes.[16] The general point here is that optimal gasoline

---

[15] The benefit of highway spending, $1 + \delta$, is (1 + the rate of return on spending)/(1 + the social discount rate).

[16] For pure transfer spending, according to Parry et al. (2009) there is an efficiency loss of 7 cents per dollar of revenue recycled ($\delta = -0.07$). This is because labor supply falls slightly

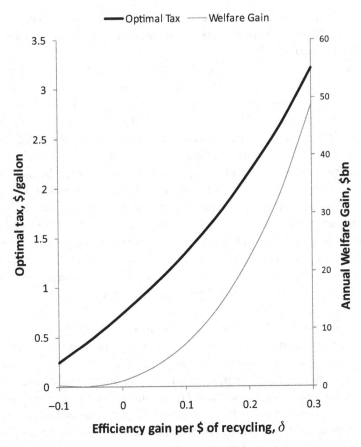

Figure 8.4. Optimal Gasoline Tax and Welfare Gains with Alternative Revenue Recycling.
Note: Efficiency gain is defined relative to withholding revenues from the economy and
therefore depends on uncompensated behavioral responses.

taxes are very sensitive to alternative forms of revenue recycling; if revenues are not used to increase efficiency, the case for higher fuel taxes is
considerably undermined. Correspondingly, annualized welfare gains from
optimizing the gasoline tax vary enormously under alternative revenue-
recycling options, from close to zero to over $30 billion (Figure 8.4).

One caveat here is that it is not always clear what the baseline is against
which the policy change should be measured. For example, fuel tax revenues
may fund a spending project that would have gone ahead anyway, even
without the fuel tax increase. In this case, fuel tax revenues effectively

as higher household income increases the demand for leisure (a normal good), thereby
exacerbating the labor tax distortion.

substitute for an increase in other distortionary taxes, rather than fund extra spending.

8.5 Optimal Taxes on Diesel for Heavy Trucks

8.5.1 Conceptual Framework

The corrective tax on diesel fuel consumed by heavy-duty trucks (i.e., single-unit and combination, commercial trucks) is given by:[17]

$$t_D^C = e_D + (\beta^T/g_D)\left\{e_M^T - t_M^T - \gamma \cdot (e_M - t_M + (e_G - t_G)/g)\right\} \quad (8.8)$$

Here, subscript D refers to diesel rather than gasoline; g_D is diesel consumption per truck mile; and e_D is external costs per gallon of diesel. Superscript T refers to trucks rather than light-duty vehicles; β^T is the portion of the marginal, price-induced, reduction in diesel that comes from reduced truck mileage; e_M^T is external costs per truck mile; and t_M^T is a possible tax per truck mile.

γ is the increase in automobile miles per unit reduction in truck miles. $\gamma > 0$ to the extent that travel speeds on congested roads increase as they are vacated by trucks (Calthrop, de Borger, and Proost 2007). If $\gamma = 0$, the corrective diesel tax would be essentially analogous to the corrective gasoline tax, with parameters related to heavy truck characteristics. One exception to this is that local emissions for trucks vary (approximately) in proportion to fuel use rather than mileage, because emissions standards are defined relative to engine capacity (specifically, grams per brake horsepower-hour) rather than mileage. In addition, road damage is a significant mileage-related externality for heavy trucks and, to lesser extent, noise.

To the extent that $\gamma > 0$, the corrective diesel tax is adjusted downwards to account for the induced increase in (fuel- and mileage-related) auto externalities. The latter are defined net of any auto mileage tolls and gasoline taxes. Net auto externalities are expressed in dollars per auto mile, then converted into dollars per gallon of diesel (via dividing by g_D), and scaled back by the portion of the reduction in diesel use that comes from reduced truck mileage, as opposed to increased fuel economy.[18]

---

[17] The formula below is adapted from Parry (2008), after aggregating his analysis, which distinguishes truck mileage by region and vehicle type.

[18] In principle, higher gasoline taxes might lead, through a fall in road congestion, to a proportionate increase in truck mileage. However, given that trucks account for a relatively small share of highway traffic, this feedback effect likely makes very little difference to the optimal gasoline tax.

We assume analogous functional forms for truck mileage and fuel/mile as in (8.3) and that γ is constant.

Finally, the general presumption is that freight is an average substitute for leisure, because essentially all heavy-truck trips are work-related, and are therefore likely to exhibit a similar degree of substitution with leisure compared with goods in general (e.g., Diamond and Mirrlees 1971). Thus, we compute the overall optimal tax using the analogous expression to (8.6), with $\eta_{GI}^{comp} = \varepsilon_{L}^{comp}$.

8.5.2 Parameters

Combusting a gallon of diesel produces about 16 percent more CO_2 than combusting a gallon of gasoline;[19] therefore, we adopt a (conservative) value of \$0.10/gallon for global warming damages from diesel (using a higher value, or zero to reflect a preexisting cap-and-trade program, would have comparable effects to those discussed for gasoline taxes). We use the same placeholder value as above, \$0.10/gallon, for oil-dependence costs.

Based on a source-apportionment study for year 2000 by the U.S. Environmental Protection Agency, FHWA (2000, Table 13) put local air pollution costs from heavy trucks at about \$0.40/gallon. We make two adjustments to this figure, which results in a cost of \$0.36/gallon. First, we multiply by 4.15/2.7, which is the ratio of the VSL for local pollution assumed previously to the VSL in FWHA (2000). Second, we multiply by 0.6 to account for the decline in heavy-truck emission rates (BTS 2008, Table 4.38).

Based on FHWA (2000), marginal congestion costs are assumed to be twice as large as for automobiles, or \$0.09/truck-mile. Trucks take up more road space and drive slower than autos, though a partly offsetting factor is that a greater share of nationwide truck mileage occurs under free flow conditions (in rural areas and at off-peak hours) than for autos.

Marginal accident costs are assumed to be 83 percent of those for autos, or \$0.029/mile, based on FHWA (2000). Although, for given speeds at impact, trucks have far greater damage potential than cars, an offsetting factor is that trucks are travelling at slower speeds and crash less often, in part because they are driven by professionals.

Road damage externalities for heavy trucks have been assessed in studies that apportion road maintenance expenditures to different vehicle classes, whereas noise costs have been estimated based on hedonic studies measuring how proximity to highways affects property values. We assume external costs

---

[19] See http://bioenergy.ornl.gov/papers/misc/energy_conv.html.

of \$0.055/mile and \$0.015/mile, respectively, based on FHWA (2000), after updating to 2007 using the consumer price index.

We assume the pre-tax price of diesel is the same as for gasoline, an initial tax of \$0.44/gallon, initial truck fuel consumption of 38 billion gallons, and fuel economy of 6 mpg.[20] Although the limited evidence available suggests that diesel fuel elasticities are in the same ballpark as gasoline price elasticities (Dahl 1993, pp. 122–123; Small and Winston 1999, Table 2.2), we might expect the fuel economy elasticity to be smaller for diesel, as technological opportunities for improving fuel economy are more limited for trucks than for cars given the high power requirements necessary to move freight (EIA 1998). We assume a diesel price elasticity of −0.25, with 40 percent and 60 percent, respectively, due to the responsiveness of fuel economy and mileage.

As regards the feedback effect on auto externalities, about 55 percent of truck travel occurs in rural areas (FHWA 2000) where congestion is minimal; therefore, a reduction in truck driving would have little impact on encouraging more auto travel. For typical urban roads, a reasonable rule of thumb appears to be that roughly 70 percent of reduced truck congestion would be offset by extra auto travel (Cervo and Hansen 2002; Calthrop, de Borger, and Proost 2007). We assume, nationwide, that 31 percent (equal to 70 percent times 0.45) of any reduction in congestion from trucks would be offset by extra auto travel. We double this, based on the assumption that two car miles are equivalent to one truck mile in terms of congestion, to obtain $\gamma = 0.62$ (Santos and Fraser 2006). If diesel taxes were increased substantially, it is highly likely that gasoline taxes would go up in tandem. Therefore, in computing the auto feedback effect in (8.8) we use the corrective gasoline tax (and fuel economy at that tax), although we also note the implications of assuming the current gasoline tax.

8.5.3 Optimal Tax Estimates

We begin with the corrective portion of the optimal diesel tax, as summarized in Table 8.2. Even though all parameters, aside from global warming and oil-dependence externalities, are notably (if not substantially) different than for gasoline, overall the corrective tax is very close to that for gasoline – \$1.15/gallon compared with \$1.23/gallon.

On the one hand, road damage and noise combined contribute \$0.26/gallon to the corrective diesel tax (and zero to the corrective gasoline tax),

---

[20] From www.eia.gov, FHWA (2003), Table MF-121T, and BTS (2008), Tables 4.13 and 4.14.

Table 8.2. *Calculations of the corrective diesel
tax (Year 2007 Dollars)*

Benchmark case	
Corrective tax, $/gallon	**1.15**
Contribution from	
global warming	0.10
oil dependence	0.10
local pollution	0.36
congestion	0.33
accidents	0.11
road damage	0.20
noise	0.06
auto feedback effect	−0.10
Miles/gallon at corrective tax	6.1
Proportionate reduction in diesel use	0.06
Welfare gain, $ billion[a]	1.3
Proportionate increase in tax revenue	2.8
With preexisting corrective mileage tax	
Corrective tax, $/gallon	**0.56**
Proportionate reduction in diesel use	0.01
Welfare gain, $ billion[a]	0.26

[a] Ignores welfare effects from broader fiscal linkages.
Sources: See discussion in text.

whereas the contribution of local pollution is higher for diesel, as emissions vary with all fuel reductions rather than just the portion from reduced mileage.

On the other hand, congestion contributes $0.33/gallon to the corrective diesel tax compared with $0.52/gallon for gasoline. Congestion per mile is twice as large for trucks as for autos, and a larger portion of the tax-induced reduction in diesel is assumed to come from reduced vehicle mileage. However, these factors are more than offset by the much lower fuel economy of trucks, which implies that a gallon reduction in diesel fuel is associated with a much smaller reduction in vehicle miles than a gallon reduction in gasoline. For the same reason, accidents play a smaller role in the corrective diesel tax. Moreover, accident costs per truck mile are roughly the same (rather than twice as large) as for an auto mile. The auto feedback effect shaves a further $0.10/gallon off the corrective diesel tax. This effect would be $0.18 if evaluated at the current, rather than corrective, gasoline tax.

Given our assumptions, the proportionate improvement in vehicle fuel economy and the proportionate reduction in fuel use, from optimizing fuel taxes, is smaller for diesel than for gasoline. Moreover, current diesel

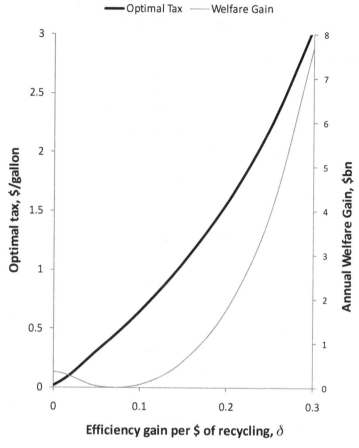

Figure 8.5. Optimal Diesel Tax and Welfare Gains with Alternative Revenue Recycling. *Note:* Efficiency gain is defined relative to withholding revenues from the economy and therefore depends on uncompensated behavioral responses.

fuel consumption is only 27 percent of that for gasoline. For these reasons, welfare gains under benchmark parameters – ignoring fiscal linkages – are $1.3 billion per year from raising diesel taxes to their corrective level, compared with $5.9 billion for the analogous gasoline tax reform.

A final point from Table 8.2 is that if mileage-related externalities were fully internalized through vehicle tolls, the corrective diesel tax is $0.56/gallon (this assumes auto externalities are fully internalized, thereby eliminating the auto feedback effect).

Figure 8.5 underscores the critical role of broader fiscal interactions for the diesel tax (under baseline parameters).

If the efficiency gain per dollar of recycled revenue is $0.15, the optimal diesel tax is $1.06, or moderately lower than the corrective tax. Thus, the net adjustment for fiscal interactions is in the opposite direction to that for the gasoline tax, reflecting the assumption that diesel is an average, rather than a relatively weak, leisure substitute. On the other hand, if the efficiency gain from revenue recycling is $0.30 per dollar (e.g., because income taxes distort spending patterns in addition to the labor market) the optimal diesel fuel tax can rise to $3/gallon. Conversely, if revenue-recycling does not increase efficiency the optimal diesel tax not only falls below its current level, but essentially falls to zero. In this case, the efficiency loss from the tax-interaction effect is large enough to offset the entire efficiency gain from externality mitigation!

8.6 Conclusion

At first glance, there appears to be a strong efficiency case for substantially increasing taxes on highway fuels – to over $1/gallon – at least for the foreseeable future, before other (more efficient) policies to largely internalize mileage-related externalities (e.g., peak-period road pricing) are widely implemented. This presumes efficient use of additional fuel tax revenues. Ideally, from an efficiency perspective, such revenues would finance reductions in distortionary income taxes, in which case the argument for higher fuel taxes is even stronger. On the other hand, the case for higher taxes is more qualified if there is some risk that revenues will not be used productively.

Our discussion ignores the distributional impact of higher fuel taxes. Studies suggest that gasoline taxes are regressive, but less so if income is measured on a lifetime, rather than annual, basis (e.g., Poterba 1991; West and Williams 2004). One approach to addressing these concerns is through adjustments to the broader tax and benefit system. Williams (2009) finds that the distributional effects of gasoline taxes can be approximately offset through such adjustments, with pretty modest overall implications for the optimal gasoline tax.

Substantially higher fuel taxes appear to have little political traction at present, but it is not difficult to think of examples of policy reforms that, at some earlier date, seemed impossible to implement (e.g., industry deregulation, use of market-based instruments for pollution control). At any rate, the economists' role is to inform about the potential net benefits from overcoming obstacles to more efficient policy.

Finally, over the long haul, the development of new technologies is critical for any effort to wean motorists off conventional fuels. Does this mean we should implement even stiffer fuel taxes? Perhaps not, as a common view among economists seems to be that innovation incentives are more efficiently addressed through supplementary technology policies, rather than raising energy taxes above levels warranted on externality and fiscal grounds (e.g., Fischer and Newell 2007; Goulder and Schneider 1999). These additional measures might include funding for basic research, inducements for applied private sector research and development, and possible interventions at the technology deployment stage, although more research is needed on the appropriate stringency and design of such supplementary measures.

APPENDIX: ANALYTICAL DERIVATIONS

Deriving Equation (2): The corrective gasoline tax. The optimal tax is derived using a standard two-step procedure. First, we solve the household optimization problem in (8.1), where externalities, and government variables, are taken as given. This yields the first-order conditions

$$\frac{u_m}{v} = \lambda(p_G + t_G)g, \ u_v = \lambda\left[(p_G + t_G)gm + c\right], \ -c'(g) = (p_G + t_G)m,$$

$$(A.1)$$

The second step is to totally differentiate the household's indirect utility function, which is simply equivalent to the expression in (8.1), with respect to the gasoline tax. In this step, economy-wide changes in externalities and the government transfer are taken into account. Using the first-order conditions in (A.1) to eliminate terms in dm/dt_G, dv/dt_G, dg/dt_G, and dX/dt_G, the total differential is given by

$$u_{E_G}E'_G\frac{dG}{dt_G} + u_{E_M}E'_M\frac{dM}{dt_G} + \lambda\left\{\frac{dGOV}{dt_G} - G\right\} \qquad (A.2)$$

The government budget constraint, equating spending with gasoline tax revenue, is $GOV = t_G G$. Totally differentiating this expression gives

$$\frac{dGOV}{dt_G} = G + t_G\frac{dG}{dt_G} \qquad (A.3)$$

From differentiating the expression for gasoline use in (8.1b)

$$\frac{dG}{dt_G} = g\frac{dM}{dt_G} + M\frac{dg}{dt_G} \qquad (A.4)$$

Equating (A.2) to zero, to obtain the corrective tax, and substituting (A.3), gives

$$t_G^C = -\frac{u_{E_G}}{\lambda}E'_G - \frac{u_{E_M}}{\lambda}E'_M\frac{dM/dt_G}{dG/dt_G} \tag{A.5}$$

Substituting expressions in (8.2b) in (A.5), gives the corrective tax formula in (8.2a), with β defined in (8.2c).

References

Blundell, Richard, and Macurdy, Thomas. 1999. Labor supply: A review of alternative approaches. In *Handbook of Labor Economics*, O. Ashenfelter and D. Card (eds.). New York: Elsevier.

Bordoff, Jason E., and Pascal J. Noel. 2008. Pay-as-you-drive auto insurance: A simple way to reduce driving-related harms and increase equity. In *The Hamilton Project*. Washington, D.C.: Brookings Institution.

Bureau of Transportation Statistics. 2008. *National Transportation Statistics 2008*. Washington, D.C.: U.S. Department of Transportation.

Brown, Stephen P.A., and Hillard G. Huntington. 2009. *Reassessing the oil security premium*. Working paper, Resources for the Future and Stanford University.

Calthrop, E., B. de Borger, and S. Proost. 2007. Externalities and partial tax reform: Does it make sense to tax road freight (but not passenger) transport? *Journal of Regional Science* 47:721–752.

Council of Economic Advisers. 2009. *Economic Report to the President*. Washington, D.C.: Council of Economic Advisors.

Cervero, R, and M. Hansen. 2002. Induced travel demand and induced transport investment: A simultaneous equation analysis. *Journal of Transport Economics and Policy* 36:469–490.

Dahl, Carol. 1993. *A Survey of Energy Demand Elasticities in Support of the Development of the NEMS*. Report prepared for the U.S. Department of Energy.

Diamond, Peter A., and James Mirrlees. 1971. Optimal taxation and public production I: Production efficiency and II: Tax rules. *American Economic Review* 61: 8–27, 261–278.

Energy Information Administration. 1998. *Impacts of the Kyoto Protocol on U.S. Energy Markets and Economic Activity*. Washington, D.C.: U.S. Department of Energy.

Federal Highway Administration. 2007. *Highway Statistics 2007*. Washington, D.C.: U.S. Department of Transportation.

Federal Highway Administration. 2003. *Highway Statistics 2003*. Washington, D.C.: U.S. Department of Transportation.

Federal Highway Administration, 2000. *Addendum to the 1997 Federal Highway Cost Allocation Study Final Report*. Washington, D.C.: U.S. Department of Transportation.

Fischer, Carolyn, and Richard G. Newell. 2008. Environmental and technology policies for climate mitigation. *Journal of Environmental Economics and Management* 55:142–162.

Fischer, Carolyn, Winston Harrington, and Ian W.H. Parry. 2007. Should corporate average fuel economy (CAFE) standards be tightened? *Energy Journal* 28:1–29.

Goulder, Lawrence H. 1995. Environmental taxation and the 'double dividend': A reader's guide. *International Tax and Public Finance* 2:157–183.

Goulder, Lawrence H., and Stephen H. Schneider. 1999. Induced technological change and the attractiveness of CO2 emissions abatement policies. *Resource and Energy Economics* 21:211–253.

Greenberg, Allen. 2009. Designing pay-per-mile auto insurance regulatory incentives. *Transportation Research Part D* 14:437–445.

Heal, Geoffrey. 2009. Climate economics: A meta-review and some suggestions for future research. *Review of Environmental Economics and Policy* 3:4–21.

Leiby, Paul N. 2007. Estimating the energy security benefits of reduced U.S. Oil Imports. Oakridge National Laboratory, ORNL-TM-2007–028.

Li, Shanjun. 2009. Traffic safety and vehicle choice: Quantifying the effects of the arms race on American roads. Discussion Paper 09–33. Washington, D.C.: Resources for the Future.

National Research Council. 2002. *Effectiveness and Impact of Corporate Average Fuel Economy (CAFE) Standards.* Washington, D.C.: National Academy Press.

Nordhaus, William D. 2007. A review of the Stern review on the economics of climate change. *Journal of Economic Literature* 45:686–702.

Nordhaus, William D. 2008. *A Question of Balance: Weighing the Options on Global Warming Policies.* New Haven: Yale University Press.

Nordhaus, William D. 2009. *An analysis of Weitzman's Dismal Theorem.* Working Paper, Yale University, New Haven, CT.

Organisation for Economic Co-operation and Development. 2009. *Energy Prices and Taxes: Quarterly Statistics.* Organization for Economic Cooperation and Development, Paris, First Quarter.

Parry, Ian W.H. 2002. Tax deductions and the marginal welfare cost of taxation. *International Tax and Public Finance* 9:531–551.

Parry, Ian W.H., 2008. How should heavy-duty trucks be taxed? *Journal of Urban Economics* 63:651–668.

Parry, Ian W.H., and Kenneth A. Small. 2005. Does Britain or the United States have the right gasoline tax? *American Economic Review* 95:1276–1289.

Parry, Ian W.H., Ramanan Laxminarayan, and Sarah E. West. 2009. Fiscal and externality rationales for alcohol taxes. *B.E. Journal of Economic Analysis & Policy* (Contributions) 9 (29): 1–45.

Poterba, James M. 1991. Is the gasoline tax regressive? *Tax Policy and the Economy* 5: 145–164.

Santos, Georgina, and Gordon Fraser. 2006. Road pricing: Lessons from London. *Economic Policy* 21:264–310.

Schrank, David, and Timothy Lomax. 2009. *The 2009 Urban Mobility Report.* College Station, Texas Transportation Institute, Texas A&M University.

Small, Kenneth A. 2009. *Energy policies for passenger transportation: A comparison of costs and effectiveness.* Working Paper, University of California, Irvine, CA.

Small, Kenneth A., and Kurt Van Dender. 2006. Fuel efficiency and motor vehicle travel: The declining rebound effect. *Energy Journal* 28:25–52.

Small, Kenneth A., and Erik Verhoef. 2007. *The economics of urban transportation.* New York: Routledge.

Small, Kenneth A., and Clifford Winston. 1999. The demand for transportation: Models and applications. In *Transportation Policy and Economics: A Handbook in Honor of John R. Meyer*, J.A. Gómez-Ibáñez, W. Tye, and C. Winston (eds.). Washington, D.C.: Brookings Institution.

Small, Kenneth A., Clifford Winston, and Carol A. Evans. 1989. *Road Work: A New Highway Pricing and Investment Policy*. Washington, D.C.: Brookings Institution.

Stern, Nicholas. 2007. *The Economics of Climate Change*. Cambridge, U.K.: Cambridge University Press.

Transportation Research Board. 2006. *The fuel tax and alternatives for transportation funding*. Special Report No. 285. Washington, D.C.: National Academies Press.

Weitzman, Martin, L. 2009. On modeling and interpreting the economics of catastrophic climate change. *Review of Economics and Statistics* 91:1–19.

West, Sarah, and Roberton C. Williams. 2004. Estimates from a consumer demand system: Implications for the incidence of environmental taxes. *Journal of Environmental Economics and Management* 47:535–558.

West, Sarah, and Roberton C. Williams. 2007. Optimal taxation and cross-price effects on labor supply: Estimates of the optimal gas tax. *Journal of Public Economics* 91:593–617.

White, Michelle. 2004. The "arms race" on American roads: The effect of SUV's and pickup trucks on traffic safety. *Journal of Law and Economics* 47:333–356.

Williams, Roberton C. III. 2009. *An estimate of the second-best optimal gasoline tax considering both efficiency and equity*. Working Paper, University of Maryland, Baltimore, MD.

Comments

Roberton C. Williams III

Introduction

Ian Parry's excellent chapter provides a valuable, highly relevant, and up-to-date assessment of the efficiency-maximizing level of gasoline and diesel fuel taxes in the United States. In doing so, it builds on work by Parry and Small (2005), which makes an even larger contribution. That earlier paper provided a careful and thorough synthesis of the literature on vehicle-related externalities, together with clear analytics on how the various externalities combine to determine the optimal gasoline tax rate (which is not simply equal to the sum of the various externalities). Parry's chapter in this volume builds on that earlier research in two respects: it updates the analysis, incorporating both the changes that have occurred over the last five years and the new research that has been done during that time; and second, it extends that same approach to consider diesel fuel use by heavy trucks.

In my comments, I will begin by reviewing what I see as the key elements of the chapter's analysis and try to provide additional intuition for the key results. In doing so, I will point out one conclusion that I think is underemphasized in Parry's chapter, which is that the gas tax isn't the best policy for addressing vehicle-related externalities: a tax on miles driven would be more efficient, and a combination of several policies could be more efficient still. I will draw out a few other implications of the analysis. I will then go on to raise a few questions about some aspects of the analysis, in particular the oil dependency and accident externalities, and the issue of distributional effects of the gas tax.

Prepared for the American Tax Policy Institute Conference on U. S. Energy Taxes.

Analysis on Multiple Margins

A key aspect of the problem that both Parry's chapter and Parry and Small (2005) have captured is that multiple margins are important in determining both gasoline (or diesel) demand and the externalities associated with it. The three most important of these are vehicle miles traveled, vehicle size, and vehicle technology; put differently, the quantity of gasoline used can decrease because people drive fewer total miles, switch to smaller cars, or switch to cars that are more fuel-efficient for a given size.

The different externalities are associated with different margins, and the various policies that might be used to reduce gasoline consumption affect these different margins in different ways. Thus, any analysis of this problem must consider the effects on each of these different margins. This makes the analysis relatively complex when considering only a single policy aimed at reducing gas consumption, and far more complex when considering a combination of two or more such policies.

One important implication of this is that the choice of policies should depend on what externalities are important, and what margins are connected to those important externalities. To see this, let's start by considering an externality that is directly tied to the amount of gasoline used, such as CO_2 emissions or oil dependency, each of which is simply proportional to the amount of gasoline consumed. For such an externality, the gas tax is an ideal instrument for correcting the externality. In this case, it doesn't matter whether a given reduction in demand comes from reduced driving, reduced vehicle size, or more fuel-efficient vehicle technology: the effect on the externality is the same. Therefore, the ideal instrument for addressing such an externality will provide incentives for reductions on all three margins. The gas tax does that, but other commonly used policies do not.

For example, fuel economy standards encourage more fuel-efficient technology and encourage a shift to smaller vehicles (if the standards are not looser for larger vehicles), but they do not provide any incentive to reduce miles driven; indeed, improved fuel efficiency actually encourages more driving, by lowering the cost per mile driven. Thus, fuel economy standards reduce consumption on two margins, but increase it on the third. Subsidies for hybrid cars are even narrower, affecting only one margin, vehicle technology. Because these policies don't address all three margins, they will tend to be less efficient in addressing an externality that is tied directly to gasoline consumption, but a gas tax perfectly targets such an externality and thus is highly efficient.

However, for an externality that is tied to one particular margin, the gas tax is a blunt instrument. For example, traffic congestion depends almost entirely on the number of miles driven. Vehicle size has little effect (one more small car has essentially the same effect on congestion as one more large car), and fuel-saving technology has no effect on congestion. When addressing this kind of externality, a policy that affects all three margins is at a disadvantage, because only one margin really matters. Here, the ideal policy would be one that directly targets the margin that matters, such as a tax on miles driven (or better still, a congestion tax, which would depend not just on miles driven, but on whether that driving occurred at rush hour in congested locations).

That example considers only one externality. When there are multiple externalities, each tied to different margins, achieving a first-best outcome requires multiple policies: one per externality (or one per margin). One would want a congestion tax to address traffic congestion, a tax on emissions of local air pollutants to address those emissions, and so on. In such a case, the gas tax – a policy that affects all margins equally – can only provide a rough approximation to the ideal.

Both this chapter and Parry and Small (2005) consider five main externalities tied to gasoline use. Two of these, CO_2 emissions and oil dependence, are tied directly to gasoline use. The other three, local air pollution, traffic congestion, and collision externalities, are all tied to miles driven,[1] and each of those three is larger than either of the first two. For diesel use by heavy trucks, the same externalities apply, plus additional externalities from road damage and noise, both of which are also linked to miles driven. Thus, most of the external damage associated with driving is tied to miles driven, not to either of the other two margins.

Given that, the ideal policy would provide more of an incentive to reduce miles driven than to cut back on either of the other two margins, but current policy in the United States is just the opposite. Gasoline taxes target all three margins, whereas other policies, such as fuel economy standards and hybrid car subsidies, primarily target vehicle technology and actually encourage driving more miles. Because it targets the wrong margins, this combination of policies is a highly inefficient way to address these externalities. Using just a gas tax would be more efficient, because it would target all margins

---

[1] One might think that local air pollution would be tied to gasoline use, but as Parry and Small point out, other regulations restrict local air pollutant emissions per mile driven. Thus, once those regulations are in place, those emissions are tied to miles driven.

equally. A tax on miles driven would be more efficient still, because it targets the margin that corresponds to the majority of the externalities, and a mix of policies, each targeting a particular externality, would be even more efficient.

However, addressing all of those potential policies is probably beyond the scope of a single chapter, and in practice, we don't see much use of mileage-based taxes. Thus, Parry's chapter focuses on finding the optimal gas tax. Nonetheless, it is valuable to keep in mind that in doing so, we are finding the optimal level of a nonoptimal policy instrument.

Multiple Margins, Multiple Externalities, and the Optimal Gas Tax

Even if we restrict the analysis to consider only the gas tax (or only the diesel tax), the issue of multiple margins and multiple externalities remains important. The contribution of a given externality to the optimal gas tax depends not only on the size of that externality, but also on the share of the gas tax–induced reduction in gas consumption that comes from the margin linked to that externality. For example, if the gas tax had no effect on miles driven and only affected vehicle size and technology, then a miles-related externality (such as congestion) would contribute nothing to the optimal gas tax, because under those conditions, the gas tax would have no effect on that externality. In contrast, if the gas tax only affected miles driven, and had no effect on vehicle size or technology, then the full amount of the externality would contribute to the optimal gas tax, because under those conditions, the gas tax would perfectly target that externality.

In practice, the gas tax affects all three margins, a case that lies between the two extremes just considered. Thus, each of the externalities contributes something to the optimal gas tax, but for an externality tied to only one margin, that contribution is only a fraction of the full amount of the externality.

The optimal gas tax also depends very strongly on what other policies are already in place, for two reasons. First, other policy instruments can correct some externalities, and thus the gas tax won't need to address those corrected externalities. If there were an optimal congestion tax, for example, that tax would fully correct the traffic congestion externality, and thus that externality would no longer play a role in determining the optimal gas tax. This would lead to a significantly lower optimal gas tax. In effect, the congestion tax replaces part of the gas tax in this case.

Second, other policies can influence the effects of the gas tax. For example, with a binding fuel economy standard, the gas tax will only affect miles driven: vehicle size and technology are already limited by the binding standard, leaving no room to adjust on those margins (unless the tax rate is so high that the standard ceases to be binding). This would make the gas tax a better-targeted policy (because the biggest externalities are linked to miles driven), and thus would imply a substantially higher gas tax. Thus, although policy makers seem to think that a tight fuel economy standard is a substitute for a higher gas tax, in fact the opposite is true: tightening the fuel economy standard raises the optimal gas tax.

Oil Dependency?

One of the externalities considered in Parry's chapter and in Parry and Small (2005) is oil dependence. Oil dependence is widely used as an argument for various policies intended to lower U.S. consumption or raise U.S. production of oil. Despite that wide usage, however, there doesn't seem to be a clear and widely accepted definition of exactly what we mean by "oil dependence." The concept clearly relates to the share of domestic oil consumption that comes from imports, and the consequences if that imported oil became more expensive or if imports were cut off entirely. However, a precise and commonly accepted definition is difficult to find.

Perhaps more importantly, it's not at all clear that oil dependence – under whatever definition one uses – is an externality. If I buy a gas-guzzling SUV, I make myself more oil-dependent: because of that purchase, the cost to me of future increases in world oil prices will be magnified. The same is true for a corporation that builds an energy-inefficient plant. In both cases, that cost is fully internalized.

A common argument for why oil dependence creates an externality is that it contributes to macroeconomic instability: the more oil-dependent the economy is, the more likely an oil price shock is to cause a recession. Under this line of reasoning, my buying an SUV creates an externality because it makes my neighbor (and every other worker in the country) very slightly more likely to become unemployed. This seems plausible, but is still a rather shaky basis for policy, given our limited understanding of the causes of macroeconomic disruptions and the widespread disagreement within the macroeconomics literature over the welfare cost of recessions.[2]

Moreover, this same argument could be used to find externalities from a tremendous range of activities, from taking out a mortgage to investing in an illiquid asset to choosing a career in which job-search costs are relatively

---

[2] Lucas (1987), for example, argues that the welfare cost of business cycles is trivial.

high. One can argue that each of those actions contributes in some small way to inflexibility in the economy, which could exacerbate macroeconomic fluctuations. Yet no one is arguing that there are externalities associated with all of those actions and that as a result they should all be taxed.

To his credit, Parry acknowledges that estimates of the oil disruption externality are highly uncertain, but he then goes on to use a value of $0.10/gallon in his calculations, based on Leiby (2007), and describes this as "probably conservative." I would argue that a conservative estimate of the oil dependency externality is zero. Fortunately, the oil dependency externality represents a relatively small portion of the estimated optimal gas tax, so this doesn't have a major effect on the chapter's results.

Accident Externalities

Parry's chapter, like Parry and Small (2005), assumes that accident externalities depend only on the number of miles traveled, not on vehicle size, which seems unrealistic. A footnote acknowledges that if higher gas taxes cause consumers to shift from light trucks to cars, there may be an additional gain because light trucks cause a larger accident externality than do cars. That footnote is a step in the right direction, but it doesn't go far enough. Why would a shift from light trucks to cars have an effect on the accident externality, but a shift from large cars to small cars not have such an effect?

Moreover, common sense and simple physics both suggest that, holding the weight of one vehicle in an accident constant, the damage to that vehicle and the risk to its occupants will be greater the heavier is the other vehicle in the accident. Thus, for a heavier vehicle, the external damage – the damage to the other car – from a given accident will be greater. Given the low levels of required liability insurance relative to the potential damage from an accident (many states require liability insurance of $20,000, as compared to a value of a statistical life in the millions of dollars), such insurance clearly can't fully internalize that external cost (therefore, differences in insurance rates across vehicles of different sizes can't fully internalize the differences in external cost).

To the extent that accident externalities depend on the weight of a vehicle, not just on miles driven, the optimal gas tax rate will be higher than what Parry estimates in his chapter.

Distributional Effects of the Gasoline Tax

The analysis in Parry's chapter focuses exclusively on the efficiency effects of changes in the gasoline tax, not on distributional effects (though he does briefly mention distributional issues in the conclusion). In practice, however, the distributional implications of a gas tax are widely cited as a reason to keep gas taxes lower.

This argument has some merit. Gasoline spending is generally a larger share of the average household budget for lower-income households than it is for higher-income households (except for the poorest households in urban areas, who often do not own cars). This means that an increase in the gas tax will be at least somewhat regressive.

Nonetheless, this effect does not justify gas tax rates that are anywhere near as low as the current rates in the United States. In a recent paper (Williams 2009), I look at the cost of using the income tax and transfer system to offset the distributional effects of a gas tax increase. Because the gas tax itself is somewhat regressive, this requires an increase in the progressivity of the rest of the tax system. That implies higher effective marginal tax rates, which have an efficiency cost. Nonetheless, that cost is relatively modest. Taking it into account lowers the estimated optimal gas tax rate by roughly 12 cents/gallon, a substantial amount, but still far smaller than the gap between current U.S. gas tax rates of roughly 40 cents/gallon and Parry's estimated optimal tax rate of $1.23/gallon.

A similar analysis for diesel fuel would be far more complicated. Most gasoline is purchased and used by individual households, so a change in gas prices shows up in household budgets directly. In contrast, most diesel fuel is used for transportation of other goods, and thus a rise in diesel prices would lead to a rise in prices of many other goods, so it would show up indirectly in many places throughout the household budget. However, this also means that the cost is likely to be roughly proportional to overall consumption, rather than being regressive. Thus, distributional considerations are likely to be less of a concern for diesel tax changes.

Conclusions

I have questioned a few elements of Parry's analysis: the existence of an oil dependency externality, the modeling of the accident externality, and the exclusive focus on efficiency with essentially no consideration of distributional effects. Although these points are important and make a significant difference for the optimal tax rate, they don't lead to any fundamental, qualitative changes in the chapter's results.

The estimates in Parry's chapter make a strong case for higher gasoline and diesel taxes as a means of addressing vehicle-related externalities. The gas tax is not the optimal policy – a tax on miles driven would be more efficient, and a combination of several policies could be more efficient still – but it is still clear that in the absence of such an alternative policy, a higher gas tax would clearly boost economic efficiency.

References

Leiby, Paul N. 2007. Estimating the energy security benefits of reduced U.S. oil imports. Oakridge National Laboratory, ORNL-TM-2007–028.

Lucas, Robert E., Jr. 1987. *Models of Business Cycles*. New York: Basil Blackwell.

Parry, Ian, and Kenneth Small. 2005. Does Britain or the United States have the right gasoline tax? *American Economic Review* 95 (4): 1276–1289.

Williams, Roberton. 2009. An estimate of the second-best optimal gasoline tax considering both efficiency and equity. Working Paper, University of Maryland and University of Texas at Austin.

NINE

State Tax Policy and Oil Production

The Role of the Severance Tax and Credits for Drilling Expenses

Ujjayant Chakravorty, Shelby Gerking, and Andrew Leach

9.1 Introduction

Although most energy-producing states have levied taxes on the value of oil, natural gas, and coal production for many years, changes in these taxes have become headline news as state governments grapple with budget shortfalls brought about by the current recession. For instance, Alaska has increased the severance tax on the value of its oil production and attempted to stimulate future production by allowing a credit against this tax for expenditures on capital items, including drilling rigs, infrastructure, exploration, and facility expansion (Alaska Department of Revenue 2008). In late 2008, California Governor Arnold Schwarzenegger proposed levying a 9.9 percent production tax on the value of most onshore oil production to help close a projected $24 billion budget deficit, but he subsequently reversed his position (Casselman 2009; Skelton 2009). The Pennsylvania legislature is considering a proposal to levy a 5 percent tax on the value of natural gas produced from the giant Marcellus shale deposit, but the bill is opposed by industry leaders who contend that it would result in 30 percent less drilling as well as revenue reductions to state and local governments totaling $880 million over the next decade (George 2009).

These measures, both enacted and proposed, raise a number of long-standing and important questions about the effects of state energy taxes that go well beyond their potential to provide a solid revenue base to support public services. Given the overlapping tax bases claimed by states and the federal government, to what extent do state energy tax increases result in lower collections of federal tax revenues, including the federal corporate income tax? Do state energy taxes restrict production and encourage "high-grading" of energy reserves and by how much? Do state taxes tilt the time path of energy production to the present or to the future? How do upstream subsidies for exploration and development work together with downstream taxes on production to influence the levels and time paths of production and tax collections? What are the implications of these taxes for the long-run sustainable use of nonrenewable natural resources? The analysis in this chapter bears directly on these questions. It also serves as a basis to examine proposed changes in federal tax policy, including the elimination of the percentage depletion allowance and the expensing of intangible drilling costs.

We adapt the Hotelling model developed by Pindyck (1978) to examine how a state's taxes and subsidies at different stages of resource exploration and production alter the behavior of oil producers and thus impact on exploration activity, additions to the reserve base, and the production of energy. In our model, returns to exploration are subject to diminishing returns, and the cost of production is affected both by the level of reserves and the level of output. Producers located in a given state are assumed to produce only a small fraction of world output and therefore face an exogenously determined price of oil. We calibrate the model using data from U.S. oil fields to evaluate the effects of alternative tax and subsidy policies on drilling and production, on tax revenue accruing to states and to the federal government, as well as on the time path of drilling expenditures and resource production.

A key result from the calibrated model is that oil production is closely linked to the size of the reserve base and is relatively insensitive to changes in oil prices. This outcome, which is broadly consistent with experience in the U.S. oil industry over the past 50 years, leads to the conclusion that the severance tax has little effect on production levels and serves mainly to redirect rents earned in the oil industry to the public sector. Thus, increases in severance taxes or a reduction in the subsidies provided to the oil and gas industry may lead to rent taxation and therefore have only marginal effects on the drilling and production of oil and few adverse impacts in terms of national security and increasing U.S. dependence on foreign oil.

Prior simulation studies (Deacon 1993; Kunce et al. 2003) also have considered aspects of these issues, but a novel feature here focuses on effects of combining subsidies for exploration and development with taxes on the value of energy production. The rationale for subsidizing exploration and development is to expand the reserve base and ultimately to stimulate oil production in much the same way as an investment tax credit (see Chirinko 2000) might increase capital formation and boost output in manufacturing. As previously indicated, this type of tax policy has been adopted by Alaska, and it has been suggested as a model for other states (Headwaters Economics

2009). It may also bear on national energy tax policy in light of the interest in stimulating drilling for new reserves.[1] The simulations suggest that a drilling expense credit may cost more than the incremental severance tax revenue obtained, although such credits may be worthwhile concessions if a state's objective is to generate greater support for increasing the severance tax rate.

The remainder of the chapter is organized into six sections. Section 9.2 reviews the issue of oil taxation in twelve major oil-producing states in the United States. Section 9.3 summarizes findings from the literature regarding temporal economic effects of state energy tax policies. Section 9.4 describes the extended Pindyck (1978) model that is used as a conceptual basis for our tax policy simulations. Section 9.5 discusses the way in which the model was parameterized. Section 9.6 presents simulation results, and Section 9.7 concludes.

9.2 Overview of State Taxation of the U.S. Oil Industry

Key taxes on nonrenewable resource development levied by state and local governments can be divided into three main groups: taxes on production, property, and income. In its simplest form, the production or severance tax is levied on the gross value (or volume) of production of the resource as it is "severed" from the ground. The severance tax is the most widely adopted state tax specifically applying to the U.S. oil industry and will receive the most attention in the discussion. State and local governments also levy property taxes on the assessed (quasi market) value of equipment *above* ground and/or reserves *beneath* the ground. Income taxes are levied against the accounting net income of extraction firms. Although these taxes are generally aimed at extracting economic rents earned by producers from the sale of nonrenewable resources, their effects on production, exploration, and development can differ substantially (see Section 9.3). The discussion in this section briefly summarizes how these taxes are applied in major oil producing U.S. states and how they interact with each other and with other taxes on energy producers levied at the federal level. A more detailed

---

[1] At the Republican National Convention in 2008, Michael Steele, former Lieutenant Governor of Maryland and currently Chairman of the Republican National Committee, underscored his view that more exploration for energy resources is needed with his now famous line, "Drill, Baby, Drill." This sentiment was echoed by Republican Vice-Presidential nominee, Sarah Palin, who as Governor of Alaska, signed legislation granting a partial credit for drilling expenses against severance tax liabilities paid at an increased tax rate. For further details, see Ball (2008).

state-by-state survey of taxation and regulation of oil and gas production is available from the Interstate Oil and Gas Compact Commission (2007) and a more up-to-date survey can be constructed from a Lexis-Nexis search of state statutes. Hellerstein (1983) provides a useful discussion of the legal basis for state taxation of natural resources.

Table 9.1 presents data on oil production, nominal (legislated) oil severance tax rates, effective severance tax rates, and nominal corporate income tax rates for the twelve U.S. states that produced the most oil in 2007.[2]

As shown, production in these states ranged from a high of 397 million barrels in Texas to a low of 20 million barrels in Utah. Nominal severance tax rates varied widely across states as well. All states except California levied a severance tax against the value of production.[3] As mentioned earlier, California is considering whether to adopt such a tax. In Alaska and Montana, nominal tax rates can exceed 10 percent. Other tax code features reflect important interstate differences.[4] Severance taxes are generally levied against the "net value" of production, where each state has its own definition of this concept. Some states, such as Wyoming, tax the value of production at the wellhead (the top of the well), whereas others, like Utah, tax the value of production at the wellfoot (the bottom of the well), which in effect allows a deduction for lifting costs. Most states subtract royalty payments (computed as a percentage of gross value of production) for production on public land in computing net production value for determining severance tax liabilities (Louisiana does not). Public land royalties are relatively more important in Alaska, Colorado, New Mexico, Utah, and Wyoming than in other states owing to their large shares of publicly owned land. State energy tax codes are subject to frequent changes as well. For instance, Alaska now allows producers to take a credit against severance tax liabilities for capital expenditures used in exploration and development, whereas this feature was not available in 2007 and thus is not reflected in Table 9.1.

In New Mexico and North Dakota, the severance tax is actually the sum of two or more different levies on net production value. In Colorado, severance taxes are paid at graduated rates that depend on the gross income of operators, and in Alaska, Oklahoma, and Utah prevailing rates depend on the price of oil. In Colorado, Kansas, and Wyoming, local governments levy a substantial tax against the value of energy production. Although this tax is generally called a property tax by tax administrators, it is in

---

[2] The year 2007 is the most recent year for which effective tax rate data could be assembled (see discussion below).

[3] California does levy a property tax on reserves in the ground (see below).

[4] See footnotes to Table 9.1.

Table 9.1. *Oil production (in Mbbl) and tax rates for selected U.S. states, 2007*

State	Production	Severance tax Nominal rate	Severance tax Effective rate	Corporate income tax rate[o]
Alaska	263,595	12.25–15%[a]	12%	1.0–9.4%
California	216,778	None	None	8.84%
Colorado	23,237	2–5%[b]	0.7%	4.63%
Kansas	36,490	4.33%[c]	3.0%[l]	4.0–7.35%
Louisiana	76,651	3.125–12.50%[d]	9.4%	4.0–8.0%
Montana	34,829	15.1%[e]	8.6%	6.75%
New Mexico	58,831	7.1%[f]	7.5%[m]	4.8–7.6%
North Dakota	45,058	5.0–11.5%[g]	–[n]	2.6–7.05%
Oklahoma	60,952	7.0%[h]	6.9%	6.0%
Texas	396,894	4.6%[i]	3.1%	1.0%[p]
Utah	19,520	3.0–5.0%[j]	2.4%	5.0%
Wyoming	54,130	4.0–6.0%[k]	5.3%	None

[a] Lower rate applies to fields in production less than 5 years; higher rate applies to fields in production more than 5 years.

[b] Rate depends on gross income of operator and excludes county ad valorem taxes at 4–10%.

[c] Excludes county ad valorem taxes of approximately 4%.

[d] Tax rate of 3.125% applies only to stripper well production.

[e] Rate applies to nonworking interest owners; working interest owners pay lower rates that vary by type of well.

[f] Rate is the sum of oil severance tax, oil school tax, and oil conservation tax; local ad valorem taxes at approximately 1.2% are excluded.

[g] Depends on the level of an oil extraction tax that varies by type of well; tax rate on stripper well production is 0%.

[h] Excludes ad valorem taxes that vary by county.

[i] Excludes county ad valorem levies and (small) state regulatory and conservation levies.

[j] Lower rate applies to first $13/bbl; higher rate applies above $13/bbl. Excludes county ad valorem levies; stripper well production is not subject to severance tax.

[k] Stripper well production taxed at 4%; other production taxed at 6%; excludes county levies at 5.9–7.7%.

[l] Effective rate is for oil and natural gas combined.

[m] Effective rate is for oil and gas combined.

[n] Insufficient information available.

[o] Tax rates depend on level of income before taxes for most states.

[p] This is the rate for a gross receipts tax that replaced the corporate income tax in 2007 (see Tax Foundation 2009a).

Sources: Production data from U.S. Department of Energy (2009b). Nominal severance tax rate data from Interstate Oil and Gas Compact Commission (2007). Effective severance tax rate data are authors' calculations (see text). State corporate income tax rate data from Tax Foundation (2009a).

effect a severance tax levied by local governments. Many states have granted innumerable exemptions and credits against state severance tax liabilities for special situations that may be encountered by operators. Production from stripper wells (wells that produce fewer than ten barrels per day), for example, is taxed at lower rates in some states than is production from better producing wells. Production from wells employing secondary or tertiary recovery methods is sometimes taxed at lower rates as well.

A further complicating feature in analyzing economic effects of state severance taxes is that states and the federal government levy other types of taxes on oil producers and tax bases interact, particularly at the state and federal levels. Except for Wyoming, all of the twelve states levy a corporate income or franchise tax that applies to oil producers. Nominal rates for this tax, taken from the Tax Foundation (2009a), are shown for each state in Table 9.1. State corporate income taxes often are levied on a similar base to that used in computing federal corporate income tax liabilities, but the state tax rates generally are lower than the top federal rates for this tax, which currently are in the 35 to 40 percent range (Tax Foundation 2009b). State corporate income tax payments are deductible against federal corporate income tax liabilities, and state and local production tax payments are deductible against both. In some states, federal corporate income tax payments are deductible in computing state corporation income taxes and in others it is not. Although local governments in most of the states utilize some form of a property tax on oil and gas extraction equipment, property taxes on reserves are levied only in relatively few states such as California and Texas.

State and local tax burdens on oil producers are endlessly compared in state tax commission and legislative hearings as industry representatives make their case for more favorable tax treatment. Yet, because of variations across states in the application of severance and other taxes, a comparison of nominal tax rates is not particularly useful. A judgment based on a comparison of nominal rates that one state's severance tax, for example, is higher than that in another state might easily be reversed once the potentially numerous exemptions, credits, incentives, deductibility, and other special features of tax law are accounted for. Instead, more meaningful comparisons across states can be obtained by computing effective tax rates expressed as the ratio of revenue collected from a particular tax to the value of production. The calculation of effective tax rates fully accounts for, without enumerating, state-specific aspects of tax treatment faced by producers and facilitates comparisons between states because the value of production is used as a common denominator.

Table 9.1 presents effective severance tax rates prevailing in 2007 for the twelve most important oil-producing states. Unfortunately, information regarding severance tax collections is neither available from a single source nor published in a common format. In consequence, data on severance tax collections needed for the numerators of the effective tax rates were obtained by searching state department of revenue reports available on the Internet and by directly contacting knowledgeable people in these agencies as questions arose. Estimates of the value of production in each state were obtained by multiplying production volumes by the average prevailing price per barrel of crude oil. State production volumes were obtained from the Energy Information Administration, U.S. Department of Energy (2009b). Average wellhead prices of oil in each state were taken from the American Petroleum Institute (2009). The price and production volume data exclude oil produced in the Outer Continental Shelf (OCS) that is not subject to state taxation. As shown in Table 9.1, among states that levy a severance tax, effective tax rates in 2007 vary from 0.7 percent in Colorado to 12 percent in Alaska. Because of the many special tax code features just discussed, these rates tend to be lower than corresponding nominal tax rates.

9.3 Prior Literature

A sizable literature deals with the economic effects of the three types of taxes discussed in the previous section. It may be useful to briefly describe this work before proceeding with the theoretical structure we assume in this chapter. Discussion is limited to intertemporal issues; thus, topics such as interstate tax shifting or "tax exporting" are ignored (Gerking and Mutti 1981; McLure 1969; Metcalf 1993). The severance tax is given the most detailed treatment because it has been widely adopted and because its effects are the focus of the simulations presented in Section 9.6.

9.3.1 Production Taxation

Hotelling's (1931) seminal analytic work considers a per unit severance tax in a model with an endogenous price (net of constant extraction costs) and the total exhaustion of fixed reserves. The severance tax is found to conserve the resource by extending the time it takes to exhaust the total pool. Herfindahl (1967) extends this result with a model that features an extraction cost function that depends on output. Under competition, the severance tax is shown to tilt production to the future (i.e., delay production), thereby extending the life of the pool. The pool is fully exhausted at a postponed terminal period.

Burness (1976) reformulates the dynamic framework by including severance tax rates that vary over time. In this model, price is exogenous, reserves are fully depleted, and extraction cost depends only on output. The general proposition derived is that the severance tax will tilt production to the future if the tax rate is held constant or rises at a rate less than the discount rate. A severance tax that rises with the discount rate will not distort the time path of production. Conrad and Hool (1984) show that introducing varying grades of the resource into the model make no difference to this result.

Levhari and Leviatan (1977) allow for an extraction cost function that depends on both current and cumulative production so that as more of the resource is extracted over time, the more it costs to produce an incremental unit. Thus, in this model, the resource may not be fully exhausted. The effect of per unit severance taxation on time to exhaustion now is ambiguous. If the resource price is constant over time, terminal time is shortened and high-grading (removing ore of the highest grade while leaving lower grade ore in the ground) may occur. Nonetheless, if tax rates vary over time, then, as Heaps (1985) demonstrates, total recovery of the resource and the economic life of the resource can either increase or decrease but in opposite directions. Because these two effects of the tax work against each other, the net impact on depletion cannot be determined.

If resource quality varies across pools but is the same within a pool, Conrad (1978, 1981) shows that mine lives are shortened and lower-quality resource is left in the ground when a per unit severance tax is levied. Krautkraemer (1990) examines the effect of production taxation in a finite reserve model when resource quality varies within a given deposit. In addition to firms choosing the rate of extraction, they also choose the marginal grade cutoff at each point in time. A production tax induces high-grading at each instant of time and not just at the end of the production program. Interestingly, a production tax reduces total resource recovery and a low-grade resource left in the ground will not be extracted, even if at some point in the future the production tax is eliminated.

Uhler (1979) includes a brief examination, for the first time, of the effects of production taxation in a model of nonrenewable natural resource extraction with both production and exploration. The possibility of exploration means that the reserve base is no longer fixed. Also, when the model allows for exploration and reserve additions, the dynamics of the process become complex and equilibrium conditions no longer have closed form solutions.

Effects of production taxation, therefore, were examined with simulations. The model was parameterized for a small oil- and gas-producing region in Alberta, Canada. When a severance tax is imposed at a constant rate, operators decrease production and exploration in all periods while the endogenous price of the resource rises.

Deacon (1993) also simulates effects of severance taxation using the model developed by Pindyck (1978) and later applied by Yücel (1986, 1989). In Deacon's formulation, the oil industry is taken to be competitive, so the time path of the resource price is treated as exogenous. In the simulations, the resource price is assumed to rise in the early years of the production program, but at a rate less than the assumed 5 percent discount rate. Similar to the analytic results derived by Burness (1976) and others in models that abstracted from exploration, the application of an ad valorem severance tax tilts production to the future in comparison to a no-tax base case. Over the life of the program, however, the tax reduces output, implying that an important effect of the production tax is to induce high-grading. In addition, simulations show that a production tax reduces drilling in all periods and that drilling shuts down prematurely in comparison to the no-tax case.

Kunce et al. (2003) also simulate effects of production taxation using the Pindyck (1978) framework, but they parameterize the model for a single state (Wyoming) rather than the nation as a whole, as was the case in the Deacon (1993) study. They consider the effect of doubling the state's production tax on oil extraction in a setting where oil producers are assumed to be price takers. A key feature of this study was to embed the production tax in a broader tax system that allowed for interactive tax bases and tax shifting between the local, state, and federal governments. Simulations demonstrate that a hypothetical doubling of Wyoming's production tax leads to reduced drilling and reduced oil production in each subsequent period. Estimated production declines, however, are comparatively modest; the response of production with respect to the tax change turns out to be highly inelastic (−0.06). Thus, the main effects of the tax increase would be to rather dramatically increase Wyoming's severance tax revenue and to reduce federal corporate income taxes paid by producers.

9.3.2 Property Taxation

Taxation of property, specifically reserves, has received little attention in the literature on production from nonrenewable resources. One reason for this may be the practical complexity of levying such taxes. Nonetheless, Hotelling (1931) demonstrates that a constant percentage tax on the value of reserves will induce firms to extract more rapidly as they attempt to "mine out from under the tax." Conrad and Hool (1981) show that a constant tax rate per unit of reserves encourages extraction of higher-grade resource in the early periods of the program, but the cutoff grades are lower, thus extending the life of the mine. The property tax is also examined by Heaps and Helliwell (1985) in a model that allows for new reserve investment. The tax is shown to tilt production to the present and to reduce investment in new deposits to avoid holding costs. Simulations by Gamponia and Mendelsohn (1985) show that a property tax on reserves results in tilting production to the present. Deacon (1993) obtains the same outcome in his simulation study and also confirms the Heaps and Helliwell (1985) result by showing that the property tax on reserves results in lower levels of drilling in the early years of the program.

9.3.3 Income Taxation

Burness (1976) analyzes a profits tax on a nonrenewable resource producer with fixed reserves and concludes that output trajectories will not change when the tax is applied at a constant rate. If the tax rate increases over time, however, firms will speed up depletion of the fixed reserve. Conrad and Hool (1984) model a progressive profits tax, finding that such a tax will not exhibit the neutrality of a flat rate profits tax with regard to the extraction path and grade selection. Deacon (1993) simulates a structure broadly similar to federal corporate income taxation with expensing of current and capitalized drilling costs. Simulated paths of extraction, drilling effort and reserves show little distortion from the no-tax base case. These results suggest that income taxation is the least distortionary among the three types of energy taxes imposed by U.S. states.

9.4 Conceptual Framework

We propose a simple dynamic model in the tradition of Hotelling (1931) and Pindyck (1978) with some modifications. The idea is to examine the producers' response when states or a social planner imposes a menu of taxes and subsidies on oil production. We consider three tax/subsidy instruments – a severance tax, a corporate income tax, and a subsidy on drilling expenditures. Producers choose the optimal amount of drilling (and therefore reserve additions) and production of oil to maximize profits.

The model is dynamic, with a known discount rate and no uncertainty. Resource producers face an output price of the commodity that is exogenously determined. Ideally, output prices should be endogenously determined through the process of dynamic optimization, as in Pindyck (1978). However, because our goal is to examine the effect of various tax regimes under assumptions of alternative petroleum prices and a single U.S. state produces only a small fraction of world output, the exogenous price assumption may be a reasonable approximation. In any case, a partial equilibrium model with endogenous prices may leave too many factors that critically affect oil prices out of the model (e.g., international financial markets, world economic growth).

Let the output price of petroleum be given by $p(t)$ where the argument t denotes time. Then the social planner imposes a set of taxes $(1 - \alpha_p)$ such that the net price received by the producer is the fraction α_p times the price.[5] Thus, the production revenue accruing to producers of energy is given by $\alpha_p p q$ where q is the quantity of oil sold by the producer. We assume that whatever is extracted is sold – there is no storage.

Because we distinguish between production and exploration, we define reserves R at any given time t and the cumulative addition to the stock of petroleum given by x. The relationship between stocks and reserves is given by the differential equation

$$\dot{R}(t) = f(w, x) - q \tag{9.1}$$

That is, the change in reserves is equal to the addition in reserves net of production, as in Pindyck (1978). The function f represents the addition to reserves as a function of drilling effort w and cumulative additions to the stock x and we assume that $f_1 > 0$; $f_{11} > 0$; $f_2 < 0$ $f_{22} > 0$ and $f_{12} < 0$. More drilling effort (w) leads to higher reserve additions, but at a decreasing rate. Higher cumulative discoveries x cause current reserve additions to decline (at a decreasing rate). It is more difficult to add to the reserve base, the higher the discoveries made in the past. Finally, the marginal effect of reserve additions as a function of drilling decline with increases in cumulative stock. For convenience we assume that the stock of resource grows linearly with drilling effort. However, the cost of drilling increases in a convex fashion with drilling effort, given by $k(w)$ where $k'(w) > 0$; $k''(w) \geq 0$ and $k(0) = 0$. Finally, the total cost of extraction is given by $c(q, R)$ with $c_1 > 0$, $c_2 > 0$, $c_2 < 0$, $c_{22} > 0$ and $c_{12} < 0$.[6] That is, the total "lifting" cost increases with quantity produced – for instance,

---

[5] The tax parameter α_p and two other tax parameters to be defined momentarily are empirically specified in the next section.

[6] In Pindyck's (1978) original formulation, both average and marginal lifting costs depended on R but not on q.

as oil is extracted from greater depths – and it also decreases concavely with current reserves. This specification follows from the view that oil is produced using reserves (a form of capital) and nonreserve inputs (i.e., physical capital other than reserves and labor), so that extraction costs are positively related to output and negatively related to reserves. The cross-partial derivative c_{12} is assumed to be negative.

We introduce two other tax/subsidy parameters in this framework, namely, the portion $(1 - \alpha_c)$ of the production cost that is deductible in computing tax liabilities, so that the net production cost faced by firms is $\alpha_c c(q, R)$ and the part $(1 - \alpha_D)$ that is deductible by the firm, which implies that the net drilling cost payable by the firm is given by $\alpha_D k(w)$. The major goals in this chapter are to examine how the three different tax/subsidy policy instruments, given by α_p, α_c and α_D, affect drilling activity, reserve additions, and production, as well as to compare their corresponding revenue and welfare implications.

Finally, given a fixed discount rate $r > 0$ the social planner solves the following problem:

$$\underset{q,w,x,R}{Max} \int_0^\infty [\alpha_p p q - \alpha_c c(q, R) - \alpha_D k(w)] e^{-rt} dt \tag{9.2}$$

which is subject to the following equations:

$$\dot{x} = w \tag{9.3}$$

and

$$\dot{R} = f(w, x) - q \tag{9.4}$$

The current value Hamiltonian for this problem is

$$H = \alpha_p p q - \alpha_c c(q, R) - \alpha_D k(w) + \lambda w + \theta[f(w, x) - q] \tag{9.5}$$

so that the first-order conditions are given by

$$\alpha_p p \leq \alpha_c c_q + \theta \ (= \ iff \ q > 0) \tag{9.6}$$

$$\theta f_w \leq \alpha_D k_w - \lambda (= \ iff \ w > 0) \tag{9.7}$$

$$\dot{\lambda} = r\lambda - \theta f_x \tag{9.8}$$

$$\dot{\theta} = r\theta + \alpha_c c_R \tag{9.9}$$

along with transversality conditions not shown here. The co-state variable λ represents the shadow price of an additional unit of discovered oil. Note that the higher the cumulative discoveries, the lower the additions to reserves. Hence, the shadow price λ will be negative. The shadow price θ represents the discounted increment to profits resulting from the addition of one unit of reserves. Reserves decrease the cost of production and therefore θ should be positive.

An important implication of the model (see equation (9.6)) is that the firm will decide to produce ($q > 0$) if the discounted after-tax wellhead oil price net of marginal extraction costs exceeds the present value of future profits from an additional unit of reserves (θ).[7] Condition (9.7) equates the marginal benefits and costs of an additional well drilled. The benefits are in the form of an increase in reserve additions, which are given by the expression θf_w. The costs are twofold: the marginal cost of drilling net of drilling subsidies denoted by the term $\alpha_D k_w$ plus the negative effect on reserve additions from an addition to the cumulative resource stock given by λ.

Equations (9.8) and (9.9) give the time path of the derivatives for the two shadow prices λ and θ. The rate of increase in the shadow price λ has two components – the discount rate r and the fact that taking out a unit of resource increases the "cost" in the future through lower marginal reserve additions. Because f_x is assumed to be negative, the first term $r\lambda$ is negative and the second term $-\theta f_x$ is positive. At least initially the latter term is likely to be large because of the high value of reserve additions, in which case $\dot{\lambda}(t)$ is likely to be positive and the value of lambda, which is negative, will decline over time. In this model, then, additions to stock adversely impact reserve formation; hence, the interpretation is completely different than in the standard Hotelling model with no exploration activity. The extra cost of drilling is that it decreases the future benefit of drilling. The time path of the marginal value of a unit of reserve θ also increases at the rate of discount but is tempered by its effect on lifting costs – additions to reserves have the added benefit of helping reduce the cost of production, net of production subsidies. This is given by the negative term $\alpha_c c_R$.

In this chapter we do not focus on the analytics of this model, which is similar to the model developed by Pindyck with some key differences. The

---

[7] Notice that condition (9.7) differs from the corresponding condition derived by Pindyck (1978) in that marginal lifting costs increase with increases in q. Consequently, rather than producing at some maximum rate subject to constraints given by reserve levels, geology, and technology, the firm pays attention to how its lifting costs are affected by the level of output.

main difference is that his production costs are independent of reserves, whereas in our case, production costs decline with cumulative reserves. Moreover, here the focus is on the three tax/subsidy instruments, and we show how they play different roles in influencing production and drilling behavior by firms.

9.5 Calibration of the Simulation Model

Simulations from the model developed in the previous section are constructed based on estimates of the drilling cost, lifting cost, and reserve additions equations, specifying values for the tax/subsidy and other parameters.

9.5.1 Equation Estimates

Estimation of $k(w)$ and $f(w, x)$ are treated together because they are used to compute the marginal cost of reserve additions (k_w/f_w), a key relationship in the model described above. Drilling cost per foot is assumed to be linearly related to footage drilled, as shown in equation (9.10):

$$k(w)/w = \phi w + u \qquad (9.10)$$

where ϕ is the parameter to be estimated and the disturbance term u is normally distributed. This specification ensures that the marginal cost of drilling is positive and increasing in footage drilled as long as $\phi > 0$. Using annual data for the United States from 1959 to 2007, with drilling cost per foot measured in year 2000 dollars and footage drilled measured in millions of feet, the least squares estimate of ϕ is 1.23 with t-statistic of 8.17.[8]

The production function for gross reserve additions is specified as

$$f(w, x) = A w^\rho e^{-\beta \cdot x} e^v \qquad (9.11)$$

where A, ρ, and β are parameters to be estimated and the disturbance term e^v is assumed lognormally distributed with mean of unity and variance σ_v^2. Equation (9.11) is similar to the one describing the discovery process proposed by Uhler (1976) and later adopted by Pindyck (1978). The idea behind this equation is that the marginal product of drilling declines as footage drilled accumulates. Estimation of equation (9.11) used annual data from seven important oil-producing U.S. states (California, Kansas,

---

[8] Data were taken from American Petroleum Institute (2009).

Louisiana, New Mexico, Oklahoma, Texas, and Wyoming) for which complete information on the requisite variables was assembled for the period 1970–97.[9] Oil reserve additions are defined as extensions, new field discoveries and new reservoir discoveries in old fields. The footage drilled variable was defined as in equation (9.10) and the cumulative footage variable was created by adding year-by-year over the sample period for each state. After taking natural logarithms of equation (9.11) and with state-effects included, we obtain least squares estimates of $\rho = 0.95$ (t-statistic $= 14.18$) and $\beta = 0.000437$ (t-statistic $= 1.37$). The value of A (28.78) was selected so that the equation predicted U.S. reserve additions in 2007. This equation shows that the marginal product of drilling (f_w) decreases with footage drilled as well as with cumulative drilling, although the coefficient of cumulative drilling is insignificant at conventional levels.

Because data on oil extraction costs are weak, $C(q, R)$ could not be econometrically estimated. Instead, this equation was calibrated for the United States with a Cobb-Douglas functional form using methods described in Deacon (1993). Results show that if the output elasticity of nonreserve inputs is 0.35, then for 2007, $C/q = 458.1(q/R)^{1.86}$. The value of 458.1 is selected so that the right-hand side will predict average U.S. operating cost per barrel in 2007 of $7.56.[10] Note that the Cobb-Douglas form implies that extraction costs rise without limit as reserves approach zero and fall as production declines.

9.5.2 Specification of Tax/Subsidy Parameters

Values for the parameters α_j ($j = p, c, D$) were specified by choosing representative rates of state and federal taxes faced by oil producers and then inserting these values into equations (9.12) through (9.14).

$$\alpha_p = (1 - \tau_{us})(1 - \tau_s)(1 - \tau_r)(1 - \tau_p) + \tau_{us}(1 - \tau_r)\gamma \quad (9.12)$$

$$\alpha_c = (1 - \tau_{us})(1 - \tau_s) \quad (9.13)$$

$$\alpha_D = \{(1 - \tau_{us}\eta - (1 - \tau_{us})\delta)\} \quad (9.14)$$

In equations (9.12), (9.13), and (9.14), τ_{us} denotes the federal corporate income tax rate, τ_s is the state corporate income tax rate, τ_r denotes the royalty rate on production from public (state and federal) land, τ_p is the

---

[9] Data were taken from American Petroleum Institute (various years).
[10] Data were taken from U.S. Department of Energy (2009a).

state severance tax rate, and δ represents the percentage of drilling costs that may be taken as a credit against state severance tax liabilities. This credit is a prominent tax code feature in Alaska. Also, γ represents the federal percentage depletion allowance weighted by the percentage of production attributable to eligible producers (nonintegrated independents), and $\eta = e + (1 - e)f$ denotes the expensed portion of current and capitalized drilling costs attributable to current period revenues for purposes of computing federal corporate income tax liabilities, where e is the percentage of current period drilling costs expensed for tax purposes and f is the present value of cost depletion deductions per unit of depletable expense (see Deacon 1993 for further details).

These equations do not capture all aspects of the tax code facing oil producers. Instead, they merely reflect important tax features and relationships between taxes affecting the oil industry in most states and at the federal level: (1) severance taxes are levied on the wellhead price of oil; (2) royalty payments for production on public land are deductible in computing state severance tax liabilities; (3) public land royalty payments, state severance taxes, and extraction costs are deductible in computing state corporate income tax liabilities; and (4) public land royalty payments, state severance taxes, and state corporate income taxes are deductible in computing federal corporate income taxes. Federal corporate income tax payments are adjusted because of the percentage depletion allowance and special treatment of drilling costs. These equations highlight interaction between tax bases and are more detailed than the corresponding treatment given by Moroney (1997) and Deacon et al. (1990). The equations incorporate the entire tax structure into the model, rather than simply analyzing one tax at a time as in Deacon (1993). Equations (9.12) through (9.14), however, ignore local taxes on the value of production as well as possible property taxes on reserves (levied by relatively few states). As noted in Section 9.2, state tax treatment of the oil industry is not uniform; the specification of the parameters α_j ($j = p, c, D$) would require reformulation to represent the tax structure of a particular state.

9.5.3 Values of Tax/Subsidy Parameters Used in Simulations

Four simulations of the model are considered in the following section. The base case simulation considers a situation in which no taxes are levied and no subsidies are allowed (No-tax Model A); the values for the tax parameters are $\alpha_p = 1$, $\alpha_c = 1$, $\alpha_D = 1$. The Low-tax Model B considers a situation in which the nominal severance tax rate is $\tau_p = 0.12$, the state corporate income tax rate is $\tau_s = 0.06$, and public land royalty payments as a fraction of total production value is $\tau_r = 0.09$. These choices for state corporate income tax and severance tax rates are broadly representative of actual nominal rates for these taxes (see Table 9.1). The public land royalty payment fraction is similar to actual values for oil-producing states in the western United States (Gerking 2005). At the federal level, the effective federal corporate income tax rate is set at $\tau_{us} = 0.30$. The current nominal depletion rate of 15 percent applies to about 60 percent of U.S. oil production; thus, $\gamma = 0.09$.[11] The expensed portion of current period drilling costs is approximately 40 percent for the industry, and the present value of depletion deductions for capitalized drilling cost can be approximated by $(q/R)/(r + (q/R))$, assuming that it is approximately 8 percent; therefore $\eta = 0.40 + (1 - 0.4)^*(0.08/(0.04 + 0.08)) = 0.8$. The parameter δ is set to zero. Thus, the tax policy parameters for Model B are $\alpha_p = 0.55$, $\alpha_c = 0.67$, $\alpha_D = 0.76$.

The High-tax Model C sets all taxes equal to their Model B values, except for the severance tax, which is set at $\tau_p = .25$. Hence, $\alpha_p = 0.47$, $\alpha_c = 0.67$, $\alpha_D = 0.76$. The Drilling Subsidy Model D sets all tax parameters equal to their Model C values, except that δ is set to 0.22, so that $\alpha_p = 0.47$, $\alpha_c = 0.67$, $\alpha_D = 0.61$.

9.5.4 Other Parameters

Each model uses a discount rate of $r = .04$, an oil price of $p = \$70$ per barrel, and is run for 110 periods at which point drilling all but ceases in the four models because it is no longer profitable. The initial value of reserves (R) was set to 20 billion barrels. This value approximates the quantity of proven reserves for the United States in 2007. The initial value of cumulative footage drilled was arbitrarily set to 2 billion feet, which is roughly equal to the cumulative footage for oil wells drilled in the United States in the past 30 years.

9.6 Discussion of Simulation Results

Results of simulations are obtained from solving the first-order equations of the model (equations (9.6) and (9.9)) after substituting values of the

---

[11] The percentage of production accounted for by nonintegrated independents was approximated by subtracting from unity the ratio of oil and natural gas liquids production by producers subject to USDOE financial reporting system (FRS) requirements to total oil and total natural gas liquids production. For 2007, this ratio was 0.612. Data were taken from U.S.Department of Energy (2009c, 2009d, 2009e).

Table 9.2. *Selected values from solutions for the four models: Year 1*

	Model A	Model B	Model C	Model D
Production in billions of barrels (q)	2.33	2.16	2.03	2.03
Drilled footage in millions of feet (w)	92.44	72.21	63.43	74.26
After-tax price per barrel received by producers ($\alpha_p P$)	$70.00	$38.50	$32.90	$32.90
After-tax marginal extraction cost of one additional barrel ($\alpha_c C_q$)	$24.03	$13.98	$12.46	$12.46
Reserve additions from drilling an additional million feet in billions of barrels (f_w)	0.0091	0.0092	0.0093	0.0092
Total reserve additions in billions of barrels (wf_w)	0.841	0.664	0.588	0.683
After-tax marginal cost of drilling one additional foot ($\alpha_D k_w$)	$227.40	$135.00	$118.59	$111.43
Beginning reserves in billions of barrels (R)	20	20	20	20
Ending reserves (R)	18.55	18.50	18.56	18.65
θ	$45.80	$24.50	$20.50	$20.50
λ	$227.00	$135.00	$119.00	$111.00

tax/subsidy parameters and specific equations for drilling costs (equation (9.10)), reserve additions (equation (9.11)), and lifting costs. Table 9.2 shows selected solution values for year 1 for the four models.

In year 1 for Model A, for example, solutions for the level of production and footage drilled are 2.3 billion barrels per year (6.4 million barrels per day) and 92.44 million feet, respectively. These values, together with initial reserves set to 20 billion barrels and $P = \$70$, imply that the marginal cost of extracting an additional barrel of oil is $c_q = \$24.03$ and the marginal cost of drilling an additional foot is $227.40. Over the course of year 1, reserves fall because production exceeds reserve additions. The present value of future profits from an additional barrel of reserves is $\theta = \$45.80$ (see equation (9.6)), and the present value of drilling cost reductions from an additional unit of reserves is the negative of $\lambda = \$227$ (see equation (9.7)). Both of these two shadow prices steadily converge toward zero over time.

Values presented in Table 9.2 for Models B and C are interpreted similarly. In these two models, production and drilling are lower than in Model A, in part because the severance tax causes prices received by producers to fall disproportionately relative to extraction and drilling costs. In Model D, production is the same as for Model C because tax rates and initial values

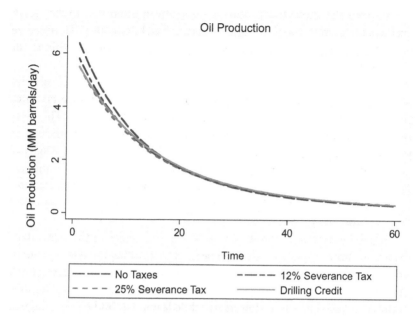

Figure 9.1. Oil production is quite insensitive to the tax structure in the U.S. case.

of reserves are the same, but footage drilled is higher because of the drilling expense subsidy. In all three models, the shadow values λ and θ converge toward zero over time, just as in Model A.

Figure 9.1 shows the time profile of oil production in millions of barrels per day for each of the four models.

In each model, production declines substantially over time. The no-tax case (Model A) shows the highest production rates. The introduction of taxes in Model B tilts production (slightly) to the future, as predicted by models of extraction from fixed reserves (see Section 9.4). Numerical calculations indicate that production rates for Model B are lower than for Model A until year 26, at which point production rates become higher for Model B than for Model A. In Model C, tilting of production to the future is more pronounced in comparison to Model A than it is for Model B because of the higher severance tax rate assumed. Production in Model C is lower in the early years of the program, but begins to exceed production in Model B by year 27. Introduction of the subsidy for drilling expenses tilts production back to the present in comparison with Model C. Model D production initially exceeds that for Model C, but is lower than that for Model C after year 48.

Figure 9.1 also shows that production is relatively insensitive to changes in tax rates and therefore to changes in prices received by operators. Cumulative production figures for the 110-year program period confirm this result (Table 9.3).

More specifically, comparing Model A with Model C, the arc elasticity of cumulative production with respect to a change in severance tax rates $((\Delta q/q)/(\Delta \tau_p/\tau_p))$ is only $(-1.4/38.7)(0.125/0.25) = -0.02$. This outcome implies that the arc elasticity of cumulative production with respect to a change in prices received by operators is $(-1.4/38.7)(56.7/-26.6) = 0.05$. Of course, these simple elasticity calculations are based on cumulative production totals and do not take the timing of production into account, but as shown in Figure 9.1, the time path of production does not differ greatly across the four models.

Oil production also would be insensitive to changes in the percentage depletion allowance rate (η) that can be used by nonintegrated independent producers in computing federal corporate income tax liabilities. As shown in equations (9.12) through (9.14), a reduction in either η or an increase in the severance tax rate τ_p lowers α_p while leaving α_c and α_D unchanged. In fact, given the values of the tax parameters used for Models B, C, and D, eliminating the percentage depletion allowance would have the same effect on production as a four percentage point increase in the severance tax. This parallel between changes in severance tax rates and the changes in the percentage depletion allowance may be of interest in light of the Obama Administration's proposal to eliminate the latter tax preference (see Krueger 2009). Of course, changes in the severance tax and changes in the oil depletion allowance will not have equivalent effects on the collection of other taxes at the state and federal levels.

Insensitivity of oil production to severance tax increases would be to some extent expected in these simulations because a key effect of the tax simply is to reduce industry profits. The assumed price of oil ($70/bbl) is relatively high by historical standards; thus, discounted profit is a relatively large percentage (80 percent) of discounted total revenue. In consequence, the array of taxes imposed in Model B can cut into profits without substantially altering drilling or production. Kunce et al. (2003) found somewhat greater responsiveness of oil production to changes in severance tax rates when setting P (P = $23) at a lower value than the one used in this study. In their simulations, which envision a lower ratio of profit to total revenue, the long-run elasticity of production to changes in the severance tax rate was −0.06.

Table 9.3. *Total drilling, production, tax collections, profits, and reserves for four models over the 110-year program*

	Model A no taxes	Model B 12% severance tax	Model C 25% severance tax	Model D 25% severance tax with drilling subsidy
Total production (in billions of barrels)	39.4	38.5	38.0	38.6
Total footage drilled (in billions of feet)	4.5	3.9	3.6	3.9
Discounted public land royalties (in billions of dollars)	$0	$131.0	$126.3	$129.3
Discounted severance tax Collections (in billions of dollars)	$0	$159.0	$319.2	$307.5
Effective severance tax Rate	0	0.109	0.228	0.212
Discounted state corporate income tax revenue (in billions of dollars)	$0	$60.9	$49.6	$50.8
Discounted federal corporate income tax revenue (in billions of dollars)	$0	$230.0	$182.5	$188.4
Discounted depletion allowance deductions (in billions of dollars)	$0	$119.2	$114.9	$117.7
Discounted pre-tax total revenue (in billions of dollars)	$1,544	$1,456	$1,403	$1,437
Discounted extraction costs (in billions of dollars)	$186.3	$151.8	$130.1	$133.0
Discounted drilling costs (in billions of dollars)	$125.6	$84.4	$68.3	$88.3
Discounted firm profits (in billions of dollars)	$1,231	$638	$527	$539
Beginning reserves (in billions of barrels)	20	20	20	20

In any case, the inelasticity of production with respect to severance tax and price changes suggests that severance tax collections computed as $s = \tau_p(1 - \tau_r)pq - \delta k(w)$ should increase roughly in proportion to changes in the tax rate when $\delta = 0$. As shown in Table 9.3, discounted (at 4 percent) severance tax collections over the 110-year program period total $159.0 billion for Model B and $319.2 billion for Model C. Effective severance tax rates for these two models are 0.109 and 0.228, respectively. These figures suggest that the arc elasticity of discounted severance tax collections with respect to a change in the effective tax rate is 0.95 (assuming unchanged royalty rates and oil prices). Model D, which includes the credit ($\delta = 0.22$) for drilling expenses, reflects smaller severance tax collections than Model C.

Table 9.3 indicates that severance tax rate increases result in lower collections of both state and federal corporate income taxes. Because of the deductibility of severance tax payments against these two taxes, discounted state corporate income tax collections fall from $60.9 billion in Model B to $49.6 billion in Model C, and discounted federal corporate income tax collections fall from $230.0 billion in Model B to $182.5 billion in Model C. Notice that the decline in federal corporate income tax collections is cushioned by declines in depletion allowance deductions ($119 billion to $114.9 billion) and in deductions for current and capitalized drilling costs. The value of these two deductions declines because both production and drilling are lower in Model D than in Model C. Also, discounted oil industry profits fall sharply when all taxes are imposed (compare Model A with Models B and C). In any case, the main effects of severance tax rate increases are to redirect (1) oil industry profits to the public sector and (2) tax payments from the federal level to the state level.

Although the specific way in which the model is parameterized may be responsible for the relative insensitivity of production to changes in oil prices and severance tax rates, results shown in Figure 9.1 and Table 9.3 are broadly consistent with U.S. experience over the past half-century. Figure 9.2 shows this by plotting total U.S. proven reserves (in billions of barrels), total U.S. production from proven reserves (in hundred millions of barrels), and the real price of crude oil (in year 2000 dollars).

Proven reserves stood at roughly 30 billion barrels from 1959 to 1970, increased to nearly 40 billion barrels in 1971 with the discovery of oil in Prudhoe Bay, and then declined steadily thereafter to 20.9 billion barrels in 2007. Over this time period, production followed a similar pattern, remaining between 8 percent and 11 percent of reserves in each year; on average, production represented 9.2 percent of reserves with standard error

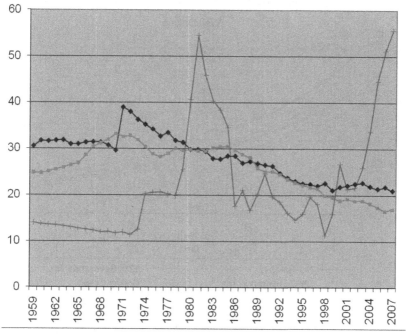

—+— Real price of oil in year 2000 dollars

—◆— Total U.S. proven oil reserves in billions of barrels

—■— Total U.S. production of oil from proved reserves in hundred million barrels

Figure 9.2. U.S. oil production has been insensitive to oil prices over the past 50 years.

of 1.34. Real crude oil prices, on the other hand, exhibited greater variability, but neither the spike in the late 1970s and early 1980s nor the price increase seen in recent years appears to have had much effect on production.

Drilling activity during the 110-year program shows greater percentage differences across the four models (see Figure 9.3 and Table 9.3) than were computed for production.

Model A has the most drilling in each year of the simulation period. Total drilling in Models B and C are lower by 13.3 percent and 20.0 percent, respectively, than in Model A, because the imposition of severance taxes reduces the future payoff from this activity. The effect of the 22 percent drilling expense credit in Model D is to increase drilling above the levels predicted for Model B, but still 13.3 percent below the level predicted for Model A. Total drilling over the 110-year simulation period (net of the starting value of 2 billion feet) is 4.5 billion feet for Model A, 3.9 billion feet for Model B, 3.6 billion feet for Model C, and 3.9 billion feet for Model D.

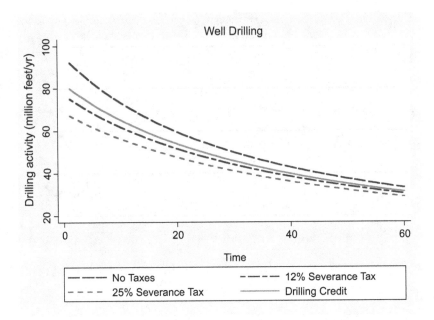

Figure 9.3. Drilling activity is more sensitive to the tax regime.

The figures presented in Table 9.3 imply that the long-run arc elasticity of footage drilled over the 110-year program with respect to the severance tax changes contemplated in Models B and C is −0.07. The corresponding price elasticity is 0.91. Thus, in percentage terms, drilling is more responsive to tax and price changes than is production. Figure 9.4 shows that these results are roughly consistent with the observed relationship between drilling footage and real oil prices (defined as in Figure 9.2) in the United States over the past 50 years.

As shown, drilling footage responds positively to changes in the real oil price, and a regression of the natural logarithm of footage drilled on the natural logarithm of the real price of crude oil yields a coefficient of the latter variable of 0.44 (t-statistic = 3.38). This estimate compares favorably with estimates produced by the simulation model.

Another perspective on the results for the time path of drilling and production can be obtained by focusing on the behavior of reserves. In all four models, initial reserves are set to 20 billion barrels. Drilling leads to annual reserve additions, and reserve additions are highest when more drilling is carried out. In consequence, reserve additions tend to be higher for Model A than for either Models B or C. Reserve additions also are higher for Model D than for Model B, again illustrating the effect of the drilling expense

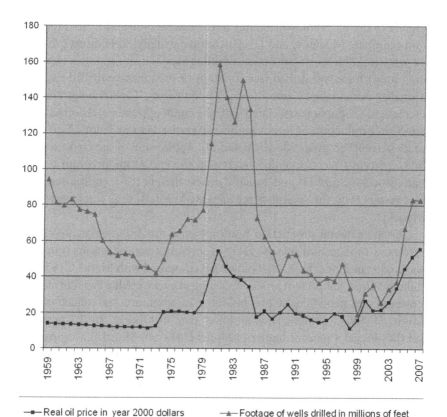

—■— Real oil price in year 2000 dollars   —▲— Footage of wells drilled in millions of feet

Figure 9.4. Price movements coincide with changes in footage of wells drilled.

subsidy. In all four models, however, annual reserve additions always are exceeded by annual production and thus reflect declining reserves over time. This outcome can be seen in Table 9.3 by comparing beginning reserves with the much smaller corresponding figures for ending reserves.[12] Moreover, this outcome is consistent with the previously discussed trends presented in Figure 9.2, which illustrate that U.S. proven reserves have declined by about 50 percent over the past half-century.

Table 9.3 presents additional information concerning the effect of the 22 percent drilling expense credit subsidy on drilling, production, reserves, and tax collections.[13] As discussed previously, the credit spurs drilling over

---

[12] The ending values for reserves reflect high-grading brought about by the severance tax, as discussed in the theoretical literature. For instance, ending reserves in Models B and C are 38 percent and 63 percent higher, respectively, than for Model A.

[13] Results presented below concerning effects of a drilling expense credit may also inform the current debate about the proposed elimination of the possibility to expense intangible

the life of the program, which adds to the reserve base and raises production (compare Models C and D). Discounted drilling expenditures rise by 29 percent ($20 billion), but because drilling expenditures rise at an increasing rate with footage drilled (see equation (9.10)), footage drilled rises by a smaller percentage (8 percent or 0.3 billion feet). The 0.6 billion barrel increase in production associated with the credit approximately offsets the effect on production of increasing the severance tax rate from 12 percent to 25 percent (compare Models B and D). Application of the credit results in 14 percent fewer remaining reserves at the end of the program (compare Models C and D) and roughly offsets the effect on ending reserves that results from the severance tax increase in Model C as compared with Model D.

The incremental production resulting from the drilling expense credit results in an increased present value of severance tax collections (gross of the credit) in Model D ($326.9 billion) as compared with Model C ($319.2 billion). Once the present value of drilling expense credits are subtracted, however, the net-of-credit present value of severance tax collections in Model D ($307.5 billion) ends up lower than in Model C by 3.7 percent, yet they are 93.4 percent higher in Model D than in Model B. Comparing Models D and C, $1.2 billion in lost severance tax revenue is regained through increased state corporate income tax collections; however, $5.9 billion in lost severance tax revenue is transferred to the federal government in the form of higher federal corporate income tax payments. In any case, the drilling expense credit results in a net loss in discounted state tax revenue of $10.5 billion. It costs about $17.50 in lost discounted state tax revenue (both severance tax and state corporate income tax) to produce an additional barrel of oil and about $35.00 of lost discounted state tax revenue to drill an additional foot. Additionally, each dollar of discounted state tax revenue lost because of the credit is associated with a $1.90 increase in drilling expenditures.

This outcome raises a question as to whether other public policy instruments, such as support for research to lower drilling costs or to increase finding rates, might spur drilling at lower cost to the state. Nonetheless, if a state's objective in granting the drilling expense credit is to gain support for increasing the severance tax rate from 12 percent to 25 percent, it is a relatively inexpensive concession. On the other hand, a state that expects the drilling expense credit to more than pay for itself through severance

---

drilling costs in computing federal corporate income tax liabilities. Both types of policies operate through α_D while leaving the other two tax parameters unchanged.

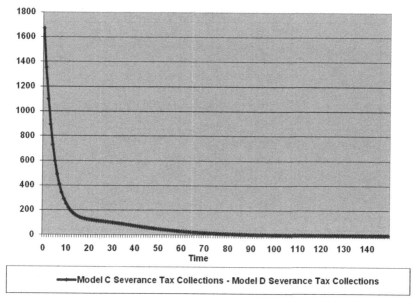

Figure 9.5. Discounted severance tax losses from the drilling expense credit accumulate over time.

tax collections will be disappointed because it simply generates too little incremental oil production. In fact, the drilling expense credit is not only cost-ineffective when evaluated over the entire program, it is cost-ineffective in each program year, as shown in Figure 9.5.

As can be seen from Table 9.2, the credit results in a 17 percent increase in drilling in year 1 (compare Models C and D), but no additional production and thus no additional revenue. Model D production begins to reflect the additional drilling in year 2 and exceeds that for Model C until year 48. During these years, severance tax losses in Model D compared to Model C are smaller than the value of the credit. As indicated, beginning in year 49, production in Model C is larger than that for Model D. Thus, in years 49 to 110, the loss in severance tax revenue in Model D compared to Model C exceeds the value of the credit.

A possible concern about these calculations is that they pertain to a model that is parameterized using U.S. oilfield data. In particular, one conjecture might be that a drilling credit might be financially more attractive in an area that has been less extensively explored, so that the marginal product of drilling in identifying new reserves would be higher. To check this idea, the simulation model was recalibrated by assuming that cumulative drilled footage prior to the start of the program was 500 million feet, rather than

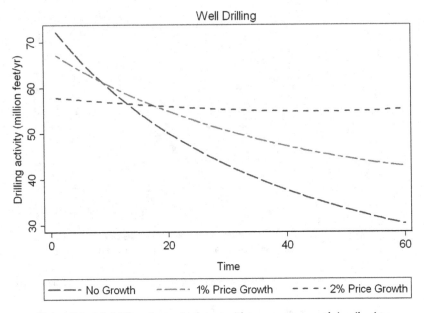

Figure 9.6. Oil drilling tilts to the future with exogenous growth in oil prices.

2 billion feet. This alteration roughly doubles the marginal product of drilling in identifying new reserves, which in turn stimulates drilling, reserve additions, and production. Therefore, Model C discounted severance tax collections are higher than those shown in Table 9.3. Model D discounted severance tax collections also are higher than in Table 9.3, but still lower than the comparable value for Model C. Thus, in both absolute and percentage terms, severance tax losses from the drilling expense credit are larger when cumulative footage drilled totals 500 million feet as compared with 2 billion feet.

It would also be of interest to construct a simulation using the actual path of oil prices over the last several decades. This price, however, exhibits sharp increases and decreases over time (see Figure 9.2), causing the simulation algorithm to break down. As a second choice, we performed a set of sensitivity analyses to reflect a forecast that oil prices will rise over time, at two exogenously given rates. Of course, with perfect foresight, prices cannot go up faster than the rate of discount, because then oil production will be postponed to the future. We thus assume exogenous growth rates in oil prices of 1 percent and 2 percent. As shown in Figure 9.6, drilling activity flattens out with a 2 percent growth in prices.

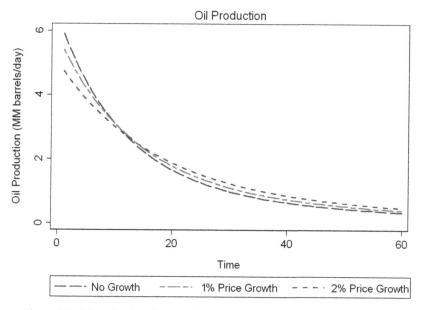

Figure 9.7. Oil production does not change appreciably with growth in oil prices.

However, oil production is relatively insensitive to oil price growth, as shown in Figure 9.7. This is because even though drilling activity shifts out to the future with an increase in prices, the decline in returns from cumulative drilling keeps production from leveling out in time. Production continues to fall, as in the case with constant prices. Figure 9.8 shows the change in reserve additions in the price growth scenario.

9.7 Concluding Remarks

This chapter described tax policies pursued by U.S. states that impact the oil industry. Three types of taxes are discussed: (1) the severance or production tax, (2) the property tax, and (3) the corporate income tax. The severance tax then is further analyzed in light of its widespread use in energy-producing states and its potential to generate revenues to support public services. The analysis is carried out using an adaptation of a conceptual model (Pindyck 1978) of exploration/development and production of exhaustible resources in which oil prices are taken as exogenous. This perspective is a useful simplification for an analysis of state taxes because no state produces enough oil to appreciably affect the world price. Simulations obtained from calibrating the model suggest that oil production volumes will be quite insensitive to

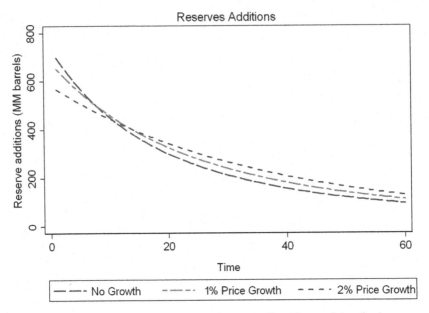

Figure 9.8. Reserve additions change only marginally with growth in oil prices.

price and severance tax rate changes. Thus, an increase in the severance tax rate is seen to generate proportionally more severance tax revenue, as its main effect is to redirect economic rents earned in the oil industry towards the public sector. An implication of this result turns out to be that the proposed elimination of the percentage depletion allowance, available to nonintegrated independent oil producers, may have much the same effect on production as a severance tax increase, although changes in the two types of tax measures may have quite different effects on the distribution of tax revenue between the state and federal levels of government.

Simulations based on the U.S. experience demonstrate that the credit for drilling expenses does turn out to increase drilling as intended. However, if the credit is applied in the United States, particularly in areas where a great deal of drilling has already occurred, its contribution to identifying new reserves may be rather limited. In other words, much of the continental United States has been extensively explored, so the chances of large oil discoveries probably are small. Simulations of the model show that the drilling expense credit does not generate enough incremental severance tax revenue to pay for itself. Additional work needs to be carried out to see whether alternative public policies to stimulate exploration and development might be more cost-effective as well as the extent to which the results presented continue to hold when the model is parameterized differently.

References

Alaska Department of Revenue. Tax Division. *Fall 2008 Revenue Sources Book*. 2008. http://www.tax.alaska.gov, 43–59.

American Petroleum Institute. 2009. *Basic Petroleum Data Book*. Washington, D.C.: American Petroleum Institute.

Ball, Jeffrey. 2008. Palin's policy: Drill, baby, drill. *Wall Street Journal*, September 4. http://blogs.wsj.com/environmentalcapital/2008/09/04/palins-policy-drill-baby-drill/.

Burness, H. Stuart. 1976. On the taxation of nonreplenishable resources. *Journal of Environmental Economics and Management* 3:289–311.

Casselman, Ben. 2009. States consider gas and oil levies. *Wall Street Journal*, June 29.

Chirinko, Robert S. 2000. Investment tax credits. CESifo Working Paper No. 243. Ifo Institute for Economic Research, Munich, Germany. https://www.cesifo-group .de /pls/guestci/.

Conrad, Robert F. 1978. Royalties, cyclical prices, and the theory of the mine. *Resources and Energy* 1:139–150.

Conrad, Robert F. 1981. Output taxes and the quantity – quality trade-off in the mining firm. *Resources and Energy* 4:207–221.

Conrad, Robert, and Bryce Hool. 1980. Resource taxation with heterogeneous quality and endogenous reserves. *Journal of Public Economics* 16:17–33.

Conrad, Robert, and Bryce Hool. 1984. Intertemporal extraction of mineral resources under variable tax rates. *Land Economics* 60:319–327.

Deacon, Robert, Stephen DeCanio, H.E. Frech III, et al. 1990. *Taxing Energy: Oil Severance Taxation and the Economy*. New York: Holmes and Meier.

Deacon, Robert. 1993. Taxation, depletion, and welfare: A simulation study of the U.S. petroleum resource. *Journal of Environmental Economics and Management* 24:159–187.

Gamponia, Villamor, and Robert Mendelsohn. 1985. The taxation of exhaustible resources. *Quarterly Journal of Economics* 100:165–181.

George, Camille. 2009. HB 1489 fair for gas industry, landowners – and taxpayers. *The Tribune-Democrat*, Johnstown, PA, August 5.

Gerking, Shelby D., and John H. Mutti. 1981. Possibilities for the exportation of production taxes: A general equilibrium analysis. *Journal of Public Economics* 16:233–252.

Gerking, Shelby. 2005. Effective tax rates on oil and gas production: A ten state comparison. Working Paper, University of Central Florida, Department of Economics.

Headwaters Economics. 2009. Impacts of energy development in Wyoming. Bozeman, MT. http://www.headwaterseconomics.org/energy.

Heaps, Terry. 1985. The taxation of nonreplenishable natural resources revisited. *Journal of Environmental Economics and Management* 12:14–27.

Heaps, Terry, and J.R. Helliwell. 1985. The taxation of natural resources. In *Handbook of Public Economics*, A.J. Auerbach and Martin Feldstein (eds.), pp. 421–472. Amsterdam: Elsevier.

Hellerstein, Walter. 1983. Legal constraints on state taxation of natural resources. In *Fiscal Federalism and the Taxation of Natural Resources*, Charles McLure and Peter Mieszkowski (eds.), pp. 135–166. Lexington, MA: Lexington Books.

Herfindahl, Orris C. 1967. Depletion and economic theory. In *Extractive Resources and Taxation*, Mason Gaffney (ed.), pp. 63–90. Madison: University of Wisconsin Press.

Hotelling, Harold. 1931. The economics of exhaustible resources. *Journal of Political Economy* 39:137–175.

Interstate Oil and Gas Compact Commission. 2007. *Summary of State Regulations and Statutes*. Oklahoma City, OK.

Krautkraemer, Jeffrey A. 1990. Taxation, ore quality selection, and the depletion of a heterogeneous deposit of a nonrenewable resource. *Journal of Environmental Economics and Management* 18:120–135.

Kunce, Mitch, Shelby Gerking, William Morgan, et al. 2003. State taxation, exploration, and production in the U.S. oil industry. *Journal of Regional Science* 43:749–770.

Kunce, Mitch, and William E. Morgan. 2005. Taxation of oil and gas in the United States. *Natural Resources Journal* 45:77–101.

Levhari, D., and N. Levitan. 1977. Notes on Hotelling's economics of exhaustible resources. *Canadian Journal of Economics* 10:177–192.

McLure, Charles. 1969. The inter-regional incidence of general regional taxes. *Public Finance* 24:457–483.

Metcalf, Gilbert E. 1993. Tax exporting, federal deductibility, and state tax structure. *Journal of Policy Analysis and Management* 12: 109–126.

Moroney, John R. 1997. *Exploration, Development, and Production: Texas Oil and Gas 1970–95*. Greenwich, CT: JAI Press.

Pindyck, Robert S. 1978. The optimal exploration and production of nonrenewable resources. *Journal of Political Economy* 86:841–861.

Skelton, George. 2009. There's revenue in those hills – and offshore. *Los Angeles Times*, August 6.

Tax Foundation. 2009a. State corporate income tax rates, 2000–2009. http://www.taxfoundation.org/taxdata/show/230.html.

Tax Foundation. 2009b. Federal corporate income tax rates, 1909–2008. http://www.taxfoundation.org/taxdata/show/2140.html.

Uhler, Russel S. 1979. The rate of petroleum extraction. In *Advances in the Economics of Energy and Resources*, Robert S. Pindyck (ed.). Greenwich, CT: JAI Press.

U.S. Department of Energy, Energy Information Administration. 2009a. *Cost Indices for Domestic Oil Field Equipment and Production Operations*. http://www.eia.doe.gov/pub/oil_gas/naturalgas/data_publications_cost_indices_equipment_production/current/coststudy.html.

U.S. Department of Energy, Energy Information Administration. 2009b. *Crude Oil Reserves, Reserve Changes, and Production*. http://tonto.eia.doe.gov/dnav/pet/pet_crd_pres_dcu_NUS_a.htm.

U.S. Department of Energy, Energy Information Administration. 2009c. *Crude Oil Production*. http://tonto.eia.gov/dnav/pet/pet_crd_crpdn_adc_mbbl_a.htm.

U.S. Department of Energy, Energy Information Administration. 2009d. *Natural Gas Liquids Proven Reserves*. http://tonto.eia.gov/dnav/ng/ng_enr_ngl_dcu_NUS_a.htm.

U.S. Department of Energy, Energy Information Administration. 2009e. *Oil and Natural Gas Production by FRS Companies by Region*. http://www.eia.doe.gov/emeu/perfpro/o&g.pdf.

U.S. Senate Finance Committee Subcommittee on Energy, Natural Resources, and Infrastructure. 2009. Testimony of Alan B. Krueger, Assistant Secretary for Economic Policy and Chief Economist, U.S. Department of Treasury, September 10. http://ustreas.gov/press/releases/tg284.htm.

Yücel, Mine K. 1986. Dynamic analysis of severance taxation in a competitive exhaustible resource industry. *Resources and Energy* 8:201–218.

Yücel, Mine K. 1989. Severance taxes and market structure in an exhaustible resource industry. *Journal of Environmental Economics and Management* 16:134–148.

TEN

The Social Costs and Benefits of U.S. Biofuel Policies with Preexisting Distortions

Harry de Gorter and David R. Just

10.1 Introduction

The primary objectives of U.S. biofuel policies are to enhance energy security (reducing dependence on oil),[1] improve the environment (mitigating global climate change and local air pollutants),[2] and increase the prosperity for agriculture (enhancing farm income and promoting rural development while reducing tax costs of farm subsidy programs).[3] In order to achieve these policy goals, several policies have been implemented, but the centerpieces of U.S. policy are federal and state biofuel consumption mandates and consumption subsidies (called *tax credits*), policies that by themselves do not discriminate against international trade. This is the focus of our chapter.

The implications of mandates and tax credits are analyzed under three different second-best constraints: a suboptimal fuel tax; adding a tax credit with a binding mandate; and interaction effects with the fiscal system in which mandates and tax credits have differential effects on government tax revenues and the size of the fiscal base. In comparing mandates to tax credits under these three preexisting distortions, this chapter does not analyze the welfare economics of policies that discriminate against trade, namely, import barriers, production subsidies, and sustainability standards.

---

[1] Rising oil prices, dwindling oil supplies, instability in both oil prices and sources of supply (political instability in Middle East and other developing country exporters), and the desire to diversify both energy use and energy sources are the primary concerns under "energy security."

[2] Negative externalities associated with traffic congestion and traffic-related accidents will be shown to be more important than other environmental effects.

[3] Biofuel policy and farm income/rural development are a double-edged sword: the tax on livestock and poultry sectors may reduce economic growth in rural areas net of the economic growth due to biofuel production.

Under each second-best constraint, we simply hold ethanol consumption (and hence ethanol and corn prices) the same.

The emerging literature on biofuels has shown that mandates are superior to tax credits (de Gorter and Just 2007, 2008a, 2009b; Lapan and Moschini 2009). In this chapter, we show this superiority is magnified by a suboptimal fuel tax, as in the United States (Parry and Small 2005), even if fuel prices decline under a mandate. This is because a mandate taxes gasoline consumption to pay for higher ethanol prices and so compensates for the suboptimal fuel tax. The benefits come in the form of reduced greenhouse gas emissions, externalities associated with miles traveled (local air pollution, traffic congestion, and traffic-related accidents), and oil dependency. On the other hand, a suboptimal fuel tax makes an ethanol tax credit even more distortionary because the tax credit lowers the fuel price, which is already too low because of the suboptimal fuel tax.

However, both policies used in combination can have perverse effects on externalities and welfare. By itself, a tax credit subsidizes ethanol consumption, but in the presence of a binding mandate, the effects are reversed and the tax credit now subsidizes gasoline consumption. This is an important result not only because many countries use subsidies in combination with biofuel mandates but also because renewable electricity faces similar policy combinations worldwide. Therefore, tax credits contradict the stated policy objectives of reducing dependency on oil and improving the environment, while providing no benefits to corn or ethanol producers.

Finally, there are implications for interactions with the fiscal system. For the same level of ethanol consumption, mandates have different impacts than tax credits on government tax revenues and fuel prices. These fiscal interaction effects can have important welfare implications, depending on how taxpayer revenues are recycled and how the tax base is affected by fuel price changes (see contributions in this volume by Parry and Williams [Chapter 8]). Although in theory a mandate can cost more in taxpayer monies, empirically we find it saves substantial tax costs for the same quantity of ethanol. This benefit has to be balanced against the cost of a mandate in reducing the tax base through relatively higher fuel prices.

The next section first provides an overview of the welfare economics of biofuel policy in general. Section 10.3 derives the optimal fuel tax–tax credit combination, whereas Section 10.4 derives the optimal fuel tax–mandate combination. Section 10.5 determines the implications of a suboptimal fuel tax, and Section 10.6 explains how adding a tax credit to a binding mandate subsidizes gasoline consumption. Section 10.7 summarizes the expected interactions with the fiscal system in terms of net effects on tax revenues and the size of the fiscal base. Section 10.8 presents simulation results of the social welfare costs and benefits from the preexisting distortions, highlighting the benefits of a mandate over a tax credit and the enormous costs of adding a tax credit to a mandate. The last section provides some concluding remarks.

10.2 Background

There is a flourishing literature on the welfare economics of biofuel policies. Some studies emphasize the benefits of ethanol policy in reducing fuel prices and tax costs of farm subsidy programs, and in improving the international terms of trade in corn exports and oil imports (Babcock 2008a; Bourgeon and Tréguer 2008; de Gorter and Just 2009a; Du, Hayes, and Baker 2008; Gardner 2007; Rajagopal et al. 2007; Schmitz, Moss, and Schmitz 2008). Other studies emphasize the impact on CO_2e emissions and vehicle miles traveled (de Gorter and Just 2008a, 2009d; Khanna, Ando, and Taheripour 2008; Lapan and Moschini 2008; Vedenov and Wetzstein 2008). The deadweight costs of the ethanol import tariff are emphasized by de Gorter and Just (2008c), Lasco and Khanna (2009), and Martinez-Gonzalez, Sheldon, and Thompson (2008). Some studies argue that ethanol policies fail to pass an overall cost-benefit test (Hahn and Cecot 2009; Metcalf 2008; Taylor and Van Doren 2007); they have an adverse impact on food prices and poverty, especially in developing countries (Mitchell 2008; Runge and Senauer 2007); and create higher greenhouse gas emissions owing to indirect land use changes (Searchinger et al. 2008).[4]

Gasoline consumption contributes to 45 percent of total oil consumption in the United States (see Table 11 in EIA 2010) and 19 percent of total CO_2e emissions (EPA 2010). Carbon dioxide emissions differ between ethanol and gasoline on a per gallon (gasoline equivalent) basis. Theoretically, there are three alternative ways to calculate CO_2. It must be recognized that all CO_2 emitted upon combustion of ethanol was originally sequestered as the corn was grown. Thus, CO_2 emissions for ethanol are net zero, whereas gasoline emits 17.94 pounds of CO_2 per gallon at combustion.[5] The emissions from any nonethanol energy used in the production of ethanol are attributed to the other fuels. This is the approach also taken by the Nobel Laureate IPCC,

---

[4] For a survey on the welfare economics of biofuel policies, see de Gorter and Just (2010).

[5] There are 115,000 BTUs in a gallon of gasoline (http://bioenergy.ornl.gov/papers/misc/energy_conv.html) and 156 pounds of CO_2 per million BTUs of gasoline (http://tonto.eia.doe.gov/ask/environment_faqs.asp), resulting in 17.94 pounds of CO_2 per gallon of gasoline.

whose guidelines used in assessing compliance with carbon limits in the Kyoto Protocol do not count CO_2 emitted from tailpipes and smokestacks when bioenergy is being used.[6]

The second approach is to measure CO_2e emissions using life-cycle accounting, a "well to wheel" measure of greenhouse gas emissions in the production of gasoline, and a "field to fuel tank" measure for ethanol production. Here, gasoline emits 25.57 pounds of CO_2e per gallon,[7] whereas ethanol emits 80 percent of that.[8] The third approach is to add CO_2e emissions due to indirect land use change to the life-cycle accounting measure, in which case ethanol emits more CO_2e than gasoline (see Hertel, Tyner, and Birur [2008] and Searchinger et al. [2008]). The latter two approaches are based on simple CO_2e balance projections that assume one gallon of ethanol (energy equivalent) replaces one gallon of gasoline, but this need not be the case – there is market "leakage." Indeed, the empirical analysis in this chapter shows leakage in ethanol production to be 52 percent. In other words, each gallon of ethanol on an energy equivalent basis replaces only 0.48 gallons of gasoline; the rest displaces gasoline. It is therefore difficult to credibly predict the true changes in emissions levels a priori. Furthermore, policies promoting ethanol will likely lead to the adoption of different – potentially dirtier – production technologies. Using the first approach by calculating ethanol's direct contribution to emissions avoids the issue of leakage and is also invariant to production technology, allowing a stable measure of how clean the particular fuel is. Further, this method avoids double counting. Using life-cycle accounting attributes some emissions to more than one fuel (e.g., if fossil fuels are used in the production of biofuels, these would count as emissions of both fossil and biofuels). Nonetheless, the life-cycle method is the most prominent in the literature and, thus, the most easily compared across studies.

In the empirical section to follow, we take the life-cycle accounting approach (an intermediate case) as the baseline case and use the other

---

[6] For a detailed argument for why ethanol is net zero in CO_2 emissions and the vagaries of using life-cycle accounting to determine CO_2e emissions, see de Gorter and Just (2009c).

[7] This number is derived by taking into account of (1) the 17.94 pounds of CO_2 emitted per gallon gasoline at combustion, (2) the estimated 95.85 grams of CO_2 per MJ for gasoline using life-cycle analysis (CARB), (3) there are 453.6 grams per pound, (4) there are 0.001052 MJ per BTU, and (5) there are 115,000 BTUs in one gallon of gasoline.

[8] The 20 percent reduction is based on the Farrell et al. (2006) study that used a meta-analysis to calculate a point estimate for CO_2e emissions for the production of U.S. corn ethanol. In response, the United States has tabled a sustainability standard that required ethanol production to reduce CO_2e relative to gasoline by 20 percent.

two options as sensitivity analysis.[9] On a per-mile-traveled basis, ethanol and gasoline are assumed to have the same value of marginal external costs from traffic congestion, local air pollutants, and traffic-related accidents.[10]

It is important to keep in mind that there are several sources of inefficiency in ethanol policy that are not analyzed in this chapter. For example, ethanol production in the United States also generates what we call "rectangular" deadweight costs. These rectangular deadweight costs are a substantial portion of the transfer to the ethanol sector. If the cost of producing ethanol is greater than the price of fuel, the gap between the fuel price and the cost of production must be covered in order for any production to take place. This gap may be bridged by taxpayers in the form of tax credits for the blending of biofuels, or by consumers if the government mandates the minimum blend of ethanol. The payment of this gap is deadweight cost because neither the producers nor consumers of biofuels can capture this payment. It is lost in the cost of producing biofuels. If this gap is high, then the effect of ethanol policy on corn prices is lower because some portion of the subsidy is eaten up to cover the gap (de Gorter and Just 2008b, 2009b). Production costs in the United States are so high that inefficiency abounds. In addition to the direct subsidies for ethanol production, corn subsidies were required historically to cover the gap between ethanol production costs and fuel prices (de Gorter and Just 2009b).

The federal government mandates the use of biofuels in the form of a Renewable Fuel Standard (RFS) of 36 billion gallons per year by 2022, to account for 20 percent of total fuel consumption. Campaign proposals by President Obama would boost this target to 60 billion gallons per year by 2030. The RFS requires 15 billion gallons to be conventional (corn-based) ethanol, but energy legislation also calls for the continuation of a tax credit for biofuels.[11] Federal and state tax credits currently total approximately 52 cents per gallon for corn ethanol (Koplow 2007), whereas a parallel program for biodiesel is worth $1.00 per gallon. A production tax credit limited to cellulosic ethanol pays out $1.01 for each gallon produced. These tax credits are worth over $28.7 billion in 2022 if the mandate is exactly filled. As

---

[9] The life-cycling approach in welfare analysis is also employed by Holland, Hughes, and Knittel (2009) and Lasco and Khanna (2009).

[10] Ethanol's contribution to local air quality is also controversial. Using life-cycle analysis, Jacobson (2009) calls it a "wash" but others argue ethanol is worse, especially corn ethanol; see Hill et al. (2009) and Hahn and Cecot (2009).

[11] In other countries, the consumption subsidy for biofuels is a tax exemption at the fuel pump while in the United States, it takes the form of a blender's subsidy. In theory, the two methods have identical effects except for specific cases in international trade (de Gorter, Just, and Kliauga 2008; Drabik, de Gorter, and Just 2009).

Table 10.1. *Effects of a mandate versus a tax credit on externalities*

	Oil dependence	Miles traveled	CO_2e emissions
Mandate	Decrease	Increase or decrease	Increase or decrease
Tax credit	Decrease	Increase	Increase or decrease
Mandate vs. tax credit (same ethanol consumption)	————	Lower with mandate	————

Source: de Gorter and Just (2008a) and Lapan and Moschini (2009).

noted earlier, subsidies and mandates by themselves do not discriminate against international trade. However, production subsidies, import tariffs (of approximately 57¢/gal.), and sustainability standards do. In addition to creating huge inefficiencies, these import barriers are inconsistent with both energy and environmental goals, because lower-cost sugar cane–based ethanol in Brazil contributes far more to reduction of CO_2e emissions than corn-based ethanol. Far less land is required, and so much lower indirect land use changes occur because Brazil not only produces twice the amount of ethanol per hectare but also crops displaced by the United States now have to be produced elsewhere (e.g., corn yields in Brazil are one-third of that of the United States) and annual net sequestration per hectare is much higher in Brazil (de Gorter and Tsur 2008). Given that ethanol production from Brazil is more economically efficient and climate-friendly than ethanol production in the United States, removal of U.S. production subsidies for corn and ethanol, and of ethanol import tariffs would save billions in CO_2e emissions alone (de Gorter and Tsur 2008; Lasco and Khanna 2009). These inefficiencies due to trade restrictions are independent of the welfare effects of mandate or tax credit analyzed in this chapter.

A key finding in the literature that is particularly important for the analysis to follow in this chapter is that a mandate is superior to a tax credit. The effects of each policy on key externalities are summarized in Table 10.1. Although gasoline consumption always declines under either a mandate or a tax credit (hence, oil dependence declines), surprisingly it is possible for total fuel consumption to increase under a mandate, depending on the relative elasticity of ethanol supply and gasoline supply (de Gorter and Just 2007, 2009b; Fischer and Newell 2008).[12] This means the change in externalities related to vehicle miles traveled and CO_2e emissions is also ambiguous. It is possible that a mandate increases CO_2e emissions even if

---

[12] Holland, Hughes, and Knittel (2009) get the same result in analyzing California's "low carbon fuel standard," which is basically the same as a blend mandate.

ethanol emits less per mile traveled than gasoline. Note, however, that a reduction in the fuel price is not a sufficient condition for CO_2e emissions to increase. The resulting change in emissions will depend not only on the ratio of emissions from the two fuels, but also on the price responsiveness of producers. If gasoline production is very price inelastic. The increase in ethanol consumption due to the mandate may not be completely offset by the reduction in gasoline consumption, potentially leading to greater emissions (de Gorter and Just 2008a; Lapan and Moschini 2009).

With a tax credit, on the other hand, fuel consumption always increases. A tax credit unambiguously increases miles traveled, but CO_2e emissions may either increase or decrease depending on the amount of the increase in ethanol consumption due to the tax credit and on ethanol's contribution to CO_2e emissions. Even though ethanol is considered to emit less CO_2e per mile traveled than gasoline, there is the chance that subsidizing ethanol may increase emissions. This is because subsidizing ethanol lowers the overall price of fuel.[13] Regardless, as the final row in Table 10.1 indicates, a mandate results in a lower level of total fuel consumption, CO_2e emissions, and miles traveled compared to a tax credit for the same quantity of ethanol.[14]

10.3 The Optimal Fuel Tax–Tax Credit Combination

Denote ξ_E and ξ_G as the CO_2e emissions per mile of fuel consumed from ethanol and gasoline, respectively, with the marginal external costs given by τ_1 dollars per mile.[15] Denote τ_2 as the per mile traveled marginal external costs due to traffic congestion, local air pollutants, and traffic-related accidents (assumed identical for ethanol and gasoline).

Consider a competitive market with a domestic supply curve for ethanol $E(P_E)$, measured in terms of contribution to vehicle miles traveled, with P_E the price to suppliers of ethanol, and a supply for oil-based gasoline $G(P_G)$, also measured in miles with P_G the market price to suppliers of gasoline. Fuel consists of only two products: ethanol and gasoline. These two are assumed to be perfect substitutes in consumption. Consumers would not be willing to pay more per mile for either fuel. Thus, in a competitive

---

[13] The resulting impact on emissions will depend also on the relative price responsiveness of fuel demand and gasoline supply; with a greater relative price elasticity of demand increasing emissions under an ethanol subsidy (see de Gorter and Just 2008a; Lapan and Moschini 2009).

[14] For full explanation of these results, see the discussion in de Gorter and Just (2008a; 2009b).

[15] As discussed in the previous section, $\xi_E = 0, 0.8 \cdot \xi_G$ or is $> \xi_G$. If the latter, then the tax credit in the analysis to follow is negative.

equilibrium, the price per mile of ethanol must equal the price per mile of gasoline: $P_E = P_G$. The domestic demand for fuel (measured in miles) is denoted by $D_F(P_F)$, where P_F is the price per mile of the blended fuel. The market equilibrium price for fuel absent a policy is thus given by P such that:

$$D_F(P) = E(P) + G(P). \qquad (10.1)$$

Now, consider the U.S. policy of charging a tax on all fuels based on volume, and then providing a tax credit for ethanol. Denote the volumetric fuel tax by t_v, measured in dollars per gallon. One gallon of ethanol produces only 70 percent of the miles achieved by a gallon of gasoline. Thus, the tax per mile traveled will be different for gasoline and ethanol. The tax per mile for gasoline is $t = t_v/MPG_G$, where MPG_G is the miles traveled per gallon of gasoline. The corresponding tax per mile traveled for ethanol is thus ϕt where $\phi = MPG_G/MPG_E \approx 1/.7$, or close to 1.4, and where MPG_E is the miles traveled per gallon of ethanol. Let t_{cv} be the tax credit per gallon of ethanol. Thus, the tax credit per mile traveled with ethanol is $t_c = t_{cv}/MPG_E$. Again, the competitive equilibrium will force the consumer price of ethanol and gasoline to be equal,

$$P_G + t = P_E + \phi t - t_c. \qquad (10.2)$$

Thus, the consumer will pay $P_G + t$, and the ethanol price in equilibrium will be given by $P_E = P_G + (1 - \phi)t + t_c$. The equilibrium under a tax and a tax credit will be given by

$$D_F(P_G + t) = E(P_G + (1 - \phi)t + t_c) + G(P_G). \qquad (10.3)$$

Thus, the price of gasoline is an implicit function of the tax and tax credit as defined by (10.3). Anytime a policy maker adjusts either the tax or tax credit, it will necessarily cause a change in P_G (and thus in the price of ethanol, the quantities of ethanol and gasoline produced, and the quantity of fuel demanded), according to the equilibrium condition in (10.3).

To find the optimal fuel tax–tax credit combination, let $V(P_F, Y, X)$ be the indirect utility function of a representative consumer, yielding the optimal utility as a function of the price of fuel, the level of income, Y, and the level of environmental externalities from CO_2e emissions and miles traveled, X. Under a fuel tax and an ethanol tax credit, assume that government tax revenues are returned lump sum to the representative consumer.

Thus, income is given by

$$Y = \pi_E(P_E) + \pi_G(P_G) + tG(P_G) + (\phi t - t_c)E(P_E), \qquad (10.4)$$

where $\pi_E(P_E)$ is the profit derived from sale of ethanol as a function of the price of ethanol, $\pi_G(P_G)$ is profit derived from the sale of gasoline as a function of the price of gasoline, and all other variables are as defined previously. Thus, to solve for the optimal tax and tax credit

$$\max_{t,\, t_c} \ V(P_F, Y, X), \qquad (10.5)$$

where $P_F = P_G + t$, according to (10.3), Y is as specified in (10.4), and the money metric externality costs associated with consuming gasoline and ethanol are defined by X:

$$X = \tau_1[\xi_E E(P_E) + \xi_G G(P_G)] + \tau_2[E(P_E) + G(P_G)]. \qquad (10.6)$$

We can then solve for the optimal tax on fuel and the tax credit for ethanol (see Section A.1 in the Appendix), finding $t^* = \tau_1\xi_G + \tau_2$ and $t_c^* = \phi t^* - t_E^*$ $= \phi(\tau_1\xi_G + \tau_2) - (\tau_1\xi_E + \tau_2)$, where the social marginal damage due to ethanol is $t_E^* = \tau_1\xi_E + \tau_2$. The optimal gasoline tax is the marginal external cost of consuming gasoline. Alternatively, the optimal ethanol tax credit is the difference between the per mile tax cost of consuming ethanol (the tax burden of paying ϕt^*) and the marginal external cost of consuming ethanol t_E^*. Thus, at the first-best optimum, the individual is charged the marginal external cost of consumption for each fuel they consume.

The intuition of how we can achieve the first best with a combination of a fuel tax and tax credit for ethanol is given in Figure 10.1. To simplify the explanation of Figure 10.1, we assume the price of gasoline P_G is fixed with the gasoline supply curve given by G. Denote the fuel demand curve by D_F and the ethanol supply curve by E. With neither a fuel tax nor an ethanol tax credit, the market price of gasoline defines the initial market (and consumer) prices for fuel P_{F0} and ethanol P_{E0}.[16] Fuel consumption equals F_0, and ethanol production is E_0. Define the gasoline demand curve by D_{G0} (the fuel demand curve D_F shifted left by the initial quantity of ethanol E_0). This generates gasoline consumption G_0.

To further simplify the analysis, assume CO_2e emissions from gasoline are the only externality given by $\tau_1\xi_G$ (ethanol is assumed to be net zero

---

[16] The ethanol price P_{E0} equals the gasoline price as all units are in gasoline equivalents. If the units were in gallons, then the market price of ethanol P_{E0} is less than P_G because consumers demand miles traveled. The per-gallon ethanol price in that case would equal P_G/ϕ.

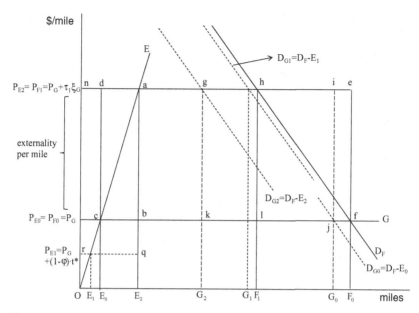

Figure 10.1. Optimal Tax Credit and Fuel Tax for CO_2 Emissions: Case of $\xi_E = \tau_2 = 0$.

in CO_2e emissions, the case where $\xi_E = 0$, and externalities due to miles traveled is assumed zero, $\tau_2 = 0$). This means initial externality costs of fuel consumption are given by area *defc*.

Imposing the optimal fuel tax $t^* = \tau_1 \xi_G$ generates a new price for gasoline P_{F1} (the market price to gasoline suppliers remains at P_G). Fuel consumption declines to F_1. Because consumers demand miles and are only willing to pay $P_G + (1 - \phi)t^*$ for ethanol, the market price to suppliers of ethanol P_{E1} declines (along with ethanol production to E_1) by $(1 - \phi)t^*$.[17] Hence, $(1 - \phi)t^*$ represents a penalty on blenders of fuel, as the government requires the payment of a *volumetric* fuel tax on all fuels but consumers are not willing to pay the excess tax for ethanol.

The optimal solution is to implement a consumption subsidy for ethanol given by the tax credit $t_c = \phi \tau_1 \xi_G$ such that the new market price for ethanol $P_{E2} = P_{E1} + \phi \tau_1 \xi_G = P_{F1}$ and ethanol production is E_2. Gasoline consumption G_2 is given by $F_1 - E_2$. Equilibrium in Figure 10.1 therefore depicts the optimal fuel tax–tax credit combination (assuming $\tau_2 = \tau_{1E} = 0$), where the fuel price equals P_{F1}, the ethanol market price equals P_{E2},

---

[17] In dollars per gallon, the market price of ethanol P_{E1} would decline by $(1 - 1/\phi)t^*$ because consumers demand miles.

the consumption of fuel equals F_1, ethanol production is E_2 and gasoline consumption equals G_2.

The optimal fuel tax–tax credit combination generates a primary welfare gain in reduced CO_2e emissions of areas *dabc* (increased ethanol consumption) and *hijl* (reduced consumption of gasoline). Fuel tax revenues are areas *ahlb + naqr*, but the tax costs of the tax credit is area *naqr*, so the net tax revenues are area *ahlb* ($= \tau_1 \xi_G \cdot G_2$). Deadweight costs in reduced fuel consumption are given by area *hfl*, whereas deadweight costs in ethanol production are area *abc*.

10.4 The Optimal Fuel Tax–Mandate Combination

Under an ethanol consumption mandate, consumers are forced to accept a specific amount of ethanol $\overline{E}$. The resulting market price for fuel will be the price that covers the average marginal cost of production for the blend

$$P_F = \frac{\overline{E} P_E(\overline{E}) + P_G G(P_G)}{\overline{E} + G(P_G)}, \tag{10.7}$$

where $P_E(E)$ is the producer price necessary to produce $\overline{E}$ amount of ethanol. The market equilibrium will thus be determined where demand for miles from fuel is equal to the supply,

$$D_F \left(\frac{\overline{E} P_E(\overline{E}) + P_G G(P_G)}{\overline{E} + G(P_G)} \right) = \overline{E} + G(P_G). \tag{10.8}$$

If we allow a volumetric fuel tax with the ethanol consumption mandate, the marginal cost of ethanol to producers becomes $P_E(\overline{E}) + \phi t$. Thus, with a mandate and a tax, the market equilibrium is determined by

$$D_F \left(\frac{(P_E(\overline{E}) + \phi t)\overline{E} + (P_G + t)G(P_G)}{\overline{E} + G(P_G)} \right) = \overline{E} + G(P_G). \tag{10.9}$$

This again defines P_G as an implicit function of the fuel tax and the ethanol mandate. Thus, as the policies change, the price of gasoline will change (and the amount of gasoline consumed) to accommodate the policy.

To find the optimal fuel tax-ethanol mandate combination, consider again the indirect utility function $V(P_F, Y, X)$. The policy maker must solve

$$\max_{\overline{E}, t} V(P_F, Y, X), \tag{10.10}$$

Table 10.2. *Optimal mandate and tax credit*

	Optimal fuel tax and ethanol policy combination	Suboptimal fuel tax
Mandate	$\overline{E} = E(P_G(t^*, t_c^*) + (1 - \phi)$ $(t^* - t_c^*) \, ; t < t^*$	$\overline{E} > E(P_G(t^*, t_c^*) + (1 - \phi)$ $(t^* + t_c^*)$
Tax credit	$t_c = \phi t^* - t_E^* \, ; t = t^*$	$t_c < \phi t^* - t_E^*$

Source: Derived in Appendix.

where

$$P_F = \frac{(P_E(\overline{E}) + \phi t)\overline{E} + (P_G + t)G(P_G)}{\overline{P} + G(P_G)} \tag{10.11}$$

$$Y = \pi_E(P_E) + \pi_G(P_G) + tG(P_G) + \phi t E(P_E) \tag{10.12}$$

and X is as given in (10.6), and where P_G is a function of the fuel tax and mandate defined implicitly by (10.9). The optimal fuel tax under the mandate (defined as t^M) can be stated in terms of the first-best fuel tax–tax credit combination (derived in the Appendix, Section A.4)

$$t^M = \frac{t^* G(P_G(t^*, t_c^*)) + (\phi t^* - t_c^*)\overline{E}}{G(P_G(t^*, t_c^*)) + \phi \overline{E}}, \tag{10.13}$$

$$\overline{E} = E(P_G(t^*, t_c^*) + (1 - \phi)t^* + t_c^*). \tag{10.14}$$

Equations (10.13) and (10.14) imply the same level of ethanol and gasoline use that was obtained in the first-best solution (using a tax and tax credit). However, the optimal fuel tax in this case is lower,

$$t^M = \frac{t^* G(P_G(t^*, t_c^*)) + (\phi t^* - t_c^*)\overline{E}}{G(P_G(t^*, t_c^*)) + \phi \overline{E}} < \frac{t^* G(P_G(t^*, t_c^*)) + \phi t^* \overline{E}}{G(P_G(t^*, t_c^*)) + \phi \overline{E}} = t^*,$$

$$\tag{10.14}$$

by the amount $t_c^* \overline{E}/(G(P_G(t^*, t_c^*)) + \phi \overline{E})$. As displayed in column 1 of Table 10.2, the optimal mandate under the optimal tax will always equal the amount of ethanol consumed under the optimal fuel tax–tax credit combination, although the optimal fuel tax will be lower. The reason for a lower optimal fuel tax is rather straightforward: the mandate is a tax on the gasoline market to pay for the higher ethanol price. Hence, a lower fuel tax is required to offset the marginal external cost of fuel consumption. The ethanol price is exactly the same as the optimal fuel tax–tax credit

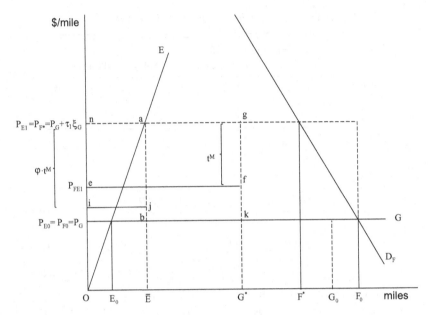

Figure 10.2. Optimal Combination of an Ethanol Mandate and Fuel Tax for CO_2 Emissions: Case of $\xi_E = \tau_2 = 0$.

combination, so one can achieve the first-best optimum, resulting in exactly the same indirect utility (shown in Section A.4 of the Appendix).[18]

The optimal fuel tax–mandate combination is depicted in Figure 10.2. As in Figure 10.1, we simplify by assuming CO_2e emissions for gasoline only ($\xi_E = 0$) and ignore the external costs due to miles traveled ($\tau_2 = 0$). The optimal ethanol mandate is $\overline{E}$ with an ethanol market price P_{E1} (generating a pre-fuel tax price of fuel equal to P_{FE1}). The optimal fuel tax with the optimal mandate is denoted by t^M. Total fuel consumption declines to F^* (gasoline consumption is $G^* = F^* - \overline{E}$). Tax revenues from ethanol sales equal area *naji* while tax revenues from gasoline are area *ngfe*.

10.5 How a Suboptimal Fuel Tax Magnifies the Superiority of a Mandate

Now that we have derived the optimal fuel tax–tax credit and fuel tax–mandate combinations, it is important to consider policy constraints

---

[18] This result holds regardless if fuel consumption increases with the mandate, because even though the mandate subsidizes fuel consumers, it still taxes gasoline consumers (and acts as a monopsony against gasoline suppliers).

imposed by politics. For example, assume it is not politically feasible to raise the gasoline tax to its optimal level in the United States (Parry and Small 2005).[19] We derive two key results in this section: a suboptimal fuel tax requires a lower tax credit and (under most conditions) a higher mandate. In other words, the superiority of a mandate is widened.

Why the Tax Credit has to Be Lowered

If we were to find the optimal ethanol tax credit when the fuel tax is held at 0, we find $t_c < -t_E^*$ (shown in Section A.3 of the Appendix). Thus, the optimal ethanol tax credit in this case is, in fact, a tax that must exceed the marginal external cost of ethanol. In this case, the instrument on ethanol is the only policy available to address the externalities associated with either fuel. The tax-reducing external effects from the consumption of ethanol is more effective than a subsidy creating secondary reductions in externalities by substituting ethanol for gasoline.

As the fuel tax exogenously decreases from the optimum, the optimal response ethanol tax credit (the tax credit that maximizes welfare given a fuel tax) decreases and eventually becomes negative once the tax is below the marginal external cost of ethanol (see Section A.3 in the Appendix). The optimal ethanol tax credit t_c is only positive if (1) CO_2e emissions decline (recall that the effect of a tax credit on CO_2e emissions is ambiguous) and (2) the social benefits of this decline in CO_2e emissions are greater than the social costs of the unambiguous increase in miles traveled with a tax credit. This will occur whenever the fuel tax exceeds the marginal external costs of consuming ethanol. A suboptimal fuel tax will lead to an optimal tax credit t_c that is below the first-best tax credit t_c^*.

Alternatively, consider a suboptimal tax credit. If we find the optimal fuel tax holding the ethanol tax credit at 0, the resulting optimal fuel tax satisfies $t^* > t > t_E^*/\phi$ (see Section A.2 in the Appendix). Thus, the optimal fuel tax will be between the marginal external cost of gasoline and the marginal external cost of ethanol (here the adjustment ϕ is due to the fact that the tax is on a volume basis). This will always result in a fuel tax that is less than the fuel tax under the jointly optimal fuel tax and ethanol tax credit, but more than the net tax on ethanol under the jointly optimal fuel tax and ethanol tax credit. In general, exogenously reducing the ethanol tax credit will always decrease the optimal fuel tax, if $t^* > t_E^* < \phi$.

---

[19] The analysis here is opposite for the case of Britain, which has a super-optimal fuel tax (Parry and Small 2005).

Why the Mandate Has to Be Increased

With a suboptimal fuel tax, the optimal ethanol mandate will be positive so long as the marginal external cost plus the marginal internal cost of ethanol is larger than the same value for gasoline within the competitive equilibrium. The level of the optimal consumption mandate $\overline{E}^*$ depends heavily on the elasticity of supply for gasoline and ethanol. In general, the optimal mandate, $\overline{E}(t)$, will result in a price of fuel that satisfies (see Section A.5 in the Appendix)

$$P_G(t, \overline{E}(t)) + t < P_F(t, \overline{E}(t)) < P_G(t, \overline{E}(t)) + t^*. \qquad (10.15)$$

If we consider lowering the tax from the optimal fuel tax–mandate combination, the direction of the change in the optimal response mandate (the mandate that maximizes welfare given a fuel tax) will be positive if we are at the optimal fuel tax–mandate combination (see the derivation in Section A.5 of the Appendix)

$$(P_G - P_E + (1 - \phi)t^M) > \left(\frac{\eta_G}{\eta_F}P_F - P_G\right)\frac{D_F}{\overline{E}\,\eta_G}. \qquad (10.16)$$

where η_G is the supply elasticity for gasoline and η_F is the demand elasticity for fuel. Both the left-hand and right-hand sides of (10.16) must be negative. Thus, decreasing the optimal response mandate is more likely to be higher than under the first-best scenario if ethanol consumption under the first best is relatively small in relation to total fuel consumption, or if both the supply elasticity for gasoline and the demand elasticity for fuel are low. This would appear to typify the current market for fuel, gasoline, and ethanol. The conditions in (10.16) are very similar to that required for an increase in the ethanol mandate to increase the price of fuel (see de Gorter and Just 2008a). Intuitively, if ethanol is a large portion of fuel consumption, increasing the mandate will necessitate a higher percentage decline in gasoline consumption. This larger percentage decline in gasoline consumption creates a much larger percentage decrease in the price of gasoline, potentially leading to a decline in total fuel price that will exacerbate the externalities from consumption of both fuels. However, externalities may increase even if the price of fuel increases with the mandate. Hence, the conditions in (10.16) are slightly more restrictive than those found by de Gorter and Just (2008a).

The intuition for why a mandate needs to be increased with a suboptimal fuel tax is depicted in Figure 10.3. As in Figures 10.1 and 10.2, we simplify by assuming CO_2e emissions for gasoline only ($\xi_E = 0$) and ignore the

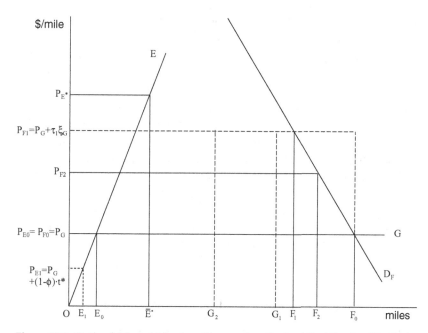

Figure 10.3. Optimal Ethanol Mandate Compared to Optimal Fuel Tax for CO_2 Emissions: Case of $\xi_E = \tau_2 = 0$.

external costs due to miles traveled ($\tau_2 = 0$). Consider first the outcome with an optimal fuel tax only ($t^* = \tau_1 \xi_G$). Fuel consumption declines to F_1 with a fuel price of P_{F1} and again, because of the *volumetric* fuel tax, ethanol prices decline to P_{E1}. Gasoline consumption is given by $G_1 (= F_1 - E_1)$.

Now consider no fuel tax and the optimal mandate becomes $\overline{E}^*$ and the corresponding fuel price is $P_{F2} (< P_{F1})$. Total fuel consumption is now F_2 and gasoline consumption is G_2. Notice that the level of ethanol production is now higher than $\overline{E}$ in Figure 10.2, the case of the optimal fuel tax–mandate combination. Ethanol prices P_{E^*} are also now higher. That is because a mandate is a tax on gasoline and a subsidy on ethanol production. It pays to overproduce ethanol with no fuel tax because a mandate compensates for the suboptimal fuel tax (unlike with a tax credit shown earlier – the lower the fuel tax, the lower the optimal tax credit). However, the optimal fuel tax cannot be achieved indirectly with a mandate alone because of the overproduction of the higher-cost ethanol.

As Table 10.2 displays, under a suboptimal fuel tax, the optimal mandate will increase, whereas the optimal tax credit will decrease. The increase in the optimal mandate implies greater ethanol consumption than under the first-best scenario. Alternatively, the lower tax credit implies less ethanol consumption than under the first-best policy.

Compared to a tax credit with a suboptimal fuel tax, a mandate is always superior so long as $t_E^* < \phi t^*$, the condition for the optimal tax credit in the first-best scenario to be positive (see the derivation in Section A.6 of the Appendix). The greater the elasticity of gasoline supply, the greater the advantage of the ethanol mandate over the tax credit in mitigating the suboptimal gasoline tax. Similarly, an inelastic demand curve will reduce the gasoline price response of a tax credit, also leading to a larger advantage of the mandate over the tax credit (see also Section A.6 of the Appendix).

Without a tax credit, the optimal fuel tax is such that $t^* > t > t_E^*/\phi$ (see Section A.2 in the Appendix). Thus, in this case, the optimal tax must fall between the optimal tax on ethanol and the optimal tax on gasoline. The optimal fuel tax with a mandate t^M draws closer to t^* as the supply elasticity of gasoline increases relative to the supply elasticity of ethanol.

10.6 What if a Tax Credit Is Added alongside a Binding Mandate?

If the tax credit determines ethanol market prices, then the mandate is dormant; however, the reverse is not true. If a mandate is binding, then the tax credit is subsidizing gasoline consumption instead (on its own, a tax credit subsidizes ethanol consumption only). This perverse effect can be explained as follows. With a binding mandate, the tax credit fails to provide any incentive to increase production of ethanol. Rather, the only way to take advantage of the subsidy is to reduce the price of the fuel (a blend of gasoline and ethanol) to compete for sales. But if the price of fuel declines, resulting in more fuel, this added fuel must be in the form of gasoline, given the binding mandate for ethanol (see de Gorter and Just [2007, 2008b, 2009a] and Lapan and Moschini [2009] for details).[20]

As a result, society loses the primary welfare gain of reduced externalities with a mandate. As the tax credit approaches the value of the ethanol price premium due to the mandate, the benefits of the mandate are dissipated. If the tax credit is equal to the ethanol price premium due to the mandate and oil prices are endogenous, then the tax credit reverses the primary welfare gain of reduced externalities of the mandate and more – it cannibalizes part of the fuel tax as well. For a formal derivation, see de Gorter and Just (2008a) and Lapan and Moschini (2009). If the mandate alone increases CO_2e emissions and miles traveled, then the tax credit in this situation

[20] For a simple, short, and intuitive explanation, see de Gorter and Just (2008d).

just make things worse. Therefore, using tax credits with mandates in place contradicts the new energy bill's stated objectives of reducing dependency on oil, improving the environment, and enhancing rural prosperity. This result is independent of the CO_2e emissions measures associated with indirect land use and life-cycle accounting that is currently in the forefront of the public debate over biofuels.

To make matters worse, production subsidies for corn and ethanol may subsidize gasoline consumption when there is a binding mandate. The reasoning is similar to that of adding a tax credit to a mandate, as discussed earlier. Unlike with a tax credit, however, a subsidy for corn and/or ethanol results in a lower ethanol wholesale price. With production subsidies for corn and ethanol, even though the market price of ethanol declines, ethanol production (and consumption) remains constant because it is determined by the mandate.[21]

This result is also important because renewable electricity faces similar policy combinations with consumption mandates (called *renewable portfolio standards*), tax credits (called *tax exemptions*), production subsidies (called *producer tax credits*) and subsidies for biomass production (e.g., for switch grass used in co-firing coal plants) (Fischer and Newell 2008). It is also important to note that even if the mandate is not binding, it otherwise could be and so represents the true opportunity cost of tax credits and production subsidies that subsidize oil consumption (Hahn and Cecot 2009).

10.7 Interactions with the Fiscal System

So far the analysis ignores interactions between biofuel policies and the broader fiscal system. There is an important literature in environmental economics in which rankings of alternative environmental policy instruments can be heavily dependent on their impact on government budget revenues and the size of the tax base (see Goulder, Parry, and Burtraw [1997]; Goulder et al. [1999]; and also Chapter 8, by Parry). So, too, the possible rankings of a biofuel mandate *versus* a tax credit can be reversed if fiscal interaction effects are taken into account.

Table 10.3 summarizes the fiscal interaction effects when comparing a mandate to a tax credit under several different scenarios. The first column summarizes our results that, in terms of social welfare when fiscal interaction

---

[21] Production of corn declines with an ethanol production subsidy but increases with a corn production subsidy. For the same per-unit subsidy, the ethanol price declines more with an ethanol production subsidy than a corn subsidy. In both cases, the consumption of nonethanol corn increases.

Table 10.3. *Effect of mandates versus tax credits on government tax revenues and fuel prices*

	Social welfare	Government tax revenues	Fuel prices
Optimal fuel tax/ethanol policy combinations	Same	Same	Same
Suboptimal fuel tax (ethanol cons. same)	Higher with mandate[a]	Higher with mandate if (a) ethanol supply more elastic than fuel demand;	Lower with tax credit
Suboptimal fuel tax[b] (max. social welfare)	Higher with mandate[a]	(b) tax credit higher than fuel tax; and (c) more inelastic gasoline supply curve	Ambiguous[c]

[a] Assuming no interactions with the fiscal system.
[b] Note that there now is a differential impact on ethanol and, hence, corn prices and farm subsidy tax costs.
[c] Ambiguous only if fuel prices decline with an increase in the mandate; otherwise, fuel prices lower with a tax credit.
Source: Calculated.

effects are ignored, social welfare is the same with the optimal fuel tax–biofuel policy combinations but that the mandate dominates in the other two cases.

The first row of Table 10.3 confirms our earlier results that the two optimal policy combinations are identical in every respect, including fiscal interaction effects. As shown in Section A.4 of the Appendix, the two policies generate identical levels of net tax revenue (income from fuel tax minus the expenditure on the tax credit). Also, all consumer and producer prices, consumption levels, and production levels are identical. Therefore, there are no differences between a mandate and a tax credit due to fiscal interactions if these biofuel policies are evaluated with the individual social optimum fuel tax combination.

Even though a mandate does not involve taxpayer expenditures (unlike a tax credit), in theory, a mandate can still result in lower net government budget revenues because of reduced tax revenues with the reduced fuel consumption. What the outcome depends on is described in Figure 10.4, where it is assumed that the tax credit equals the fuel tax and the supply curve for gasoline is flat. A mandate to achieve the same ethanol production as the tax credit results in a higher fuel price P_{FM} and lower fuel consumption F_M such that area $c + d$ equals area $a + b$. Area e represents the loss in tax revenues due to reduced total fuel consumption and can exceed taxpayer

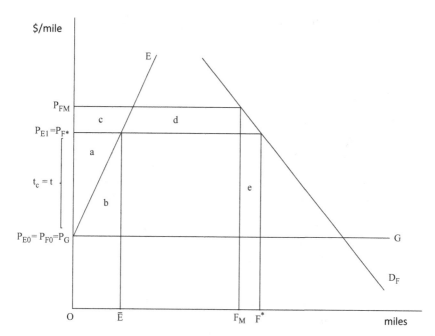

Figure 10.4. Taxpayer Costs: Mandate and Tax Credit Compared.

cost of the tax credit of area $a + b$ if fuel demand is sufficiently more elastic than the ethanol supply elasticity. But we find empirically that fuel demand is sufficiently inelastic relative to ethanol supply such that a mandate saves taxpayer costs. Furthermore, the tax credit exceeds the fuel tax, making it less likely a mandate involves more tax revenues compared to a tax credit for the same ethanol quantity. Lastly, removing the assumption of a perfectly elastic gasoline supply further widens the superiority of a mandate in saving tax costs.[22]

However, the benefits in taxpayer savings depend upon how the revenues are used and on how fuel prices are affected (the latter impacting the size of the tax base). As shown in the last column of Table 10.3, fuel prices are lower with a tax credit than with a mandate, with the same ethanol quantity in the case of a suboptimal fuel tax. This reduces the tax base and can offset the benefits of lower tax costs. In the case of the fuel market, Parry (Chapter 8) argues that it is more likely that the benefits of reduced tax costs dominate.

[22] To understand this latter point, consider the case of a vertical gasoline supply curve. Total fuel consumption is the same with a mandate and tax credit. Hence, there are no fuel tax revenues lost, so the more inelastic the gasoline supply curve, *ceteris paribus*, the less likely the mandate foregoes fuel tax revenues.

Table 10.4. *Parameters used in empirical simulations*

Benchmark Case	
Externalities	
CO$_2$e emissions life-cycle	
lb per gallon gasoline	25.57
lb per gallon ethanol	0.8·25.57
Price of CO$_2$e emissions ($/ton Nordhaus)	10
Oil dependence (¢/gal.)	10
Traffic congestion (¢/mile)	52
Local air pollution (¢/mile)	12
Accidents (¢/mile)	41
Efficiency gain per $ of recyling (¢)	30
Parameters	
Fuel tax (¢/gal.)	41
Fuel demand elasticity	−0.4
Response from improved fuel economy	$\beta = 0.5$
Initial miles per gallon	22.3
Ethanol supply elasticity	4,2,3 (2007; 2015; 2022)
Domestic oil supply elasticity	0.2
OPEC supply elasticity	2.375
Excess demand elasticity for oil in rest of world	−0.86
Sensitivity Analysis	
Price of CO$_2$e emissions ($/ton Stern)	80
Efficiency gain per $ of recyling (¢)	0
Response from improved fuel economy	$\beta = 0.67$
Initial miles per gallon	30.4

Source: Parry (Chapter 8); Leiby (2007); estimated.

10.8 Empirical Simulations

We calibrate a simple stylized model of the U.S. gasoline and ethanol market for the years 2007, 2015, and 2022 to determine the potential significance of the social deadweight costs due to ethanol mandates and tax credits. The assumed values of key parameters are summarized in Table 10.4. Life-cycle emissions are taken from the recent ruling of the California Air Resources Board on California's "low carbon fuel standard" where ethanol emissions are assumed to be 80 percent of those for gasoline, based on our discussion earlier. The assumed values for the price of CO$_2$e, oil dependence, traffic congestion, local air pollution, and accidents are taken from Parry (Chapter 8). The efficiency gain per dollar of revenue recycled is taken from Parry (see Figure 8.5 in Chapter 8). The fuel tax, fuel demand elasticity, response from improved fuel economy, and initial miles per gallon are taken from Parry (Chapter 8).

The supply curve for ethanol is defined as the horizontal difference between the supply of corn and the demand for nonethanol corn. Thus, the elasticity of ethanol supply is given by $\eta_E^S = \eta_C^S S_C / S_C^E - \eta_{NE}^D S_C^{NE} / S_C^E$, where η_C^S is the supply elasticity for corn, η_{NE}^D is the demand elasticity for nonethanol corn (domestic and export sales), S_C is the production of corn, S_C^E is the corn used as an input to ethanol production, and S_C^{NE} is corn used for nonethanol purposes. Because ethanol's share of total corn production is expected to decline and bottom out in 2015 (Babcock 2008b), we estimate different ethanol supply elasticities for each year. The elasticities assumed in the U.S. corn market are as follows: 0.2, −0.2, and −1.0 for supply, nonethanol domestic demand, and export demand, respectively.[23] Using observed or forecast quantities for the various years and the assumed parameter values, the estimated supply elasticities for ethanol are 4, 2, and 3 for 2007, 2015, and 2022, respectively.

The import supply elasticity for gasoline is derived from the negative of the formula used for the ethanol supply curve, with assumed values of elasticities of domestic supply of gasoline, OPEC supply, and excess demand for gasoline in the rest of the world taken from Leiby (2007). The OPEC supply elasticity of 2.375 is the midpoint of the range given in Leiby (2007).

The values for sensitivity analysis (price of CO_2e emissions, efficiency gain per dollar of recycling, response from improved fuel economy, and initial miles per gallon) are taken from Parry (Chapter 8). The market price for gasoline was $2.00 per gallon in 2007 and is estimated to be $2.50 per gallon in 2015 and 2022. The estimated market prices for ethanol, P_E, is equal to $\lambda(P_G + t) - t + t_c$ where λ is the ratio of miles per gallon of ethanol relative to gasoline and with an assumed value of 0.70, P_G is the price of gasoline, t denotes the volumetric fuel tax and t_c is the tax credit for ethanol (de Gorter and Just 2008b). The weighted average biofuel tax credit is $0.570, $0.658, and $0.796 per gallon for 2007, 2015, and 2022, respectively.

The likelihood of the mandate binding depends on the level of the tax credit itself. If the tax credit is high enough to bind, the true social opportunity cost is still a mandate that could otherwise generate the same level of ethanol consumption. In the empirical analysis to follow, we use the level of ethanol generated by the tax credit in each year to analyze the trade-offs between a tax credit, a mandate, or no policy at all. In other words, a

---

[23] These parameters are well within the range of a vast literature in agricultural economics that reports estimates of various supply and demand elasticities.

mandate is set to reproduce ethanol production and prices that otherwise would occur with the observed tax credit.

The results of these simulations on changes in key market parameters are presented in Table 10.5, and welfare changes are given in Table 10.6. A negative value in Table 10.6 represents a social gain. The first set of results in Table 10.6 shows the effects of a tax credit alone. The only social benefits of a tax credit are in improved terms of trade in oil imports and reduced oil dependence. Theoretically, CO_2e emissions can decline but are found empirically to increase. The efficiency gain per dollar of recycling is assumed to be 30 cents (see Figure 8.5 in Chapter 8). Others argue that it may be zero (e.g., Kaplow 2004) but Parry (Chapter 8) cites literature that 30 cents on the dollar is a more accurate estimate for parameters pertaining to the transportation fuel sector. Overall, tax credits are estimated to have generated a $300 million improvement in social welfare in 2007, but net social losses of $1.1 and $1.5 billion are predicted for 2015 and 2022, respectively.

The second set of results in Table 10.6 shows the effects of a mandate alone. Social benefits are substantial. Although not necessary in theory, gasoline market prices and total fuel consumption decline, as do miles traveled, and CO_2e emissions increase. The estimated market parameters are such that a mandate generates benefits ranging from $2.5 billion in 2007 to $9.5 billion in 2022.

The last set of results in Table 10.6 shows the effect of implementing a mandate instead of a tax credit to achieve the same level of ethanol consumption. This simulates the reverse of adding a tax credit to a binding mandate. Therefore, there are social benefits in all categories, with welfare gains of $2.2, $5.5, and $11 billion in 2007, 2015, and 2022, respectively. Note that the social costs of adding a tax credit to a mandate are greater than the benefits of a mandate alone (e.g., $11 billion *versus* $9.5 billion in 2022). This is because the tax credit cannibalizes all of the social benefits of a mandate and part of the fuel tax.

The last two rows of Table 10.6 provide some sensitivity analysis. The forward-looking case for vehicle miles traveled allows for a higher response in miles traveled to fuel price changes because of fuel economy regulations (see Chapter 8). This somewhat increases the costs of a tax credit and the benefits of a mandate. Some argue fuel economy regulations make miles traveled completely sensitive to fuel price changes (i.e., the response parameter β should equal one). Row [11] in Table 10.6 presents the effects of assuming that the price of CO_2 is $80 per ton, as in Stern (2007). The last row provides the range of welfare losses or gains that includes the outcomes

Table 10.5. *Market effects of a tax credit versus a mandate*

Changes in …	Tax credit vs. no policy			Mandate vs. no policy			Mandate instead of tax credit[a]		
	2007	2015	2022	2007	2015	2022	2007	2015	2022
[1] Gasoline price (¢/gal.)	-0.0081	-0.0126	-0.0269	-0.0093	-0.0155	-0.0323	-0.0012	-0.0029	-0.0054
[2] Fuel price (¢/gal.)	-0.0081	-0.0126	-0.0269	0.0248	0.0633	0.1119	0.0329	0.0758	0.1388
[3] Ethanol price (¢/gal.)	0.56	0.65	0.78	0.56	0.65	0.78	0	0	0
[4] Ethanol consumption (bil. gals.)	7.7	10.5	24.7	7.7	10.5	24.7	0	0	0
[5] Fuel consumption (bil. gals.)	0.19	0.26	0.62	-0.58	-1.37	-2.68	-0.76	-1.63	-3.30
[6] World oil consumption (bil. gals.)	-4.0	-5.5	-12.9	-4.6	-6.8	-15.5	-0.6	-1.3	-2.6
[7] Oil imports (bil. gals.)	-4.7	-6.5	-15.5	-5.4	-8.0	-18.5	-0.7	-1.5	-3.1
[8] Taxpayer costs ($ bil.)	4.7	12.8	25.4	0.3	0.7	1.4	-4.4	-12.1	-24.0

[a] Ethanol prices and consumption are held equal to that with a tax credit (the inverse of adding a tax credit to a mandate).

Source: Calculated.

Table 10.6. *Social costs and benefits of a tax credit versus a mandate*

Changes in . . .	Tax credit vs. no policy			Mandate vs. no policy			Mandate instead of tax credit[a]		
	2007	2015	2022	2007	2015	2022	2007	2015	2022
Social deadweight costs ($ bil.)									
[1] International terms of trade	−1.5	−2.3	−5.1	−1.7	−2.9	−6.2	−0.2	−0.5	−1.0
[2] Oil dependency	−0.40	−0.58	−1.48	−0.47	−0.73	−1.79	−0.07	−0.15	−0.31
[3] CO_2 emissions ($10/ton Nordhaus)	0.03	0.05	0.11	−0.04	−0.11	−0.21	−0.08	−0.16	−0.33
[4] Efficiency gain per $ of recycling (30¢)	1.4	3.8	7.6	0.09	0.20	0.41	−1.3	−3.6	−7.2
Vehicle miles traveled (VMT)									
[5] Local air pollution	0.02	0.03	0.07	−0.07	−0.16	−0.32	−0.09	−0.20	−0.40
[6] Traffic congestion	0.10	0.14	0.32	−0.30	−0.71	−1.39	−0.40	−0.85	−1.72
[7] Traffic accidents	0.08	0.11	0.26	−0.24	−0.56	−1.10	−0.31	−0.67	−1.35
[8] Deadweight cost triangles[b]	0.001	0.002	0.012	0.014	0.064	0.241	0.013	0.062	0.229
[9] Total[c]	−0.3	1.1	1.5	−2.5	−4.4	−9.5	−2.2	−5.5	−11.0
[10] Forward looking VMT (higher fuel economy)	0.11	0.16	0.38	−0.35	−0.83	−1.63	−0.47	−0.99	−2.01
[11] CO_2 emissions (life-cycle; $80/ton Stern)	0.28	0.39	0.92	−0.33	−0.90	−1.69	−0.61	−1.29	−2.61
Range of Best/worst[a]	−1.7/0	−2.7/1.5	−6.1/2.4	−2.8/−2.5	−5.3/−4.4	−11.2/−9.5	−2.8/−0.9	−6.8/−1.9	−13.6/−3.8

[a] Ethanol prices and consumption are held equal to that with a tax credit (the inverse of adding a tax credit to a mandate).
[b] Of domestic gasoline supply and fuel demand only.
[c] Excludes costs of traffic accidents as that offsets current fuel tax.
[d] Includes possibility of no efficiency gain per $of recycling in row [4].
Source: Calculated.

in the baseline as well as those produced by the sensitivity analysis (the latter reflected by the results in rows [10] and [11] and by the possibility of no efficiency gain per dollar of recycling, zero emissions from ethanol at combustion, or inclusion of CO_2e emissions resulting from indirect land use change with ethanol production).

Overall, the results in Table 10.6 show how the change in terms of trade in oil imports and fiscal interaction effects are significantly larger than the other potential sources of deadweight costs we have analyzed. Even though gasoline prices do not change much, the sheer volume of oil imports generates social benefits that are relatively large; likewise for fiscal interaction effects, although the range of best/worst given at the bottom of Table 10.6 includes the possibility that there are no benefits of a mandate in saving taxpayer monies (revenues are not recycled).

Part of the reason for the lower values of cost and benefits associated with oil dependence and CO_2e emissions is allowance for leakages. Although oil consumption declines in the transportation sector, the latter accounts for only 45 percent of total domestic oil consumption, so part of the gains are offset by increased consumption of oil in other parts of the domestic economy. The same occurs for CO_2e emissions, except we also allow for international leakages (world oil price declines, so CO_2e emissions increase in the rest of the world). Furthermore, we assume ethanol production only reduces CO_2 emissions by 20 percent because of life-cycle accounting. For these three reasons, the values for oil dependence and CO_2e emissions are dampened significantly.

Finally, it should be emphasized that the estimates of deadweight cost triangles are for fuel demand and domestic oil production only. We ignore the deadweight costs in the domestic ethanol and corn sectors because these distortions are caused by policies that discriminate against trade. Mandates and tax credits by themselves do not discriminate against trade. We hold ethanol production constant in each of our simulations. To estimate the social costs of not having any domestic ethanol production requires analysis, as in Lasco and Khanna (2009) and de Gorter and Tsur (2008).

10.9 Concluding Remarks

Emerging literature on the welfare economics of biofuel policies shows that a mandate is superior to a consumption subsidy. This chapter builds on this literature by assessing three important preexisting constraints: a suboptimal fuel tax, a binding ethanol mandate, and a wage tax. In each case, an ethanol mandate is found to be even more superior to an ethanol consumption subsidy. In both the theoretical and empirical analysis, we abstract from the welfare effects of policies that discriminate against international trade and so ignore deadweight costs in the U.S. ethanol production and corn sectors. Our focus instead has been in comparing a mandate to a consumption subsidy, holding ethanol consumption fixed in each case.

We present numerical estimates for the first time that compare the effects of a mandate *versus* a consumption subsidy and also the relative importance of the three second-best constraints. Our empirical findings show that the welfare superiority of a mandate over a consumption subsidy can be quite large with each of the preexisting distortions.

It is particularly important to highlight the effect of adding a consumption subsidy to a mandate; the benefits of a mandate are wiped out and more because subsidies cannibalize the positive effects of a mandate and fuel tax, thereby contradicting the objectives of renewable energy policy. Therefore, hybrid instruments that combine policies can cause severe adverse policy interaction effects. Not only do most countries use these two policies in concert, these same combinations of policies have also been adopted world-wide for renewable electricity. With the growing momentum for expanded renewable energy mandates and subsidies of various forms, the choice of policy instrument made by policy makers is therefore crucial.

Although the effects of each policy and their interactions are shown to be complex, once understood, a set of relatively clear policy implications emerge. This clear picture on biofuel policies is atypical in the debate comparing alternative policy instruments in the environmental economics literature, in which the choice of environmental policy instrument (e.g., a carbon tax *versus* cap and trade) is normally deemed as inherently difficult because of competing criteria (see Goulder and Parry [2008] for a discussion). See also contributions in this volume by Weisbach and Kaplow on the functional equivalence between a price- *versus* quantity-based environmental policy. The current debate on appropriate environmental policy for global climate change is often about whether the use of a carrot or a stick, or both, is appropriate. Stern (2009, p. 28) argues, for example, that we need both: "No doubt, a combination of tax policies and quotas should be used." This appears not to hold in the case of a biofuel mandate *versus* a subsidy. Clearly, renewable energy policies are proving to be unique, as the stick of a mandate is better than the carrot of a subsidy, and governments should *never* use both.

These conclusions are extremely relevant to the current policy thrust behind recent energy and farm legislation, the stimulus bill, and the proposed climate change bill to develop new clean renewable energy sources by expanding the smorgasbord of subsidies and mandates. The increased resolve of the U.S. government to promote alternative energy sources and combat climate change has also led to a bevy of new policy proposals, including cap and trade, carbon offsets, "green" tariffs, and producer rebates. These will add to the several layers of incentives and regulations of current policies, themselves combined without being coordinated, and not well understood to date. This means that there will be even more complex economic interactions between biofuel, environmental, and energy policies – a priority for future research.

APPENDIX

A.1 The Optimal Fuel Tax and Ethanol Tax Credit Combination

Finding the optimal fuel tax and ethanol tax credit involves solving

$$\max_{t, t_c} \ V(P_F, Y, X) \tag{A.1}$$

subject to

$$P_F = P_G + t, \tag{A.2}$$

$$P_E = P_G + (1 - \phi)t + t_c, \tag{A.3}$$

$$Y = \pi_E(P_E) + \pi G(P_G) + tG(P_G) + (\phi t - t_c)E(P_G), \tag{A.4}$$

$$X = \tau_1[\xi_E E(P_E) + \xi_G G(P_E)] + \tau_2[E(P_E) + G(P_G)], \tag{A.5}$$

where P_G is a function of t and t_c implicitly defined by the market equilibrium condition

$$D_F(P_G + t) = E(P_G + (1 - \phi)t + t_e) + G(P_G). \tag{A.6}$$

Equations (A.2) through (A.5) can readily be substituted into (A.1). Thus, the first-order conditions are given by

$$
V_P \cdot \left(\frac{dP_G}{dt} + 1 \right)
$$
$$
+ V_Y \cdot \left(\left(\frac{dP_G}{dt} + 1 - \phi \right) \pi'_E + \frac{dP_G}{dt} \pi'_G + G + t \frac{dP_G}{dt} G' \right.
$$
$$
\left. + \phi E + (\phi t - t_c) \left(\frac{dP_G}{dt} + 1 - \phi \right) E' \right)
$$
$$
+ V_X \cdot \left(\tau_1 \left[\xi_E \left(\frac{dP_G}{dt} + 1 - \phi \right) E' + \xi_G \frac{dP_G}{dt} G' \right] \right.
$$
$$
\left. + \tau_2 \left[\left(\frac{dP_G}{dt} + 1 - \phi \right) E' + \frac{dP_G}{dt} G' \right] \right) = 0 \tag{A.7}
$$

and

$$V_P \cdot \frac{dP_G}{dt_c} + V_Y \cdot \left(\left(\frac{dP_G}{dt_c} + 1 \right) \pi'_E + \frac{dP_G}{dt_c} \pi'_G + t \frac{dP_G}{dt_c} G' \right.$$

$$- E + (\phi t - t_c) \left(\frac{dP_G}{dt_c} + 1 \right) E' \Bigg)$$

$$+ V_X \cdot \left(\tau_1 \left[\xi_E \left(\frac{dP_G}{dt_c} + 1 \right) E' + \xi_G \frac{dP_G}{dt_c} G' \right] \right.$$

$$+ \tau_2 \left[\left(\frac{dP_G}{dt_c} + 1 \right) E' + \frac{dP_G}{dt_c} G' \right] \Bigg) = 0. \tag{A.8}$$

Here, a prime denotes a derivative with respect to a sole argument, and a subscript denotes a derivative with respect to the noted argument. By substituting elasticity equivalents

$$E' = \frac{\eta_E E}{P_E} = \frac{\eta_E E}{(P_G + (1 - \phi)t + t_c)}, \tag{A.9}$$

$$G' = \frac{\eta_G G}{P_G}, \tag{A.10}$$

into (A.7) and (A.8), recognizing that $\pi'_E = E$ and $\pi'_G = G$, by Hotelling's Lemma we obtain

$$\left(V_P + V_Y \left[E + G + t \frac{\eta_G G}{P_G} + (\phi t - t_c) \frac{\eta_E E}{(P_G + (1 - \phi)t + t_c)} \right] \right.$$
$$\left. + V_X \left[(\tau_1 \xi_E + \tau_2) \frac{\eta_E E}{(P_G + (1 - \phi)t + t_c)} + (\tau_1 \xi_G + \tau_2) \frac{\eta_G G}{P_G} \right] \right) \frac{dP_G}{dt}$$

$$+ V_P + V_Y \left[(1 - \phi)E + G + \phi E + (\phi t - t_c) \frac{(1 - \phi)\eta_E E}{(P_G + (1 - \phi)t + t_c)} \right]$$

$$+ V_X \left[(\tau_1 \xi_E + \tau_2) \frac{(1 - \phi)\eta_E E}{(P_G + (1 - \phi)t + t_c)} \right] = 0 \tag{A.7'}$$

$$\left(V_P + V_Y \left[E + G + t \frac{\eta_G G}{P_G} + (\phi t - t_c) \frac{\eta_E E}{(P_G + (1 - \phi)t + t_c)} \right] \right.$$
$$\left. + V_X \left[(\tau_1 \xi_E + \tau_2) \frac{\eta_E E}{(P_G + (1 - \phi)t + t_c)} + (\tau_1 \xi_G + \tau_2) \frac{\eta_G G}{P_G} \right] \right) \frac{dP_G}{dt_c}$$

$$+ V_Y \left(E - E + (\phi t - t_c) \frac{\eta_E E}{(P_G + (1 - \phi)t + t_c)} \right)$$

$$+ V_X \left[(\tau_1 \xi_E + \tau_2) \frac{\eta_E E}{(P_G + (1 - \phi)t + t_c)} \right] = 0. \tag{A.8'}$$

Because marginal external effects are measured in terms of monetary costs, $V_X/V_Y = -1$. Dividing (A.7') and (A.8') by V_Y, recognizing that $V_P/V_Y = -D_F = -E - G$, we can rewrite (A.7') and (A.8') as

$$[t - (\tau_1 \xi_G + \tau_2)] \frac{\eta_G G}{P_G} \frac{dP_G}{dt}$$

$$+ [\phi t - t_c - (\tau_1 \xi_E + \tau_2)] \frac{\eta_E E}{(P_G + (1 - \phi)t + t_c)} \left(\frac{dP_G}{dt} + 1 - \phi \right) = 0. \quad \text{(A.7'')}$$

$$[t - (\tau_1 \xi_G + \tau_2)] \frac{\eta_G G}{P_G} \frac{dP_G}{dt_c}$$

$$+ [\phi t - t_c - (\tau_1 \xi_E + \tau_2)] \frac{\eta_E E}{(P_G + (1 - \phi)t + t_c)} \left(\frac{dP_G}{dt} + 1 \right) = 0.$$

$$\text{(A.8'')}$$

Both first-order conditions imply the similar relationships, with the only difference being the policy instrument with which the price of gasoline is differentiated and the ϕ appearing in the last term of (A.7''). Totally differentiating (A.6), substituting $D_F' = \frac{\eta_F D_F}{P_F} = \frac{\eta_F D_F}{P_G + t} < 0$ and collecting terms we obtain

$$\frac{dP_G}{dt} = - \frac{\left[\dfrac{\eta_F D_F}{P_G + t} - \dfrac{(1 - \phi)\eta_E E}{(P_G + (1 - \phi)t + t_c)} \right]}{\left[\dfrac{\eta_F D_F}{P_G + t} - \dfrac{\eta_E E}{(P_G + (1 - \phi)t + t_c)} - \dfrac{\eta_G G}{P_G} \right]} < 0 \quad \text{(A.11)}$$

and

$$\frac{dP_G}{dt_c} = - \frac{\dfrac{\eta_E E}{(P_G + (1 - \phi)t + t_c)}}{\left[\dfrac{\eta_F D_F}{P_G + t} - \dfrac{\eta_E E}{(P_G + (1 - \phi)t + t_c)} - \dfrac{\eta_G G}{P_G} \right]} < -1. \quad \text{(A.12)}$$

The numerators of the expressions in the inequalities (A.11) and (A.12) will not generally be equal, implying that it is extremely unlikely that (A.7'') and (A.8'') could be satisfied unless the terms of (A.7'') and (A.8'') in square brackets are equal to zero.[24] Thus, the optimal tax and tax credit combination, $t^* = \tau_1 \xi_G + \tau_2$ and $t_c^* = \phi t^* - t_E^* = \phi(\tau_1 \xi_G + \tau_2) - (\tau_1 \xi_E + \tau_2)$.

---

[24] For another solution to exist, the tax and tax credit would be required to satisfy $\frac{\eta_F D_F}{(2 - \phi)\eta_E E} = \frac{P_G + t}{(P_G + (1 - \phi)t + t_c)}$ as well as (A.7'') and (A.8''). With two unknowns and three equations, this can only happen on a set of measure zero.

A.2 Finding the Optimal Tax without a Tax Credit

Finding the optimal tax with no tax credit involves solving

$$\max_{t} V(P_F, Y, X) \tag{A.13}$$

subject to (A.2) through (A.5) with $t_c = 0$, with P_G now an implicit function of t defined by (A.6), again with $t_c = 0$. The resulting first-order condition is (compare with A.7'')

$$[t - t^*] \frac{\eta_G G}{P_G} \frac{dP_G}{dt} + [\phi t - t_E^*] \frac{\eta_E E}{(P_G + (1 - \phi)t + t_c)} \left(\frac{dP_G}{dt} + 1 + \phi \right) = 0, \tag{A.7'''}$$

where t^* is the optimal tax (which is equal to the marginal external cost of consuming gasoline) and t_E^* is the marginal external cost of consuming ethanol. Totally differentiating (A.6) we find dP_G/dt to have the same formula as given in (A.9), except that now $t_c = 0$. From (A.9) we find

$$1 + \phi + \frac{dP_G}{dt} = \frac{\left[\phi \dfrac{\eta_F D_F}{P_G + t} - (\phi + 1) \dfrac{\eta_G G}{P_G} \right]}{\left[\dfrac{\eta_F D_F}{P_G + t} - \dfrac{\eta_E E}{(P_G + (1 - \phi)t)} - \dfrac{\eta_G G}{P_G} \right]} > 0. \tag{A.14}$$

Also recall that $dP_G/dt < 0$. The optimal tax in this case must be between t^* and t_E/ϕ. To see this, first suppose that $t^* > t_E^*/\phi$. Evaluating the left-hand side of (A.7''') at $t = t_E^*/\phi$ makes the first term positive and the second term zero; thus, the function is increasing in the tax. If we evaluate at $t = t^*$, the first term is positive and the second is negative; thus, the function is decreasing in the tax. Given that second-order conditions hold globally and that the function is continuous, it must be that $t^* > t > \frac{t_E^*}{\phi}$. Hence, in this case (which is representative of the apparent external costs) the optimal tax without a tax credit is less than the optimal tax under the jointly optimal tax credit. Alternatively, if $t^* < t_E^*/\phi$, the same logic implies $t^* < t < \frac{t_E^*}{\phi}$, and thus a higher tax than under the optimal tax and tax credit combination.

A.3 Optimal Tax Credit without a Suboptimal Fuel Tax

Finding the optimal tax credit with a fixed fuel tax involves solving

$$\max_{t_c} V(P_F, Y, X) \tag{A.15}$$

subject to (A.2) through (A.5), with P_G now an implicit function of t_c defined by (A.6). The resulting first-order condition is (compare with A.8'')

$$\frac{dV}{dt_c} = - [t - t^*] \frac{\eta_G\, G}{P_G} \frac{dP_G}{dt_c}$$

$$- [\phi t - t_c - t_E^*] \frac{\eta_E\, E}{(P_G + (1 - \phi)t + t_c)} \left(\frac{dP_G}{dt_c} + 1 \right) = 0 \qquad (A.8''')$$

where t^* and t_E^* are as defined previously – the marginal external cost of consuming gasoline and ethanol, respectively. Note that in deriving the left-hand side of (A.8''') we are careful to preserve the sign from the original derivative. By totally differentiating (A.6) with t set equal to zero, we can find the value of dP_g/dt_c that is appropriate for this policy. This differentiation results in exactly the condition in (A.10), only with t set exogenously. Consider first the case where $t = 0$. From (A.10), we know that $dP_G/dt_c + 1 < 0$. This and (A.8''') implies that $(-t_c - t_E^*)$ must be positive. Thus, $t_c < -t_E^*$. Hence, the optimal tax credit without a tax is in fact negative and exceeds the marginal external cost of ethanol.

In general, consider starting with the optimal tax and tax credit combination, and then lowering t to see the impact on the first-order condition in (A.8'''). If we start with the optimal combination (see Section A.1 of the Appendix for a derivation), equation (A.8''') must equal zero. By lowering t, $[t - t^*]$ becomes negative, making the first term of (A.8''') negative. Also, lowering t will make $[\phi t - t_c - t_E^*]$ negative, thus making the second term negative. Hence, the derivative of welfare with respect to the tax credit is negative. This implies that decreasing the tax will result in a lower optimal tax credit.

A.4 Finding the Optimal Combination of a Tax and a Mandate

To find the optimal tax and mandate, we must solve

$$\max_{\overline{E}, t} V(P_F, Y, X), \qquad (A.16)$$

where

$$P_F = \frac{(P_E(\overline{E}) + \phi t)\overline{E} + (P_G + t)G(P_G)}{\overline{E} + G(P_G)} \qquad (A.17)$$

$$Y = \pi_E(P_E(\overline{E})) + \pi_G(P_G) + t[G(P_G) + \phi\overline{E}] \qquad (A.18)$$

$$X = \tau_1[\xi_E\overline{E} + \xi_G G(P_G)] + \tau_2[\overline{E} + G(P_G)], \qquad (A.19)$$

and where P_G is a function of the tax and mandate defined implicitly by

$$D_F\left(\frac{(P_E(\overline{E}) + \phi t)\overline{E} + (P_G + t)G(P_G)}{\overline{E} + G(P_G)}\right) = \overline{E} + G(P_G). \qquad (A.20)$$

Equations (A.17) through (A.19) can be substituted into (A.12). Note that under the optimal tax and tax credit, the indirect utility function is

$$V(P_G(t^*, t_c^*) + t^*, Y, X), \qquad (A.21)$$

where (see (A.4) and (A.5))

$$Y = \pi_E(P_G(t^*, t_c^*) + (1 - \phi)t^* + t_c^*) + \pi_G(P_G(t^*, t_c^*))$$
$$+ t^* G(P_G(t^*, t_c^*)) + (\phi t^* - t_c^*)E(P_G(t^*, t_c^*) + (1 - \phi)t^* + t_c^*), \qquad (A.22)$$

$$X = \tau_1[\xi_G E(P_G(t^*, t_c^*) + (1 - \phi)t^* + t_c^*) + \xi_G G(P_G(t^*, t_c^*))]$$
$$+ \tau_2[E(P_G(t^*, t_c^*) + (1 - \phi)t^* + t_c^*) + G(P_G(t^*, t_c^*))]. \qquad (A.23)$$

Note again that because the optimal tax and tax credit is equivalent to charging a separate tax on ethanol and gasoline, this achieves the first-best optimum. We can show that an equivalent level of indirect utility is obtained by setting the consumption mandate

$$\overline{E} = E(P_G(t^*, t_c^*) + (1 - \phi)t^* + t_c^*), \qquad (A.24)$$

with producer price for ethanol equal to $P_E = P_G(t^*, t_c^*) + (1 - \phi)t^* + t_c^*$, and setting the tax so that the price of fuel is equal to $P_F = P_G(t^*, t_c^*) + t^*$. Note that this is the same price of fuel under the optimal tax and tax credit combination; thus, the same amount of fuel must be demanded and consumed. Further, because the identical amount of fuel is consumed, and the identical amount of ethanol, this must result in an identical amount of gasoline, $G(P_G(t^*, t_c^*))$. The necessary tax solves that,

$$P_F = \frac{(P_G(t^*, t_c^*) + (1 - \phi)t^* + t_c^* + \phi t)\overline{E} + (P_G(t^*, t_c^*) + t)G}{\overline{E} + G}$$
$$= P_G(t^*, t_c^*) + t^*, \qquad (A.25)$$

or,

$$t^M = \frac{t^* G(P_G(t^*, t_c^*)) + (\phi t^* - t_c^*)\overline{E}}{G(P_G(t^*, t_c^*)) + \phi\overline{E}}. \qquad (A.26)$$

This policy combination results in the indirect utility

$$V(P_G(t^*, t_c^*) + t^*, Y, X), \qquad (A.27)$$

where (see equations (A.18) and (A.19))

$$
\begin{aligned}
Y &= \pi_E(P_G(t^*, t_c^*) + (1-\phi)t^* + t_c^*) + \pi_G(P_G(t^*, t_c^*)) \\
&\quad + t^M[G(P_G(t^*, t_c^*)) + \phi E(P_G(t^*, t_c^*) + (1-\phi)t^* + t_c^*)] \\
&= \pi_E(P_G(t^*, t_c^*) + (1-\phi)t^* + t_c^*) + \pi_G(P_G(t^*, t_c^*)) \\
&\quad + t^* G(P_G(t^*, t_c^*)) + (\phi t^* - t_c^*)E(P_G(t^*, t_c^*) + (1-\phi)t^* + t_c^*), \quad \text{(A.28)}
\end{aligned}
$$

$$
\begin{aligned}
X &= \tau_1[\xi_E E(P_G(t^*, t_c^*) + (1-\phi)t^* + t_c^*) + \xi_G G(P_G(t^*, t_c^*))] \\
&\quad + \tau_2[E(P_G(t^*, t_c^*) + (1-\phi)t^* + t_c^*) + G(P_G(t^*, t_c^*))]. \quad \text{(A.29)}
\end{aligned}
$$

Here, (A.27), (A.28), and (A.29) result in identical values for P_F, Y, and X, and thus the maximand V, as in (A.1). Because this is the maximum attainable value of V, this combination of tax and mandate must be the optimum values solving (A.21).

A.5 Finding the Optimal Mandate Holding the Fuel Tax Constant

To find the optimal mandate without a tax, we must solve

$$
\max_{\overline{E}} V(P_F, Y, X), \quad \text{(A.30)}
$$

where

$$
P_F = \frac{(P_E(\overline{E}) + \phi t)\overline{E} + (P_G + t)G(P_G)}{\overline{E}\,G(P_G)}. \quad \text{(A.31)}
$$

$$
Y = \pi_E(P_E(\overline{E})) + \pi_G(P_G) + t[G(P_G) + \phi\overline{E}]. \quad \text{(A.32)}
$$

$$
X = \tau_1[\xi_E \overline{E} + \xi_G G(P_G)]\tau_2[\overline{E} + G(P_G)], \quad \text{(A.33)}
$$

and where P_G is a function of the mandate defined implicitly by

$$
D_F\left(\frac{(P_E(\overline{E}) + \phi t)\overline{E} + (P_G + t)G(P_G)}{\overline{E} + G(P_G)}\right) = \overline{E} + G(P_G). \quad \text{(A.34)}
$$

The first-order condition is given by

$$
V_P \cdot \left[\frac{\left[\overline{E}P_E' + P_E + t + \frac{dP_G}{d\overline{E}}G + (P_G + t)\,G'\frac{dP_G}{d\overline{E}}\right](\overline{E}+G) - \left[1 + G'\frac{dP_G}{d\overline{E}}\right]((P_E + \phi t)\overline{E} + (P_G + t)\,G)}{(\overline{E}+G)^2} \right]
$$

$$
+ V_Y \cdot \left[\pi_E' P_E' + \pi_G'\frac{dP_G}{d\overline{E}} + tG'\frac{dP_G}{d\overline{E}} + \phi t\right] + V_X \cdot \left[(\tau_1\xi_E + \tau_2) + (\tau_1\xi_G + \tau_2)\,G'\frac{dP_G}{d\overline{E}}\right] = 0.
$$

$$
\text{(A.35)}
$$

Dividing by V_Y, and employing elasticity formulas, Hotelling's Lemma, $V_P/V_Y = -D_F = -E - G$, the previous definitions of t^*, t_E^*, and the identity $V_X/V_Y = -1$ (as discussed in Section A.1 of the Appendix), we obtain

$$-P_F + P_E + (1 - \phi)t + t_E^* - (P_F - P_G - t^*)\eta_G \frac{G}{P_G}\frac{dP_G}{dE} = 0. \quad \text{(A.36)}$$

Note that in deriving the left-hand side of (A.36) we are careful to preserve the sign. Thus, a value of the left-hand side that is positive implies that increasing $\overline{E}$ will increase welfare. If the tax were optimal given the tax credit, then $P_F\left(t^*, \overline{E}\left(t^*\right)\right) = P_G\left(t^*, \overline{E}\left(t^*\right)\right) + t^*$, from the previous section. Thus, evaluating (A.36) at this point we find

$$- P_F + P_E + (1 - \phi)t^* + t_E^* = 0. \quad \text{(A.37)}$$

If we were to lower t from t^* holding all else constant, P_F would decline, increasing the first term of (A.36). In (A.36), $(1 - \phi) < 0$, so reducing t will also increase the third additive term. The terms P_E and t_E^* will remain constant (the former because the mandate remains constant). Thus, if the last term also increases, it must be that the (A.36) becomes positive as the tax is lowered below the optimal level, implying a higher optimal ethanol mandate. By totally differentiating (A.34) with respect to P_G and $\overline{E}$, we obtain

$$\frac{dP_G}{d\overline{E}} = -\frac{\left[D_F'\dfrac{dP_F}{d\overline{E}} - 1\right]}{\left[D_F'\dfrac{dP_F}{dP_G} - G'\right]} \quad \text{(A.38)}$$

which must be negative so long as the equilibrium is stable (in other words, as long as the demand for fuel has a more negative slope than the supply of fuel blend; see de Gorter and Just [2008a]). Thus, the optimal ethanol mandate must increase as the tax decreases if $P_F - P_G$ decreases as t is lowered from A.36. Totally differentiating (A.34) with respect to P_G and t obtains

$$\frac{dP_G}{dt} = -\frac{D_F' \cdot (\phi\overline{E} + G)}{\left[D_F' \cdot \left(G + \dfrac{(P_G - P_E + (1 - \phi)t)\overline{E}G'}{(\overline{E} + G)}\right) - G'(\overline{E} + G)\right]}, \quad \text{(A.39)}$$

or, substituting elasticities

$$\frac{dP_G}{dt} = -\frac{\frac{\eta_F}{P_F}(\phi\overline{E} + G)}{\left[\frac{\eta_F}{P_F}\left(G + (P_G - P_E + (1-\phi)t)\overline{E}\eta_G\frac{G}{(\overline{E}+G)P_G}\right) - \eta_G\frac{G}{P_G}\right]}.$$

(A.40)

Alternatively, differentiating the formula for P_F and substituting elasticities obtains

$$\frac{dP_F}{dt} = \frac{(\phi\overline{E} + G) + \left[(P_G - P_E + (1-\phi)t)\frac{G\overline{E}\eta_G}{(\overline{E}+G)P_G} + G\right]\frac{dP_G}{dt}}{(\overline{E}+G)}.$$

(A.41)

Combining (A.40) and (A.41) and simplifying terms obtains

$$\frac{d(P_F - P_G)}{dt} = \frac{(\phi\overline{E} + G)}{(\overline{E}+G)}$$

$$+ \frac{\frac{\eta_F}{P_F}\left(\phi\overline{E} + G - \frac{\eta_F}{P_F}\frac{(\phi\overline{E}+G)}{(\overline{E}+G)}\left[G + (P_G - P_E + (1-\phi)t)\overline{E}\eta_G\frac{G}{(\overline{E}+G)P_G}\right]\right)}{\left[\frac{\eta_F}{P_F}\left(G + (P_G - P_E + (1-\phi)t)\overline{E}\eta_G\frac{G}{(\overline{E}+G)P_G}\right) - \eta_G\frac{G}{P_G}\right]}$$

(A.42)

or,

$$\frac{d(P_F - P_G)}{dt} = \frac{(\phi\overline{E} + G)}{(\overline{E}+G)}\left[\frac{\left(-\eta_G\frac{G}{P_G} + \frac{\eta_F}{P_F}(\overline{E}+G)\right)}{\left[\frac{\eta_F}{P_F}\left(G + (P_G - P_E + (1-\phi)t)\overline{E}\eta_G\frac{G}{(\overline{E}+G)P_G}\right) - \eta_G\frac{G}{P_G}\right]}\right].$$

(A.43)

Note that the first multiplicative term is positive, whereas the numerator in the square brackets must be negative. The denominator will also be negative if

$$(P_G - P_E + (1-\phi)t) > \left(\frac{\eta_G}{\eta_F}P_F - P_G\right)\frac{D_F}{\overline{E}\eta_G},$$

(A.44)

implying that (A.43) is positive. Thus, if (A.44) holds where $t = t^*$, then a suboptimal tax will result in an increased mandate. This condition will hold if the left-hand side is not too negative. Note that both sides of (A.44) are negative. Thus, (A.44.) will hold, for example, if the optimal ethanol mandate is low relative to fuel demand, the optimal tax-mandate combination will not create too large a wedge between gasoline and ethanol prices. This condition is very similar to the requirements for the fuel price to increase when the ethanol mandate is increased (see de Gorter and Just [2008a]).

A.6 Welfare as the Fuel Tax Is Lowered Under the Tax Credit and the Mandate

Under both the optimal tax–tax credit combination and the optimal tax-mandate combination, the same level of welfare is achieved. Thus, we can determine the impact on welfare of reducing the fuel tax under each biofuel policy by simply differentiating welfare with respect to the tax and evaluating at the optimal policy. Consider first the optimal tax credit given an exogenously set fuel tax. If we begin by evaluating at the optimal tax (first best), the welfare is given by

$$V(P_g(t^*, t_c^*) + t^*, Y, X) \tag{A.45}$$

where

$$
\begin{aligned}
Y &= \pi_E(P_E(t^*, t_c^*)) + \pi_G(P_G(t^*, t_c^*)) + t^* G(P_G(t^*, t_c^*)) \\
&\quad + (\phi t^* - t_c^*) E(P_E(t^*, t_c^*)) \\
X &= \tau_1[\xi_E E(P_E(t^*, t_c^*)) + \xi_G G(P_G(t^*, t_c^*))] \\
&\quad + \tau_2[E(P_E(t^*, t_c^*)) + G(P_G(t^*, t_c^*))].
\end{aligned}
\tag{A.46}
$$
$$\tag{A.47}$$

Differentiating (A.45) with respect to the tax yields

$$
\begin{aligned}
\frac{dV}{dt} &= V_P \cdot \left(\frac{dP_g}{dt} + 1 \right) + V_Y \cdot \left(\pi'_E \frac{dP_E}{dt} + \pi'_G \frac{dP_g}{dt} + G + t^* G' \frac{dP_g}{dt} \right. \\
&\quad \left. + \phi E + (\phi t^* - t_c^*) E' \frac{dP_E}{dt} \right) \\
&\quad + V_X \cdot \left(\tau_1 \left(\xi_E E' \frac{dP_E}{dt} + \xi_G G' \frac{dP_G}{dt} \right) + \tau_2 \left(E' \frac{dP_E}{dt} + G' \frac{dP_G}{dt} \right) \right) \\
&= V_P \cdot \left(\frac{dP_g}{dt} + 1 \right) + V_Y \cdot \left(\left(E + t_E^* \eta_E \frac{E}{P_E} \right) \frac{dP_E}{dt} \right. \\
&\quad \left. + \left(G + t^* \eta_G \frac{G}{P_g} \right) \frac{dP_g}{dt} + G + \phi E \right) \\
&\quad + V_X \cdot \left(t_E^* \eta_E \frac{E}{P_E} \frac{dP_E}{dt^*} + t^* \eta_G \frac{G}{P_g} \frac{dP_G}{dt^*} \right).
\end{aligned}
\tag{A.48}
$$

If instead we evaluate the optimal mandate response to a tax with the initial tax given by the optimal tax-mandate combination, we obtain welfare

$$V(P_F(t^M, \overline{E}), Y, X) \tag{A.49}$$

where

$$P_F(t^M, \overline{E}) = \frac{(P_E(\overline{E}) + \phi t^M)\overline{E} + (P_G(t^M, \overline{E}) + t^M)G(P_G(t^M, \overline{E}))}{\overline{E} + G(P_G(t^M, \overline{E}))} \tag{A.50}$$

$$Y = \pi_E(P_E(\overline{E})) + \pi_G(P_G(t^M, \overline{E})) + t^M[G(P_G(t^M, \overline{E})) + \phi\overline{E}] \tag{A.51}$$

$$X = \tau_1[\xi_E \overline{E} + \xi_G G(P_G(t^M, \overline{E}))] + \tau_2[\overline{E} + G(P_G(t^M, \overline{E}))]. \tag{A.52}$$

Differentiating (A.49) with respect to the tax yields

$$
\begin{aligned}
\frac{dV}{dt} &= V_P \cdot \left(\frac{(\phi\overline{E} + G)(\overline{E} + G) + \frac{dP_G}{dt^M}\left[(\overline{E} + G)G + (P_G - P_E + t^M - \phi t^M)G'\overline{E} \right]}{(\overline{E} + G)^2} \right) \\
&\quad + V_Y \cdot \left(\pi_G' \frac{dP_G}{dt^M} + G + \phi\overline{E} + t^M G' \frac{dP_G}{dt^M} \right) + V_X \cdot (\tau_1 \xi_G + \tau_2) G' \frac{dP_G}{dt^M} \\
&= V_P \cdot \left(\frac{(\phi\overline{E} + G)(\overline{E} + G) + \frac{dP_G}{dt^M}\left[(\overline{E} + G)G + (P_G - P_E + t^M - \phi t^M)\frac{\eta_G G}{P_G}\overline{E} \right]}{(\overline{E} + G)^2} \right) \\
&\quad + V_Y \cdot \left(\left(G + t^M \frac{\eta_G G}{P_G} \right) \frac{dP_G}{dt^M} + G + \phi\overline{E} \right) + V_X \cdot t^* \frac{\eta_G G}{P_G} \frac{dP_G}{dt^M}
\end{aligned}
\tag{A.53}
$$

Thus, in order for the mandate to provide a higher level of welfare, it must be the case that the derivative with respect to the tax under the tax credit is larger (a steeper decline) than under the mandate, or

$$
\begin{aligned}
&V_P \cdot \left(\frac{(\phi\overline{E} + G)(\overline{E} + G) + \frac{dP_G}{dt^M}\left[(\overline{E} + G)G + (P_G - P_E + t^M - \phi t^M)\frac{\eta_G G}{P_G}\overline{E} \right]}{(\overline{E} + G)^2} \right) \\
&+ V_Y \cdot \left(\left(G + t^* \frac{\eta_G G}{P_G} \right) \frac{dP_G}{dt^M} + G + \phi\overline{E} \right) + V_X \cdot t^* \frac{\eta_G G}{P_G} \frac{dP_G}{dt^M} \\
&< V_P \cdot \left(\frac{dP_g}{dt^*} + 1 \right) + V_Y \cdot \left(\left(E + t_E^* \eta_E \frac{E}{P_E} \right) \frac{dP_E}{dt^*} + \left(G + t^* \eta_G \frac{G}{P_g} \right) \frac{dP_g}{dt^*} + G + \phi E \right) \\
&+ V_X \cdot \left(t_E^* E' \frac{dP_E}{dt^*} + t^* \eta_G \frac{G}{P_g} \frac{dP_G}{dt^*} \right).
\end{aligned}
\tag{A.54}
$$

Dividing both sides of (A.54) by V_Y, employing common identities, and canceling like terms allows us to rewrite (A.54) as

$$\left(1 - \phi - \frac{dP_E}{dt^*} + \frac{dP_g}{dt^*} - \frac{dP_G}{dt^M} \left(P_G - P_E + (1-\phi)t^M \right) \frac{\eta_G G}{P_G(\overline{E} + G)} \right) < 0 \tag{A.55}$$

Substituting $P_E = P_G(t^*, t_c^*) + (1 - \phi)t^* + t_c^*$ and $dP_E/dt^* = dP_G/dt^* + (1 - \phi)$ into (A.47) obtains

$$-\frac{dP_G}{dt^M}\left((1 - \phi)(t^M - t^*) - t_c^*\right)\frac{\eta_G G}{P_G(\overline{E} + G)} < 0 \tag{A.56}$$

Note that $dP_G/dt^M < 0$, $\eta_G G/\left[P_G(\overline{E} + G)\right] > 0$. Thus, (A.48) will hold only if

$$(1 - \phi)(t^M - t^*) < t_c^*. \tag{A.57}$$

Substituting in the definition of t^M from (A.26) and the definition of t_c^*, and canceling terms obtains

$$t_E^* < t^*\phi, \tag{A.57}$$

which requires that the marginal external cost of consuming ethanol is below the marginal tax burden of consuming ethanol under the optimal tax–tax credit combination. This is the same requirement that is necessary for a positive tax credit.

References

Babcock, Bruce A. 2008a. Distributional implications of U.S. ethanol policy. *Review of Agricultural Economics* 30 (3): 533–542.

Babcock, Bruce A. 2008b. Situation, outlook and some key research questions pertaining to biofuels. Paper presented at the annual meeting of the USDA Economic Research Service. Conference on Energy and Agriculture: Emerging Policy and R&D Issues. Washington, D.C., March 7.

Bourgeon, Jean-Marc, and David Tréguer. 2008. Killing two birds with one stone: The United States and the European Union biofuel program. Paper presented at the XIIth Congress of the European Association of Agricultural Economists, Ghent, Belgium, August 26–29.

California Air Resources Board (CARB). 2009. *Proposed Regulation to Implement the Low Carbon Fuel Standard.* March 5.

de Gorter, Harry, David R. Just, and Erika M. Kliauga. 2008. Measuring the "subsidy" component of biofuel tax credits and exemptions. Paper presented at the annual meeting of the International Trade Research Consortium, Scottsdale, Arizona, December 7–9.

de Gorter, Harry, and Yacov Tsur. 2008. Towards a genuine sustainability criterion for biofuel production. Background paper for World Bank Report *Low Carbon, High Growth*, Augusto de la Torre, Pablo Fajnzylberg, and John Nash (eds.), July 31. http://aem.cornell.edu/research/researchpdf/wp/Cornell_AEM_wp0912.pdf.

de Gorter, Harry, David R. Just, and Qinwen Tan. 2009. The social optimal import tariff and tax credit for ethanol with farm subsidies. *Agricultural and Resource Economics Review* 38 (1): 65–77.

de Gorter, Harry, and David R. Just. 2007. The law of unintended consequences: How the U.S. biofuel tax credit with a mandate subsidizes oil consumption and has no impact on ethanol consumption. Working Paper No. 2007–20, Department of Applied Economics and Management, Cornell University, Ithaca, NY.

de Gorter, Harry, and David R. Just. 2008a. The welfare economics of the U.S. ethanol consumption mandate and tax credit. Unpublished working paper, Department of Applied Economics and Management, Cornell University, Ithaca, NY.

de Gorter, Harry, and David R. Just. 2008b. 'Water' in the U.S. ethanol tax credit and mandate: Implications for rectangular deadweight costs and the corn-oil price relationship. *Review of Agricultural Economics* 30 (3): 397–410.

de Gorter, Harry, and David R. Just. 2008c. The economics of the U.S. ethanol import tariff with a blend mandate and tax credit. *Journal of Agricultural & Food Industrial Organization* 6 (2, article 6): http://www.bepress.com/jafio/vol6/iss2/art6.

de Gorter, Harry, and David R. Just. 2008d. The forgotten flaw in biofuels policy: How tax credits in the presence of mandates subsidize oil consumption. Resources for the Future Policy Commentary, http://www.rff.org/Publications/WPC/Pages/08_06_09_Forgotten-Flaw-in-Biofuels.aspx, June 9.

de Gorter, Harry, and David R. Just. 2009a. The welfare economics of a biofuel tax credit and the interaction effects with price contingent farm subsidies. *American Journal of Agricultural Economics* 91 (2): 477–488.

de Gorter, Harry, and David R. Just. 2009b. The economics of a blend mandate for biofuels. *American Journal of Agricultural Economics* 91 (3): 738–750.

de Gorter, Harry, and David R. Just. 2009c. Why sustainability standards for biofuel production make little economic sense. Cato Institute *Policy Analysis* no. 647 (October): http://www.cato.org/pubs /pas/pa647.pdf.

de Gorter, Harry, and David R. Just. 2010. The social costs and benefits of biofuels: The intersection of environmental, energy and agricultural policy. *Applied Economic Perspectives and Policy* 32 (1): 4–32.

Drabik, Dusan, Harry de Gorter, and David R. Just. 2009. The economics of a blenders tax credit versus a tax exemption: The case of U.S. splash & dash biodiesel exports to the European Union. Working Paper 2009–22, AgFoodTrade.

Du, Xiaodong, Dermot J. Hayes, and Mindy L. Baker. 2008. Ethanol: A welfare-increasing market distortion? Working Paper 08-WP 480, Center for Agricultural and Rural Development (CARD), Iowa State University, Ames, IA.

Environmental Protection Agency. 2009. *Changes to Renewable Fuel Standard Program. Proposed Rule40 CFR Part 80 Regulation of Fuels and Fuel Additives*, May 26.

Environmental Protection Agency. 2010. *U.S. Greenhouse Gas Inventory*, Table ES-2 http://www.epa.gov/clim atechange/emissions/downloads/08_ES.pdf last accessed 01/06/10.

Energy Information Administration. 2009. *Annual Energy Outlook 2010 Early Release, Report #DOE/EIA-0383*, http://www.eia.doe.gov/oiaf/aeo/aeoref_tab.html.

Farrell A., R. Plevin, B. Turner, et al. 2006. Ethanol can contribute to energy and environmental goals. *Science* 311 (5760): 506–508.

Fischer, Carolyn, and Richard G. Newell. 2008. Environmental and technology policies for climate mitigation. *Journal of Environmental Economics and Management* 55 (2): 142–162.

Gardner, Bruce. 2007. Fuel ethanol subsidies and farm price support. *Journal of Agricultural and Food Industrial Organization* 5 (2): Article 2.

Goulder, Lawrence H., Ian W. H. Parry, Roberton C. Williams III, et al. 1999. The cost-effectiveness of alternative instruments for environmental protection in a second-best setting. *Journal of Public Economics* 72 (3): 329–360.

Goulder, Lawrence H., Ian W. H. Parry, and Dallas Burtraw. 1997. Revenue-raising vs. other approaches to environmental protection: The critical significance of pre-existing tax distortions. *RAND Journal of Economics* 28 (4): 708–731.

Goulder, Lawrence H., and Ian W. H. Parry. 2008. Instrument choice in environmental policy. *Review of Environmental Economics and Policy* 2 (2): 152–174.

Hahn, Robert, and Caroline Cecot. 2009. The benefits and costs of ethanol: An evaluation of the government's analysis. *Journal of Regulatory Economics* 35 (3): 275–295.

Hertel, Thomas W., Wallace E. Tyner, and Dileep Birur. 2008. Biofuels for all? Understanding the global impacts of multinational mandates. GTAP Working Paper 51, Center for Global Trade Analysis, Department of Agricultural Economics, Purdue University, West Lafayette, IN.

Hill, J., S. Polasky, E. Nelson, et al. 2009. Climate change and health costs of air emissions from biofuels and gasoline. *Proceedings of the National Academy of Sciences* 106 (6): 2077–2082.

Holland, Stephen P., Jonathan E. Hughes, and Christopher R. Knittel. 2009. Greenhouse gas reductions under low carbon fuel standards? *American Economic Journal: Economic Policy* 1 (1): 106–146.

Intergovernmental Panel on Climate Change. 2007. 2006 IPCC guidelines for national greenhouse gas inventories. Paper presented at the National Greenhouse Gas Inventories Programme, Institute for Global Environmental Strategies, Tokyo, Japan.

Jacobson, Mark Z. 2009. Review of solutions to global warming, air pollution, and energy security. *Energy Environmental Science* 2:148–173.

Kaplow, Louis. 2004. On the (ir)relevance of distribution and labor supply distortion to government policy. *Journal of Economic Perspectives* 18 (4): 159–175.

Khanna, Madhu, Amy W. Ando, and Farzad Taheripour. 2008. Welfare effects and unintended consequences of ethanol subsidies. *Review of Agricultural Economics* 30 (3): 411–421.

Koplow, Doug. 2007. Ethanol – At what cost? Government support for ethanol and biodiesel in the United States. 2007 Update. Geneva, Switzerland: Global Subsidies Initiative of the International Institute for Sustainable Development, October.

Lapan, H., and G. Moschini. 2009. Biofuel policies and welfare: Is the stick of mandates better than the carrot of subsidies? Working Paper No. 09010, Department of Economics, Iowa State University, Ames, IA.

Lasco, Christine, and Madhu Khanna. 2009. Welfare effects of biofuels trade policy in the presence of environmental externalities. Paper presented at the ASSA Meetings, San Francisco, January. http://ssrn.com/abstract=1367101.

Leiby, Paul N. 2007. Estimating the energy security benefits of reduced U.S. oil imports. Oak Ridge National Laboratory ORNL/TM-2007/028 Oak Ridge, TN, February 28.

Martinez-Gonzalez, Ariadna, Ian M. Sheldon, and Stanley Thompson. 2007. Estimating the welfare effects of U.S. distortions in the ethanol market using a partial equilibrium trade model. *Journal of Agricultural & Food Industrial Organization* 5 (2): Article 5.

Metcalf, Gilbert. 2008. Using tax expenditures to achieve energy policy goals. *American Economic Review Papers and Proceedings* 98 (4): 90–94.

Mitchell, Donald. 2008. A note on rising food prices. Policy Research Working Paper 4682, Development Prospects Group, the World Bank.

Nordhaus, William D. 2007. A review of the Stern Review on the economics of climate change. *Journal of Economic Literature* 45 (3): 686–702.

Parry, Ian W. H., and Kenneth Small. 2005. Does Britain or the United States have the right gasoline tax? *American Economic Review* 95 (4): 1276–1289.

Rajagopal, Deepak, Steven E. Sexton, David Roland-Holst, et al. 2007. Challenge of biofuel: Filling the tank without emptying the stomach? *Environmental Research Letters* 2 (November):1–9.

Runge, C. Ford, and Benjamin Senauer. 2007. How biofuels could starve the poor. *Foreign Affairs* 86 (3): 41–53.

Schmitz, A., C. B. Moss, and T. G. Schmitz. 2007. Ethanol: No free lunch. *Journal of Agricultural and Food Industrial Organization* 5 (2): Article 3.

Searchinger, Timothy D., Ralph E. Heimlich, Richard A. Houghton, et al. 2008. Use of U.S. croplands for biofuels increases greenhouse gases through emissions from land use change. *Science* 319(5867): 1238–1240. DOI: 10.1126/science.1151861.

Stern, Nicholas. 2009. Imperfections in the economics of public policy, imperfections in markets, and climate change. Presidential Lecture for the European Economic Association, Barcelona, August.

Stern, Nicholas. 2007. *The Economics of Climate Change: The Stern Review.* New York: Cambridge University Press.

Taylor, Jerry, and Peter Van Doren. 2007. The ethanol boondoggle. *The Milken Institute Review*, First Quarter:17–27.

Vedenov, Dmitry, and Michael Wetzstein. 2008. Toward an optimal US ethanol fuel subsidy. *Energy Economics* 30:2073–2090.

Comments

Brent Yacobucci

I found the substance of the chapter by de Gorter and Just a useful addition to the policy discussion surrounding biofuels incentives. The potentially perverse effects of a double incentive of fuel mandates and tax incentives has not been as thoroughly treated as it perhaps should be. I doubt that most policy makers are aware of the idea that the authors demonstrate: that providing tax incentives for biofuels at the same time as the government requires the use of those fuels leads to greater overall fuel consumption than would otherwise occur in the absence of the tax incentive.

As the authors show, if a renewable fuel mandate – an ethanol mandate in gasoline in the simplified model of the chapter – is binding, then a lower ethanol tax rate does not further incentivize ethanol consumption. That level of consumption has been set by the mandate. Therefore, the lower ethanol tax rate – a result of the blender's tax credit in federal law – leads to a lower effective price for motor fuel in general, which promotes more motor fuel demand. As a result, demand for gasoline is higher, as the supply and demand of ethanol are pegged at the mandate. That is not to say that the mandate or the tax incentive alone will lead to higher gasoline consumption, but that in the presence of a mandate, gasoline consumption is expected to be higher if there is an ethanol tax credit than in the absence of such a credit.

Independently, both the mandate and the tax credit lead to higher ethanol consumption, but a tax credit on top of a binding mandate creates no additional demand for ethanol. If the tax credit were high enough, then that would lead to greater consumption of ethanol, but in that case, the mandate would no longer be binding. Only one policy, either the mandate or the tax incentive, will set ethanol demand. The authors discuss how, for

---

Comments and opinions are the author's own and do not represent the views of the Congressional Research Service or the U.S. Congress.

purposes of reducing greenhouse gas emissions, a tax rate could be set that would be based on the per-mile greenhouse gas emissions of ethanol relative to gasoline, and then optimized to balance the social costs of greenhouse gas emissions. Likewise, an optimal mandate level could be set that would achieve the same goal.

However, it should be noted that real-world effects may differ from this simplified model for several reasons, which will be discussed later. These factors complicate the situation and include questions of whether the mandate is truly binding, what the optimal level of a biofuels tax would be if greenhouse gas reductions was the ultimate goal of a tax, and what other greenhouse gas policies may interact with the mandate and/or tax. In most cases, these are not criticisms of the substance of the chapter, but suggestions on how to expand the discussion for the future.

The Value of ξ

In discussing the optimal tax level, the authors assume that the per-mile greenhouse gas emissions from gasoline are constant, equal to ξ_G. Next, the authors present two possible scenarios for emissions from fuel ethanol, one in which per-mile emissions of ethanol are 20 percent lower than gasoline and one in which net ethanol emissions are zero: $\xi_E = 0.8 \times \xi_G$ and $\xi_E = 0$, respectively. From these values of ξ_E the optimal greenhouse gas emission–based tax or mandate can be set for a particular value of the social cost of carbon.[1]

However, there is ongoing debate over the actual greenhouse gas emissions of biofuels, including ethanol. Because the life cycle varies for biofuels produced from various feedstocks, through different processes, and with different chemical and energy inputs, the values for ξ_E (or ξ_B for biodiesel, or ξ_X for other fuels) could vary widely from fuel to fuel. Therefore, the value of ξ would need to represent an average of all biofuels in the market, or there would need to be individual terms for each fuel or fuel pathway.

This issue of assessing the life-cycle emissions of biofuels is of key interest at the Environmental Protection Agency (EPA). The EPA must quantify the emissions for all renewable fuels under the Renewable Fuel Standard (RFS) that was established in the Energy Policy Act of 2005 (P.L. 109–58) and expanded in the Energy Independence and Security Act of 2007 (EISA,

---

[1] The values for the social cost of carbon vary widely. See Richard Tol. The social cost of carbon: trends, outliers, and catastrophes. *Economics: The Open-Access, Open-Assessment E-Journal*, vol. 2, 2008–25.

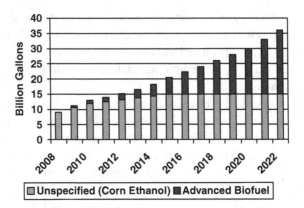

Figure 10.5. Expanded Renewable Fuel Standard under EISA.

P.L. 110–140).[2] The RFS mandates a substantial increase in biofuels use – from roughly 8 billion gallons in 2007 to 36 billion gallons in 2022. Further, most of this increase must come from "advanced biofuels" – biofuels with at least a 50 percent reduction in life-cycle greenhouse gas emissions relative to gasoline. (Figure 10.5 shows the mandated levels under EISA.)

Thus, for advanced biofuels, $\xi_A \leq 0.5 \times \xi_G$. Further, within that advanced biofuel mandate, by 2022 the majority of the advanced biofuels must be cellulose-based, with at least a 60 percent reduction in greenhouse gas emissions relative to gasoline. (Figure 10.6 shows the sub-mandates for various fuels under the larger advanced biofuel mandate.)

Thus, for cellulosic biofuels, $\xi_C \leq 0.4 \times \xi_G$.

However, as shown in Figure 10.7, the EPA's preliminary assessment of different biofuels' life-cycle greenhouse gas emissions for the Agency's proposed rule making shows widely different emissions profiles for various fuels, as compared to gasoline. Furthermore, EPA's proposed rule – and the methodology that underlies it – has been widely criticized by many stakeholders.

Some of these stakeholders question particular portions of the EPA's analysis, whereas others question the validity of any attempt to quantify a biofuel's life-cycle emissions, especially when EISA requires that EPA consider both direct emissions (emissions from the production of agricultural feedstocks, refinery emissions, etc.) and indirect emissions (including any indirect effects of changes in land use).

---

[2] EPA. Regulation of Fuels and Fuel Additives: Changes to Renewable Fuel Standard Program – Notice of Proposed Rulemaking, 74 Federal Register 24903–25143.

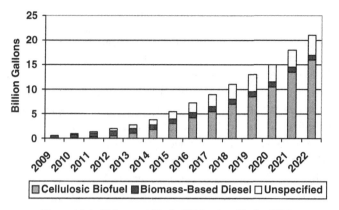

Figure 10.6. "Advanced Biofuel" Mandate Under EISA.

To completely model the ideal tax or mandate level, the actual life-cycle emissions of all biofuels would need to be incorporated into the model. Further, as each of these fuels also has different production costs and energy content, each would have its own supply curve, further complicating any model.

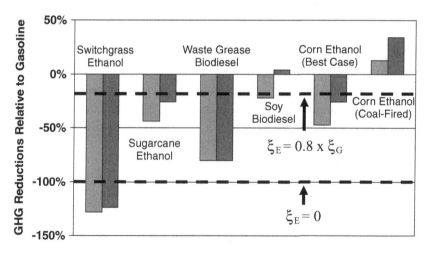

Figure 10.7. EPA Estimates for Life-Cycle Emissions from Various Biofuels U.S. EPA, EPA Lifecycle Analysis of Greenhouse Gas Emissions from Renewable Fuels, May 2009. http://www.epa.gov/otaq/renewablefuels/420f09024.htm. The two values for each fuel represent two different accounting methods proposed by EPA. The first considers emissions changes over a 100-year life cycle with a 0 percent discount rate. The second uses a 30-year life cycle and a 2 percent discount rate. Values for ξ were added by the author.

How Certain Is the Mandate?

One inherent assumption in the authors' analysis is that the mandate is credible and certain. However, it is unclear how firm fuel suppliers assume the mandate will be. In the absence of adequate biofuel supply, production capacity, or feedstock supply, the EPA has the authority to partially or fully waive various parts of the RFS. For example, the EPA can waive the requirement for biomass-based diesel fuel in a given year if there is inadequate feedstock to produce the fuel. If a feedstock producer or fuel supplier has reason to believe that the EPA will grant a waiver, that may limit investment in the capital or commodities to produce biofuels.[3]

Using a concrete example, the RFS mandate for cellulosic biofuels begins at 100 million gallons in 2010. However, looking at existing and proposed refineries, it is unclear that the United States will have 100 million gallons of cellulosic biofuel production *capacity* by the end of 2010, let alone 100 million gallons of actual production. This raises the question of whether the EPA will grant a partial waiver to the cellulosic biofuel mandate? Further, if the EPA were to grant a waiver from the 2010 requirement, would that lead to reduced investment in 2010 that would lead to a shortfall in 2011 capacity, necessitating a waiver in that year? It is conceivable that the EPA's waiver authority could lead to a cascade of waivers that result in diminished investment – a "self-fulfilling prophecy" requiring partial waivers every year because the mandate is not credible. Between the conference and the publication of this volume, the EPA finalized regulations significantly lowering the 2010 cellulosic mandate from 100 million gallons to 6.5 million gallons. For 2011, the EPA has proposed a cellulosic mandate between 5.0 and 17.1 million gallons, well below the scheduled 2011 mandate of 250 million gallons (see http://www.epa.gov/otaq/fuels/renewablefuels/420f10043 .pdf).

If the mandate is not as credible as has been assumed, tax incentives on top of the mandates could help provide a backstop against more significant shortfalls in production capacity.

Other Potential Policies

Perhaps the key policy proposal outside of biofuels mandates and tax incentives that could interact with them would be an explicit policy to reduce economy-wide greenhouse gas emissions. In the One hundred-eleventh

---

[3] See Brent D. Yacobucci. Waiver Authority Under the Renewable Fuel Standard (RFS) – CRS Report RS22870, May 5, 2008.

Congress, proposals to establish a cap-and-trade system have received the most attention, although carbon taxes have also been proposed. Under legislation passed by the House and currently under consideration in the Senate, biofuels would be exempt from carbon controls placed on petroleum fuels. Effectively, if the cap-and-trade proposals were modeled as carbon taxes, $\xi_B = 0$. However, the cost of producing biofuels would likely increase with the cost of chemical inputs that are subject to the program (e.g., fossil fuels, fertilizer). The level of the cost increase would depend on the feedstock/fuel pathway.

The overall effect of the cap-and-trade system would be to effectively raise the tax rate on petroleum fuels relative to biofuels at the same time that overall fuel prices increased. The net effect is unclear, but if the price margin caused by the cap-and-trade program were large enough, the RFS mandate would no longer be binding.[4] However, most economic modeling of cap-and-trade legislation indicates that carbon prices do not reach high enough levels to promote significant reductions in transportation sector emissions from the baseline, and that fuel producers effectively purchase reductions from other sectors.[5]

Because cap-and-trade policies alone are not enough to stimulate emissions reductions in the transportation sector, policies to directly reduce the carbon content of fuels have been proposed. For example, the state of California is in the process of finalizing regulations to require a 10 percent reduction in the carbon content of transportation fuels by 2020.[6] (Similar standards have been proposed in the U.S. Congress, but have not been approved by either the House or the Senate.) A low-carbon fuel standard would effectively provide an incentive for lower-carbon fuels based on their reduction from baseline gasoline or diesel fuel. For example, if a fuel were able to achieve a 20 percent reduction from gasoline $\xi = 0.8 \times \xi_G$ and were able to command a premium of X, then a fuel with zero greenhouse gas emissions ($\xi = 0$) would be able to command a premium of 5X – the greater the emissions reduction, the more valuable the fuel.

---

[4] The Energy Information Administration's (EIA) modeling of the House bill (H.R. 2454) showed that the Renewable Electricity Standard (RES, analogous to the RFS) is not binding under the cap-and-trade system. That is to say that the increase in the price of carbon stimulates more renewable electricity production than would the RES mandate. EIA. Energy Market and Economic Impacts of H.R. 2454, the American Clean Energy and Security Act of 2009, August 4, 2009, p. 23. http://www.eia.doe.gov/oiaf/servicerpt/hr2454/index.html.

[5] See EPA. EPA Analysis of the American Clean Energy and Security Act of 2009, June 23, 2009, p. 11. http://www.epa.gov/climatechange/economics/pdfs/HR2454_Analysis.pdf.

[6] http://www.arb.ca.gov/regact/2009/lcfs09/lcfs09.htm.

Thus, the assessment of life-cycle greenhouse gas emissions would be of key importance. It should be noted that a low-carbon fuel standard would not be an explicit biofuels mandate; biofuels would need to compete with other alternatives (e.g., electricity for electric vehicles, compressed natural gas, hydrogen) based on their carbon content. In fact, in California's proposed regulations, some corn-based ethanol fuels have *higher* emissions than gasoline, penalizing those fuels as opposed to incentivizing them.

Conclusion

The chapter by de Gorter and Just does a good job of highlighting a potentially perverse situation in which combined biofuels incentives effectively incentivize conventional fuels. However, the overall effects of those policies become more complicated as other policies – mainly policies to control carbon emissions – are layered on top of those existing policies.

Index

Printed in the United States
By Bookmasters